THE ENCYCLOPEDIA OF
SOUPS & STEWS

THE ENCYCLOPEDIA OF SOUPS & STEWS

OVER 300 HEARTY RECIPES FOR EVERY SEASON

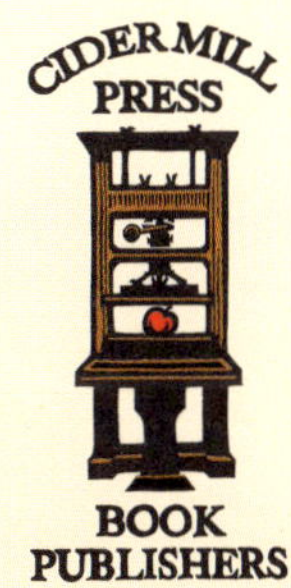

The Encyclopedia of Soups & Stews

 • 13-Digit ISBN: 978-1-40035-299-9 • 10-Digit ISBN: 1-40035-299-1 • This book may be ordered by mail from the publisher. Please include $5.99 for postage and handling. Please support your local bookseller first! • Books published by Cider Mill Press Book Publishers are available at special discounts for bulk purchases in the United States by corporations, institutions, and other organizations. For more information, please contact the publisher. • Cider Mill Press Book Publishers • "Where good books are ready for press" • 501 Nelson Place • Nashville, Tennessee 37214, USA • cidermillpress.com • HarperCollins Publishers, Macken House, 39/40 Mayor Street Upper, Dublin 1, D01 C9W8, Ireland (https://www.harpercollins.com) • Typography: Hansief, Freight Sans, Freight Serif • Images on pages 21, 69, 77, & 259 used under official license from Shutterstock. All other images courtesy of Cider Mill Press. • Printed in Malaysia • 25 26 27 28 29 SEA 5 4 3 2 1 • First Edition

CONTENTS

INTRODUCTION

THE ONLY UNIVERSAL DISH

The world contains countless cuisines, techniques, and ingredients. These differences might be due to availability, religious beliefs, etc., but there's no debate that food varies drastically from culture to culture.

But there is one thing that bonds them all—every single culture has some form of soup.

However, what each culture thinks of soup also varies. They can be thick or thin, can feature seafood, meat, or vegetables, and can even be clarified with gastronomic ingredients, as consommé is.

Whatever they contain, soups have been around for some time. Broths show up in the historical record around the year 1000 CE, and in the 15th century, soup dishes known as potages became a staple in the lives of peasants around the world. In fact, soups are such a vital part of what we eat that the word stems from the same Latin word that supper does: *suppare*.

SOUP IN CULTURE

Soups came to be known as something that promotes healing—so much so that they essentially were the health care system until the advent of modern medicine. Medical textbooks of the time read more like diet books. In China, snakes were used to make soups that were believed to help with joint pain. The meat of a strong animal was thought to strengthen a weak man. And special, protein-rich soups featuring pigs' feet were prepared for mothers following a successful childbirth, the idea being that the added protein would bolster milk production.

Of course, there is the age-old belief in chicken soup's healing capabilities. This stems from the Ancient Greeks, who recommended the meat of hens and roosters, and broth made from their bones, for many treatments. As it turns out, scientists have confirmed that this was not just an ancient superstition. Chicken actually contains a compound called carnosine that slows or blocks the migration of white blood cells, which reduces the amount of inflammation in the respiratory tract that results from the common cold. Researchers have also found that chicken soup may improve one's ability to deflect a virus and weaken it upon entry into the body. On top of all this, it also allows mucus to escape the body more freely, which keeps airways clear and eases the effects of congestion. So, with chicken soup, as with most things, it turns out that the Ancient Greeks, and your mother, have it right.

COLD SOUPS

When you think of soup, you no doubt picture a steaming bowl, ready to provide comfort on a cold day. But cold soups have their place in the world as well and are versatile enough to serve as an appetizer, a main course, or even a dessert.

Skeptical? Well, if you think about it, the contemporary smoothie is technically a soup—a liquid concoction of fruits and vegetables.

And there are a few cold soups that are as classic as any of their warmer counterparts. For instance, Vichyssoise is a classic summer soup that was created in the early 1900s by Louis Diat, a French expatriate who was then chef at the Ritz-Carlton in New York City. A thick soup made of boiled and puréed leeks, onions, potatoes, cream, and chicken stock, it is traditionally served cold, but is also lovely hot. Vichyssoise is a perfect start to a great meal, as it is tasty and easy on the stomach.

Another classic cold soup is Gazpacho, which has spread far from its country of origin—Spain—to provide refreshment all over the world on hot summer days. Originally just bread, garlic, oil, and vinegar ground into a paste with a mortar and pestle, gazpacho is a great example of how quickly and drastically soups can evolve.

And mentioned earlier, Borscht is an extremely popular soup throughout Eastern Europe. A well-made Borscht provides a wonderful sour taste that distracts you from how nourishing it is.

SOUP IN THE MODERN KITCHEN

Soups are not just placeholders on a menu. They are often the key to running a successful restaurant: one that provides the customer with a memorable experience, and does so without waste.

This is because soups are a great way to use trimmings and unused parts. Many chefs use a vegetable scrap bucket. It's a way to cut costs, sure. But it's also a way to experiment with a particular dish and add a bit more complexity.

From the bucket of vegetable trimmings, you can make a beautiful, rich vegetable stock that becomes the foundation for a number of soups. In fact, the resulting stock can be so lovely that, so long as time isn't a factor, you could elect to ignore the Vegetable Stock recipe on page 441 and make yours with the trimmings and peels that you've saved.

And don't think those trimmings are only for vegetable stock. They're also great for adding flavor to chicken, beef, and fish stock. The same goes for the leftover bits of a chicken: it doesn't look like much, but you can make a stock from the carcass and the legs, braise the thighs to use in a chicken noodle soup, and even make a pâté from the innards. Do this, and you've managed to save yourself a bundle, all while making your future meals far more enjoyable. This is an invaluable habit to get into—both for your wallet and for your creativity in the kitchen.

Soups also make for a great amuse-bouche or intermezzo (palate cleanser) at a restaurant, allowing the chef to keep the customer happy and entertained while they work through a five-course, prix fixe menu. Not to say that soup can't be more than just a distraction. It's also the perfect lunch. On a cold, crisp fall day, there's nothing better than warming your body, soul, and mind with a bowl of soup and a roll. As long as the soup's good, that's heaven.

Soup is also a good way to celebrate the season, and enjoy ingredients when they are fresh. In spring, it's time to pile the fiddleheads, peas, broccoli, and fava beans into a pot and get to work. In the summer, it's time to highlight corn, spinach, and bell peppers. And during the fall and winter, we move on to the heartier vegetables such as sweet potatoes, pumpkin, and squash.

THE MOTHER SOUPS

BROTHS

Made from meat, poultry, fish, or vegetables, a broth is a clear soup that can be consumed "as is" or used as the base in stews, soups, sauces, and braised dishes. The aroma of the broth is intended to stimulate one's appetite. They should be translucent to golden brown, with a rich, well-balanced flavor.

CONSOMMÉS

The key to a great consommé is a perfectly balanced and flavorful stock that has been clarified with a raft (made from lean meats, egg whites, tomatoes, and aromatics). When making consommé, remember this: The raft is there to develop flavor, not provide it. It cannot compensate for a weak stock. A well-made consommé will be rich in flavor, translucent, and completely free of fat.

VEGETABLE SOUPS

The key to these soups is cooking the vegetables so that the flavor of the vegetables penetrates the base. This preparation will make the soup slightly cloudy and incredibly flavorful. Think of French Onion Soup as a perfect example of this group.

CREAM SOUPS AND VELOUTES

Traditionally, a cream soup is thickened with both cream and a roux (a combination of butter and flour). A veloute is a stock that has been thickened with a roux, cream, and eggs. Cream soups are luxurious both for the customer and the kitchen, since they can be prepared in advance and reheated to serve. Not so for veloutes, which need to be finished with the egg and served right away.

When making these soups, make sure to add the cream at the last possible moment, so that it does not curdle. Though tradition demands it, some try to avoid using a roux in these soups whenever possible, preferring to cook them low and slow in order to thicken them.

PUREED SOUPS

Pureed soups are similar to the cream soups, but more appropriate to dried beans, lentils, and starchy vegetables such as squash, potatoes, and carrots. These soups should not be strained and should have a slightly coarse texture. You'll know you've done well with one of these when the flavor is robust and the soup is not too watery and not too thick.

BISQUES

A combination of both pureed and cream soups, a bisque is traditionally made with crustaceans, which are used both in the cooking process and in garnishing the dish. A bisque is typically thickened with rice.

STORING AND REHEATING

One of the best things about soups is that not only are they OK to reheat, they are often even better the second and third time around. So make a double batch and enjoy some for lunch the following day, or use what remains to surprise your friends and neighbors with a little treat.

If you don't have a chest freezer, we highly recommend picking one up, since it will allow you to prepare a number of items in advance. If you're worried about the cost, keep an eye on Craigslist, where they pop up for free on occasion, so long as you're willing to handle transportation.

STOCKS

Flavorful stocks are a crucial piece to preparing these soups, so you're going to want to make a big batch every time. If you do this, and freeze whatever you don't use immediately, you'll never be stuck with grocery store stock again—meaning your soups will never lack flavor, body, or character.

Stocks freeze very well, and if you can vacuum seal the bags you store them in, much the better. If you don't have this option, make sure to leave a little space in your container before placing it in the freezer, because the water in the stock will expand as it freezes. You can also use an ice cube tray to store your stocks, a method that comes in handy if you just want to use a little bit in a pan sauce.

Here's how you do it: When you're cooking a protein, you start it in a sauté pan and then finish it in the oven. Hang onto the juices the protein leaves behind, deglaze it with whatever wine you've chosen to enjoy with your meal, and then add a couple stock cubes and some aromatics—voila! You've got a delicious sauce to top your protein with.

Your freezer will also come in handy for storing the components you use to make the stocks. After roasting a chicken for dinner, you probably won't have the time or the energy to toss that carcass into a pot and whip up a stock. No problem! Just wrap up the carcass and toss it into the freezer until you have some time. Do the same with your vegetable trimmings and you'll always be well on the way toward a delicious soup.

STORING SOUP

When storing a soup, be sure not to place them in the refrigerator while they are still hot. Let them cool to room temperature to avoid the development of any bacteria and prevent the temperature inside your refrigerator from rising to unsafe levels.

Not only that, depending on the size of your leftover soup, you can create an "igloo" effect, where the outsides will cool first and insulate the interior, slowing its ability to cool.

And if you are preparing a soup ahead of time and planning to reheat it for dinner the next day, make sure you leave out any fragile ingredients—such as finishing herbs—before storing in the fridge. Instead, you'll want to add these when you reheat the soup.

REHEATING

Chefs don't often recommend using a microwave, but soup is the exception. Not to finish the soup, but using it to raise the temperature and adjust the viscosity before heating.

Once it's on the stovetop, you want to go slowly. Since soups will often coagulate when chilled due to the gelatin in the stock, you want it to thin out gradually and evenly—otherwise, you risk burning ingredients in the soup or curdling the cream.

PREPARING THE DAY BEFORE

Letting a pot of soup sit overnight allows the harsh flavors to soften, the ingredients to take on the flavors of the broth, and everything to harmonize.

Because of this, preparing them ahead of time is a great idea—except for those that are thickened with eggs, those colored by their ingredients (specifically gentle herb and spinach soups), and those containing fragile seafood.

But even these exceptions can be worked around. For soups that are thickened with eggs or feature delicate seafood, leave these ingredients out until you reheat it the next day. Soups that soak up the color of their ingredients should be frozen if not enjoyed in 24 hours, so that the chlorophyll can stabilize and the color will last.

WARMING BOWLS

When appropriate, it is very important to serve your soups in prewarmed bowls. Most china or pottery will hold a significant temperature for an extended period of time. After investing the effort to prepare a beautiful soup, it's best to extend its life by presenting and enjoying it in a warm serving dish. This will retain the soup's appropriate temperature.

PASTA, NOODLES & DUMPLINGS

Pasta Fagioli

YIELD: 4 SERVINGS / **ACTIVE TIME:** 15 MINUTES / **TOTAL TIME:** 30 MINUTES

- 2 TABLESPOONS EXTRA-VIRGIN OLIVE OIL
- 1 ONION, FINELY DICED
- 2 CARROTS, PEELED AND GRATED
- 2 CELERY STALKS, FINELY DICED
- 1 GARLIC CLOVE, MINCED
- 4 CUPS CHICKEN STOCK (SEE PAGE 440)
- 1 (14 OZ.) CAN OF DICED TOMATOES, DRAINED
- 2 TABLESPOONS HERBES DE PROVENCE
- 1 CUP ELBOW MACARONI
- 1 (14 OZ.) CAN OF PINTO BEANS, DRAINED AND RINSED
- SALT AND PEPPER, TO TASTE
- PARMESAN CHEESE, GRATED, FOR GARNISH

1. Place the olive oil in a medium pot and warm it over medium heat. Add the onion, carrots, celery, and garlic and cook, stirring frequently, until they have softened, about 5 minutes. Add the stock, tomatoes, and herbes de Provence and bring to a boil.
2. Reduce the heat so that the soup simmers, add the pasta, and cook until it is al dente, 8 to 10 minutes.
3. Add the beans and cook for 5 minutes. Season the soup with salt and pepper and ladle it into warmed bowls. Garnish with Parmesan and serve.

Kimchi Ramen

YIELD: 4 SERVINGS / **ACTIVE TIME:** 10 MINUTES / **TOTAL TIME:** 30 MINUTES

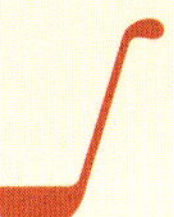

NOODLES FROM 2 PACKETS OF RAMEN

¼ CUP EXTRA-VIRGIN OLIVE OIL

2 SHIITAKE MUSHROOMS, STEMMED AND FINELY DICED

2 CUPS KIMCHI, FINELY CHOPPED

1 CUP KIMCHI LIQUID

6 CUPS CHICKEN STOCK (SEE PAGE 440)

½ TEASPOON CHILI POWDER, OR TO TASTE

1 TEASPOON SUGAR

1 TABLESPOON SESAME OIL

SALT AND PEPPER, TO TASTE

SCALLIONS, SLICED THIN, FOR GARNISH

1. Cook the noodles according to the instructions on the package and then set them aside.
2. Place the olive oil in a medium pot and warm it over medium-high heat. Add the mushrooms and cook, stirring occasionally, for 3 minutes. Add the kimchi, kimchi liquid, stock, chili powder, sugar, and sesame oil and bring to a boil.
3. Reduce the heat so that the soup simmers and cook for 5 minutes. Season the soup with salt and pepper.
4. Divide the noodles among warmed bowls and ladle the soup over the top. Garnish with scallions and serve.

Chicken Meatball Soup with Farfalle & Spinach

YIELD: 8 SERVINGS / **ACTIVE TIME:** 35 MINUTES / **TOTAL TIME:** 1 HOUR

FOR THE MEATBALLS

1 CUP FRESH BREAD CRUMBS

1 LB. GROUND CHICKEN

1 CUP FRESHLY GRATED PARMESAN CHEESE

3 TABLESPOONS TOMATO PASTE

1 HANDFUL OF FRESH PARSLEY, CHOPPED

3 LARGE EGGS

SALT AND PEPPER, TO TASTE

2 TABLESPOONS EXTRA-VIRGIN OLIVE OIL

FOR THE SOUP

2 TABLESPOONS EXTRA-VIRGIN OLIVE OIL

2 LEEKS, TRIMMED, RINSED WELL, AND CHOPPED

SALT AND PEPPER, TO TASTE

5 GARLIC CLOVES, SLICED THIN

8 CUPS CHICKEN STOCK (SEE PAGE 440)

5 CARROTS, PEELED AND SLICED

½ LB. FARFALLE

2 HANDFULS OF BABY SPINACH LEAVES

¼ CUP GRATED PARMESAN CHEESE, PLUS MORE FOR GARNISH

1. To begin preparations for the meatballs, place the bread crumbs, chicken, Parmesan, tomato paste, parsley, and eggs in a mixing bowl, season with salt and pepper, and work the mixture with your hands until thoroughly combined. Working with wet hands, form the mixture into ½-inch balls.
2. Place the olive oil in a large skillet and warm it over medium heat. Working in batches to avoid crowding the pan, add the meatballs and cook, turning them occasionally, until they are browned all over. Transfer the browned meatballs to a paper towel–lined plate to drain.
3. To begin preparations for the soup, place the olive oil in a Dutch oven and warm it over medium heat. Add the leeks, season with salt and pepper, and cook, stirring frequently, until they are translucent, about 3 minutes. Reduce the heat to low, cover the pot, and cook, stirring occasionally, until the leeks are very soft, about 15 minutes.
4. Add the garlic, cook for 1 minute, and then stir in the stock, carrots, and meatballs. Raise the heat to medium-high and bring the soup to a gentle boil. Reduce the heat to medium-low and simmer the soup until the meatballs are cooked through and the carrots are tender, about 15 minutes.
5. Add the farfalle and cook until tender, about 8 minutes. Remove the Dutch oven from heat and stir in the spinach and Parmesan. Cover the pot and let it rest until the spinach has wilted, about 5 minutes.
6. Ladle the soup into warmed bowls, garnish each portion with additional Parmesan, and serve.

Creamy Vegetable Soup with Turkey Dumplings

YIELD: 4 SERVINGS / **ACTIVE TIME:** 45 MINUTES / **TOTAL TIME:** 4 HOURS AND 15 MINUTES

FOR THE BROTH

1 LEFTOVER TURKEY CARCASS

2 CELERY STALKS, FINELY DICED

2 CARROTS, PEELED AND DICED

1 ONION, FINELY DICED

2 TEASPOONS FRESH THYME

2 BAY LEAVES

6 BLACK PEPPERCORNS

FOR THE SOUP

2 TABLESPOONS EXTRA-VIRGIN OLIVE OIL

1 ONION, FINELY DICED

2 CELERY STALKS, FINELY DICED

1 CELERIAC, TRIMMED AND FINELY DICED

2 PARSNIPS, PEELED AND FINELY DICED

1 TEASPOON FINELY CHOPPED FRESH ROSEMARY

½ CUP WHITE WINE

4 CUPS TURKEY BROTH

1 CUP HEAVY CREAM

SALT AND PEPPER, TO TASTE

TURKEY DUMPLINGS (SEE PAGE 472), FOR SERVING

1. To prepare the broth, bring all of the ingredients to a boil in a large pot. Reduce the heat so that the broth simmers and cook until the flavor has developed to your liking, at least 3½ hours. Skim off any excess fat, strain the broth through a fine-mesh sieve, and set it aside.
2. To begin preparations for the soup, place the olive oil in a medium pot and warm it over medium heat. Add the onion, celery, celeriac, and parsnips and cook, stirring occasionally, until they are tender, about 10 minutes. Add the rosemary and cook, stirring frequently, for 2 minutes.
3. Add the wine and broth and bring the soup to a boil. Reduce the heat so that the soup simmers and cook until the vegetables are tender, about 30 minutes.
4. Transfer the soup to a food processor, pulse until smooth, and strain it into a clean pot through a fine-mesh sieve. Bring the soup to a simmer, add the heavy cream, and season with salt and pepper.
5. Ladle the soup into warmed bowls and serve with the Turkey Dumplings.

Avgolemono

YIELD: 4 TO 6 SERVINGS / **ACTIVE TIME:** 15 MINUTES / **TOTAL TIME:** 45 MINUTES

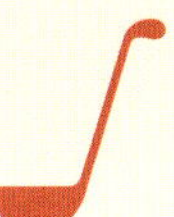

8 CUPS CHICKEN STOCK (SEE PAGE 440)

½ CUP ORZO

3 EGGS

JUICE OF 1 LEMON

1 TABLESPOON COLD WATER

SALT AND PEPPER, TO TASTE

1 LEMON, SLICED THIN, FOR GARNISH

FRESH DILL, CHOPPED, FOR GARNISH

1. Place the stock in a large saucepan and bring it to a boil. Reduce the heat so that the stock simmers. Add the orzo and cook until tender, about 5 minutes.
2. Strain the stock and orzo over a large bowl. Set the orzo aside. Return the stock to the pan and bring it to a simmer.
3. Place the eggs in a mixing bowl and beat until scrambled and frothy. Stir in the lemon juice and cold water. While stirring constantly, add approximately ½ cup of the stock to the egg mixture. Stir another cup of stock into the egg mixture and then stir the tempered eggs into the saucepan. Reduce the heat to low and be careful not to let the stock come to boil once you add the egg mixture.
4. Return the orzo to the soup. Cook, stirring continually, until everything is warmed through, about 2 minutes. Season with salt and pepper, ladle the soup into warmed bowls, and garnish each portion with slices of lemon and dill.

Vietnamese Pho

YIELD: 4 SERVINGS / **ACTIVE TIME:** 30 MINUTES / **TOTAL TIME:** 3 HOURS AND 50 MINUTES

2 LBS. BEEF OR CHICKEN BONES

¼ CUP EXTRA-VIRGIN OLIVE OIL

SALT AND PEPPER, TO TASTE

1 SMALL YELLOW ONION, HALVED

1-INCH PIECE OF FRESH GINGER, UNPEELED

2 CINNAMON STICKS

3 STAR ANISE PODS

SEEDS OF 2 CARDAMOM PODS, CRUSHED

1 TABLESPOON BLACK PEPPERCORNS

5 WHOLE CLOVES

1 TABLESPOON CORIANDER SEEDS

1 TABLESPOON FENNEL SEEDS

1 CUP FRESH CILANTRO, CHOPPED

8 CUPS WATER

1 TABLESPOON FISH SAUCE

1 TABLESPOON HOISIN SAUCE

1 TEASPOON SRIRACHA

3 OZ. RICE NOODLES

1 JALAPEÑO CHILE PEPPER, SLICED, FOR GARNISH

BEAN SPROUTS, FOR GARNISH

LIME WEDGES, FOR SERVING

FRESH THAI BASIL, FOR GARNISH

1. Preheat the oven to 375°F. Place the bones on a baking sheet, drizzle half of the olive oil over them, and season with salt and pepper. Toss to combine, place the pan in the oven, and roast until the bones are browned, about 20 minutes. Remove the bones from the oven and set them aside.
2. Place the remaining olive oil in a small skillet and warm it over medium heat. Add the onion and ginger and cook, stirring occasionally, until they are lightly charred, 10 to 15 minutes.
3. Place the cinnamon, star anise, cardamom, peppercorns, cloves, coriander seeds, and fennel seeds in a large nonstick skillet and toast over medium heat until they release a fragrant aroma, 2 to 3 minutes, shaking the pan frequently.
4. Place the bones, onion-and-ginger mixture, toasted spices, cilantro, and water in a large pot and bring to a boil, stirring occasionally. Reduce the heat so that the soup simmers, cover the pot with a lid, and cook for 3 hours.
5. Strain the soup into another large pot, add the fish sauce, hoisin, black pepper, and sriracha, and stir to combine. Place the pot over medium-low heat and simmer.
6. Bring water to a boil in a medium pot. Add salt, let the water return to a boil, and add the noodles. Cook until the noodles are al dente, 6 to 8 minutes. Drain the noodles, rinse them under cold water, and let them cool.
7. Divide the noodles among the serving bowls. Ladle the soup into each of the bowls, garnish with the sliced jalapeño, bean sprouts, lime wedges, and Thai basil, and serve.

Polpette di Ricotta in Brodo

YIELD: 4 SERVINGS / **ACTIVE TIME:** 40 MINUTES / **TOTAL TIME:** 1 HOUR

1½ CUPS RICOTTA CHEESE (MADE FROM SHEEP'S MILK PREFERRED), DRAINED

¼ CUP GRATED PARMESAN CHEESE

⅔ CUP BREAD CRUMBS

2 HANDFULS OF FRESH PARSLEY, FINELY CHOPPED

1 EGG

SALT AND PEPPER, TO TASTE

6 CUPS VEGETABLE STOCK (SEE PAGE 441)

1. Place all of the ingredients, except for the stock, in a mixing bowl and stir until well combined. Place the mixture in the refrigerator and chill for 30 minutes.
2. Place the stock in a medium saucepan and bring it to a boil.
3. Form the mixture into 1-oz. balls and slip them into the stock. Cook the ricotta balls for 10 minutes.
4. Ladle the soup into warmed bowls and enjoy.

Virtù Teramane

YIELD: 4 SERVINGS / **ACTIVE TIME:** 1 HOUR AND 30 MINUTES / **TOTAL TIME:** 24 HOURS

SALT, TO TASTE

3 CUPS FRESH SPINACH

1 SMALL ZUCCHINI, CHOPPED

1 HEAD OF ENDIVE, CHOPPED

1 CARROT, PEELED AND CHOPPED

1 CELERY STALK, CHOPPED

¾ CUP DRIED CHICKPEAS, SOAKED OVERNIGHT AND DRAINED

¾ CUP LENTILS

1 CUP DRIED FAVA BEANS, SOAKED OVERNIGHT AND DRAINED

⅔ CUP DRIED SPLIT PEAS

2 OZ. LARD, CHOPPED

1 ONION, FINELY DICED

1 GARLIC CLOVE

5 OZ. PANCETTA, CUBED

1 TEASPOON CHOPPED FRESH PARSLEY

2 TOMATOES, CHOPPED

8 CUPS CHICKEN STOCK OR BEEF STOCK (SEE PAGE 441 OR 442)

½ LB. SHORT-FORMAT PASTA (MIX OF DRIED SEMOLINA PASTA AND HOMEMADE EGG PASTA RECOMMENDED)

PECORINO CHEESE, GRATED, FOR GARNISH

1. Bring water to a boil in a large saucepan. Add salt and the spinach, zucchini, endive, carrot, and celery and cook for 5 minutes. Drain the vegetables and let them cool. When they are cool enough to handle, squeeze them to remove as much water as possible and set them aside.
2. Place the chickpeas, lentils, beans, and split peas in separate saucepans, cover them with water, and cook until they just start to soften—the cook times will differ for each legume. Drain the legumes and set them aside.
3. Place the lard in a large saucepan and warm it over medium heat. Add the onion, garlic, and pancetta and cook, stirring frequently, until the pancetta's fat starts to render.
4. Remove the garlic from the pan and discard it. Add the parsley and tomatoes and cook, stirring occasionally, until the tomatoes start to collapse, about 15 minutes.
5. Add the stock and cooked vegetables to the pan and cook for 10 minutes.
6. Add the pasta and legumes and cook until they are tender, about 30 minutes.
7. Ladle the soup into warmed bowls, garnish each portion with pecorino, and enjoy.

Fast Pho

YIELD: 4 SERVINGS / **ACTIVE TIME:** 15 MINUTES / **TOTAL TIME:** 30 MINUTES

SALT, TO TASTE

3 OZ. RICE NOODLES

2 CINNAMON STICKS

3 STAR ANISE PODS

SEEDS OF 2 CARDAMOM PODS, CRUSHED

1 CUP FINELY CHOPPED FRESH CILANTRO

5 WHOLE CLOVES

1 TABLESPOON CORIANDER SEEDS

1 TABLESPOON FENNEL SEEDS

2 TABLESPOONS EXTRA-VIRGIN OLIVE OIL

1 YELLOW ONION, FINELY DICED

1-INCH PIECE OF FRESH GINGER, PEELED AND MINCED

6 CUPS BEEF STOCK (SEE PAGE 442)

1 TABLESPOON FISH SAUCE

1 TABLESPOON HOISIN SAUCE

1 TEASPOON SRIRACHA

1 JALAPEÑO CHILE PEPPER, SLICED THIN, FOR GARNISH

BEAN SPROUTS, FOR GARNISH

FRESH THAI BASIL, FINELY CHOPPED, FOR GARNISH

LIME WEDGES, FOR SERVING

1. Bring water to a boil in a medium pot. Add salt, let the water return to a boil, and add the noodles. Cook until they are al dente, 8 to 10 minutes. Drain the noodles, rinse them under cold water, and set them aside.
2. Place the cinnamon, star anise, cardamom, cilantro, cloves, and seeds in a small skillet and toast over medium heat, stirring continually, until the mixture is fragrant, 2 to 3 minutes. Remove the pan from heat and set the mixture aside.
3. Place the olive oil in a clean medium pot and warm it over medium heat. Add the onion and ginger and cook, stirring occasionally, until they have softened, about 5 minutes. Add the spice mixture and stock, stir to combine, and bring to a boil.
4. Reduce the heat so that the soup simmers and cook for 10 minutes. Strain the soup into a clean pot through a fine-mesh sieve. Bring the soup to a simmer and stir in the fish sauce, hoisin, and sriracha.
5. Divide the noodles among warmed bowls and ladle the soup over the top. Garnish with the jalapeño, bean sprouts, and Thai basil and serve with lime wedges.

Lasagna Soup

YIELD: 4 SERVINGS / **ACTIVE TIME:** 20 MINUTES / **TOTAL TIME:** 45 MINUTES

SALT, TO TASTE

12 LASAGNA NOODLES, BROKEN

2 TABLESPOONS EXTRA-VIRGIN OLIVE OIL

1 ONION, FINELY DICED

1 LB. GROUND ITALIAN SAUSAGE

2 GARLIC CLOVES, MINCED

2 TEASPOONS DRIED OREGANO

2 TABLESPOONS TOMATO PASTE

4 CUPS BEEF STOCK (SEE PAGE 442)

2 (14 OZ.) CANS OF CRUSHED TOMATOES

¼ CUP GRATED PARMESAN CHEESE

¼ CUP HEAVY CREAM

½ CUP FINELY CHOPPED FRESH BASIL, PLUS MORE FOR GARNISH

RICOTTA CHEESE, FOR GARNISH

1. Bring water to a boil in a large pot. Add salt, let the water return to a boil, and add the lasagna noodles. Cook until they are al dente, 8 to 10 minutes. Drain the noodles, rinse them under cold water, and set them aside.
2. Place the olive oil in a medium pot and warm it over medium heat. Add the onion and cook, stirring occasionally, until it has softened, about 5 minutes. Add the sausage, garlic, and oregano and cook, stirring frequently, until the sausage has browned, about 5 minutes.
3. Add the tomato paste, stock, and tomatoes and bring to a boil. Reduce the heat so that the soup simmers and cook for 10 minutes. Stir in the noodles, Parmesan, cream, and basil and cook until the cheese has melted, about 2 minutes.
4. Ladle the soup into warmed bowls, garnish with ricotta and additional basil, and serve.

Chicken Liver & Pasta Soup

YIELD: 4 SERVINGS / **ACTIVE TIME:** 25 MINUTES / **TOTAL TIME:** 55 MINUTES

2 TABLESPOONS EXTRA-VIRGIN OLIVE OIL

½ CUP CHICKEN LIVERS, SLICED INTO ¼-INCH PIECES

4 GARLIC CLOVES, MINCED

2 TABLESPOONS WHITE WINE

1 TABLESPOON FINELY CHOPPED FRESH PARSLEY

1 TABLESPOON FINELY CHOPPED FRESH MARJORAM

1 TABLESPOON FINELY CHOPPED SAGE

1 TEASPOON FRESH THYME

6 FRESH BASIL LEAVES, CHOPPED

6 CUPS CHICKEN STOCK (SEE PAGE 440)

2 CUPS PEAS

1 CUP FARFALLE

3 SCALLIONS, TRIMMED AND SLICED

SALT AND PEPPER, TO TASTE

CRUSTY BREAD, FOR SERVING

1. Place the olive oil in a small skillet and warm it over medium-high heat. Add the livers and garlic and cook, stirring occasionally, until the livers are golden brown, about 3 minutes. Add the wine and cook until it evaporates. Add the parsley, marjoram, sage, thyme, and basil, stir to combine, and cook for about 2 minutes. Remove the pan from heat and set it aside.
2. Bring the stock to a boil in a large saucepan. Add the peas, reduce the heat so that the stock simmers, and cook for 5 minutes. Return the stock to a boil over medium heat, add the farfalle, and reduce the heat so that it simmers. Cook until the pasta is al dente, about 10 minutes.
3. Add the chicken liver mixture and scallions, stir to combine, and cook for about 3 minutes. Season with salt and pepper, divide the soup among the serving bowls, and serve with crusty bread.

Macaroni & Cheese Soup

YIELD: 4 SERVINGS / **ACTIVE TIME:** 15 MINUTES / **TOTAL TIME:** 40 MINUTES

SALT AND PEPPER, TO TASTE

1½ CUPS ELBOW MACARONI

¼ CUP UNSALTED BUTTER

1 ONION, FINELY DICED

2 CARROTS, PEELED AND FINELY DICED

2 CELERY STALKS, FINELY DICED

2 TABLESPOONS ALL-PURPOSE FLOUR

4 CUPS CHICKEN STOCK (SEE PAGE 440)

2 CUPS WHOLE MILK

4 CUPS SHREDDED SHARP CHEDDAR CHEESE

1. Bring water to a boil in a large pot. Add salt, let the water return to a boil, and add the macaroni. Cook until it is al dente, 8 to 10 minutes. Drain the macaroni, rinse it under cold water, and set it aside.
2. Place the butter in a medium pot and melt it over low heat. Add the onion, carrots, and celery and cook, stirring occasionally, until they have softened, about 5 minutes.
3. Add the flour and cook, stirring continually, for 5 minutes. Add the stock and milk and bring to a boil. Reduce the heat so that the soup simmers and cook for 10 minutes.
4. Remove the pot from heat, stir in the macaroni and cheddar, and season the soup with salt and pepper.
5. Ladle the soup into warmed bowls and serve.

Five-Spice & Chicken Ramen

YIELD: 4 SERVINGS / **ACTIVE TIME:** 35 MINUTES / **TOTAL TIME:** 1 HOUR

16 CUPS CHICKEN STOCK (SEE PAGE 440)

4 GARLIC CLOVES, MINCED

2-INCH PIECE OF FRESH GINGER

½ CUP SOY SAUCE

2 TEASPOONS WORCESTERSHIRE SAUCE

1 TEASPOON FIVE-SPICE POWDER

⅛ TEASPOON CHILI POWDER

SALT AND PEPPER, TO TASTE

1 TABLESPOON SUGAR (OPTIONAL)

½ LB. UDON NOODLES

2 TABLESPOONS SESAME OIL

2 BONELESS, SKINLESS CHICKEN BREASTS, CUT INTO 1-INCH CUBES

1 CUP CANNED CORN, DRAINED

1 CUP SPINACH

SCALLIONS, CHOPPED, FOR GARNISH

1 SHEET OF NORI, SHREDDED, FOR GARNISH

4 HARD-BOILED EGGS, FOR SERVING

1. Place the stock, garlic, ginger, soy sauce, Worcestershire sauce, five-spice powder, and chili powder in a large saucepan, stir to combine, and bring to a boil. Reduce the heat so that the broth simmers and cook for about 5 minutes. Turn off the heat and season the broth with salt, pepper, and the sugar (if desired).
2. Bring water to a boil in a medium pot. Add salt, let the water return to a boil, and add the noodles. Cook until the noodles are al dente, 8 to 10 minutes. Drain the noodles and set them aside.
3. Place the sesame oil in a medium skillet and warm it over medium heat. Add the chicken, season it with salt and pepper, and cook until it is browned on both sides and cooked through, 10 to 12 minutes. Add the noodles, corn, and spinach and cook, stirring occasionally, for about 2 minutes. Remove the skillet from heat.
4. Strain the broth into another large saucepan and bring it to a boil.
5. Divide the noodle mixture among the serving bowls and add broth to each bowl. Garnish with scallions and shredded nori and serve with the hard-boiled eggs.

Wagon Wheel Soup

YIELD: 4 SERVINGS / **ACTIVE TIME:** 15 MINUTES / **TOTAL TIME:** 30 MINUTES

SALT AND PEPPER, TO TASTE

1 CUP WAGON WHEEL PASTA

2 TABLESPOONS EXTRA-VIRGIN OLIVE OIL

1 CUP FINELY DICED ONION

1 LB. GROUND BEEF

4 CUPS TOMATO SAUCE (SEE PAGE 458)

½ TEASPOON GROUND DRIED OREGANO

2 CUPS BEEF STOCK (SEE PAGE 442)

2 CUPS CANNED KIDNEY BEANS, DRAINED AND RINSED

1. Bring water to a boil in a medium pot. Add salt, let the water return to a boil, and add the pasta. Cook until it is al dente, 8 to 10 minutes. Drain the pasta and set it aside.
2. Place the olive oil in a medium pot and warm it over medium heat. Add the onion and cook, stirring occasionally, until it has softened, about 5 minutes.
3. Add the beef and cook, breaking it up with a wooden spoon, until it has browned, about 5 minutes. Add the sauce, oregano, stock, and beans, bring to a simmer, and cook for 10 minutes.
4. Stir in the pasta and season with salt and pepper.
5. Ladle the soup into warmed bowls and serve.

ran straight away
to Mr. McGregor's
garden, and
ate some
radishes.
Now run
along, and don't
get into mischief.

Italian Wedding Soup

YIELD: 4 SERVINGS / **ACTIVE TIME:** 30 MINUTES / **TOTAL TIME:** 1 HOUR AND 15 MINUTES

FOR THE MEATBALLS

¾ LB. GROUND CHICKEN

⅓ CUP PANKO

1 GARLIC CLOVE, MINCED

2 TABLESPOONS FINELY CHOPPED FRESH PARSLEY

¼ CUP PARMESAN CHEESE, GRATED

1 TABLESPOON WHOLE MILK

1 EGG, BEATEN

⅛ TEASPOON FENNEL SEEDS

⅛ TEASPOON RED PEPPER FLAKES

½ TEASPOON PAPRIKA

SALT AND PEPPER, TO TASTE

FOR THE SOUP

2 TABLESPOONS EXTRA-VIRGIN OLIVE OIL

1 ONION, FINELY DICED

2 CARROTS, PEELED AND FINELY DICED

1 CELERY STALK, FINELY DICED

6 CUPS CHICKEN STOCK (SEE PAGE 440)

¼ CUP WHITE WINE

½ CUP SHORT-FORMAT PASTA

2 TABLESPOONS FINELY CHOPPED FRESH DILL

6 OZ. BABY SPINACH

SALT AND PEPPER, TO TASTE

PARMESAN CHEESE, GRATED, FOR GARNISH

1. To begin preparations for the meatballs, preheat the oven to 375°F. Place all of the ingredients in a large mixing bowl and mix until fully combined. Form the mixture into 16 meatballs. Place the balls on a baking sheet, place them in the oven, and cook until they are browned and cooked through, 15 to 25 minutes, turning them as necessary. Remove the meatballs from the oven and let them cool.
2. To begin preparations for the soup, place the olive oil in a medium pot and warm it over medium heat. Add the onion, carrots, and celery and cook, stirring occasionally, until they have softened, about 5 minutes. Add the stock and wine and bring the mixture to a boil.
3. Reduce the heat so that the broth simmers, add the pasta, and cook until it is al dente, about 8 minutes. Add the meatballs and cook until they are warmed through, about 5 minutes. Add the dill and spinach and cook until the spinach has wilted, about 2 minutes. Remove the pot from heat.
4. Ladle the soup into warmed bowls and season with salt and pepper. Garnish with Parmesan and serve.

Chickpea & Pasta Soup

YIELD: 4 SERVINGS / **ACTIVE TIME:** 15 MINUTES / **TOTAL TIME:** 24 HOURS

6 CUPS WATER

1¼ CUPS DRIED CHICKPEAS, SOAKED OVERNIGHT, DRAINED, AND RINSED

1 TABLESPOON DRIED KOMBU

3 GARLIC CLOVES

2 TABLESPOONS EXTRA-VIRGIN OLIVE OIL, PLUS MORE FOR GARNISH

1 SPRIG OF FRESH ROSEMARY

1 CUP SHORT-FORM PASTA

1 TEASPOON FINELY CHOPPED FRESH ROSEMARY

SALT AND PEPPER, TO TASTE

CRUSTY BREAD, FOR SERVING

1. Place the water, chickpeas, seaweed, and garlic in a medium saucepan, bring to a simmer, and cover the pot. Cook until the chickpeas are tender, 1 to 1½ hours. Remove one-quarter of the cooked chickpeas and set them aside.
2. Pour the rest of the mixture into a food processor and puree. Set the puree aside.
3. Place the olive oil in a medium pot and warm it over medium-high heat. Add the sprig of rosemary and cook until fragrant, about 2 minutes. Remove the sprig of rosemary from the pan and discard it. Add the reserved chickpeas, puree, and pasta and cook until the pasta is al dente, 8 to 10 minutes.
4. If the soup is too thick for your liking, add water until it has the desired consistency. Add the chopped rosemary and season with salt and pepper.
5. Ladle the soup into warmed bowls, garnish with additional olive oil, and serve with crusty bread.

Chicken Parm Soup

YIELD: 4 SERVINGS / **ACTIVE TIME:** 20 MINUTES / **TOTAL TIME:** 1 HOUR

2 TABLESPOONS EXTRA-VIRGIN OLIVE OIL

2 BONELESS, SKINLESS CHICKEN BREASTS, CHOPPED

SALT AND PEPPER, TO TASTE

1 ONION, CHOPPED

2 GARLIC CLOVES, MINCED

1 TEASPOON RED PEPPER FLAKES

¼ CUP TOMATO PASTE

1 (14 OZ.) CAN OF DICED TOMATOES, WITH THEIR LIQUID

6 CUPS CHICKEN STOCK (SEE PAGE 440)

2 CUPS PENNE

2 CUPS SHREDDED MOZZARELLA CHEESE

1 CUP GRATED PARMESAN CHEESE, PLUS MORE FOR GARNISH

FRESH BASIL, CHOPPED, FOR GARNISH

1. Place the olive oil in a medium pot and warm it over medium-high heat. Season the chicken with salt and pepper, place it in the pan, and cook for 5 minutes. Turn the chicken over, add the onion and garlic, and cook, stirring occasionally, until the onion has softened, about 5 minutes. Add the red pepper flakes, tomato paste, tomatoes, and stock and bring the soup to a boil.
2. Reduce the heat so that the soup simmers and cook for 10 minutes. Add the penne and cook until al dente, 8 to 10 minutes.
3. Add the mozzarella and Parmesan, stir until they have melted, and season with salt and pepper.
4. Ladle the soup into warmed bowls, garnish with basil and additional Parmesan, and serve.

Khao Soi Gai with Rice Noodles

YIELD: 4 SERVINGS / **ACTIVE TIME:** 30 MINUTES / **TOTAL TIME:** 1 HOUR

1 TEASPOON SESAME OIL

1 THAI CHILE PEPPER, STEMMED, SEEDED, AND CHOPPED

2 SHALLOTS, QUARTERED, PLUS MORE, SLICED, FOR GARNISH

4 GARLIC CLOVES, MINCED

1 LEMONGRASS STALK, CRUSHED

1 TEASPOON LIME ZEST

1-INCH PIECE OF FRESH GALANGAL ROOT, PEELED AND MINCED

1-INCH PIECE OF FRESH GINGER, PEELED AND MINCED

1 BUNCH OF FRESH CILANTRO

1 TEASPOON CORIANDER SEEDS

SEEDS OF 1 CARDAMOM POD

PINCH OF KOSHER SALT, PLUS MORE TO TASTE

1½ TABLESPOONS SHRIMP PASTE

1 CUP EXTRA-VIRGIN OLIVE OIL

4 OZ. RICE NOODLES

2 (14 OZ.) CANS OF COCONUT MILK

1 CUP CHICKEN STOCK (SEE PAGE 440)

2 TABLESPOONS SUGAR

4 CHICKEN LEGS, SEPARATED INTO DRUMSTICKS AND THIGHS

FISH SAUCE, TO TASTE

BLACK PEPPER, TO TASTE

LIME WEDGES, FOR SERVING

1. Place the sesame oil in a large skillet and warm it over medium-low heat. Add the chile, shallots, garlic, lemongrass, lime zest, galangal root, ginger, cilantro, coriander seeds, and cardamom, reduce the heat to low, and cook, stirring occasionally, until the mixture becomes fragrant, 2 to 3 minutes.
2. Transfer the mixture to a mortar and add the salt and shrimp paste. Use a pestle to grind the mixture into a smooth paste.
3. Place the olive oil in a Dutch oven and warm it over medium-high heat until it reaches 325°F. Add one-quarter of the noodles and fry until they are crispy, 5 to 8 minutes. Transfer the fried noodles to a paper towel–lined plate to drain and season with salt.
4. Place 1 tablespoon of the olive oil from the Dutch oven and 2 tablespoons of the creamy fat from the top of the coconut milk in a medium pot and warm them over high heat until the coconut fat begins to smoke. Add the paste and cook, stirring continually, for 45 seconds.
5. Reduce the heat to medium, add the remaining coconut milk, the stock, and the sugar, and stir to combine. Add the chicken and cook, stirring occasionally, until the chicken is tender and cooked through (the interior is 165°F), about 30 minutes.
6. Bring water to a boil in a medium pot. Add salt, let the water return to a full boil, and add the remaining uncooked noodles. Cook until they are al dente, 6 to 8 minutes.
7. Drain the noodles and divide them among the serving bowls. Season the soup with fish sauce, salt, and pepper, and ladle it into each bowl. Garnish with additional shallots and the fried rice noodles and serve with lime wedges.

Miso Ramen with Spicy Bean Sprout Salad

YIELD: 4 SERVINGS / **ACTIVE TIME:** 20 MINUTES / **TOTAL TIME:** 45 MINUTES

FOR THE SALAD

¾ LB. BEAN SPROUTS

1 TABLESPOON BLACK SESAME SEEDS

2 GREEN ONIONS, SLICED THIN

2 TABLESPOONS SESAME OIL

2 TEASPOONS SOY SAUCE

⅛ TEASPOON RED PEPPER FLAKES

PINCH OF GROUND GINGER

ZEST OF 1 ORANGE

FOR THE SOUP

2 TABLESPOONS SESAME OIL

4 GARLIC CLOVES, MINCED

2-INCH PIECE OF FRESH GINGER, PEELED AND MINCED

2 SHALLOTS, FINELY DICED

½ LB. GROUND PORK

2 TEASPOONS CHILI BEAN PASTE

6 TABLESPOONS WHITE MISO

¼ CUP SESAME SEEDS, TOASTED AND GROUND INTO A PASTE

2 TABLESPOONS SUGAR

2 TABLESPOONS SAKE

8 CUPS CHICKEN STOCK (SEE PAGE 440)

SALT AND PEPPER, TO TASTE

½ LB. RAMEN NOODLES

PICKLED RED GINGER, FOR GARNISH

4 POACHED EGGS, FOR GARNISH

1. To begin preparations for the salad, bring water to a boil in a medium pot. Add the bean sprouts and cook until tender, about 2 minutes. Drain the bean sprouts, pat them dry with paper towels, and let them cool.
2. Place the sprouts and the remaining ingredients in a salad bowl, toss to combine, and set the salad aside.
3. To begin preparations for the soup, place the sesame oil in a medium pot and warm it over medium heat. Add the garlic, ginger, and shallots and cook, stirring occasionally, until fragrant, about 2 minutes.
4. Add the pork, raise the heat to medium-high, and cook until the pork is lightly browned, about 5 minutes, breaking it up with a wooden spoon. Add the chili paste, miso, sesame seed paste, sugar, sake, and stock, stir to combine, and bring the soup to a boil. Reduce the heat so that it simmers and season with salt and pepper.
5. Bring water to a boil in a medium pot. Add salt, let the water return to a full boil, and add the noodles. Cook until they are al dente, 6 to 8 minutes.
6. Drain the noodles and divide them among the serving bowls. Ladle the soup over the noodles, top each portion with some of the salad, and garnish with pickled red ginger and a poached egg.

Leftover Turkey Pasta Soup

YIELD: 4 SERVINGS / **ACTIVE TIME:** 20 MINUTES / **TOTAL TIME:** 45 MINUTES

2 TABLESPOONS EXTRA-VIRGIN OLIVE OIL

1 ONION, CHOPPED

2 CELERY STALKS, CHOPPED

2 CARROTS, PEELED AND CHOPPED

6 CUPS TURKEY STOCK (SEE PAGE 446)

1 BAY LEAF

1 TEASPOON FINELY CHOPPED FRESH ROSEMARY

½ CUP ORZO

2 CUPS LEFTOVER TURKEY MEAT, CHOPPED

1 TEASPOON FINELY CHOPPED FRESH PARSLEY

SALT AND PEPPER, TO TASTE

1. Place the olive oil in a medium pot and warm it over medium heat. Add the onion, celery, and carrots and cook, stirring occasionally, until they have softened, about 5 minutes.
2. Add the stock, bay leaf, and rosemary and bring the soup to a boil. Reduce the heat so that it simmers and cook for 10 minutes. Add the orzo and cook until it is al dente, 8 to 10 minutes. Stir in the turkey and parsley and cook until the turkey is warmed through.
3. Ladle the soup into warmed bowls, season with salt and pepper, and serve.

Old-Fashioned Chicken & Dumpling Soup

YIELD: 4 SERVINGS / **ACTIVE TIME:** 30 MINUTES / **TOTAL TIME:** 1 HOUR AND 30 MINUTES

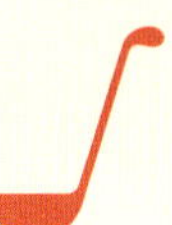

FOR THE BROTH

1 TABLESPOON EXTRA-VIRGIN OLIVE OIL

½ ONION, FINELY DICED

1 CARROT, PEELED AND FINELY DICED

1 CELERY STALK, FINELY DICED

1 TEASPOON FRESH THYME

4 CUPS CHICKEN STOCK (SEE PAGE 440)

SALT AND PEPPER, TO TASTE

FRESH PARSLEY, CHOPPED, FOR GARNISH

FOR THE DUMPLINGS

4 BREAD SLICES, DICED

½ CUP FINELY CHOPPED FRESH PARSLEY

1¼ CUPS ALL-PURPOSE FLOUR, PLUS MORE AS NEEDED

1 TEASPOON BAKING POWDER

½ CUP WHOLE MILK

1 EGG

¼ CUP UNSALTED BUTTER, MELTED

1 CUP COOKED CHICKEN MEAT, DICED

SALT AND PEPPER, TO TASTE

1. To begin preparations for the broth, place the olive oil in a medium pot and warm it over medium heat. Add the onion and cook, stirring occasionally, until it has softened, about 5 minutes. Add the carrot and celery and cook, stirring occasionally, until the carrot has softened, about 5 minutes.
2. Add the thyme and stock and bring the soup to a boil. Reduce the heat so that the soup simmers, season with salt and pepper, and cook until the carrot is tender, about 20 minutes.
3. To begin preparations for the dumplings, place the bread and parsley in a food processor and pulse until combined. Transfer the mixture to a mixing bowl, add the flour and baking powder, and stir to combine. Add the milk, egg, butter, and chicken, season with salt and pepper, and work the mixture until it comes together as a smooth dough. Add a few drops of water to the mixture if it is having trouble coming together as a dough.
4. Place the dough on a flour-dusted work surface and knead it until it is smooth. Pinch off small pieces of the dough and drop them into the simmering soup.
5. Cook until the dumplings are cooked through, about 10 minutes. Remove the pot from heat and let the soup rest for 5 minutes.
6. Ladle the soup into warmed bowls, garnish with parsley, and serve.

Pork & Crab Wonton Soup

YIELD: 4 SERVINGS / **ACTIVE TIME:** 40 MINUTES / **TOTAL TIME:** 1 HOUR

FOR THE BROTH

1 TABLESPOON SESAME OIL, PLUS MORE FOR GARNISH

1 ONION, FINELY DICED

2 CARROTS, PEELED AND FINELY DICED

2 GARLIC CLOVES, MINCED

1 CUP MIRIN

4 CUPS CRAB STOCK (SEE PAGE 452)

1 LEMONGRASS STALK, CRUSHED

1 TABLESPOON SOY SAUCE

1 TABLESPOON FISH SAUCE

SALT AND PEPPER, TO TASTE

SESAME SEEDS, TOASTED, FOR GARNISH

FRESH CILANTRO, CHOPPED, FOR GARNISH

1 SHEET OF NORI, SHREDDED, FOR GARNISH

FOR THE WONTONS

¼ LB. CANNED LUMP CRABMEAT, PICKED OVER AND CHOPPED

¼ LB. GROUND PORK, COOKED

1 TABLESPOON MINCED SHALLOTS

1 TABLESPOON FINELY CHOPPED FRESH CHIVES

1 TABLESPOON FISH SAUCE

2 TABLESPOONS WHITE MISO

2 TABLESPOONS CHOPPED RADISH

1 TABLESPOON TOASTED SESAME SEEDS

1 TEASPOON SESAME OIL

1 TEASPOON SHERRY

12 WONTON WRAPPERS

---

1. To begin preparations for the broth, place the sesame oil in a medium pot and warm it over medium heat. Add the onion and carrots and cook, stirring occasionally, until they have softened, about 5 minutes. Add the garlic and cook, stirring frequently, for 2 minutes.
2. Add the mirin, stock, lemongrass, soy sauce, and fish sauce, bring the soup to a simmer, and cook for 10 minutes.
3. To begin preparations for the wontons, place all of the ingredients, except for the wonton wrappers, in a bowl and stir until well combined.
4. Place 2 teaspoons of the wonton mixture in the center of each wonton wrapper. Moisten a finger with cold water and rub it around the entire edge of each wrapper. Bring the corners of each wrapper together and pinch to seal the wontons.
5. Remove the lemongrass from the soup and discard it.
6. Bring the soup to a boil and add the wontons. Reduce the heat so that the soup simmers and cook until the wontons float to the surface, about 5 minutes.
7. Place three wontons into each serving bowl and ladle the soup over the top. Season with salt and pepper, garnish with toasted sesame seeds, cilantro, additional sesame oil, and nori, and serve.

Tomato Soup with Cheddar Cheese Dumplings

YIELD: 4 SERVINGS / **ACTIVE TIME:** 30 MINUTES / **TOTAL TIME:** 1 HOUR

FOR THE SOUP

2 TABLESPOONS EXTRA-VIRGIN OLIVE OIL

1 ONION, CHOPPED

2 LBS. TOMATOES, CHOPPED

2 CARROTS, PEELED AND CHOPPED

2 TABLESPOONS FINELY CHOPPED FRESH PARSLEY, PLUS MORE FOR GARNISH

½ TEASPOON FRESH THYME

5 CUPS CHICKEN STOCK (SEE PAGE 440)

6 TABLESPOONS HEAVY CREAM, PLUS MORE FOR GARNISH

SALT AND PEPPER, TO TASTE

PARMESAN CHEESE, SHAVED, FOR GARNISH

FOR THE DUMPLINGS

¾ CUP ALL-PURPOSE FLOUR, PLUS MORE AS NEEDED

1 TEASPOON BAKING POWDER

¼ TEASPOON KOSHER SALT

⅓ CUP SHREDDED SHARP CHEDDAR CHEESE

½ CUP BUTTERMILK

3 TABLESPOONS FINELY CHOPPED FRESH PARSLEY

1. To begin preparations for the soup, place the olive oil in a medium pot and warm it over medium heat. Add the onion and cook, stirring occasionally, until it has softened, about 5 minutes. Add the tomatoes, carrots, parsley, thyme, and stock, bring to a simmer, and cook until the carrots are tender, about 20 minutes. Remove the pot from heat.
2. Pour the soup into a food processor and puree it. Strain the soup back into the pot, add the cream, and stir to combine. Bring to a gentle simmer and season with salt and pepper.
3. To begin preparations for the dumplings, place the flour, baking powder, and salt in a mixing bowl and stir to combine. Add the cheese, buttermilk, and parsley and work the mixture until it comes together as a dough. Add a few drops of water to the mixture if it is having trouble coming together as a dough.
4. Place the dough on a flour-dusted work surface and knead it until it is smooth. Pinch off small pieces of the dough and drop them into the simmering soup.
5. Cook until the dumplings are cooked through, about 10 minutes. Remove the pot from heat and let the soup cool for 5 minutes.
6. Ladle the soup into warmed bowls, garnish with shaved Parmesan and additional parsley and cream, and serve.

Tomato Soup with Cheddar Cheese Dumplings

SEE PAGE 39

Pork & Shrimp Wonton Soup

YIELD: 4 SERVINGS / **ACTIVE TIME:** 40 MINUTES / **TOTAL TIME:** 1 HOUR

FOR THE BROTH

1 TABLESPOON SESAME OIL

1 ONION, FINELY DICED

2 CARROTS, PEELED AND FINELY CHOPPED

2 GARLIC CLOVES, MINCED

1 CUP SAKE

4 CUPS CHICKEN STOCK (SEE PAGE 440)

1 LEMONGRASS STALK, CRUSHED

1 TABLESPOON SOY SAUCE

1 TABLESPOON FISH SAUCE

SALT AND PEPPER, TO TASTE

SHALLOTS, SLICED THIN, FOR GARNISH

BEAN SPROUTS, FOR GARNISH

FRESH CILANTRO, CHOPPED, FOR GARNISH

FOR THE WONTONS

¼ LB. SHRIMP, SHELLED, DEVEINED, AND FINELY CHOPPED

½ LB. COOKED GROUND PORK

1 TABLESPOON CHOPPED SHALLOTS

1 TABLESPOON FINELY CHOPPED FRESH CHIVES

1 TABLESPOON FISH SAUCE

2 TABLESPOONS WHITE MISO

1 TABLESPOON SHRIMP PASTE

2 TABLESPOONS DICED RADISH

1 TABLESPOON TOASTED SESAME SEEDS

1 TEASPOON SESAME OIL

1 TEASPOON SHERRY

12 WONTON WRAPPERS

1. To begin preparations for the broth, place the sesame oil in a medium pot and warm it over medium heat. Add the onion and carrots and cook, stirring occasionally, until they have softened, about 5 minutes. Add the garlic and cook, stirring frequently, for 2 minutes.
2. Add the sake, stock, lemongrass, soy sauce, and fish sauce, bring the soup to a simmer, and cook for 10 minutes.
3. To begin preparations for the wontons, place all of the ingredients, except for the wonton wrappers, in a bowl and stir until well combined.
4. Place 2 teaspoons of the wonton mixture in the center of each wonton wrapper. Moisten a finger with cold water and rub it around the entire edge of each wrapper. Bring the corners of each wrapper together and pinch to seal the wontons.
5. Remove the lemongrass from the soup and discard it.
6. Bring the soup to a boil and add the wontons. Reduce the heat so that the soup simmers and cook until the wontons float to the surface, about 5 minutes. Season with salt and pepper.
7. Place three wontons into each serving bowl and ladle the soup over the wantons. Garnish with shallots, bean sprouts, and cilantro and serve.

Pork Teriyaki & Red Miso Ramen

YIELD: 6 SERVINGS / **ACTIVE TIME:** 30 MINUTES / **TOTAL TIME:** 2 HOURS AND 30 MINUTES

FOR THE BROTH

1½ LBS. PORK BONES

1 ONION, FINELY DICED

2-INCH PIECE OF FRESH GINGER, PEELED AND MINCED

¼ CUP SOY SAUCE

1 CUP MIRIN

1 TABLESPOON BROWN SUGAR

1 CUP WATER

3 TABLESPOONS EXTRA-VIRGIN OLIVE OIL

1¼ LBS. PORK TENDERLOIN, CHOPPED INTO 1-INCH PIECES

SALT AND PEPPER, TO TASTE

⅔ CUP RED MISO

4 SCALLIONS, SLICED THIN

6 HARD-BOILED EGGS, HALVED

BAMBOO SHOOTS, FOR GARNISH

NORI, SHREDDED, FOR GARNISH

CHILI OIL, FOR GARNISH

FOR THE BEAN SPROUTS AND NOODLES

¾ LB. RAMEN NOODLES

½ LB. BEAN SPROUTS

1 TABLESPOON SESAME OIL

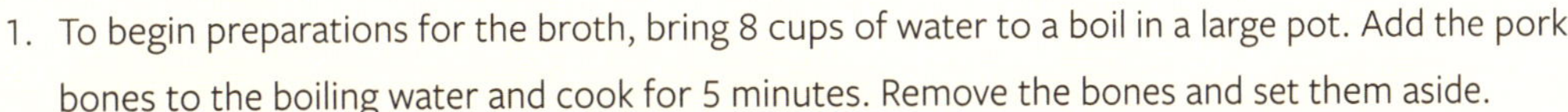

1. To begin preparations for the broth, bring 8 cups of water to a boil in a large pot. Add the pork bones to the boiling water and cook for 5 minutes. Remove the bones and set them aside.
2. Bring 12 cups of water to a boil in another large pot. Add the pork bones, onion, and ginger, reduce the heat so that the broth simmers, and cook for 1 hour and 30 minutes.
3. Place the soy sauce, mirin, brown sugar, and water in a mixing bowl and mix until fully combined.
4. Place 2 tablespoons of the olive oil in a large skillet and warm it over medium-high heat. Add the pork and cook, stirring occasionally, until it is lightly browned, about 5 minutes. Add the mirin mixture, reduce the heat to low, and cook until the pork is cooked through, about 25 minutes, stirring occasionally. Remove the skillet from heat and let it cool.
5. To begin preparations for the bean sprouts and noodles, bring water to a boil in 2 medium pots.
6. Add salt to one of the pots, let the water return to a full boil, and add the noodles. Cook until they are al dente, 6 to 8 minutes. Add the sprouts to the other pot, let the water return to a boil, and cook for 1 minute. Drain the noodles and sprouts and place them in a mixing bowl. Add the sesame oil, stir until thoroughly combined, and set the mixture aside.
7. Once the broth has finished cooking, strain it through a fine-mesh sieve. Place 1 cup of the broth in a medium skillet and bring it to a boil. Remove the pan from heat, add the red miso, and stir until it has dissolved.
8. Place the remaining olive oil in a medium pot and warm it over medium-high heat. Add the scallions and cook for 1 minute, stirring occasionally. Add the remaining broth and bring the soup to a boil.
9. Reduce the heat so that the soup simmers, add the miso mixture, and stir until everything is thoroughly combined. Turn off the heat and season with salt and pepper.
10. Divide the pork, eggs, bean sprouts, and noodles among the serving bowls and ladle the soup over the top. Garnish with bamboo shoots, nori, and chili oil and serve.

Pasta e Lattuga

YIELD: 4 SERVINGS / **ACTIVE TIME:** 10 MINUTES / **TOTAL TIME:** 25 MINUTES

8 CUPS WATER

SALT, TO TASTE

½ LB. MACARONI OR OTHER SHORT-FORMAT PASTA

1 HEAD OF ROMAINE LETTUCE, WASHED AND CHOPPED

2 TABLESPOONS EXTRA-VIRGIN OLIVE OIL, FOR GARNISH

1. Bring the water to a boil in a large saucepan. Add salt—less than you would for a typical pasta dish.
2. Add the pasta and lettuce and cook until the pasta is al dente, following the instructions on the pasta packaging.
3. Ladle the soup into warmed bowls, top each portion with some of the olive oil, and enjoy.

Pot Sticker Soup

YIELD: 4 SERVINGS / **ACTIVE TIME:** 30 MINUTES / **TOTAL TIME:** 1 HOUR

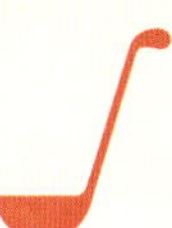

FOR THE POT STICKERS

6 OZ. COOKED GROUND PORK OR MINCED SHRIMP

½ CUP FINELY CHOPPED CABBAGE

1 TABLESPOON MINCED FRESH GINGER

4 SCALLIONS, TRIMMED AND SLICED

1 TABLESPOON SOY SAUCE

¼ CUP WATER

24 WONTON WRAPPERS

1 EGG, BEATEN

2 TABLESPOONS EXTRA-VIRGIN OLIVE OIL

FOR THE SOUP

6 CUPS CHICKEN STOCK (SEE PAGE 440)

3 CUPS SHREDDED SAVOY CABBAGE

2 CUPS DICED SHIITAKE MUSHROOMS

1 CARROT, PEELED AND JULIENNED

½ CUP PEAS

2 TABLESPOONS SOY SAUCE

SALT AND PEPPER, TO TASTE

SCALLION GREENS, FOR GARNISH

SESAME OIL, FOR GARNISH

1. To begin preparations for the pot stickers, place the pork or shrimp, cabbage, ginger, scallions, soy sauce, and half of the water in a large mixing bowl and stir until well combined.
2. Place 1 teaspoon of the mixture in the center of each wonton wrapper. Moisten a finger with the beaten egg and rub it around the edge of each wrapper. Bring the corners of each wrapper together and pinch to seal.
3. Place the olive oil in a large skillet and warm it over medium-high heat. Add the pot stickers and cook until they are lightly browned, about 2 minutes. Add the remaining water, cover the skillet, and steam for 3 minutes. Remove the skillet from heat and set the pot stickers aside.
4. To begin preparations for the soup, bring the stock to a boil in a medium pot. Add the cabbage, mushrooms, and carrot and cook for 3 minutes. Add the peas and cook until all of the vegetables are cooked through, about 2 minutes. Add the soy sauce, season with salt and pepper, and remove the pot from heat.
5. Divide the pot stickers among the serving bowls and ladle the soup over the top. Garnish with scallion greens and sesame oil and serve.

Portobello Mushroom Ravioli in Beet Soup

YIELD: 4 SERVINGS / **ACTIVE TIME:** 1 HOUR / **TOTAL TIME:** 1 HOUR AND 45 MINUTES

FOR THE PASTA DOUGH

1 CUP "00" PASTA FLOUR

⅛ TEASPOON KOSHER SALT

1 CUP EGG YOLKS

1 TEASPOON EXTRA-VIRGIN OLIVE OIL

FOR THE FILLING

1 TABLESPOON UNSALTED BUTTER

2 CUPS DICED PORTOBELLO MUSHROOMS

1 FRESH SHALLOT, FINELY CHOPPED

1 GARLIC CLOVE, MINCED

1 TEASPOON FRESH THYME

2 TABLESPOONS MASCARPONE CHEESE

SALT AND PEPPER, TO TASTE

FOR THE RAVIOLI

1 CUP ALL-PURPOSE FLOUR

1 EGG, BEATEN

1 TABLESPOON WATER

FOR THE SOUP

1 TABLESPOON EXTRA-VIRGIN OLIVE OIL

1 ONION, FINELY DICED

2 GARLIC CLOVES, MINCED

1 TEASPOON FENNEL SEEDS

1 BEET, PEELED AND FINELY DICED

6 CUPS CHICKEN STOCK (SEE PAGE 440)

¼ CUP ORANGE JUICE

SALT AND PEPPER, TO TASTE

FENNEL FRONDS, FOR GARNISH

1. To begin preparations for the pasta dough, place the pasta flour and salt in a small mixing bowl and stir until well combined. Pour the mixture onto a work surface and make a well in the center of it. Place the egg yolks and olive oil in the well and combine the mixture with your hands. Knead the dough until it is smooth, about 5 minutes. Cover the dough with plastic wrap and let it rest at room temperature for 30 minutes.
2. To begin preparations for the filling, place the butter in a medium skillet and melt it over medium heat. Add the mushrooms and cook for 5 minutes, stirring occasionally. Add the shallot, garlic, and thyme and cook, stirring occasionally, until the shallot has softened, about 5 minutes. Remove the skillet from heat, strain the mixture, and let it cool.
3. Place the vegetable mixture and mascarpone in a small mixing bowl and stir until well combined. Season with salt and pepper and set the filling aside.
4. To begin preparations for the ravioli, gently sprinkle the all-purpose flour over a large ravioli tray. Place the egg and water in a small mixing bowl and whisk until well combined
5. Feed the pasta dough into a pasta maker to create thin sheets (about ⅙-inch thick). Place half of the sheets in the ravioli tray and add 1 teaspoon of filling to the center of each rectangle. Moisten a finger with the egg wash and run it along the edges of each rectangle.
6. Place the remaining sheets of pasta on top of each of the filled sheets, press on the edges of each ravioli to seal and cut them, and cover them with plastic wrap. Set the ravioli aside.
7. To begin preparations for the soup, place the olive oil in a large pot and warm it over medium heat. Add the onion, garlic, and fennel seeds and cook, stirring occasionally, until the onion has softened, about 5 minutes. Add the beet and cook for 5 minutes, stirring occasionally.

8. Add the stock and orange juice and bring the soup to a boil. Reduce the heat so that the soup simmers and cook until the beet is tender, about 15 minutes. Season with salt and pepper and return to a boil. Drop the ravioli into the soup and cook until they are cooked through, about 3 minutes.
9. Ladle the soup into warmed bowls, garnish with fennel fronds, and serve.

Pork Wonton Soup

YIELD: 4 TO 6 SERVINGS / **ACTIVE TIME:** 30 MINUTES / **TOTAL TIME:** 1 HOUR AND 15 MINUTES

1 TABLESPOON CANOLA OIL

¾ LB. GROUND PORK

1 TEASPOON CORNSTARCH

2 TABLESPOONS MIRIN

4 FRESH SCALLIONS, CHOPPED

1 TABLESPOON TOASTED SESAME SEEDS

1½ TABLESPOONS SOY SAUCE

1 TEASPOON MINCED FRESH GINGER

2 TEASPOONS SESAME OIL

½ TEASPOON SUGAR

SALT AND PEPPER, TO TASTE

24 WONTON WRAPPERS

1 EGG, BEATEN

6 CUPS CHICKEN STOCK (SEE PAGE 440)

1 CARROT, PEELED AND SLICED THIN

4 BOK CHOY, SEPARATED INTO INDIVIDUAL LEAVES

24 SUGAR SNAP PEAS

SCALLION GREENS, FOR GARNISH

EDIBLE FLOWERS, FOR GARNISH

1. Place the canola oil in a large skillet and warm it over medium heat. Add the pork and cook until it is cooked through, 8 to 10 minutes, breaking it up with a wooden spoon. Remove the pan from heat and let the pork cool.
2. Place the cornstarch and mirin in a large mixing bowl and mix until well combined. Add the pork, scallions, sesame seeds, soy sauce, ginger, sesame oil, and sugar and stir to combine. Season with salt and pepper and chill the mixture in the refrigerator for 30 minutes.
3. Place 1 tablespoon of the pork mixture in the center of each wonton wrapper. Moisten a finger with the beaten egg and rub it around the entire edge of each wrapper. Bring the corners of each wrapper together and pinch to seal. Chill the wontons in the refrigerator.
4. Bring the stock to a boil in a medium pot. Reduce the heat so that the stock simmers and season with salt and pepper. Add the carrot and bok choy and cook for 3 minutes, stirring occasionally. Add the snap peas and cook until the vegetables are tender, about 3 minutes. Remove the vegetables from the broth with a strainer and set them aside.
5. Bring the broth back to a simmer and add the wontons in two batches. Cook each batch until the wontons float to the surface, about 5 minutes. Remove the wontons with a strainer and set them aside.
6. Divide the vegetables and wontons among the serving bowls and ladle the broth over the top. Garnish with scallion greens and edible flowers and serve.

Shrimp & Pork Wonton Soup

YIELD: 4 SERVINGS / **ACTIVE TIME:** 40 MINUTES / **TOTAL TIME:** 1 HOUR AND 30 MINUTES

6 CUPS HAM STOCK (SEE PAGE 447)

1 ONION, FINELY DICED

1 GARLIC CLOVE, MINCED

1 CINNAMON STICK

2 STAR ANISE PODS

2 WHOLE CLOVES

1 RED THAI CHILE PEPPER, CHOPPED

2 SCALLIONS, TRIMMED AND SLICED

1 TABLESPOON FISH SAUCE

1 TABLESPOON SOY SAUCE

PORK & SHRIMP WONTONS (SEE PAGE 42)

SALT AND PEPPER, TO TASTE

SCALLION GREENS, FOR GARNISH

1. Bring the stock to a boil in a medium pot. Add the onion, garlic, cinnamon, star anise, cloves, and chile, reduce the heat so that the broth simmers, and cook for 10 minutes, stirring occasionally. Remove the pot from heat and let the broth steep for 30 minutes.
2. Strain the broth through a fine-mesh sieve, place it in a clean medium pot, and bring to a simmer. Add the scallions, fish sauce, soy sauce, and wontons and cook until the wontons float to the surface of the soup, about 5 minutes. Season with salt and pepper.
3. Ladle the soup into warmed bowls, garnish with scallion greens, and serve.

Vegetarian Ramen

YIELD: 4 SERVINGS / **ACTIVE TIME:** 30 MINUTES / **TOTAL TIME:** 1 HOUR

1 OZ. KOMBU, SLICED

4 DRIED SHIITAKE MUSHROOMS, FINELY DICED

¼ CUP TOASTED SESAME SEEDS, PLUS MORE FOR GARNISH

2 TABLESPOONS SESAME OIL

4 GARLIC CLOVES, MINCED

2-INCH PIECE OF FRESH GINGER, PEELED AND MINCED

4 SCALLIONS, TRIMMED AND SLICED

2 TABLESPOONS CHILI BEAN PASTE

2 TABLESPOONS WHITE MISO

¼ CUP SAKE

3 CUPS UNSWEETENED SOY MILK

SALT AND PEPPER, TO TASTE

½ LB. RAMEN NOODLES

BEAN SPROUTS, FOR GARNISH

SCALLION GREENS, FOR GARNISH

4 POACHED EGGS, FOR SERVING

1. Bring water to a boil in a large pot. Remove the pot from heat, add the kombu, and let it soak for 20 minutes.
2. Remove the kombu from the pot and score its surface gently with a knife.
3. Return the kombu to the pot and bring the water to a boil. Remove the kombu from the pot and discard it. Add the mushrooms and return the broth to a boil. Remove the pan from heat and let the broth rest until it has cooled completely.
4. Strain the broth through a fine-mesh sieve and set it aside. Using a mortar and pestle, grind the sesame seeds into a smooth paste. Set the paste aside.
5. Place the sesame oil in a medium pot and warm it over medium heat. Add the garlic and ginger and cook, stirring frequently, for 2 minutes. Add the scallions, chili bean paste, and miso and cook, stirring frequently, for 1 minute. Add the sake and cook, stirring occasionally, until half of it has evaporated.
6. Add the broth, sesame seed paste, and soy milk and bring the soup to a simmer. Season with salt and pepper, remove the pot from heat, and let the soup rest.
7. Bring water to a boil in a medium pot. Add salt, let the water return to a full boil, and add the noodles. Cook until they are al dente, 6 to 8 minutes. Drain the noodles and divide them among the serving bowls.
8. Ladle the soup over the noodles, garnish with additional toasted sesame seeds, bean sprouts, and scallion greens, and serve with the poached eggs.

Vietnamese Noodle Soup

YIELD: 6 SERVINGS / **ACTIVE TIME:** 15 MINUTES / **TOTAL TIME:** 35 MINUTES

1 LB. RICE NOODLES

2 TABLESPOONS EXTRA-VIRGIN OLIVE OIL

2-INCH PIECE OF FRESH GINGER, PEELED AND SLICED THIN

3 JALAPEÑO CHILE PEPPERS, STEMMED, SEEDED, AND SLICED

4 SCALLIONS, TRIMMED AND CHOPPED

1 LEMONGRASS STALK, BRUISED AND CHOPPED

1 TABLESPOON FISH SAUCE

2 TEASPOONS CHILI GARLIC SAUCE

1 TEASPOON SOY SAUCE

4 CUPS CHICKEN STOCK (SEE PAGE 440)

½ LB. MUSHROOMS, SLICED

1 TEASPOON WHITE PEPPER

1 CUP FRESH BASIL

1 CUP FRESH MINT

SALT AND PEPPER, TO TASTE

5 OZ. FRESH SPINACH, CHOPPED

1 CUP CHOPPED FRESH CILANTRO

2 CUPS BEAN SPROUTS

1 LB. MEDIUM SHRIMP, SHELLS REMOVED, DEVEINED

1. Place the rice noodles in a bowl and cover them with boiling water. Soak until they are al dente, following the instructions on the packaging. Drain the noodles and set them aside.

2. Place the olive oil in a Dutch oven and warm it over medium heat. Add the ginger, jalapeños, scallions, and lemongrass and cook, stirring occasionally, for 4 minutes. Reduce the heat to medium-low and add the remaining ingredients, except for the spinach, cilantro, bean sprouts, and shrimp. Bring to a simmer and cook for about 10 minutes.

3. Stir in the spinach, cilantro, bean sprouts, and shrimp and cook until the shrimp turn pink and are cooked through, 3 to 5 minutes.

4. Divide the rice noodles among the serving bowls, ladle the soup over them, and enjoy.

Noodle Soup with Crab Balls

YIELD: 6 SERVINGS / **ACTIVE TIME:** 15 MINUTES / **TOTAL TIME:** 1 HOUR AND 40 MINUTES

FOR THE CRAB BALLS

1 LB. FRESH LUMP CRABMEAT, PICKED OVER

¾ CUP BREAD CRUMBS

½ CUP CHOPPED FRESH CILANTRO

1 LARGE EGG, BEATEN

2 TEASPOONS FRESH LEMON JUICE

1 TEASPOON KOSHER SALT

½ TEASPOON BLACK PEPPER

FOR THE SOUP

¼ CUP AVOCADO OIL

6 GARLIC CLOVES, SLICED

1-INCH PIECE OF FRESH GINGER, PEELED AND GRATED

1 LEMONGRASS STALK, TRIMMED AND BRUISED

½ LB. MUSHROOMS, SLICED

SALT, TO TASTE

6 CUPS CHICKEN STOCK (SEE PAGE 440)

¾ LB. RICE NOODLES

2 TABLESPOONS SOY SAUCE

FRESH CILANTRO, CHOPPED, FOR GARNISH

1. To prepare the crab balls, place all of the ingredients in a mixing bowl and work the mixture with your hands until well combined. Form heaping tablespoons of the mixture into balls, place the crab balls on a plate, and cover them with plastic wrap. Chill the crab balls in the refrigerator for 1 hour.

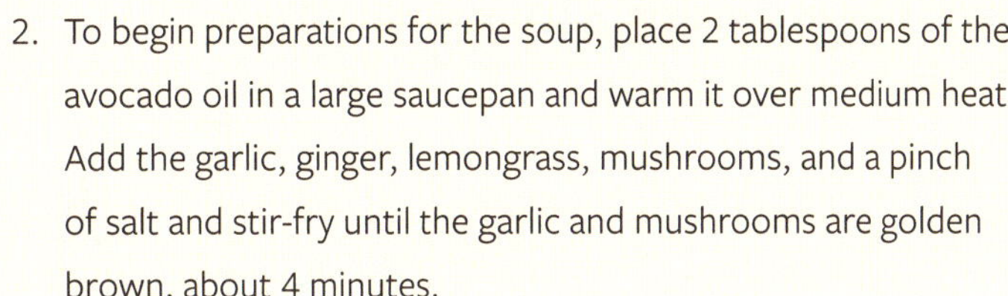

2. To begin preparations for the soup, place 2 tablespoons of the avocado oil in a large saucepan and warm it over medium heat. Add the garlic, ginger, lemongrass, mushrooms, and a pinch of salt and stir-fry until the garlic and mushrooms are golden brown, about 4 minutes.
3. Add the stock, bring the soup to a boil, and then reduce the heat so that it simmers. Add the rice noodles and cook until they are tender, about 6 minutes.
4. While the noodles are cooking, place the remaining avocado oil in a large skillet and warm it over medium heat. Add the crab balls to the skillet and cook until they are golden brown, 4 to 6 minutes, turning them as necessary.
5. Add the crab balls to the soup, along with the soy sauce, and cook until they are cooked through, about 3 minutes.
6. Ladle the soup into warmed bowls, garnish each portion with cilantro, and enjoy.

Elk Soup with Gnocchi

YIELD: 4 SERVINGS / **ACTIVE TIME:** 1 HOUR / **TOTAL TIME:** 3 HOURS

2 TABLESPOONS EXTRA-VIRGIN OLIVE OIL

3 LBS. ELK BONES (NECK OR BACK BONES)

5 CUPS WATER

2 BAY LEAVES

3 ALLSPICE BERRIES

½ TEASPOON KOSHER SALT, PLUS MORE TO TASTE

2 TABLESPOONS BREAD CRUMBS

¾ LB. GROUND ELK SHOULDER

1 EGG

BLACK PEPPER, TO TASTE

PAPRIKA, TO TASTE

½ CELERIAC, PEELED AND DICED

3 CARROTS, PEELED AND DICED

3 CUPS MUSHROOMS

1 ONION, DICED

4 ROMA TOMATOES, DICED

¾ LB. GNOCCHI

FRESH PARSLEY, CHOPPED, FOR GARNISH

1. Place the olive oil in a large saucepan and warm it over medium-high heat. Add the elk bones and cook, stirring occasionally, until they are starting to brown.
2. Add the water, bay leaves, allspice, and salt and bring the mixture to a simmer. Cook for 2 hours, skimming off any impurities that rise to the top.
3. Strain the stock into a clean saucepan and bring it to a simmer.
4. Place the bread crumbs, elk, and egg in a bowl, season the mixture with salt, pepper, and paprika, and work the mixture with your hands until it is thoroughly combined. Form the mixture into small balls and add them to the stock, along with the celeriac, carrots, mushrooms, onion, and tomatoes. Bring the soup to a simmer and cook for 10 minutes.
5. Add the gnocchi to the soup and cook until the meatballs and gnocchi are cooked through, 5 to 7 minutes.
6. Ladle the soup into warmed bowls, garnish each portion with parsley, and serve.

Thai Coconut Soup with Lobster Wontons

YIELD: 4 SERVINGS / **ACTIVE TIME:** 30 MINUTES / **TOTAL TIME:** 1 HOUR

FOR THE WONTONS

1½ CUPS CANNED LUMP LOBSTER, PICKED OVER AND CHOPPED

1 SCALLION, TRIMMED AND SLICED

SALT AND PEPPER, TO TASTE

24 WONTON WRAPPERS

1 EGG, BEATEN

FOR THE SOUP

1 TABLESPOON SESAME OIL

2 TABLESPOONS RED THAI CURRY PASTE

2 TEASPOONS SUGAR

3 TABLESPOONS FISH SAUCE

1 (14 OZ.) CAN OF COCONUT MILK

FRESH LIME JUICE, TO TASTE

SALT AND PEPPER, TO TASTE

THAI CHILE PEPPERS, STEMMED, SEEDED, AND SLICED, FOR GARNISH

FRESH CILANTRO, CHOPPED, FOR GARNISH

1. To begin preparations for the wontons, place the lobster and scallion in a mixing bowl, season with salt and pepper, and stir to combine.
2. Place 1 tablespoon of filling in the center of each wonton wrapper. Moisten a finger with the egg and then rub it around the entire edge of each wrapper. Bring the corners of the wrapper together and pinch to seal the wontons. Chill the wontons in the refrigerator.
3. To begin preparations for the soup, place the sesame oil in a medium pot and warm it over low heat. Add the curry paste and cook, stirring frequently, for 5 minutes. Add the sugar, fish sauce, and coconut milk and cook, stirring frequently, for 4 minutes. Season with lime juice, salt, and pepper, remove the pot from heat, and let the soup rest.
4. Bring water to a boil in a large pot. Working in two batches to avoid overcrowding the pot, add the wontons to the boiling water and cook until they float to the surface, about 3 minutes. Remove the wontons with a strainer and set them aside.
5. Divide the wontons among the serving bowls and ladle the soup over the top. Garnish with chile peppers and cilantro and serve.

Simple Dumpling Soup

YIELD: 4 SERVINGS / **ACTIVE TIME:** 30 MINUTES / **TOTAL TIME:** 1 HOUR

FOR THE DUMPLINGS

1 CUP ALL-PURPOSE FLOUR, PLUS MORE AS NEEDED

½ TEASPOON BAKING POWDER

½ TEASPOON KOSHER SALT

½ TABLESPOON EXTRA-VIRGIN OLIVE OIL

1 EGG

6 TABLESPOONS WATER

1 TABLESPOON FINELY CHOPPED FRESH CHIVES

FOR THE SOUP

2 TABLESPOONS UNSALTED BUTTER

4 SLICES OF THICK-CUT BACON, FINELY DICED

1 ONION, FINELY DICED

4 CUPS PEELED AND DICED POTATOES

6 CUPS CHICKEN STOCK (SEE PAGE 440)

SALT AND PEPPER, TO TASTE

1. To begin preparations for the dumplings, place the flour, baking powder, and salt in a mixing bowl and mix until well combined. Add the olive oil, egg, water, and chives and work the mixture until it comes together as a smooth dough. Place the dough on a flour-dusted work surface and knead until it is smooth. Cover the dough with plastic wrap and set it aside.
2. To begin preparations for the soup, place the butter in a medium pot and melt it over medium heat. Add the bacon and onion and cook, stirring occasionally, until the bacon is crispy and the onion has softened, about 5 minutes. Add the potatoes and cook, stirring occasionally, for 3 minutes.
3. Add the stock and bring it to a boil. Reduce the heat so that the soup simmers and cook until the potatoes are tender, about 15 minutes. Season with salt and pepper.
4. Pinch off pieces of the dough and drop them into the simmering soup. Cook until the dumplings are cooked through, about 10 minutes. Remove the pot from heat and let the soup rest for 5 minutes.
5. Ladle the soup into warmed bowls and serve.

Spicy Shoyu Ramen

YIELD: 4 SERVINGS / **ACTIVE TIME:** 30 MINUTES / **TOTAL TIME:** 1 HOUR AND 15 MINUTES

2 TABLESPOONS SESAME OIL

4 GARLIC CLOVES, MINCED

3-INCH PIECE OF FRESH GINGER, PEELED AND MINCED

2 TABLESPOONS CHILI BEAN SAUCE

3 CUPS CHICKEN STOCK (SEE PAGE 440)

3 CUPS DASHI STOCK (SEE PAGE 448)

¼ CUP SOY SAUCE

1 TABLESPOON SAKE

SALT AND PEPPER, TO TASTE

2 TEASPOONS SUGAR

½ LB. RAMEN NOODLES

4 POACHED EGGS

SICHUAN PEPPERCORN & CHILE OIL (SEE PAGE 458)

FRESH SCALLION FRONDS, FOR GARNISH

1. Place the sesame oil in a medium pot and warm it over medium heat. Add the garlic and ginger and cook, stirring frequently, until they are fragrant, about 2 minutes. Add the chili bean sauce and cook for 1 minute, stirring occasionally.
2. Add the stocks, soy sauce, and sake and bring the soup to a boil. Reduce the heat so that the soup simmers and cook for 5 minutes. Season with salt, pepper, and sugar, turn off the heat, and let the soup sit.
3. Bring water to a boil in a medium pot. Add salt, let the water return to a full boil, and add the noodles. Cook until they are al dente, 6 to 8 minutes. Drain the noodles and divide them among warmed serving bowls.
4. Bring the broth to a boil and ladle it over the noodles. Top each portion with a poached egg and Sichuan Peppercorn & Chile Oil. Garnish with scallion fronds and serve.

Tomato Alphabet Soup

YIELD: 4 SERVINGS / **ACTIVE TIME:** 15 MINUTES / **TOTAL TIME:** 30 MINUTES

SALT AND PEPPER, TO TASTE

1 CUP ALPHABET PASTA

¼ CUP UNSALTED BUTTER

2 ONIONS, FINELY DICED

4 CARROTS, PEELED AND FINELY DICED

2 CELERY STALKS, FINELY DICED

3 CUPS VEGETABLE STOCK (SEE PAGE 441)

2 TEASPOONS FINELY CHOPPED FRESH BASIL

4 (14 OZ.) CANS OF DICED TOMATOES, DRAINED

1. Bring water to a boil in a medium pot. Add salt, let the water return to a boil, and add the pasta. Cook until it is al dente, 8 to 10 minutes. Drain the pasta and set it aside.
2. Place the butter in a medium pot and melt it over medium heat. Add the onions, carrots, and celery and cook, stirring occasionally, until they have softened, about 5 minutes. Add the stock, basil, and tomatoes and bring to a boil.
3. Reduce the heat so that the soup simmers and cook for 10 minutes.
4. Transfer the soup to a food processor, pulse until smooth, and strain it into a clean pot through a fine-mesh sieve. Bring the soup to a simmer, add the pasta, and season with salt and pepper.
5. Ladle the soup into warmed bowls and serve.

Tomato Soup with Chickpeas & Pasta

YIELD: 4 SERVINGS / **ACTIVE TIME:** 20 MINUTES / **TOTAL TIME:** 45 MINUTES

2 TABLESPOONS EXTRA-VIRGIN OLIVE OIL

1 ONION, FINELY DICED

2 GARLIC CLOVES, MINCED

2 (28 OZ.) CANS OF STEWED TOMATOES, PUREED

2 TEASPOONS FRESH THYME

4 CUPS CHICKEN STOCK (SEE PAGE 440)

½ CUP SHORT-FORMAT PASTA

1 (14 OZ.) CAN OF CHICKPEAS, DRAINED AND RINSED

¼ CUP FINELY CHOPPED FRESH PARSLEY

¼ CUP GRATED PARMESAN CHEESE, PLUS MORE FOR GARNISH

SALT AND PEPPER, TO TASTE

FRESH BASIL, CHOPPED, FOR GARNISH

1. Place the olive oil in a large pot and warm it over medium heat. Add the onion and cook, stirring occasionally, until it has softened, about 5 minutes. Add the garlic and cook, stirring frequently, for 2 minutes.
2. Add the tomatoes, thyme, and stock and bring the soup to a boil. Reduce the heat so that the soup simmers, add the pasta, and cook until it is al dente, 8 to 10 minutes. Add the chickpeas, parsley, and cheese and cook for 3 minutes.
3. Season with salt and pepper and divide the soup among the serving bowls. Garnish with additional Parmesan and basil and serve.

VEGETABLES

Corn & Plantain Soup

YIELD: 4 SERVINGS / **ACTIVE TIME:** 15 MINUTES / **TOTAL TIME:** 40 MINUTES

¼ CUP UNSALTED BUTTER

1 ONION, FINELY DICED

2 GARLIC CLOVES, MINCED

2 RIPE PLANTAINS, PEELED AND SLICED

2 PLUM TOMATOES, FINELY DICED

5 CUPS CORN KERNELS

1 TEASPOON FINELY CHOPPED FRESH TARRAGON

4 CUPS CHICKEN STOCK (SEE PAGE 440)

1 TABLESPOON FINELY DICED JALAPEÑO CHILE PEPPER

⅛ TEASPOON FRESHLY GRATED NUTMEG

SALT AND PEPPER, TO TASTE

1. Place the butter in a medium pot and melt it over medium heat. Add the onion and garlic and cook, stirring frequently, until the onion has softened, about 5 minutes. Add the plantains, tomatoes, corn, and tarragon and cook, stirring occasionally, for 5 minutes.
2. Add the stock, jalapeño, and nutmeg and bring the soup to a boil. Reduce the heat so that the soup simmers and cook until the plantains are tender, about 10 minutes.
3. Season with salt and pepper, divide the soup among the serving bowls, and serve.

Purple Cauliflower Soup

YIELD: 4 SERVINGS / **ACTIVE TIME:** 15 MINUTES / **TOTAL TIME:** 45 MINUTES

¼ CUP UNSALTED BUTTER

1 ONION, FINELY DICED

1 HEAD OF PURPLE CAULIFLOWER, CUT INTO FLORETS AND FINELY CHOPPED

½ CUP PEELED AND FINELY DICED BEETS

4 CUPS VEGETABLE STOCK (SEE PAGE 441)

2 CUPS HEAVY CREAM

SALT AND PEPPER, TO TASTE

PARMESAN CHEESE, GRATED, FOR GARNISH

1. Place the butter in a medium pot and melt it over medium heat. Add the onion, cauliflower, and beets and cook, stirring occasionally, until the onion has softened, about 5 minutes. Add the stock and bring to a boil.
2. Reduce the heat so that the soup simmers and cook for 5 minutes. Add the cream, stir to combine, and cook for 10 minutes.
3. Transfer the soup to a food processor, pulse until smooth, and strain it into a clean pot through a fine-mesh sieve. Bring the soup to a simmer.
4. Ladle the soup into warmed bowls, garnish with Parmesan, and serve.

Spicy Tortilla Soup

YIELD: 4 SERVINGS / **ACTIVE TIME:** 30 MINUTES / **TOTAL TIME:** 1 HOUR AND 30 MINUTES

1½ OZ. DRIED PASILLA CHILE PEPPERS, STEMMED AND SEEDED

1 TOMATO

2 GARLIC CLOVES, UNPEELED

6 CUPS CHICKEN STOCK (SEE PAGE 440)

2 CUPS PLUS 1 TABLESPOON EXTRA-VIRGIN OLIVE OIL

1 ONION, FINELY DICED

½ TEASPOON KOSHER SALT

8 CORN TORTILLAS, CUT INTO ¼-INCH-WIDE STRIPS

4 CUPS RED SWISS CHARD, SLICED THIN

MONTEREY JACK CHEESE, GRATED, FOR GARNISH

LIME WEDGES, FOR SERVING

1. Preheat the oven to 350°F. Bring water to a boil in a small pot. Reduce the heat under the boiling water to low, add the chiles, and simmer for 20 minutes. Drain the chiles and place them in a food processor.
2. Place the tomato in a baking dish, place it in the oven, and roast for 10 minutes. Remove the tomato from the oven and set it aside.
3. Place the garlic in a small, dry skillet and toast over medium heat, turning occasionally, until it is charred, about 15 minutes. Remove the garlic from the skillet and let it cool. When it is cool enough to handle, peel and mince the garlic.
4. Add the garlic, the tomato and its juices, and 1 cup of the stock to the food processor and pulse until combined. Strain the puree through a fine-mesh sieve and set it aside.
5. Place 1 tablespoon of the olive oil in a medium pot and warm it over medium heat. Add the onion and cook, stirring occasionally, until the onion has softened, about 5 minutes. Add the puree and remaining stock and bring to a boil. Reduce the heat so that the soup simmers and cook for 30 minutes.
6. Place the remaining olive oil in a Dutch oven and warm it to 350°F. Gently slip the tortillas into the hot oil and fry until they are crispy, gently stirring as necessary. Transfer the fried tortilla strips to a paper towel–lined plate to drain.
7. Stir the Swiss chard into the soup and cook for 5 minutes.
8. Divide the soup among the serving bowls and top each portion with the fried tortilla strips. Garnish with Monterey Jack and serve with lime wedges.

Apple & Rutabaga Soup

YIELD: 6 SERVINGS / **ACTIVE TIME:** 25 MINUTES / **TOTAL TIME:** 45 MINUTES

¼ CUP UNSALTED BUTTER

1 CUP FINELY DICED ONION

1 CUP PEELED AND DICED APPLE

1 CUP PEELED AND DICED RUTABAGA

1 CUP PEELED AND DICED BUTTERNUT SQUASH

1 CUP PEELED AND DICED CARROTS

1 CUP PEELED AND DICED SWEET POTATO

4 CUPS VEGETABLE STOCK (SEE PAGE 441)

3 CUPS HEAVY CREAM

SALT, TO TASTE

CAYENNE PEPPER, TO TASTE

FRESH ROSEMARY, CHOPPED, FOR GARNISH

1. Place the butter in a medium pot and melt it over medium heat. Add the onion, apple, rutabaga, squash, carrots, and sweet potato and cook, stirring occasionally, until the vegetables have softened, about 10 minutes.
2. Add the stock and bring the soup to a boil. Reduce the heat so that the soup simmers and cook until the vegetables are tender, about 20 minutes.
3. Transfer the soup to a food processor, pulse until smooth, and strain back into the pot through a fine-mesh sieve. Bring the soup to a simmer, add the heavy cream, and season with salt and cayenne pepper.
4. Ladle the soup into warmed bowls, garnish with rosemary, and serve.

Spring Pea Soup with Lemon Ricotta

YIELD: 4 SERVINGS / **ACTIVE TIME:** 15 MINUTES / **TOTAL TIME:** 15 MINUTES

12 CUPS WATER

1 TABLESPOON PLUS 2 TEASPOONS KOSHER SALT

1 CUP RICOTTA CHEESE

¼ CUP HEAVY CREAM

2 TABLESPOONS LEMON ZEST

6 STRIPS OF LEMON PEEL

3 CUPS PEAS

3 SHALLOTS, DICED

6 FRESH MINT LEAVES, PLUS MORE FOR GARNISH

1. Place the water and 1 tablespoon of the salt in a saucepan and bring to a boil over medium heat.
2. Place the ricotta, cream, lemon zest, and remaining salt in a food processor and puree until smooth. Season to taste and set the mixture aside.
3. Add the strips of lemon peel to the saucepan, along with the peas and shallots. Cook for 2 minutes, until the peas are just cooked through.
4. Drain, making sure to reserve 2 cups of the cooking liquid, and immediately transfer the peas, strips of lemon peel, and shallots to a blender. Add the mint leaves and half of the reserved cooking liquid and puree until the desired consistency is achieved, adding more cooking liquid as needed.
5. Season to taste, ladle into warmed bowls, and place a spoonful of the lemon ricotta into each bowl. Garnish with additional mint and serve immediately, as the brilliant green color starts to fade as the soup cools.

Artichoke Soup with Fennel Seed Yogurt

YIELD: 4 SERVINGS / **ACTIVE TIME:** 20 MINUTES / **TOTAL TIME:** 45 MINUTES

1 TABLESPOON EXTRA-VIRGIN OLIVE OIL

1 TABLESPOON UNSALTED BUTTER

6 ARTICHOKE HEARTS, SLICED THIN

1 GARLIC CLOVE, MINCED

1 ONION, FINELY DICED

1 CUP RIESLING

1 TEASPOON FRESH THYME

4 CUPS HEAVY CREAM

1 CUP VEGETABLE STOCK (SEE PAGE 441)

SALT AND PEPPER, TO TASTE

FRESH DILL, CHOPPED, FOR GARNISH

FENNEL SEED YOGURT (SEE PAGE 459), FOR SERVING

1. Place the olive oil and butter in a medium pot and warm the mixture over medium heat. Add the artichoke hearts, garlic, and onion and cook, stirring occasionally, for 10 minutes.
2. Add the wine and thyme and cook until the wine has been reduced by half, about 5 minutes. Add the cream and stock and bring the soup to a simmer. Cook for 10 minutes.
3. Transfer the soup to a food processor, pulse until smooth, and strain the soup back into the pot through a fine-mesh sieve.
4. Season the soup with salt and pepper and ladle it into warmed bowls. Garnish with dill and serve with Fennel Seed Yogurt.

Asparagus & Pea Soup

YIELD: 6 SERVINGS / **ACTIVE TIME:** 30 MINUTES / **TOTAL TIME:** 1 HOUR AND 30 MINUTES

2 TABLESPOONS UNSALTED BUTTER

1 LEEK, TRIMMED, RINSED WELL, AND FINELY DICED

¾ LB. ASPARAGUS, TRIMMED AND FINELY DICED, TIPS RESERVED

1 CUP PEAS

1 TABLESPOON FINELY CHOPPED FRESH PARSLEY

5 CUPS VEGETABLE STOCK (SEE PAGE 441)

½ CUP HEAVY CREAM

ZEST OF 1 LEMON, PLUS MORE FOR GARNISH

SALT AND PEPPER, TO TASTE

FRESH MINT, FINELY CHOPPED, FOR GARNISH

PARMESAN CHEESE, GRATED, FOR GARNISH

PARMESAN CRISPS (SEE PAGE 459), FOR SERVING

1. Place the butter in a medium pot and melt it over medium heat. Add the leek and cook, stirring occasionally, until it has softened, about 5 minutes. Add the asparagus, peas, and parsley and cook, stirring occasionally, for 3 minutes.
2. Add the stock and bring the soup to a boil. Reduce the heat so that the soup simmers and cook until the vegetables are tender, 6 to 8 minutes. Transfer the soup to a food processor, pulse until smooth, and strain it into a clean pot through a fine-mesh sieve.
3. Add the cream and lemon zest to the soup, season with salt and pepper, and bring it to a simmer.
4. Bring water to a boil in a small pot. Add salt, let the water return to a boil, and add the reserved asparagus tips. Cook until they are tender, about 3 minutes. Drain the asparagus tips, rinse them under cold water, and set them aside.
5. Ladle the soup into warmed bowls, garnish with mint, Parmesan, additional lemon zest, and the asparagus tips, and serve with Parmesan Crisps.

Basil Vichyssoise

YIELD: 4 SERVINGS / **ACTIVE TIME:** 45 MINUTES / **TOTAL TIME:** 1 HOUR AND 30 MINUTES

¼ CUP UNSALTED BUTTER

1 ONION, FINELY DICED

2 LEEKS, TRIMMED, RINSED WELL, AND FINELY DICED

1 POTATO, PEELED AND FINELY DICED

1 BAY LEAF

4 CUPS CHICKEN STOCK (SEE PAGE 440)

1½ TEASPOONS FRESH LEMON JUICE

2 TABLESPOONS RED WINE VINEGAR

1 CUP FRESH BASIL, CHOPPED, PLUS MORE FOR GARNISH

1 CUP HEAVY CREAM

SALT AND PEPPER, TO TASTE

1. Place the butter in a medium pot and melt it over medium heat. Add the onion and leeks and cook, stirring occasionally, until they have softened, about 5 minutes. Add the potato and bay leaf and cook, stirring occasionally, for 5 minutes. Add the stock, bring to a simmer, and cook until the potato is tender, about 15 minutes.
2. Stir in the lemon juice and vinegar, place the soup in a food processor, and pulse until combined. Strain the soup through a fine-mesh sieve and chill it in the refrigerator.
3. Add the basil to the soup, transfer the soup to a food processor, and pulse until smooth. Place the soup in a mixing bowl, add the cream, and stir until fully combined. Season with salt and pepper and chill the soup in the refrigerator for at least 1 hour.
4. Divide the soup among the serving bowls, garnish with additional basil, and serve.

Broccoli & Cheddar Soup with Parmesan Crisps

YIELD: 4 SERVINGS / **ACTIVE TIME:** 15 MINUTES / **TOTAL TIME:** 30 MINUTES

2 TABLESPOONS EXTRA-VIRGIN OLIVE OIL

1 ONION, FINELY DICED

¼ CUP UNSALTED BUTTER

¼ CUP ALL-PURPOSE FLOUR

2 CUPS WHOLE MILK

2 CUPS CHICKEN STOCK (SEE PAGE 440)

1½ CUPS BROCCOLI FLORETS, CHOPPED

1 CARROT, PEELED AND JULIENNED

2 CELERY STALKS, FINELY DICED

2 CUPS GRATED SHARP CHEDDAR CHEESE

SALT AND PEPPER, TO TASTE

PARMESAN CRISPS (SEE PAGE 459), FOR SERVING

1. Place the olive oil in a medium pot and warm it over medium heat. Add the onion and cook, stirring occasionally, until it has softened, about 5 minutes. Add the butter and let it melt, about 1 minute.

2. Gradually add the flour, stirring frequently, and cook for 3 minutes. Add the milk and stock, stirring continually, and bring the soup to a boil. Reduce the heat so it simmers, add the broccoli, carrot, and celery, and cook until the vegetables are tender, 10 to 15 minutes. Add the cheddar and stir until it has melted.

3. Season with salt and pepper, ladle the soup into warmed bowls, and serve with Parmesan Crisps.

Eggplant & Zucchini Soup

YIELD: 4 SERVINGS / **ACTIVE TIME:** 20 MINUTES / **TOTAL TIME:** 1 HOUR AND 15 MINUTES

1 LARGE EGGPLANT, PEELED AND CHOPPED

2 LARGE ZUCCHINI, CHOPPED

1 ONION, CHOPPED

3 GARLIC CLOVES, MINCED

2 TABLESPOONS EXTRA-VIRGIN OLIVE OIL

3 CUPS CHICKEN STOCK (SEE PAGE 440)

1 TABLESPOON FINELY CHOPPED FRESH OREGANO

1 TABLESPOON CHOPPED FRESH MINT, PLUS MORE FOR GARNISH

SALT AND PEPPER, TO TASTE

TZATZIKI (SEE PAGE 460), FOR SERVING

PITA BREAD (SEE PAGE 460), FOR SERVING

MINTY PICKLED CUCUMBERS (SEE PAGE 461), FOR SERVING

1. Preheat the oven to 425°F. Place the eggplant, zucchini, onion, and garlic in a baking dish, drizzle the olive oil over the mixture, and gently stir to coat. Place in the oven and roast for 30 minutes, removing to stir occasionally.
2. Remove from the oven and let the vegetables cool briefly.
3. Place half of the roasted vegetables in a food processor. Add the stock and blitz until pureed. Place the puree in a medium saucepan, add the remaining roasted vegetables, and bring to a boil.
4. Stir in the oregano and mint and season with salt and pepper. Cook for 2 minutes and ladle into warmed bowls. Garnish with additional mint and serve with the Tzatziki, Pita Bread, and Minty Pickled Cucumbers.

Tunisian Butternut Squash Soup

YIELD: 12 SERVINGS / **ACTIVE TIME:** 30 MINUTES / **TOTAL TIME:** 2 HOURS

1 LARGE BUTTERNUT SQUASH, HALVED AND SEEDED

1 TEASPOON HARISSA SAUCE (SEE PAGE 461)

1 TEASPOON KOSHER SALT

½ TEASPOON BLACK PEPPER

¼ CUP FRESH LEMON JUICE

1 TABLESPOON LEMON ZEST

1½ TEASPOONS LIME ZEST

2 TABLESPOONS EXTRA-VIRGIN OLIVE OIL

2 PARSNIPS, PEELED AND CUBED

2 TABLESPOONS AVOCADO OIL

3 SMALL SHALLOTS, DICED

3 GARLIC CLOVES, SLICED

8 CUPS CHICKEN STOCK (SEE PAGE 440)

1. Preheat the oven to 400°F. Place the butternut squash on an aluminum foil–lined baking sheet, cut side up.
2. Place the harissa, salt, pepper, lemon juice, lemon zest, lime zest, and olive oil in a bowl and stir until combined.
3. Spread some of the mixture over the squash. Place the parsnips around the squash, drizzle the remaining harissa mixture over them, and toss to coat.
4. Place the pan in the oven and roast until the squash and parsnips are fork-tender, about 1 hour. Remove from the oven and let the vegetables cool for 20 minutes.
5. Place the avocado oil in a large saucepan and warm it over medium heat. Add the shallots and cook, stirring frequently, until they are translucent, about 3 minutes. Add the garlic and cook, stirring frequently, until fragrant, about 1 minute.
6. Scoop the squash's flesh into a food processor, add the parsnips and some of the stock, and blitz until smooth.
7. Add the puree to the saucepan, add the remaining stock, and simmer until the flavor has developed to your liking, about 25 minutes.
8. Taste, adjust the seasoning as necessary, and ladle the soup into warmed bowls.

Roasted Corn & Red Pepper Soup

YIELD: 4 SERVINGS / **ACTIVE TIME:** 30 MINUTES / **TOTAL TIME:** 1 HOUR AND 45 MINUTES

3 CUPS FRESH CORN KERNELS

2 TABLESPOONS EXTRA-VIRGIN OLIVE OIL

SALT, TO TASTE

3 RED BELL PEPPERS

¼ CUP UNSALTED BUTTER

½ CUP HEAVY CREAM

½ CUP MILK

1. Preheat the oven to 375°F. Place the corn in a single layer on a large baking sheet and drizzle the olive oil over it. Season with salt, place the pan in the oven, and roast until the corn starts to darken and caramelize, 12 to 18 minutes. Remove the corn from the oven, set it aside, and raise the oven's temperature to 425°F.
2. Place the bell peppers on a separate baking sheet and place them in the oven. Cook, while turning occasionally, until the skins are blistered all over, about 30 minutes. Remove from the oven and let cool. When cool enough to handle, remove the skins and seeds and discard. Set the peppers aside.
3. Place the corn, peppers, butter, cream, and milk in a saucepan and bring to a simmer over medium heat, stirring frequently. Simmer for 20 minutes, making sure that it does not come to a boil. After simmering for 20 minutes, remove the soup from heat and let it cool for 10 minutes.
4. Transfer the soup to a blender and puree until smooth. If the soup has cooled too much, return it to the saucepan and cook until warmed through. If not, ladle the soup into warmed bowls and enjoy.

Saffron, Tomato & Fennel Soup

YIELD: 12 TO 16 SERVINGS / **ACTIVE TIME:** 5 MINUTES / **TOTAL TIME:** 25 MINUTES

2 TABLESPOONS EXTRA-VIRGIN OLIVE OIL

½ CUP DICED ONIONS

¼ CUP DICED PARSNIPS

¼ CUP DICED CELERY

¼ CUP DICED FENNEL (RESERVE FENNEL FRONDS AND STALK)

2 TABLESPOONS SLICED GARLIC

3 BAY LEAVES

1½ TABLESPOONS KOSHER SALT, PLUS MORE TO TASTE

1 TABLESPOON BLACK PEPPER, PLUS MORE TO TASTE

1 CUP WHITE WINE

1 TEASPOON SAFFRON THREADS

8 CUPS HIGH-QUALITY TOMATO JUICE

1 TABLESPOON FRESH OREGANO

2 TABLESPOONS CHOPPED FRESH BASIL

2 TABLESPOONS CHOPPED FRESH PARSLEY

1 TABLESPOON FRESH LEMON JUICE

1 TABLESPOON RED WINE VINEGAR

1. Place the olive oil in a saucepan and warm it over medium heat. Add the onions, parsnips, celery, fennel, garlic, bay leaves, salt, and pepper and cook, stirring frequently, until the onions are translucent, about 3 minutes.
2. Deglaze the pan with the wine, scraping up any browned bits from the bottom of the pan. Bring the wine to a simmer and then stir in the saffron threads, the tomato juice, and all of the fresh herbs. Return the soup to a simmer and let it cook for 10 minutes.
3. Stir in the lemon juice and vinegar, season the soup with salt and pepper, ladle it into warmed bowls, and enjoy.

Sweet Pea Soup

YIELD: 4 SERVINGS / **ACTIVE TIME:** 10 MINUTES / **TOTAL TIME:** 20 MINUTES

2 TABLESPOONS UNSALTED BUTTER

1 LEEK, TRIMMED, RINSED WELL, AND FINELY DICED

1 ONION, FINELY DICED

4 CUPS VEGETABLE STOCK (SEE PAGE 441)

1½ LBS. FROZEN PEAS

1 CUP CRÈME FRAÎCHE

SALT AND PEPPER, TO TASTE

1. Place the butter in a medium pot and melt it over medium heat. Add the leek and onion and cook, stirring occasionally, until they have softened, about 5 minutes. Add the stock and bring to a boil.
2. Reduce the heat so that the soup simmers, add the peas, and cook for 5 minutes. Transfer the soup to a food processor, pulse until smooth, and strain it into a clean pot through a fine-mesh sieve. Bring the soup to a simmer, stir in the crème fraîche, and season with salt and pepper.
3. Ladle the soup into warmed bowls and serve.

Acorn Squash Soup

YIELD: 4 SERVINGS / **ACTIVE TIME:** 15 MINUTES / **TOTAL TIME:** 30 MINUTES

1 TABLESPOON EXTRA-VIRGIN OLIVE OIL

8 SLICES OF THICK-CUT BACON, CHOPPED

2 ACORN SQUASH, PEELED, SEEDED, AND GRATED

1 ONION, FINELY DICED

2 APPLES, PEELED AND GRATED

1 TEASPOON CHINESE FIVE-SPICE POWDER

¼ TEASPOON CAYENNE PEPPER

4 CUPS CHICKEN STOCK (SEE PAGE 440)

2 CUPS HEAVY CREAM

SALT AND PEPPER, TO TASTE

FENNEL, SHAVED, FOR GARNISH

ORANGE ZEST, FOR GARNISH

1. Place the olive oil in a medium pot and warm it over medium heat. Add the bacon and cook, stirring occasionally, until it is crispy, about 8 minutes. Remove the bacon from the pot and place it on a paper towel–lined plate to drain.
2. Add the squash and onion to the pot and cook, stirring occasionally, until they have softened, about 5 minutes. Add the apples, five-spice powder, cayenne, and stock, and three-quarters of the bacon and bring to a boil. Reduce the heat so that the soup simmers and cook for 10 minutes.
3. Transfer the soup to a food processor, pulse until smooth, and strain it into a clean pot through a fine-mesh sieve. Bring the soup to a simmer, stir in the cream, and cook for 5 minutes.
4. Season the soup with salt and pepper and ladle it into warmed bowls. Garnish with fennel, orange zest, and the remaining bacon and serve.

Creamed Parsnip Soup with Pesto

YIELD: 4 SERVINGS / **ACTIVE TIME:** 15 MINUTES / **TOTAL TIME:** 30 MINUTES

2 TABLESPOONS UNSALTED BUTTER

1 ONION, FINELY DICED

1 GARLIC CLOVE, MINCED

2 TEASPOONS FRESH THYME

5 PARSNIPS, PEELED AND GRATED

6 CUPS VEGETABLE STOCK (SEE PAGE 441)

2 CUPS HEAVY CREAM

SALT AND PEPPER, TO TASTE

FRESH PARSLEY, FINELY CHOPPED, FOR GARNISH

PESTO (SEE PAGE 462), FOR SERVING

1. Place the butter in a medium pot and melt it over medium heat. Add the onion, garlic, and thyme and cook, stirring frequently, until the onion has softened, about 5 minutes. Add the parsnips and cook, stirring occasionally, for 5 minutes. Add the stock and bring the soup to a boil.
2. Reduce the heat so that the soup simmers and cook for 10 minutes.
3. Transfer the soup to a food processor, pulse until smooth, and strain it into a clean pot through a fine-mesh sieve. Bring the soup to a simmer and stir in the cream. Season with salt and pepper and cook for 5 minutes.
4. Ladle the soup into warmed bowls, garnish with parsley, and serve with the Pesto.

Cream of Broccoli Soup

YIELD: 4 SERVINGS / **ACTIVE TIME:** 15 MINUTES / **TOTAL TIME:** 30 MINUTES

2 TABLESPOONS UNSALTED BUTTER

1 TABLESPOON EXTRA-VIRGIN OLIVE OIL

1 ONION, FINELY DICED

1 HEAD OF BROCCOLI, CUT INTO FLORETS AND FINELY CHOPPED

1 TEASPOON FRESH THYME

1 TEASPOON FINELY CHOPPED FRESH ROSEMARY

4 CUPS CHICKEN STOCK OR VEGETABLE STOCK (SEE PAGE 440 OR 441)

2 CUPS HEAVY CREAM

SALT AND PEPPER, TO TASTE

1. Place the butter and olive oil in a medium pot and warm the mixture over medium heat. Add the onion and cook, stirring occasionally, until it has softened, about 5 minutes.
2. Add the broccoli, thyme, and rosemary and cook, stirring frequently, for 3 minutes. Add the stock and bring to a boil. Reduce the heat so that the soup simmers and cook for 5 minutes.
3. Add the cream and cook until the broccoli is tender, about 10 minutes.
4. Transfer the soup to a food processor, pulse until smooth, and strain it into a clean pot through a fine-mesh sieve. Bring the soup to a simmer and season with salt and pepper.
5. Ladle the soup into warmed bowls and serve.

Baked Potato Soup

YIELD: 4 SERVINGS / **ACTIVE TIME:** 20 MINUTES / **TOTAL TIME:** 1 HOUR AND 30 MINUTES

2 LARGE IDAHO POTATOES, HALVED LENGTHWISE

¼ CUP UNSALTED BUTTER

⅓ CUP ALL-PURPOSE FLOUR

4 CUPS WHOLE MILK

1 CUP SHREDDED CHEDDAR CHEESE, PLUS MORE FOR GARNISH

½ CUP SOUR CREAM

SALT AND PEPPER, TO TASTE

FRESH SCALLIONS, SLICED THIN, FOR GARNISH

CRISPY COOKED BACON, CHOPPED, FOR GARNISH

1. Preheat the oven to 400°F. Place the potatoes in a baking dish, place them in the oven, and bake until they are tender, about 1 hour.
2. Remove the potatoes from the oven and let them cool slightly. Scoop out the flesh, mash until it is smooth, and set the mashed potatoes aside.
3. Place the butter in a medium pot and melt it over medium heat. Add the flour and milk and cook, stirring continually, until the mixture thickens, about 5 minutes.
4. Stir in the potatoes and cheddar and cook until the cheese has melted. Remove the pan from heat, stir in the sour cream, and season with salt and pepper.
5. Ladle the soup into warmed bowls, garnish with scallions, bacon, and additional cheddar, and serve.

Broccoli & Stilton Soup

YIELD: 4 SERVINGS / **ACTIVE TIME:** 30 MINUTES / **TOTAL TIME:** 45 MINUTES

2 TABLESPOONS UNSALTED BUTTER

1 ONION, FINELY DICED

1 LEEK, TRIMMED, RINSED WELL, AND FINELY DICED

8 CUPS BROCCOLI FLORETS, CHOPPED

1 SMALL POTATO, PEELED AND DICED

3 CUPS CHICKEN STOCK (SEE PAGE 440)

1 CUP SPINACH

1 CUP WHOLE MILK

¼ CUP HEAVY CREAM

6 OZ. STILTON CHEESE, RIND REMOVED

SALT AND PEPPER, TO TASTE

TOASTED PEANUTS, CHOPPED, FOR GARNISH

1. Place the butter in a large pot and melt it over medium heat. Add the onion and leek and cook, stirring occasionally, until they have softened, about 5 minutes. Add the broccoli, potato, and stock and bring the soup to a boil.
2. Reduce the heat so that the soup simmers and cook until the vegetables are tender, 10 to 15 minutes.
3. Transfer the soup to a food processor, add the spinach, and pulse until smooth. Strain the soup into a clean pot through a fine-mesh sieve and add the milk and cream. Bring the soup to a simmer, add the Stilton, and stir until it has melted. Season the soup with salt and pepper.
4. Ladle the soup into warmed bowls, garnish with toasted peanuts, and serve.

Fiddlehead Fern Soup

YIELD: 4 SERVINGS / **ACTIVE TIME:** 30 MINUTES / **TOTAL TIME:** 1 HOUR

3 TABLESPOONS UNSALTED BUTTER

1 ONION, FINELY DICED

1 GARLIC CLOVE, MINCED

1 LB. FIDDLEHEAD FERNS

4 CUPS VEGETABLE STOCK (SEE PAGE 441)

1 CUP HEAVY CREAM

SALT AND PEPPER, TO TASTE

FRESH CHIVES, CHOPPED, FOR GARNISH

CRÈME FRAÎCHE, FOR SERVING

1. Place the butter in a medium pot and melt it over medium heat. Add the onion, garlic, and fiddleheads and cook, stirring occasionally, until the onion has softened, about 5 minutes. Add the stock and bring the soup to a boil.
2. Transfer the soup to a food processor, pulse until smooth, and strain the soup into a clean pot through a fine-mesh sieve. Add the cream, bring the soup to a simmer, and season with salt and pepper.
3. Ladle the soup into warmed bowls, garnish with chives, and serve with crème fraîche.

Artichoke à la Barigoule

YIELD: 4 SERVINGS / **ACTIVE TIME:** 30 MINUTES / **TOTAL TIME:** 1 HOUR AND 30 MINUTES

2 CUPS BABY ARTICHOKES IN OLIVE OIL, DRAINED AND QUARTERED, OIL RESERVED

½ LB. BUTTON MUSHROOMS, SLICED THIN

1 LEEK, TRIMMED, HALVED, RINSED WELL, AND SLICED THIN

1 GARLIC CLOVE, MINCED

2 ANCHOVIES IN OLIVE OIL, DRAINED AND FINELY CHOPPED

½ TEASPOON FRESH THYME

2 TABLESPOONS ALL-PURPOSE FLOUR

¼ CUP DRY VERMOUTH

4 CUPS CHICKEN STOCK (SEE PAGE 440), PLUS MORE AS NEEDED

½ CUP PEELED AND CHOPPED CELERIAC

1 BAY LEAF

½ CUP HEAVY CREAM

1½ TABLESPOONS CHOPPED FRESH TARRAGON

1 TEASPOON CHAMPAGNE VINEGAR

SALT AND PEPPER, TO TASTE

1. Place 2 tablespoons of the olive oil reserved from the artichokes in a medium saucepan and warm it over medium heat. Add the artichokes and cook, stirring occasionally, until they are lightly caramelized, about 5 minutes. Remove the pan from heat, transfer the artichokes to a plate, and let them cool.
2. Place the pan back over medium heat and add the mushrooms. Cover the pan and cook for 5 minutes. Remove the cover and cook until most of the liquid the mushrooms release has evaporated, about 5 minutes.
3. Add another tablespoon of the reserved oil and the leek and cook, stirring occasionally, until it has softened, about 5 minutes. Stir in the garlic, anchovies, and thyme and cook, stirring continually, for 1 minute.
4. Stir in the flour, cook for 1 minute, and then add the vermouth. Cook until the alcohol has been cooked off, 1 to 2 minutes.
5. While whisking, gradually add the stock. When all of the stock has been incorporated, add the celeriac and bay leaf, along with the artichokes, and bring the mixture to a boil. Reduce the heat and simmer until the celeriac is tender, 10 to 15 minutes, adding more stock if the level of liquid starts to look a bit too low.
6. Remove the pan from heat, remove the bay leaf, and discard it. Stir in the cream, tarragon, and vinegar, season the soup with salt and pepper, ladle it into warmed bowls, and enjoy.

Canh Bap Cai Cuon

YIELD: 4 SERVINGS / **ACTIVE TIME:** 40 MINUTES / **TOTAL TIME:** 2 HOURS AND 30 MINUTES

FOR THE BROTH

6 CUPS CHICKEN STOCK (SEE PAGE 440)

1½-INCH PIECE OF FRESH GINGER, PEELED AND MINCED

2 TABLESPOONS FISH SAUCE

2 TABLESPOONS SOY SAUCE

2 TEASPOONS FRESH THYME

¼ TEASPOON SALT

FOR THE SOUP

8 SAVOY CABBAGE LEAVES

4 SCALLIONS, TRIMMED AND SLICED, GREENS AND WHITES SEPARATED

¼ CUP DRIED WOOD EAR MUSHROOMS, SOAKED IN WARM WATER FOR 30 MINUTES, DRAINED, AND FINELY DICED

4 OZ. GROUND PORK

4 OZ. SHRIMP, SHELLED, DEVEINED, AND FINELY DICED

1 THAI CHILE PEPPER, STEMMED, SEEDED, AND SLICED

2 TABLESPOONS FISH SAUCE

1 TABLESPOON SOY SAUCE

FRESH WATERCRESS, FOR GARNISH

1 JALAPEÑO CHILE PEPPER, FINELY SLICED, FOR GARNISH

1. To begin preparation for the broth, place all of the ingredients in a large pot and bring to a boil. Remove the pot from heat and let the broth rest for 1 hour. Strain the broth through a fine-mesh sieve and set it aside.
2. To begin preparations for the soup, bring water to a boil in a large pot. Add the cabbage leaves to the boiling water and cook for 2 minutes. Remove the cabbage leaves from the pot, rinse them under cold water, and set them aside.
3. Add the scallion greens to the boiling water and cook for 1 minute. Remove the scallion greens from the pot and rinse them under cold water. Place the cabbage leaves and scallion greens on a paper towel–lined plate and let them dry.
4. Place the mushrooms, pork, shrimp, scallion whites, Thai chile, fish sauce, and soy sauce in a mixing bowl and mix until fully combined. Place 1 tablespoon of the filling on the bottom of each cabbage leaf, roll the leaves up, and tie them closed with the scallion greens.
5. Bring the broth to a boil in a large pot. Reduce the heat so that it simmers, add the cabbage leaves to the soup, and cook for 20 minutes.
6. Place two cabbage leaves in each warmed bowl and ladle the soup over the top. Garnish with watercress and the jalapeño and serve.

Caldo Verde

YIELD: 4 SERVINGS / **ACTIVE TIME:** 25 MINUTES / **TOTAL TIME:** 1 HOUR

1 TABLESPOON EXTRA-VIRGIN OLIVE OIL

¼ LB. CHORIZO, SLICED INTO ¼-INCH PIECES

½ ONION, FINELY DICED

4 GARLIC CLOVES, MINCED

3 POTATOES, PEELED AND FINELY DICED

1 BAY LEAF

6 CUPS VEGETABLE STOCK (SEE PAGE 441)

1 LB. SAVOY CABBAGE, SLICED INTO THIN STRIPS

SALT AND PEPPER, TO TASTE

FRESH DILL, CHOPPED, FOR GARNISH

PAPRIKA OIL (SEE PAGE 462), FOR SERVING

1. Place the olive oil in a large pot and warm it over medium heat. Add the chorizo and cook, stirring occasionally, until it begins to brown, about 5 minutes. Remove the chorizo from the pan and set it aside.
2. Add the onion and cook, stirring occasionally, until it has softened, about 5 minutes. Add the garlic and cook, stirring frequently, for 2 minutes. Add the potatoes, bay leaf, and stock and bring the soup to a boil. Reduce the heat so that the soup simmers and cook until the potatoes are tender, about 20 minutes.
3. Remove the pot from heat and discard the bay leaf. Transfer the soup to a food processor, pulse until smooth, and return the soup to the pot. Add the chorizo and cabbage and bring the soup to a boil. Reduce the heat so that the soup simmers, cook for 5 minutes, and season with salt and pepper.
4. Ladle the soup into warmed bowls, garnish with dill, and serve with the Paprika Oil.

Caldo Verde

SEE PAGE 91

Carrot & Ginger Soup

YIELD: 4 TO 6 SERVINGS / **ACTIVE TIME:** 25 MINUTES / **TOTAL TIME:** 1 HOUR

¼ CUP UNSALTED BUTTER

2 ONIONS, FINELY DICED

6 CUPS PEELED AND DICED CARROTS

¼ CUP PEELED AND MINCED GINGER

ZEST AND JUICE OF 2 ORANGES

1 CUP WHITE WINE

8 CUPS VEGETABLE STOCK (SEE PAGE 441), PLUS MORE AS NEEDED

SALT AND PEPPER, TO TASTE

FRESH DILL, CHOPPED, FOR GARNISH

GREEK YOGURT, FOR GARNISH

1. Place the butter in a medium pot and melt it over medium heat. Add the onions and cook, stirring occasionally, until they have softened, about 5 minutes. Add the carrots, ginger, and orange zest and cook, stirring occasionally, until the carrots have softened, about 5 minutes.
2. Add the orange juice and wine and cook, stirring occasionally, until they have evaporated. Add the stock and bring the soup to a boil. Reduce the heat so that the soup simmers and cook until the vegetables are tender, 10 to 15 minutes.
3. Transfer the soup to a food processor, pulse until smooth, and strain it into a clean pot through a fine-mesh sieve. Season with salt and pepper. Add more stock to the soup if it is too thick for your liking.
4. Ladle the soup into warmed bowls, garnish with dill and yogurt, and serve.

Celeriac & Roasted Garlic Soup

YIELD: 4 SERVINGS / **ACTIVE TIME:** 45 MINUTES / **TOTAL TIME:** 1 HOUR AND 15 MINUTES

1 HEAD OF GARLIC

1 TABLESPOON EXTRA-VIRGIN OLIVE OIL

2 TABLESPOONS UNSALTED BUTTER

½ ONION, FINELY DICED

8 CUPS TRIMMED AND FINELY DICED CELERIAC

1 TEASPOON FRESH THYME

1 TEASPOON FINELY CHOPPED FRESH ROSEMARY

1 CUP WHITE WINE

2 CUPS CHICKEN STOCK (SEE PAGE 440)

4 CUPS HEAVY CREAM

SALT AND PEPPER, TO TASTE

SCALLION GREENS, SLICED, FOR GARNISH

1. Preheat the oven to 350°F. Cut the bottom off the head of garlic and place it in a baking dish. Drizzle the olive oil over it, place it in the oven, and roast until the cloves are tender and golden brown, about 30 minutes. Remove the dish from the oven and let it cool. When it is cool enough to handle, peel the garlic and set it aside.
2. Place the butter in a medium pot and melt it over medium heat. Add the onion and celeriac and cook, stirring occasionally, until the onion has softened, about 5 minutes. Add the thyme and rosemary and cook, stirring frequently, for 5 minutes.
3. Add the wine, stock, and roasted garlic and bring the soup to a boil. Reduce the heat so that the soup simmers, add the cream, and cook until the celeriac is tender, about 15 minutes.
4. Transfer the soup to a food processor, pulse until smooth, and strain it into a clean pot through a fine-mesh sieve. Bring the soup to a boil and season with salt and pepper.
5. Ladle the soup into warmed bowls, garnish with scallion greens, and serve.

Caramelized Onion Soup

YIELD: 4 SERVINGS / **ACTIVE TIME:** 30 MINUTES / **TOTAL TIME:** 1 HOUR

¼ CUP UNSALTED BUTTER

6 SPANISH ONIONS, FINELY DICED

2 GARLIC CLOVES, MINCED

1 TEASPOON FRESH THYME

½ CUP RIESLING

½ CUP MADEIRA

4 CUPS HEAVY CREAM

SALT AND PEPPER, TO TASTE

CROUTONS (SEE PAGE 463), FOR SERVING

1. Place the butter in a medium pot and melt it over the lowest heat. Add the onions and cook, stirring occasionally, until they are caramelized, about 30 minutes. Add water as needed if the onions start sticking to the pot.
2. Add the garlic, thyme, Riesling, and Madeira and cook, stirring occasionally, until the liquid has reduced by half. Add the cream, bring the soup to a simmer, and cook for 10 minutes.
3. Transfer the soup to a food processor, pulse until smooth, and return it to the pot. Season the soup with salt and pepper.
4. Ladle the soup into warmed bowls and serve with the Croutons.

Celeriac & Truffle Soup

YIELD: 4 SERVINGS / **ACTIVE TIME:** 25 MINUTES / **TOTAL TIME:** 1 HOUR AND 15 MINUTES

2 TABLESPOONS UNSALTED BUTTER

½ ONION, FINELY DICED

8 CUPS TRIMMED AND FINELY DICED CELERIAC

1 TEASPOON FRESH THYME

1 TEASPOON FINELY CHOPPED FRESH ROSEMARY

2 CUPS CHICKEN STOCK (SEE PAGE 440)

1 CUP WHITE WINE

¼ CUP BLACK TRUFFLE PASTE, PLUS MORE FOR GARNISH

4 CUPS HEAVY CREAM

SALT AND PEPPER, TO TASTE

WHITE TRUFFLE OIL, FOR GARNISH

CELERY LEAVES, FOR GARNISH

1. Place the butter in a medium pot and melt it over medium heat. Add the onion and celeriac and cook, stirring occasionally, until the onion has softened, about 5 minutes. Add the thyme and rosemary and cook, stirring frequently, for 5 minutes.
2. Add the stock, wine, and truffle paste and bring the soup to a boil. Reduce the heat so that the soup simmers, add the cream, and cook until the celeriac is tender, about 15 minutes.
3. Transfer the soup to a food processor, pulse until smooth, and strain it into a clean pot through a fine-mesh sieve. Bring the soup to a boil and season with salt and pepper.
4. Ladle the soup into warmed bowls, garnish with additional truffle paste, truffle oil, and celery leaves, and serve.

Celery Bisque

YIELD: 6 SERVINGS / **ACTIVE TIME:** 15 MINUTES / **TOTAL TIME:** 1 HOUR AND 5 MINUTES

¼ CUP UNSALTED BUTTER

1 ONION, FINELY DICED

½ LEEK, TRIMMED, RINSED WELL, AND FINELY DICED

2 CELERY STALKS, FINELY DICED

1 BAY LEAF

1 POTATO, PEELED AND FINELY DICED

1 CELERIAC, TRIMMED AND FINELY DICED

4 CUPS CHICKEN STOCK (SEE PAGE 440)

1 CINNAMON STICK

½ CUP HEAVY CREAM

FRESHLY GRATED NUTMEG, TO TASTE

SALT AND PEPPER, TO TASTE

1. Place the butter in a medium pot and melt it over medium heat. Add the onion, leek, and celery and cook, stirring occasionally, until the onion has softened, about 5 minutes. Add the bay leaf, potato, and celeriac and cook, stirring occasionally, for 5 minutes.
2. Add the stock and cinnamon and bring the soup to a boil. Reduce the heat so that the soup simmers and cook until the potato and celeriac have softened, about 15 minutes. Remove the cinnamon stick from the pot and discard it.
3. Transfer the soup to a food processor, pulse until smooth, and strain it back into the pot through a fine-mesh sieve. Bring the soup to a simmer, add the cream, and season with nutmeg, salt, and pepper.
4. Ladle the soup into warmed bowls and serve.

Sweet & Sour Beet Soup

YIELD: 4 SERVINGS / **ACTIVE TIME:** 20 MINUTES / **TOTAL TIME:** 2 HOURS

2 TABLESPOONS UNSALTED BUTTER

1 ONION, FINELY DICED

6 CUPS PEELED AND FINELY DICED BEETS

2 CELERY STALKS, FINELY DICED

1 RED BELL PEPPER, STEMMED, SEEDED, AND FINELY DICED

2 APPLES, PEELED AND FINELY DICED

6 CUPS VEGETABLE STOCK (SEE PAGE 441)

1 TEASPOON CUMIN

1 TEASPOON FRESH THYME

2 BAY LEAVES

½ CUP SOUR CREAM, PLUS MORE FOR GARNISH

½ CUP HEAVY CREAM

2 TEASPOONS FRESH LEMON JUICE

SALT AND PEPPER, TO TASTE

FRESH DILL, CHOPPED, FOR GARNISH

1. Place the butter in a large pot and melt it over medium heat. Add the onion, beets, celery, bell pepper, and apples and cook, stirring occasionally, until they have softened, about 5 minutes.
2. Add the stock, cumin, thyme, and bay leaves and bring the soup to a boil. Reduce the heat so that the soup simmers and cook until the vegetables are tender, about 30 minutes.
3. Transfer the soup to a food processor, pulse until smooth, and strain it into a clean pot through a fine-mesh sieve.
4. Add the sour cream, cream, and lemon juice and bring the soup to a simmer. Season with salt and pepper and chill the soup in the refrigerator for 1 hour.
5. Ladle the soup into chilled bowls, garnish with additional sour cream and dill, and serve.

Corn Chowder

YIELD: 4 TO 6 SERVINGS / **ACTIVE TIME:** 25 MINUTES / **TOTAL TIME:** 2 HOURS AND 15 MINUTES

6 EARS OF CORN, HUSKED, KERNELS REMOVED, AND COBS RESERVED

4 OZ. BACON, FINELY DICED

1 ONION, FINELY DICED

3 GARLIC CLOVES, MINCED

2 POTATOES, PEELED AND FINELY DICED

4 CUPS HEAVY CREAM

SALT AND PEPPER, TO TASTE

1. Bring water to a boil in a large pot. Add the reserved corn cobs to the boiling water, reduce the heat so that the water simmers, and cook for 1 hour. Strain the stock and set 4 cups of it aside.
2. Place the bacon in a large pot and warm it over medium heat, stirring occasionally, until the fat renders. Add the onion and garlic and cook, stirring frequently, until the onion has softened, about 5 minutes. Add the potatoes and corn kernels and cook, stirring occasionally, until they have softened, about 10 minutes.
3. Add the corn stock and cook until the soup has reduced by one-third, about 15 minutes. Reduce the heat so that the soup gently simmers, add the cream, and cook for 30 minutes.
4. Season the soup with salt and pepper, ladle it into warmed bowls, and serve.

Butternut Squash & Apple Cider Soup

YIELD: 4 SERVINGS / **ACTIVE TIME:** 30 MINUTES / **TOTAL TIME:** 1 HOUR AND 20 MINUTES

1 TABLESPOON EXTRA-VIRGIN OLIVE OIL

1 ONION, FINELY DICED

1 LB. BUTTERNUT SQUASH, PEELED AND FINELY DICED

1 APPLE, PEELED AND FINELY DICED

2 TABLESPOONS CALVADOS

½ CUP APPLE CIDER

2 CUPS CHICKEN STOCK (SEE PAGE 440)

SALT AND PEPPER, TO TASTE

TOASTED PUMPKIN SEEDS, FOR GARNISH

1. Place the olive oil in a medium pot and warm it over medium heat. Add the onion and cook, stirring occasionally, until it has softened, about 5 minutes. Add the squash and apple and cook, stirring occasionally, until the squash has softened, 5 to 10 minutes.
2. Add the Calvados and cook, stirring occasionally, until it evaporates. Add the cider and stock and bring the soup to a boil. Reduce the heat so that the soup simmers and cook until the squash is tender, about 20 minutes.
3. Transfer the soup to a food processor, pulse until smooth, and strain it into a clean pot through a fine-mesh sieve. Bring the soup to a simmer and season with salt and pepper.
4. Ladle the soup into warmed bowls, garnish with toasted pumpkin seeds, and serve.

Spicy Tomato & Egg Drop Soup

YIELD: 4 SERVINGS / **ACTIVE TIME:** 20 MINUTES / **TOTAL TIME:** 45 MINUTES

2 TABLESPOONS EXTRA-VIRGIN OLIVE OIL

4 SHALLOTS, FINELY DICED

2 GARLIC CLOVES, MINCED

2 THAI CHILE PEPPERS, STEMMED, SEEDED, AND CHOPPED

8 TOMATOES, FINELY DICED

1 TABLESPOON SUGAR

6 TABLESPOONS FISH SAUCE

4 MAKRUT LIME LEAVES

6 CUPS CHICKEN STOCK (SEE PAGE 440)

2 EGGS, BEATEN

SALT AND PEPPER, TO TASTE

SCALLION GREENS, CHOPPED, FOR GARNISH

SICHUAN PEPPERCORN & CHILE OIL (SEE PAGE 458), FOR SERVING

1. Place the olive oil in a medium pot and warm it over medium heat. Add the shallots, garlic, and chiles and cook, stirring frequently, until the mixture is fragrant, about 3 minutes. Add the tomatoes, sugar, fish sauce, lime leaves, and stock and bring the soup to a boil.
2. Reduce the heat so that the soup simmers and cook for 15 minutes. Add the eggs, season with salt and pepper, and cook until the soup begins to thicken, 3 to 5 minutes.
3. Ladle the soup into warmed bowls, garnish with scallion greens, and serve with the Sichuan Peppercorn & Chile Oil.

Cream of Cauliflower Soup

YIELD: 4 SERVINGS / **ACTIVE TIME:** 15 MINUTES / **TOTAL TIME:** 45 MINUTES

2 TABLESPOONS UNSALTED BUTTER

1 TABLESPOON EXTRA-VIRGIN OLIVE OIL

½ ONION, FINELY DICED

1 HEAD OF CAULIFLOWER, CUT INTO FLORETS

1 TEASPOON FRESH THYME

1 TEASPOON FINELY CHOPPED FRESH ROSEMARY

1 CUP CHARDONNAY

1 CUP VEGETABLE STOCK (SEE PAGE 441)

2 CUPS HEAVY CREAM

SALT AND PEPPER, TO TASTE

FRESH PEA TENDRILS, FOR GARNISH

TOASTED ALMONDS, CHOPPED, FOR GARNISH

1. Place the butter and olive oil in a medium pot and warm the mixture over medium heat. Add the onion and cauliflower and cook, stirring occasionally, until the onion has softened, about 5 minutes. Add the thyme and rosemary and cook, stirring frequently, for 3 minutes.
2. Add the wine and stock and bring the soup to a boil. Reduce the heat so that the soup simmers and cook for 5 minutes. Add the cream and simmer until the cauliflower is tender, about 20 minutes.
3. Transfer the soup to a food processor, pulse until smooth, and strain it into a clean pot through a fine-mesh sieve. Bring the soup to a simmer and season it with salt and pepper.
4. Ladle the soup into warmed bowls, garnish with pea tendrils and toasted almonds, and serve.

Cream of Tomato Soup

YIELD: 4 SERVINGS / **ACTIVE TIME:** 30 MINUTES / **TOTAL TIME:** 1 HOUR AND 15 MINUTES

2 TABLESPOONS UNSALTED BUTTER

1 ONION, FINELY DICED

2 LBS. TOMATOES, FINELY DICED

2 CARROTS, PEELED AND FINELY DICED

5 CUPS CHICKEN STOCK (SEE PAGE 440)

2 TABLESPOONS FRESHLY CHOPPED PARSLEY

½ TEASPOON FRESH THYME

6 TABLESPOONS HEAVY CREAM

SALT AND PEPPER, TO TASTE

1. Place the butter in a large pot and melt it over medium heat. Add the onion and cook, stirring occasionally, until it has softened, about 5 minutes. Add the tomatoes, carrots, stock, parsley, and thyme and bring to a boil. Reduce the heat so that the soup simmers and cook until the vegetables are tender, about 20 minutes.
2. Transfer the soup to a food processor, pulse until smooth, and strain it back into the pot through a fine-mesh sieve. Bring the soup to a simmer and season it with salt and pepper.
3. Ladle the soup into warmed bowls and serve.

French Onion Soup

YIELD: 4 SERVINGS / **ACTIVE TIME:** 30 MINUTES / **TOTAL TIME:** 1 HOUR AND 15 MINUTES

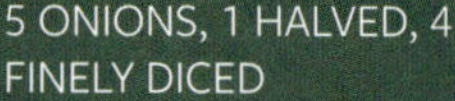

5 ONIONS, 1 HALVED, 4 FINELY DICED

2 TABLESPOONS EXTRA-VIRGIN OLIVE OIL

½ CUP SHERRY

1 TABLESPOON WORCESTERSHIRE SAUCE

2 TEASPOONS FRESH THYME

8 CUPS CHICKEN STOCK (SEE PAGE 440)

SALT AND PEPPER, TO TASTE

4 SLICES OF SOURDOUGH BREAD

1½ CUPS GRATED GRUYÈRE CHEESE

1. Prepare a gas or charcoal grill for medium-high heat (about 450°F). Place the halved onion on the grill, cut sides down, and cook until it is lightly charred, about 6 minutes. Turn the halves over and cook until they are just tender, about 5 minutes. Remove the onion from the grill and set it aside.
2. Place the olive oil in a medium pot and warm it over the lowest-possible heat. Add the remaining onions and cook, stirring occasionally, until they have caramelized, about 30 minutes. Add a splash of water occasionally if the onions start sticking to the pot.
3. Add the sherry and Worcestershire sauce and cook, stirring occasionally, until the liquid has reduced by half, about 10 minutes. Add the thyme and stock and cook until the liquid has reduced by half, about 20 minutes.
4. Preheat the oven to its broiler setting and season the soup with salt and pepper. Ladle the soup into oven-safe bowls and cover each bowl with a slice of sourdough bread and the Gruyère. Place the bowls in the oven and broil until the cheese has melted, 1 to 2 minutes. Remove the bowls from the oven and serve.

Eggplant Soup with Gremolata

YIELD: 4 SERVINGS / **ACTIVE TIME:** 30 MINUTES / **TOTAL TIME:** 1 HOUR

1 TABLESPOON EXTRA-VIRGIN OLIVE OIL

2 SHALLOTS, FINELY DICED

1 GARLIC CLOVE, MINCED

1 EGGPLANT, PEELED AND FINELY DICED

4 CUPS CHICKEN STOCK (SEE PAGE 440)

½ CUP HEAVY CREAM

2 TABLESPOONS FINELY CHOPPED FRESH PARSLEY

SALT AND PEPPER, TO TASTE

GREMOLATA (SEE PAGE 463), FOR SERVING

1. Place the olive oil in a large pot and warm it over medium heat. Add the shallots and garlic and cook, stirring frequently, until the shallots have softened, about 5 minutes. Add the eggplant and cook, stirring occasionally, until it has softened, about 10 minutes. Add the stock, bring the soup to a simmer, and cook for 10 minutes.
2. Transfer the soup to a food processor, pulse until smooth, and strain the soup into a clean pot through a fine-mesh sieve. Add the cream and parsley, bring the soup to a simmer, and season it with salt and pepper.
3. Ladle the soup into warmed bowls and serve with the Gremolata.

Forest Mushroom Soup

YIELD: 4 SERVINGS / **ACTIVE TIME:** 20 MINUTES / **TOTAL TIME:** 1 HOUR

1¼ CUPS UNSALTED BUTTER

1 ONION, FINELY DICED

2 GARLIC CLOVES, MINCED

⅓ CUP MADEIRA

½ LB. WILD MUSHROOMS, FINELY DICED

5 OZ. PORTOBELLO MUSHROOMS, FINELY DICED

4 CUPS MUSHROOM STOCK (SEE PAGE 449)

1 CUP HEAVY CREAM

1 TABLESPOON WORCESTERSHIRE SAUCE

SALT AND PEPPER, TO TASTE

SAUTÉED MUSHROOMS, FOR GARNISH

FRESH PARSLEY, CHOPPED, FOR GARNISH

1. Place the butter in a medium pot and melt it over medium heat. Add the onion and garlic and cook, stirring frequently, until the onion has softened, about 5 minutes. Add the Madeira and cook, stirring occasionally, until it evaporates, 5 to 10 minutes. Add the mushrooms and cook, stirring occasionally, until they have softened, about 5 minutes.
2. Add the stock and bring the soup to a boil. Reduce the heat so that the soup simmers and cook for 10 minutes.
3. Transfer the soup to a food processor, pulse until smooth, and strain it into a clean pot through a fine-mesh sieve. Add the cream and Worcestershire sauce, season with salt and pepper, and bring the soup to a simmer.
4. Ladle the soup into warmed bowls, garnish with sautéed mushrooms and parsley, and serve.

Green Asparagus Soup

YIELD: 4 SERVINGS / **ACTIVE TIME:** 30 MINUTES / **TOTAL TIME:** 1 HOUR

- 2 TABLESPOONS EXTRA-VIRGIN OLIVE OIL
- 3 CUPS FINELY DICED ASPARAGUS, WOODY ENDS DISCARDED
- 2 TABLESPOONS UNSALTED BUTTER
- 1 ONION, FINELY DICED
- 1 LEEK, TRIMMED, RINSED WELL, AND FINELY DICED
- 2 CELERY STALKS, FINELY DICED
- 1 POTATO, PEELED AND FINELY DICED
- 1 BAY LEAF
- 4 CUPS CHICKEN STOCK (SEE PAGE 440)
- ¾ CUP HEAVY CREAM
- SALT AND PEPPER, TO TASTE
- LEMON SLICES, FOR SERVING

1. Place the olive oil in a large skillet and warm it over medium-high heat. Add the asparagus and cook, stirring occasionally, until it has softened slightly, about 4 minutes. Reserve 12 asparagus tips for garnish and set the rest of the asparagus aside.
2. Place the butter in a medium pot and melt it over medium heat. Add the onion, leek, and celery and cook, stirring occasionally, until they have softened, about 5 minutes. Add the potato and bay leaf and cook, stirring occasionally, for 5 minutes.
3. Add the stock and bring the soup to a boil. Reduce the heat so that the soup simmers and cook until the potato is tender, about 15 minutes. Add the asparagus and cook until it has softened, about 5 minutes.
4. Transfer the soup to a food processor, pulse until smooth, and strain it back into the pot through a fine-mesh sieve. Add the cream, bring the soup to a simmer, and season with salt and pepper.
5. Ladle the soup into warmed bowls, garnish with the reserved asparagus tips, and serve with lemon slices.

Irish Leek & Cashel Blue Cheese Soup

YIELD: 6 SERVINGS / **ACTIVE TIME:** 30 MINUTES / **TOTAL TIME:** 1 HOUR

¼ CUP UNSALTED BUTTER

2 TABLESPOONS EXTRA-VIRGIN OLIVE OIL

3 LEEKS, TRIMMED, RINSED WELL, AND FINELY DICED

½ LB. CASHEL BLUE CHEESE, CRUMBLED

2 TABLESPOONS ALL-PURPOSE FLOUR

MUSTARD, TO TASTE, PLUS MORE FOR GARNISH

6 CUPS CHICKEN STOCK (SEE PAGE 440)

BLACK PEPPER, TO TASTE

FRESH CHIVES, CHOPPED, FOR GARNISH

1. Place the butter and olive oil in a medium pot and warm the mixture over medium-low heat. Add the leeks and cook, stirring occasionally, until they have softened, about 5 minutes. Add the cheese and cook, stirring frequently, until it has melted, about 5 minutes. Add the flour, season with mustard, and cook, stirring continually, for 2 minutes.
2. Gradually add the stock, stirring continually, and bring the soup to a boil. Reduce the heat so that the soup simmers and cook for 10 minutes. Season the soup with pepper.
3. Ladle the soup into warmed bowls, garnish with chives and additional mustard, and serve.

Heart of Palm Soup

YIELD: 4 SERVINGS / **ACTIVE TIME:** 20 MINUTES / **TOTAL TIME:** 45 MINUTES

2 TABLESPOONS UNSALTED BUTTER

2 TEASPOONS EXTRA-VIRGIN OLIVE OIL

1 ONION, FINELY DICED

1 LEEK, TRIMMED, RINSED WELL, AND FINELY DICED

1 TABLESPOON ALL-PURPOSE FLOUR

6 CUPS CHICKEN STOCK (SEE PAGE 440)

¾ LB. POTATOES, PEELED AND FINELY DICED

2 (14 OZ.) CANS OF HEART OF PALM, DRAINED AND FINELY DICED

1 CUP HEAVY CREAM

SALT AND PEPPER, TO TASTE

FRESH CHIVES, CHOPPED, FOR GARNISH

CAYENNE PEPPER, FOR GARNISH

1. Place the butter and olive oil in a medium pot and warm the mixture over medium heat. Add the onion and leek and cook, stirring occasionally, until they have softened, about 5 minutes. Sprinkle the flour over the vegetables and cook, stirring continually, for 2 minutes.
2. Add the stock and potatoes and bring the soup to a boil. Reduce the heat so that the soup simmers and cook for 10 minutes. Add the hearts of palm and cook until the potatoes are tender, about 10 minutes.
3. Transfer the soup to a food processor, pulse until smooth, and strain it into a clean pot through a fine-mesh sieve. Bring the soup to a simmer, add the cream, and season with salt and pepper. Let the soup return to a gentle simmer.
4. Ladle the soup into warmed bowls, garnish with chives and cayenne pepper, and serve.

Coconut & Spinach Soup

YIELD: 4 SERVINGS / **ACTIVE TIME:** 20 MINUTES / **TOTAL TIME:** 45 MINUTES

3 TABLESPOONS UNSALTED BUTTER

1 ONION, FINELY DICED

16 CUPS SPINACH, CHOPPED

4 CUPS VEGETABLE STOCK (SEE PAGE 441)

1 TABLESPOON ALL-PURPOSE FLOUR

2 CUPS COCONUT MILK

SALT AND PEPPER, TO TASTE

FRESHLY GRATED NUTMEG, TO TASTE, PLUS MORE FOR GARNISH

FRESH CHIVES, CHOPPED, FOR GARNISH

TOASTED ALMONDS, CHOPPED, FOR GARNISH

UNSWEETENED SHREDDED COCONUT, FOR GARNISH

1. Place 2 tablespoons of the butter in a medium pot and melt it over medium heat. Add the onion and cook, stirring occasionally, until it has softened, about 5 minutes. Reduce the heat to low, add the spinach, and cook, stirring occasionally, until it has wilted, about 5 minutes. Add the stock and bring the soup to a boil.
2. Transfer the soup to a food processor, pulse until smooth, and strain it through a fine-mesh sieve. Set it aside.
3. Place the remaining butter in a clean medium pot and melt it over medium heat. Add the flour and cook, stirring continually, for 2 minutes. Add the soup and coconut milk and cook, stirring occasionally, for 5 minutes. Season the soup with salt, pepper, and nutmeg.
4. Ladle the soup into warmed bowls, garnish with chives, almonds, coconut, and additional nutmeg, and serve.

Mexican Roasted Garlic Soup

YIELD: 4 SERVINGS / **ACTIVE TIME:** 20 MINUTES / **TOTAL TIME:** 1 HOUR

FOR THE GARLIC CONFIT

½ CUP EXTRA-VIRGIN OLIVE OIL

CLOVES FROM 1 HEAD OF GARLIC, MINCED

FOR THE SOUP

5 CUPS CHICKEN STOCK (SEE PAGE 440)

SALT AND PEPPER, TO TASTE

2 EGGS, LIGHTLY BEATEN

FLESH OF 1 AVOCADO, FINELY DICED, FOR GARNISH

3 OZ. QUESO FRESCO OR FETA CHEESE, CRUMBLED, FOR GARNISH

1 TOMATO, FINELY DICED, FOR GARNISH

4 CHIPOTLES EN ADOBO, SEEDED AND SLICED THIN, FOR GARNISH

FRESH CILANTRO, FOR GARNISH

CROUTONS (SEE PAGE 463), FOR SERVING

1. To begin preparations for the garlic confit, place the olive oil in a small skillet and warm it over the lowest-possible heat. Add the garlic and cook until it has softened, about 15 minutes. Remove the pan from heat, strain the garlic, and set the confit aside.
2. To begin preparations for the soup, place the garlic and stock in a medium pot, bring to a simmer, and cook for 20 minutes.
3. Transfer the soup to a food processor, pulse until smooth, and strain it into a clean pot through a fine-mesh sieve. Bring the soup to a simmer and season it with salt and pepper. Remove the pot from heat, add the eggs, and whisk until well combined.
4. Ladle the soup into warmed bowls, garnish with avocado, queso fresco or feta, tomato, chipotles en adobo, and cilantro, and serve with the Croutons.

Miso Broth with Crispy Wonton Strips

YIELD: 4 SERVINGS / **ACTIVE TIME:** 30 MINUTES / **TOTAL TIME:** 1 HOUR

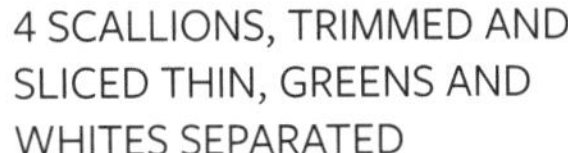

4 SCALLIONS, TRIMMED AND SLICED THIN, GREENS AND WHITES SEPARATED

¼ CUP CHOPPED FRESH CILANTRO

1-INCH PIECE OF FRESH GINGER, PEELED AND MINCED

1 STAR ANISE POD

1 CINNAMON STICK

SEEDS OF 4 CARDAMOM PODS

1 BAY LEAF

½ TEASPOON RED PEPPER FLAKES

4 CUPS DASHI STOCK (SEE PAGE 448)

3 BOK CHOY, SLICED LENGTHWISE

¼ CUP RED MISO

2 TABLESPOONS SOY SAUCE

THAI CHILE PEPPERS, SEEDED AND SLICED THIN, FOR GARNISH

CRISPY WONTON STRIPS (SEE PAGE 464), FOR SERVING

1. Place the scallion greens, cilantro, ginger, star anise, cinnamon stick, cardamom, bay leaf, red pepper flakes, and stock in a large pot and bring to a boil. Reduce the heat so that the soup simmers and cook for 10 minutes.
2. Strain the broth into a clean pot through a fine-mesh sieve and bring the broth to a simmer. Add the bok choy and cook for 5 minutes. Add the scallion whites and cook for 2 minutes.
3. Place the miso and 1 tablespoon of the broth in a small mixing bowl and stir until fully combined. Add the miso mixture and soy sauce to the pot and stir to combine.
4. Ladle the soup into warmed bowls, garnish with chiles, and serve with the Crispy Wonton Strips.

Parsnip & Pear Soup

YIELD: 4 TO 6 SERVINGS / **ACTIVE TIME:** 30 MINUTES / **TOTAL TIME:** 1 HOUR AND 15 MINUTES

2 TABLESPOONS UNSALTED BUTTER

4 CUPS PEELED AND FINELY DICED PARSNIPS

1 ONION, FINELY DICED

1 CUP PEELED AND FINELY DICED PEAR

1 GARLIC CLOVE, MINCED

1 TEASPOON FRESH THYME

½ CUP WHITE WINE

8 CUPS CHICKEN STOCK (SEE PAGE 440)

SALT AND PEPPER, TO TASTE

BLUE CHEESE, CRUMBLED, FOR GARNISH

POACHED PEARS (SEE PAGE 465), FOR SERVING

1. Place the butter in a medium pot and melt it over medium heat. Add the parsnips, onion, pear, garlic, and thyme and cook, stirring occasionally, until they have softened, about 10 minutes.
2. Add the wine and cook until it has completely evaporated. Add the stock, bring the soup to a simmer, and cook until the parsnips are tender, about 30 minutes.
3. Transfer the soup to a food processor, pulse until smooth, and strain it into the pot through a fine-mesh sieve. Season the soup with salt and pepper.
4. Ladle the soup into warmed bowls, garnish with blue cheese, and serve with the Poached Pears.

Parsnip Soup with Butternut Squash Bread

YIELD: 6 SERVINGS / **ACTIVE TIME:** 30 MINUTES / **TOTAL TIME:** 1 HOUR AND 10 MINUTES

2 TABLESPOONS UNSALTED BUTTER

6 CUPS PEELED AND FINELY DICED PARSNIPS

1 CARROT, PEELED AND FINELY DICED

½ ONION, FINELY DICED

1 CELERY STALK, FINELY DICED

8 CUPS VEGETABLE STOCK (SEE PAGE 441)

1 BAY LEAF

2 CUPS HEAVY CREAM

SALT AND PEPPER, TO TASTE

FRESHLY GRATED NUTMEG, TO TASTE

BUTTERNUT SQUASH BREAD (SEE PAGE 464), SLICED, FOR SERVING

1. Place the butter in a large pot and melt it over medium heat. Add the parsnips, carrot, onion, and celery and cook, stirring occasionally, until they have softened, about 5 minutes.
2. Add the stock and bay leaf and bring the soup to a boil. Reduce the heat so that the soup simmers and cook until the vegetables are tender, about 20 minutes. Remove the bay leaf from the pot and discard it.
3. Transfer the soup to a food processor, pulse until smooth, and strain it back into the pot through a fine-mesh sieve. Add the cream, season with salt, pepper, and nutmeg, and bring the soup to a simmer.
4. Ladle the soup into warmed bowls and serve with the Butternut Squash Bread.

Roasted Pumpkin Mole Soup

YIELD: 4 SERVINGS / **ACTIVE TIME:** 20 MINUTES / **TOTAL TIME:** 1 HOUR AND 30 MINUTES

1 (3 LB.) PUMPKIN, HALVED AND SEEDED, ½ CUP SEEDS RINSED WELL AND RESERVED

1½ TABLESPOONS EXTRA-VIRGIN OLIVE OIL

1 TEASPOON BROWN SUGAR

½ TEASPOON CUMIN

¼ TEASPOON KOSHER SALT

1 ANCHO CHILE PEPPER, SOAKED IN WARM WATER, DRAINED, AND SLICED THIN

1 TABLESPOON MOLE PASTE

¼ CUP WATER

2 CUPS BUTTERMILK

SALT AND PEPPER, TO TASTE

FRESH CHIVES, CHOPPED, FOR GARNISH

SOUR CREAM, FOR SERVING

1. Preheat the oven to 450°F. Place the pumpkin halves in a baking dish, flesh side down, drizzle 1 tablespoon of the olive oil over them, place the dish in the oven, and roast until the pumpkin is tender, about 30 minutes. Remove the dish from the oven and let the pumpkin cool. Once the pumpkin has cooled, scoop out its flesh and set it aside.
2. Lower the oven's temperature to 325°F. Place the pumpkin seeds, brown sugar, cumin, salt, and remaining olive oil in a small mixing bowl and toss until the seeds are thoroughly coated. Place the seeds on a baking sheet, place it in the oven, and toast the seeds for 8 minutes. Remove the pan from the oven and let the seeds cool.
3. Place the pumpkin and chile in a food processor and pulse until smooth.
4. Place the mole paste and water in a small pot and cook, stirring continually, until the mixture becomes smooth, about 5 minutes. Remove the pot from heat and set the mixture aside.
5. Place the pumpkin puree, mole sauce, and buttermilk in a large pot and bring the soup to a simmer while stirring continually. Season the soup with salt and pepper.
6. Ladle the soup into warmed bowls, garnish with the toasted pumpkin seeds and chives, and serve with sour cream.

Saffron & Sunchoke Soup

YIELD: 4 SERVINGS / **ACTIVE TIME:** 30 MINUTES / **TOTAL TIME:** 1 HOUR AND 30 MINUTES

2 TABLESPOONS EXTRA-VIRGIN OLIVE OIL

1 ONION, FINELY DICED

1 GARLIC CLOVE, MINCED

2 CUPS PEELED AND FINELY DICED SUNCHOKES

4 CUPS CHICKEN STOCK (SEE PAGE 440)

PINCH OF SAFFRON THREADS, PLUS MORE FOR GARNISH

JUICE OF ½ LEMON

FRESH PARSLEY, CHOPPED, FOR GARNISH

TOASTED SLIVERED ALMONDS, FOR GARNISH

1. Place the olive oil in a medium pot and warm it over medium heat. Add the onion and cook, stirring occasionally, until it has softened, about 5 minutes. Add the garlic and sunchokes and cook, stirring occasionally, for 5 minutes.
2. Add the stock and bring the soup to a boil. Reduce the heat so that the soup simmers and cook for 15 minutes. Add the saffron and lemon juice and cook until the sunchokes are tender, about 15 minutes.
3. Transfer the soup to a food processor and pulse until smooth. Strain the soup back into the pot through a fine-mesh sieve and bring it to a simmer.
4. Ladle the soup into warmed bowls, garnish with additional saffron, parsley, and toasted almonds, and serve.

Fire-Roasted Pepper Soup

YIELD: 4 SERVINGS / **ACTIVE TIME:** 30 MINUTES / **TOTAL TIME:** 1 HOUR

4 RED BELL PEPPERS, STEMMED, SEEDED, AND HALVED

¼ CUP UNSALTED BUTTER

1 ONION, FINELY DICED

1 TEASPOON FINELY CHOPPED FRESH ROSEMARY

5 CUPS CHICKEN STOCK (SEE PAGE 440)

2 TABLESPOONS TOMATO PASTE

1 TEASPOON PAPRIKA

⅛ TEASPOON CAYENNE PEPPER

½ CUP SOUR CREAM, PLUS MORE FOR GARNISH

SALT AND PEPPER, TO TASTE

HERB CRACKERS, FOR SERVING

1. Prepare a gas or charcoal grill for medium-high heat (about 450°F). Place the bell peppers on the grill, cut sides down, and cook until they are lightly charred, about 6 minutes. Turn them over and cook until they are just tender, about 5 minutes. Remove the peppers from the grill and let them cool slightly.
2. Place the butter in a medium pot and melt it over medium heat. Add the onion and rosemary and cook, stirring occasionally, until the onion has softened, about 5 minutes.
3. Add the roasted peppers, stock, tomato paste, paprika, and cayenne and bring the soup to a boil. Reduce the heat so that the soup simmers and cook for 15 minutes.
4. Transfer the soup to a food processor, pulse until smooth, and strain it into a clean pot through a fine-mesh sieve. Stir in the sour cream, season with salt and pepper, and bring the soup to a simmer.
5. Ladle the soup into warmed bowls, garnish with additional sour cream, and serve with herb crackers.

Borscht

YIELD: 4 TO 6 SERVINGS / **ACTIVE TIME:** 30 MINUTES / **TOTAL TIME:** 1 HOUR AND 15 MINUTES

1½ TABLESPOONS UNSALTED BUTTER

1 ONION, FINELY DICED

4 CUPS PEELED AND FINELY DICED BEETS

1 CARROT, PEELED AND FINELY DICED

1 CELERY STALK, FINELY DICED

2 TOMATOES, FINELY DICED

SACHET D'ÉPICES (SEE PAGE 465), WITH 2 GARLIC CLOVES ADDED

6 CUPS BEEF STOCK (SEE PAGE 442)

½ CUP BEET KVASS

SALT AND PEPPER, TO TASTE

SOUR CREAM, FOR GARNISH

FRESH PARSLEY, CHOPPED, FOR GARNISH

1. Place the butter in a large pot and melt it over medium heat. Add the onion and cook, stirring occasionally, until it has softened, about 5 minutes. Add the beets, carrot, and celery and cook, stirring occasionally, for 5 minutes. Add the tomatoes and cook, stirring occasionally, for 2 minutes.
2. Add the Sachet d'Épices and stock and bring the soup to a boil. Reduce the heat so that the soup simmers and cook until the vegetables are tender, about 1 hour.
3. Add the kvass, season with salt and pepper, and stir to combine.
4. Ladle the soup into warmed bowls, garnish with sour cream and parsley, and serve.

Carrot & Ginger Bisque

YIELD: 4 TO 6 SERVINGS / **ACTIVE TIME:** 20 MINUTES / **TOTAL TIME:** 45 MINUTES

- 2 TABLESPOONS UNSALTED BUTTER
- 1 LARGE ONION, SLICED
- 5 GARLIC CLOVES, SLICED
- 2 OZ. FRESH GINGER, PEELED AND SLICED
- 2 LBS. CARROTS, PEELED AND CHOPPED
- SALT AND PEPPER, TO TASTE
- 6 CUPS CHICKEN STOCK (SEE PAGE 440)
- 1 CUP HEAVY CREAM
- 1 CUP CRÈME FRAÎCHE
- TOASTED NUTS, FOR GARNISH
- HERB OIL (SEE PAGE 466), FOR GARNISH

1. Place the butter in a medium saucepan and melt it over medium heat. Add the onion, garlic, and ginger and cook, stirring frequently, until they have softened, about 5 minutes.
2. Add the carrots, season with salt and pepper, and add the stock. Bring the soup to a boil, reduce the heat, and let the soup simmer until the carrots are tender, about 15 minutes.
3. Add the heavy cream and half of the crème fraîche and gently simmer the soup for 10 minutes.
4. Strain the soup, reserving the liquid. Transfer the solids to a blender and puree until smooth, using the reserved liquid to reach the desired consistency. Taste the soup and adjust the seasoning as necessary.
5. Pour the soup into warmed bowls, garnish each portion with toasted nuts, Herb Oil, and the remaining crème fraîche, and serve.

Baby Spinach & Yogurt Soup

YIELD: 4 SERVINGS / **ACTIVE TIME:** 20 MINUTES / **TOTAL TIME:** 1 HOUR

2 TABLESPOONS EXTRA-VIRGIN OLIVE OIL

1 ONION, FINELY DICED

12 CUPS BABY SPINACH

2 SCALLIONS, TRIMMED AND SLICED

3 TABLESPOONS LONG-GRAIN RICE

3 CUPS VEGETABLE STOCK (SEE PAGE 441)

1 GARLIC CLOVE, MINCED

1½ CUPS YOGURT

SALT AND PEPPER, TO TASTE

1. Place the olive oil in a large pot and warm it over medium heat. Add the onion and cook, stirring occasionally, until it has softened, about 5 minutes. Add 8 cups of the spinach, cover the pot, and cook until all the spinach has wilted, about 5 minutes. Add the scallions, rice, and stock, bring the soup to a simmer, and cook until the rice is fully cooked, about 18 minutes.
2. Transfer the soup to a food processor, add the garlic and remaining spinach, and pulse until smooth. Strain the soup into a clean pot through a fine-mesh sieve, bring it to a simmer, and add the yogurt.
3. Season the soup with salt and pepper, ladle it into warmed bowls, and serve.

Tomato & Basil Soup

YIELD: 4 TO 6 SERVINGS / **ACTIVE TIME:** 45 MINUTES / **TOTAL TIME:** 1 HOUR AND 30 MINUTES

2 TABLESPOONS EXTRA-VIRGIN OLIVE OIL

2 TABLESPOONS UNSALTED BUTTER

1 ONION, FINELY DICED

2 LBS. TOMATOES, FINELY DICED

1 GARLIC CLOVE, MINCED

3 CUPS VEGETABLE STOCK (SEE PAGE 441)

½ CUP WHITE WINE

3 TABLESPOONS TOMATO PASTE

SALT AND PEPPER, TO TASTE

½ CUP CHOPPED FRESH BASIL, PLUS MORE FOR GARNISH

1 CUP HEAVY CREAM

ROMANO CHEESE, GRATED, FOR GARNISH

1. Place the olive oil and butter in a medium pot and warm the mixture over medium heat. Add the onion and cook, stirring occasionally, until it has softened, about 5 minutes. Add the tomatoes and garlic and cook, stirring frequently, for 2 minutes. Add the stock, wine, and tomato paste and bring the soup to a boil. Reduce the heat so that the soup simmers, season with salt and pepper, and cook for 20 minutes.
2. Transfer the soup to a food processor, add the basil, and pulse until smooth. Strain the soup into a clean pot through a fine-mesh sieve, add the cream, and bring it to a simmer.
3. Ladle the soup into warmed bowls, garnish with additional basil and Romano cheese, and serve.

Sweet Potato Soup

YIELD: 4 TO 6 SERVINGS / **ACTIVE TIME:** 25 MINUTES / **TOTAL TIME:** 55 MINUTES

1½ TABLESPOONS UNSALTED BUTTER

1 SMALL ONION, FINELY DICED

5 CUPS CHICKEN STOCK (SEE PAGE 440)

½ TEASPOON CURRY POWDER, PLUS MORE FOR GARNISH

10 CUPS PEELED AND FINELY DICED SWEET POTATOES

2 TABLESPOONS MAPLE SYRUP

2 TEASPOONS FRESH THYME

PINCH OF CAYENNE PEPPER

2 CUPS HEAVY CREAM

2 PINCHES OF FRESHLY GRATED NUTMEG

SALT AND PEPPER, TO TASTE

FRESH CILANTRO, CHOPPED, FOR GARNISH

CRÈME FRAÎCHE, FOR SERVING

1. Place the butter in a medium pot and melt it over medium heat. Add the onion and cook, stirring occasionally, until it has softened, about 5 minutes. Add the stock, curry powder, potato, syrup, thyme, and cayenne and bring the soup to a boil. Reduce the heat so that the soup simmers and cook until the potatoes are tender, about 25 minutes.
2. Transfer the soup to a food processor, pulse until smooth, and strain back into the pot through a fine-mesh sieve. Bring the soup to a simmer, add the cream and nutmeg, and season with salt and pepper.
3. Ladle the soup into warmed bowls, garnish with additional curry powder and cilantro, and serve with crème fraîche.

Vegetable Soup with Israeli Couscous

YIELD: 4 TO 6 SERVINGS / **ACTIVE TIME:** 15 MINUTES / **TOTAL TIME:** 45 MINUTES

2 TABLESPOONS EXTRA-VIRGIN OLIVE OIL

1 ONION, FINELY DICED

1 LARGE CARROT, PEELED AND DICED

1 (14 OZ.) CAN OF DICED TOMATOES

5 GARLIC CLOVES, MINCED

6 CUPS VEGETABLE STOCK (SEE PAGE 441)

1¼ CUPS ISRAELI COUSCOUS

¼ TEASPOON CUMIN

2 TABLESPOONS CHOPPED FRESH CILANTRO

⅛ TEASPOON CAYENNE PEPPER

SALT AND PEPPER, TO TASTE

1. Place the olive oil in a large pot and warm it over medium heat. Add the onion and carrot and cook, stirring occasionally, until the onion has softened, about 5 minutes.
2. Add the tomatoes, garlic, stock, couscous, cumin, cilantro, and cayenne, season with salt and pepper, and bring the soup to a boil. Reduce the heat so that the soup simmers and cook until the couscous is tender, about 8 to 12 minutes.
3. Ladle the soup into warmed bowls and serve.

Truffled Mushroom Consommé

YIELD: 4 SERVINGS / **ACTIVE TIME:** 25 MINUTES / **TOTAL TIME:** 1 HOUR AND 15 MINUTES

2 CARROTS, PEELED AND DICED

1 ONION, FINELY DICED

2 CELERY STALKS, FINELY DICED

½ LB. GROUND CHICKEN

6 OZ. TOMATOES, FINELY DICED

6 CUPS MUSHROOM STOCK (SEE PAGE 449)

SACHET D'ÉPICES (SEE PAGE 465), 1 WHOLE CLOVE AND 1 ALLSPICE BERRY ADDED

5 EGG WHITES, BEATEN

SALT AND PEPPER, TO TASTE

FRESH PARSLEY, CHOPPED, FOR GARNISH

TRUFFLE OIL, FOR GARNISH

TRUFFLE PASTE, FOR GARNISH

1. Place the carrots, onion, celery, chicken, tomatoes, stock, Sachet d'Épices, and egg whites in a large pot, bring the soup to a simmer, and cook for 45 minutes.
2. Strain the soup into a clean pot through a fine-mesh sieve, bring the soup to a boil, and season with salt and pepper.
3. Ladle the soup into warmed bowls, garnish with parsley, truffle oil, and truffle paste, and serve.

Easy Minestrone

YIELD: 4 TO 6 SERVINGS / **ACTIVE TIME:** 45 MINUTES / **TOTAL TIME:** 1 HOUR AND 30 MINUTES

2 TABLESPOONS EXTRA-VIRGIN OLIVE OIL

1 GARLIC CLOVE, MINCED

2 ONIONS, FINELY DICED

1 CARROT, PEELED AND FINELY DICED

½ LEEK, TRIMMED, RINSED WELL, AND FINELY DICED

1 YELLOW BELL PEPPER, SEEDED AND FINELY DICED

1 RED BELL PEPPER, SEEDED AND FINELY DICED

1 ZUCCHINI, FINELY DICED

6 CUPS TOMATO JUICE

½ TEASPOON FRESH THYME

½ TEASPOON FINELY CHOPPED FRESH ROSEMARY

SALT AND PEPPER, TO TASTE

PARMESAN CHEESE, GRATED, FOR GARNISH

1. Place the olive oil in a large pot and warm it over medium heat. Add the garlic, onions, carrot, and leek and cook, stirring occasionally, until the onions have softened, about 5 minutes. Add the bell peppers and cook, stirring occasionally, for 5 minutes. Add the zucchini and cook, stirring occasionally, for 3 minutes.
2. Add the tomato juice, thyme, and rosemary and bring the soup to a boil. Reduce the heat so that the soup simmers and cook until the vegetables are tender, about 20 minutes. Season the soup with salt and pepper.
3. Ladle the soup into warmed bowls, garnish with Parmesan cheese, and serve.

Watercress & Buttermilk Soup

YIELD: 4 SERVINGS / **ACTIVE TIME:** 25 MINUTES / **TOTAL TIME:** 1 HOUR AND 15 MINUTES

2 TABLESPOONS EXTRA-VIRGIN OLIVE OIL

1 ONION, FINELY DICED

1 POTATO, PEELED AND FINELY DICED

5 CUPS CHOPPED WATERCRESS, STEMS RESERVED, PLUS MORE FOR GARNISH

2 CUPS VEGETABLE STOCK (SEE PAGE 441)

1½ CUPS BUTTERMILK

SALT AND PEPPER, TO TASTE

POPPY SEED YOGURT (SEE PAGE 467), FOR SERVING

1. Place the olive oil in a medium pot and warm it over medium heat. Add the onion and cook, stirring occasionally, until it has softened, about 5 minutes. Add the potato and cook, stirring occasionally, for 8 minutes. Add the watercress stems and stock and bring the soup to a boil.
2. Reduce the heat so that the soup simmers and cook until the potato is tender, about 10 minutes. Add the watercress and cook for 2 minutes.
3. Transfer the soup to a food processor, pulse until smooth, and strain it into a clean pot through a fine-mesh sieve. Bring the soup to a simmer, add the buttermilk, and season with salt and pepper.
4. Ladle the soup into warmed bowls, garnish with additional watercress, and serve with the Poppy Seed Yogurt.

Shiitake & Laksa Soup

YIELD: 4 SERVINGS / **ACTIVE TIME:** 30 MINUTES / **TOTAL TIME:** 1 HOUR AND 30 MINUTES

4 CUPS VEGETABLE STOCK (SEE PAGE 441)

1¼ CUPS FINELY DICED DRIED SHIITAKE MUSHROOMS

1 CUP HOT WATER

3 DRIED PASILLA CHILE PEPPERS, STEMMED, SEEDED, AND FINELY DICED

1 LEMONGRASS STALK, CRUSHED AND SLICED THIN

½ TEASPOON TURMERIC

1 TABLESPOON PEELED AND MINCED FRESH GALANGAL

1 ONION, FINELY DICED

½ TABLESPOON SHRIMP PASTE

1 TABLESPOON EXTRA-VIRGIN OLIVE OIL

1 TABLESPOON TAMARIND PASTE

1 TABLESPOON JAGGERY

SALT AND PEPPER, TO TASTE

3 OZ. RICE NOODLES

FRESH CUCUMBER, SLICED THIN, FOR GARNISH

FRESH MINT, FOR GARNISH

1. Bring the stock to a boil in a medium pot. Remove the pot from heat, add the mushrooms, and let the broth rest for 20 minutes. Strain the broth through a fine-mesh sieve and reserve the mushrooms and broth.
2. Place the water and chiles in a small mixing bowl and soak the peppers for 5 minutes. Strain the mixture through a fine-mesh sieve and reserve the peppers and ½ cup of the soaking liquid.
3. Place the soaked peppers, reserved soaking liquid, lemongrass, turmeric, galangal, onion, and shrimp paste in a food processor and pulse until the mixture is a smooth paste.
4. Place the olive oil in a medium pot and warm it over low heat. Add the tamarind paste and cook, stirring occasionally, until fragrant, about 5 minutes. Add the mushroom broth and jaggery, bring the soup to a simmer, and cook for 25 minutes.
5. Bring water to a boil in a large pot. Add salt, let the water return to a boil, and add the noodles. Cook until the noodles are al dente, 8 to 10 minutes. Drain the noodles, rinse them under cold water, and let them cool.
6. Strain the soup into the pot through a fine-mesh sieve, add the mushrooms, and bring the soup to a simmer. Season the soup with salt and pepper.
7. Divide the noodles among warmed bowls and ladle the soup over the top. Garnish with cucumber and mint and serve.

Onion & White Port Soup

YIELD: 4 TO 6 SERVINGS / **ACTIVE TIME:** 15 MINUTES / **TOTAL TIME:** 45 MINUTES

¼ CUP EXTRA-VIRGIN OLIVE OIL

5 ONIONS, FINELY DICED

SALT AND PEPPER, TO TASTE

1 GARLIC CLOVE, MINCED

1 TEASPOON FRESH THYME

1 CUP WHITE PORT

4 CUPS HEAVY CREAM

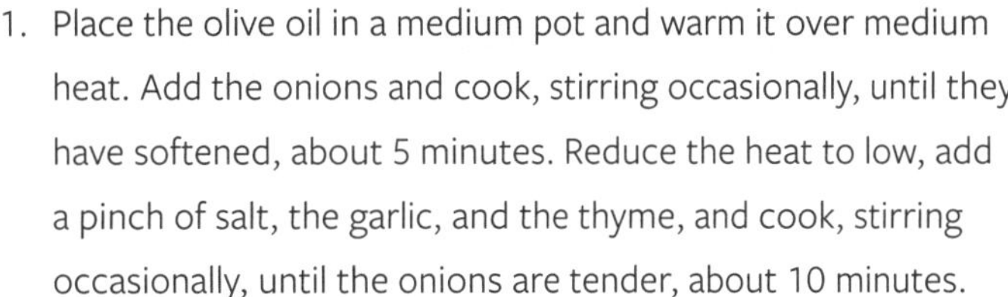

1. Place the olive oil in a medium pot and warm it over medium heat. Add the onions and cook, stirring occasionally, until they have softened, about 5 minutes. Reduce the heat to low, add a pinch of salt, the garlic, and the thyme, and cook, stirring occasionally, until the onions are tender, about 10 minutes.

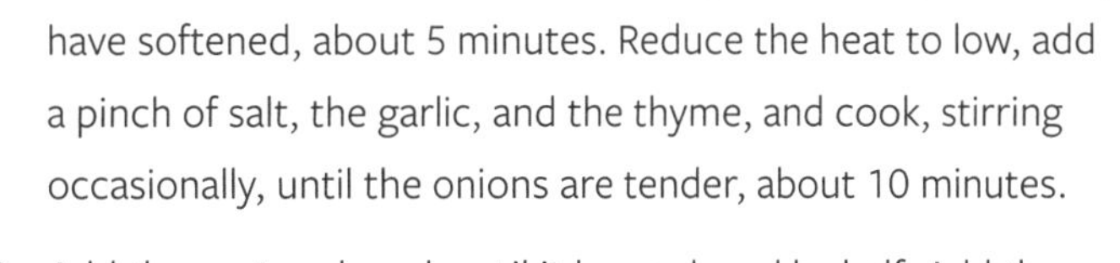

2. Add the port and cook until it has reduced by half. Add the cream and bring the soup to a boil. Reduce the heat so that the soup simmers and cook for 15 minutes.
3. Transfer the soup to a food processor, pulse until smooth, and strain it back into the pot through a fine-mesh sieve. Bring the soup to a simmer and season with salt and pepper.
4. Ladle the soup into warmed bowls and serve.

Potato & Leek Soup

YIELD: 4 TO 6 SERVINGS / **ACTIVE TIME:** 25 MINUTES / **TOTAL TIME:** 1 HOUR

½ CUP UNSALTED BUTTER

1 LEEK, WHITE PART ONLY, RINSED WELL AND SLICED

1 SMALL ONION, SLICED

5 GARLIC CLOVES, SLICED

SALT, TO TASTE

3 LARGE POTATOES, PEELED AND CHOPPED

4 CUPS MILK

1 TEASPOON SHERRY VINEGAR

½ CUP CRÈME FRAÎCHE

½ CUP HEAVY CREAM

1. Place the butter in a medium saucepan and melt it over medium heat. Add the leek, onion, and garlic, season with salt, and cook, stirring frequently, until the onion and leek are translucent, about 3 minutes.
2. Add the potatoes and milk, season with salt, and bring to a gentle simmer. Reduce the heat to low and cook until the potatoes are tender, 15 to 20 minutes.
3. Drain the vegetables, reserving the milk. Add the vegetables to a blender, along with the sherry vinegar, crème fraîche, and cream, and puree until smooth, adding the reserved milk as needed to get the desired consistency.
4. Taste the soup, adjust the seasoning as necessary, and serve.

Yellow Split Pea Soup

YIELD: 4 SERVINGS / **ACTIVE TIME:** 30 MINUTES / **TOTAL TIME:** 1 HOUR AND 30 MINUTES

¼ CUP EXTRA-VIRGIN OLIVE OIL

2 RED ONIONS, FINELY DICED

½ CUP DRIED YELLOW SPLIT PEAS, RINSED AND DRAINED

6 CUPS CHICKEN STOCK (SEE PAGE 440)

1 TEASPOON DRIED OREGANO

1 TABLESPOON RED WINE VINEGAR

2 TABLESPOONS CAPERS, DRAINED AND RINSED

SALT AND PEPPER, TO TASTE

SPRIGS OF FRESH OREGANO, FOR GARNISH

TOMATO SAUCE (SEE PAGE 458), FOR SERVING

1. Place the olive oil in a large pot and warm it over medium heat. Add the onions and cook, stirring occasionally, until they have softened, about 5 minutes. Add the peas and cook, stirring continually, for 2 minutes. Add 4 cups of the stock, cover the pot, and bring the soup to a boil.
2. Reduce the heat so that the soup simmers, uncover the pot, and cook until most of the stock has evaporated, about 1 hour.
3. Transfer the soup to a food processor, add the remaining stock, and pulse until smooth. Strain the soup back into the pot through a fine-mesh sieve. Bring the soup to a simmer, add the oregano, vinegar, and capers, and season with salt and pepper.
4. Ladle the soup into warmed bowls, garnish with sprigs of fresh oregano, and serve with the Tomato Sauce.

White Tomato Soup with Basil Oil

YIELD: 4 SERVINGS / **ACTIVE TIME:** 45 MINUTES / **TOTAL TIME:** 24 HOURS

10 TOMATOES, FINELY DICED

1 TEASPOON FRESH THYME

1 STAR ANISE POD

1 TABLESPOON RICE

2 CUPS HEAVY CREAM

SALT AND PEPPER, TO TASTE

BASIL OIL (SEE PAGE 466), FOR SERVING

1. Place the tomatoes in a food processor, pulse until smooth, and place them in a fine-mesh sieve that is positioned over a large bowl. Let the tomatoes drain overnight.
2. Place the strained tomato water, thyme, star anise, and rice in a medium pot and cook over medium heat, stirring occasionally, until the water has been reduced by half. Add the cream and cook for 30 minutes. Remove the star anise from the pot and discard it.
3. Transfer the soup to a food processor, pulse until smooth, and strain it back into the pot through a fine-mesh sieve. Bring the soup to a simmer and season with salt and pepper.
4. Ladle the soup into warmed bowls and serve with the Basil Oil.

Havuç Çorbası

YIELD: 6 SERVINGS / **ACTIVE TIME:** 20 MINUTES / **TOTAL TIME:** 1 HOUR

8 CUPS CHICKEN STOCK (SEE PAGE 440)

5 CUPS PEELED AND DICED CARROTS

2 TEASPOONS SUGAR

1 TEASPOON CINNAMON

SALT AND PEPPER, TO TASTE

2 TABLESPOONS UNSALTED BUTTER

2 TABLESPOONS ALL-PURPOSE FLOUR

½ CUP WARM MILK

3 EGG YOLKS, BEATEN

TOASTED PISTACHIOS, CHOPPED, FOR GARNISH

1. Bring the stock and carrots to a boil in a medium pot. Add the sugar and cinnamon, season with salt and pepper, and reduce the heat so that the soup simmers. Cook until the carrots are tender, about 30 minutes.
2. Transfer the broth to a food processor, pulse until smooth, and strain it through a fine-mesh sieve. Set the broth aside.
3. Place the butter in a clean medium pot and melt it over low heat. Add the flour and cook, stirring continually, for 3 minutes. Add the milk and cook, stirring continually, until the mixture thickens, about 3 minutes. Add the broth and bring the soup to a simmer.
4. Add the egg yolks and cook, stirring frequently, until the soup thickens.
5. Ladle the soup into warmed bowls, garnish with toasted pistachios, and serve.

Rutabaga & Fig Soup

YIELD: 4 SERVINGS / **ACTIVE TIME:** 20 MINUTES / **TOTAL TIME:** 1 HOUR

2 TABLESPOONS EXTRA-VIRGIN OLIVE OIL

1 ONION, CHOPPED

4 CUPS PEELED AND CHOPPED RUTABAGAS

1 TABLESPOON HONEY

4 CUPS VEGETABLE STOCK (SEE PAGE 441)

1 TEASPOON FRESH THYME

16 FRESH FIGS

1 CUP BUTTERMILK

SALT AND PEPPER, TO TASTE

SPICY CHICKPEAS (SEE PAGE 467), FOR SERVING

1. Place the olive oil in a medium saucepan and warm it over medium heat. Add the onion and rutabagas and cook, stirring occasionally, until the onion is soft, about 10 minutes.
2. Stir in the honey, stock, thyme, and figs and bring the soup to a boil.
3. Reduce the heat so that the soup simmers and cook until the rutabagas are tender, about 20 minutes.
4. Transfer the soup to a food processor or blender and blitz until smooth. Place the soup in a clean saucepan, add the buttermilk, and bring to a simmer.
5. Season the soup with salt and pepper, ladle into warmed bowls, and serve with the Spicy Chickpeas.

Vegetarian Gumbo

YIELD: 4 TO 6 SERVINGS / **ACTIVE TIME:** 30 MINUTES / **TOTAL TIME:** 1 HOUR

- 1 TABLESPOON EXTRA-VIRGIN OLIVE OIL
- 1 ONION, FINELY DICED
- 2 GARLIC CLOVES, MINCED
- 1 CELERY STALK, FINELY DICED
- 1 GREEN BELL PEPPER, STEMMED, SEEDED, AND FINELY DICED
- ¼ HEAD OF CABBAGE, CHOPPED
- ½ TEASPOON FINELY CHOPPED FRESH OREGANO
- ½ TEASPOON FRESH THYME
- 1 BAY LEAF
- 6 CUPS VEGETABLE STOCK (SEE PAGE 441)
- 2 CUPS COLLARD GREENS, FINELY CHOPPED
- 2 CUPS SPINACH, FINELY CHOPPED
- 1 BUNCH OF WATERCRESS
- ¾ LB. TOFU, DRAINED AND FINELY DICED
- ¼ CUP FINELY CHOPPED FRESH PARSLEY
- ½ TEASPOON ALLSPICE
- PINCH OF CAYENNE PEPPER
- SALT AND PEPPER, TO TASTE

1. Place the olive oil in a large pot and warm it over medium heat. Add the onion, garlic, celery, and bell pepper and cook, stirring occasionally, until the onion has softened, about 5 minutes. Add the cabbage, oregano, thyme, and bay leaf and cook, stirring occasionally, for 5 minutes. Add the stock and bring the soup to a boil.
2. Reduce the heat so that the soup simmers and cook for 5 minutes. Add the collard greens and cook for 5 minutes. Add the spinach, watercress, and tofu and cook for 2 minutes. Add the parsley, allspice, and cayenne pepper, season with salt and pepper, and cook for 2 minutes.
3. Ladle the soup into warmed bowls and serve.

Vegan Tom Yam Goong

YIELD: 4 SERVINGS / **ACTIVE TIME:** 20 MINUTES / **TOTAL TIME:** 45 MINUTES

¼ CUP EXTRA-VIRGIN OLIVE OIL

1 ONION, FINELY DICED

1 GARLIC CLOVE, MINCED

6 CUPS VEGETABLE STOCK (SEE PAGE 441)

JUICE OF 2 LIMES

3 MAKRUT LIME LEAVES

3 THAI CHILE PEPPERS, STEMMED, SEEDED, AND SLICED

¼ CUP CHOPPED FRESH CILANTRO, PLUS MORE FOR GARNISH

1 LEMONGRASS STALK, CRUSHED

1 TABLESPOON SUGAR

¾ LB. TOFU, DRAINED AND FINELY DICED

¼ CUP FISH SAUCE

8 SHIITAKE MUSHROOMS, STEMMED AND FINELY DICED

SALT AND PEPPER, TO TASTE

FRESH WATERCRESS, FOR GARNISH

FRESH BEAN SPROUTS, FOR GARNISH

1. Place half of the olive oil in a medium pot and warm it over medium heat. Add the onion and garlic and cook, stirring occasionally, until the onion has softened, about 5 minutes. Add the stock, lime juice, lime leaves, peppers, cilantro, lemongrass, and sugar and bring the soup to a boil. Reduce the heat so that the soup simmers and cook for 20 minutes.
2. Place the remaining olive oil in a medium skillet and warm it over medium heat. Add the tofu and cook, stirring occasionally, until it is lightly browned, about 4 minutes. Remove the tofu from the pan, let it cool, and set it aside.
3. Strain the soup into a clean pot through a fine-mesh sieve, bring it to a simmer, and add the tofu, fish sauce, and mushrooms. Cook the soup for 4 minutes and season it with salt and pepper.
4. Ladle the soup into warmed bowls, garnish with watercress, bean sprouts, and additional cilantro, and serve.

Tomato & Eggplant Soup

YIELD: 4 SERVINGS / **ACTIVE TIME:** 30 MINUTES / **TOTAL TIME:** 1 HOUR AND 30 MINUTES

½ CUP EXTRA-VIRGIN OLIVE OIL

2 EGGPLANTS, TRIMMED AND CUT INTO ¾-INCH CUBES

1 ONION, CHOPPED

2 GARLIC CLOVES, MINCED

2 TEASPOONS RAS EL HANOUT

½ TEASPOON CUMIN

4 CUPS CHICKEN STOCK (SEE PAGE 440), PLUS MORE AS NEEDED

1 (14 OZ.) CAN OF CRUSHED TOMATOES

⅓ CUP RAISINS

¼ CUP PINE NUTS, TOASTED

2 TEASPOONS FRESH LEMON JUICE

SALT AND PEPPER, TO TASTE

FRESH CILANTRO, CHOPPED, FOR GARNISH

EGGPLANT & PINE NUT RAGOUT (SEE PAGE 468), FOR SERVING

1. Place 1 tablespoon of the olive oil in a large saucepan and warm it over medium heat. Add the eggplants, cover the pan, and cook, stirring occasionally, for 5 minutes. Remove the cover and cook, stirring occasionally, until the eggplants are browned, about 10 minutes.
2. Add 2 tablespoons of the olive oil to the pan, along with the onion, and cook, stirring occasionally, until the onion has softened, about 5 minutes. Stir in the garlic, ras el hanout, and cumin and cook, stirring continually, for 1 minute.
3. Add the stock, tomatoes, raisins, and pine nuts and bring the soup to a boil. Reduce the heat and simmer the soup until the flavor has developed to your liking, about 20 minutes.
4. Remove the pan from heat and let the soup cool for 10 minutes.
5. Place the soup in a blender and puree until smooth, adding more stock if the soup seems too thick.
6. Place the soup in a clean saucepan and warm it over medium-low heat. Stir in the lemon juice and season with salt and pepper.
7. Ladle the soup into warmed bowls, drizzle some of the remaining olive oil over each portion, and garnish with cilantro. Add a dollop of the Eggplant & Pine Nut Ragout to each bowl and enjoy.

Hot & Sour Soup

YIELD: 4 SERVINGS / **ACTIVE TIME:** 30 MINUTES / **TOTAL TIME:** 45 MINUTES

3 TABLESPOONS CORNSTARCH

1 CUP WATER

1 TABLESPOON SESAME OIL

½ CUP FINELY DICED ONION

2 TEASPOONS PEELED AND MINCED GINGER

2 GARLIC CLOVES, MINCED

2 TABLESPOONS FINELY DICED CELERY

¼ CUP CHOPPED GREEN BEANS

¼ CUP PEELED AND FINELY DICED CARROT

¼ CUP FINELY DICED MUSHROOMS

½ CUP CHOPPED CABBAGE

¼ CUP SEEDED AND FINELY DICED GREEN BELL PEPPER

4 CUPS VEGETABLE STOCK (SEE PAGE 441)

3 TABLESPOONS SOY SAUCE

1 TEASPOON WHITE VINEGAR

SALT AND PEPPER, TO TASTE

FRESH BEAN SPROUTS, FOR GARNISH

FRESH SCALLIONS, CHOPPED, FOR GARNISH

1. Place the cornstarch and water in a small mixing bowl and stir until well combined. Set the slurry aside.
2. Place the sesame oil in a medium pot and warm it over medium heat. Add the onion, ginger, garlic, and celery and cook, stirring occasionally, until the onion has softened, about 5 minutes. Add the green beans, carrot, mushrooms, cabbage, and bell pepper and cook, stirring occasionally, for 1 minute. Add the stock and bring the soup to a boil.
3. Reduce the heat so that the soup simmers and add the soy sauce and vinegar. Gradually add the slurry to the soup, stir until it is fully combined, and cook, stirring frequently, until the soup has thickened, about 5 minutes. Season the soup with salt and pepper.
4. Ladle the soup into warmed bowls, garnish with bean sprouts and scallions, and serve.

Vegan Laksa Curry Soup

YIELD: 4 TO 6 SERVINGS / **ACTIVE TIME:** 20 MINUTES / **TOTAL TIME:** 45 MINUTES

1 TABLESPOON EXTRA-VIRGIN OLIVE OIL

LAKSA CURRY PASTE (SEE PAGE 470)

2 CUPS FINELY DICED SHIITAKE MUSHROOMS

1 CUP PEELED AND DICED CARROTS

¼ CUP FINELY DICED RED BELL PEPPER

¼ CUP FINELY DICED GREEN BELL PEPPER

¼ CUP FINELY DICED ZUCCHINI

¼ CUP FINELY DICED SUMMER SQUASH

4 CUPS VEGETABLE STOCK (SEE PAGE 441)

1 (14 OZ.) CAN OF COCONUT MILK

½ LB. RICE NOODLES

1 CUP CHOPPED KALE

½ LB. TOFU, DRAINED AND CUBED

1 TABLESPOON SOY SAUCE

1 TABLESPOON FRESH LIME JUICE

1 TEASPOON SUGAR

SALT AND PEPPER, TO TASTE

THAI CHILE PEPPERS, STEMMED, SEEDED, AND SLICED THIN, FOR GARNISH

FRESH CILANTRO, CHOPPED, FOR GARNISH

1. Place the olive oil in a medium pot and warm it over medium heat. Add the curry paste and cook, stirring continually, for 2 minutes. Add the mushrooms and cook, stirring frequently, for 2 minutes.

2. Add the carrots, bell peppers, zucchini, and squash and cook, stirring occasionally, until they have softened, about 5 minutes. Add the stock and coconut milk and bring the soup to a boil.

3. Reduce the heat so that the soup simmers, add the noodles, and cook for 10 minutes.

4. Add the kale and tofu, stir to combine, and cook for 2 minutes. Stir in the soy sauce, lime juice, and sugar and season with salt and pepper.

5. Ladle the soup into warmed bowls, garnish with chiles and cilantro, and serve.

Tofu, Shiitake & Ginger Soup

YIELD: 4 SERVINGS / **ACTIVE TIME:** 20 MINUTES / **TOTAL TIME:** 1 HOUR AND 30 MINUTES

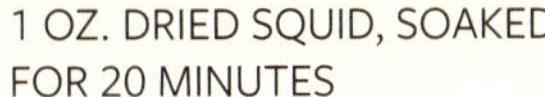

1 OZ. DRIED SQUID, SOAKED FOR 20 MINUTES

3-INCH PIECE OF FRESH GINGER, PEELED AND MINCED

¼ CUP FISH SAUCE

10 BLACK PEPPERCORNS

2 STAR ANISE PODS

6 WHOLE CLOVES

SEEDS OF 2 CARDAMOM PODS

2 CINNAMON STICKS

2 TABLESPOONS FINELY CHOPPED FRESH CILANTRO, PLUS MORE FOR GARNISH

6 CUPS CHICKEN STOCK (SEE PAGE 440)

1 TABLESPOON EXTRA-VIRGIN OLIVE OIL

1 SHALLOT, FINELY DICED

2 THAI CHILE PEPPERS, STEMMED, SEEDED, AND SLICED THIN

4 CUPS FINELY DICED SHIITAKE MUSHROOMS

¾ LB. TOFU, DRAINED AND CUBED

1 (14 OZ.) CAN OF DICED TOMATOES, DRAINED AND FINELY CHOPPED

SALT AND PEPPER, TO TASTE

1. Place the squid, ginger, fish sauce, peppercorns, star anise, cloves, cardamom, cinnamon sticks, cilantro, and 4 cups of the stock in a large pot and bring to a boil. Reduce the heat so that the soup simmers and cook for 20 minutes.
2. Remove the pot from heat and let the broth steep for 30 minutes.
3. Strain the broth through a fine-mesh sieve and set it aside.
4. Place the olive oil in a medium pot and warm it over medium heat. Add the shallot and cook, stirring occasionally, until it has softened, about 5 minutes. Add the prepared broth, the remaining stock, and the chiles and bring the soup to a simmer.
5. Add the mushrooms, tofu, and tomatoes and cook for 10 minutes.
6. Season with salt and pepper and ladle the soup into warmed bowls. Garnish with additional cilantro and serve.

Curried Carrot & Spinach Soup

YIELD: 4 SERVINGS / **ACTIVE TIME:** 20 MINUTES / **TOTAL TIME:** 45 MINUTES

1 TABLESPOON EXTRA-VIRGIN OLIVE OIL

1 ONION, FINELY DICED

1 GARLIC CLOVE, MINCED

2 TABLESPOONS CURRY POWDER

6 CUPS VEGETABLE STOCK (SEE PAGE 441)

1 THAI CHILE PEPPER, STEMMED, SEEDED, AND SLICED THIN

ZEST AND JUICE OF 1 LIME

2 TABLESPOONS SOY SAUCE

¼ CUP JAGGERY

2 MAKRUT LIME LEAVES

1 CARROT, PEELED AND FINELY DICED

2 CUPS SPINACH

¾ LB. TOFU, DRAINED AND FINELY DICED

SALT AND PEPPER, TO TASTE

1. Place the olive oil in a medium pot and warm it over medium heat. Add the onion, garlic, and curry powder and cook, stirring occasionally, until the onion has softened, about 5 minutes. Add the stock, chile, lime zest, lime juice, soy sauce, jaggery, and lime leaves and bring the soup to a boil.
2. Reduce the heat so that the soup simmers and cook for 10 minutes.
3. Add the carrot and cook until it is tender, 15 to 20 minutes.
4. Add the spinach and tofu, season with salt and pepper, and cook until the tofu is warmed through.
5. Ladle the soup into warmed bowls and serve.

LEGUMES, NUTS & GRAINS

Barley & Sausage Soup

YIELD: 4 SERVINGS / **ACTIVE TIME:** 20 MINUTES / **TOTAL TIME:** 1 HOUR AND 30 MINUTES

2 TABLESPOONS EXTRA-VIRGIN OLIVE OIL

1 LB. GROUND ITALIAN SAUSAGE

1 ONION, FINELY DICED

2 GARLIC CLOVES, MINCED

1 TEASPOON FINELY CHOPPED FRESH BASIL

1 TEASPOON FINELY CHOPPED FRESH OREGANO

1 TEASPOON FRESH THYME

8 CUPS CHICKEN STOCK (SEE PAGE 440)

1 CARROT, PEELED AND DICED

¼ CUP PEARL BARLEY

10 OZ. SPINACH, CHOPPED

SALT AND PEPPER, TO TASTE

CRUSTY BREAD, FOR SERVING

1. Place the olive oil in a medium pot and warm it over medium-high heat. Add the sausage, onion, and garlic and cook, stirring frequently, until the sausage has browned, about 5 minutes. Add the basil, oregano, thyme, and stock and bring the soup to a boil.
2. Reduce the heat so that the soup simmers and add the carrot and barley. Reduce the heat to its lowest setting, cover the pot, and cook until the barley is tender, about 1 hour.
3. Add the spinach and cook until it has wilted, about 5 minutes. Season the soup with salt and pepper.
4. Ladle the soup into warmed bowls and serve with crusty bread.

Zuppa Gallurese

YIELD: 4 SERVINGS / **ACTIVE TIME:** 20 MINUTES / **TOTAL TIME:** 1 HOUR

6 CUPS BEEF STOCK (SEE PAGE 442)

7 OZ. PECORINO CHEESE, GRATED

3 TABLESPOONS CHOPPED FRESH PARSLEY

1 TEASPOON CHOPPED MIXED HERBS

¼ TEASPOON CINNAMON

¼ TEASPOON FRESHLY GRATED NUTMEG

2.2 LBS. DAY-OLD BREAD, SLICED THIN

1 LB. CACIOCAVALLO CHEESE, SLICED THIN

1. Place the stock in a saucepan and warm it over medium heat.
2. Place the pecorino, parsley, herbs, cinnamon, and nutmeg in a bowl and stir to combine.
3. Preheat the oven to 350°F. Layer some of the bread on the bottom of a 13 x 9–inch baking pan. Top with some of the caciocavallo and the pecorino mixture and prick the cheese with a fork. Continue the layering process until all of these ingredients have been used up.
4. Pour the stock over the dish, place it in the oven, and bake until the gallurese is golden brown, about 30 minutes.
5. Remove the gallurese from the oven and let it rest for 20 minutes before serving.

Zuppa di Castagne Sarda

YIELD: 4 SERVINGS / **ACTIVE TIME:** 1 HOUR / **TOTAL TIME:** 3 HOURS

1 LB. CHESTNUTS

6 OZ. LARD, CHOPPED

1 ONION, FINELY DICED

6 CUPS WATER, PLUS MORE AS NEEDED

SALT, TO TASTE

¾ LB. SHORT-FORMAT PASTA

1. Preheat the oven to 160°F. Peel the chestnuts, place them on a baking sheet, and roast them for 20 minutes. Remove the chestnuts from the oven, remove the nuts, and set them aside.
2. Place the lard in a large saucepan and warm it over medium heat. Add the onion and cook, stirring occasionally, until it has softened, about 5 minutes.
3. Add the chestnuts and water, season with salt, and partially cover the pan. Bring the soup to a simmer, reduce the heat to low, and cook for 1½ hours.
4. Add the pasta and cook until it is al dente, following the instructions on the pasta packaging, adding more water if needed.
5. Ladle the soup into warmed bowls and enjoy.

Chicken Quinoa Soup

YIELD: 4 SERVINGS / **ACTIVE TIME:** 20 MINUTES / **TOTAL TIME:** 45 MINUTES

½ CUP QUINOA

1 TABLESPOON EXTRA-VIRGIN OLIVE OIL

2 CHICKEN BREASTS, SLICED INTO ½-INCH PIECES

1 ONION, FINELY DICED

2 CARROTS, PEELED AND DICED

2 CELERY STALKS, FINELY DICED

½ CUP FINELY DICED GREEN BELL PEPPER

2 GARLIC CLOVES, MINCED

4 CUPS CHICKEN STOCK (SEE PAGE 440)

1 BAY LEAF

2 TEASPOONS FRESH THYME

1 TEASPOON FINELY CHOPPED FRESH OREGANO

1 CUP FINELY CHOPPED KALE

SALT AND PEPPER, TO TASTE

1. Cook the quinoa according to the directions on the package. Spread the cooked quinoa evenly on a baking sheet, let it cool completely, and set it aside.
2. Place the olive oil in a medium pot and warm it over medium heat. Add the chicken and cook, stirring occasionally, until it is browned all over, about 5 minutes. Remove the chicken from the pot and set it aside.
3. Add the onion, carrots, celery, and bell pepper to the pot and cook, stirring occasionally, until the onion has softened, about 5 minutes. Add the garlic and cook, stirring occasionally, for 2 minutes. Add the stock, bay leaf, thyme, and oregano and bring the soup to a boil.
4. Reduce the heat so that the soup simmers, add the chicken, and cook for 10 minutes. Add the quinoa and kale and cook until the chicken is cooked through and the kale is tender, about 5 minutes.
5. Remove the bay leaf from the pot, discard it, and season the soup with salt and pepper.
6. Ladle the soup into warmed bowls and serve.

Cashew Soup

YIELD: 4 SERVINGS / **ACTIVE TIME:** 25 MINUTES / **TOTAL TIME:** 1 HOUR AND 15 MINUTES

2 TABLESPOONS UNSALTED BUTTER

½ CUP FINELY DICED CELERY, LEAVES RESERVED FOR GARNISH

2 TABLESPOONS FINELY DICED LEEK

1 TABLESPOON FINELY DICED SHALLOT

1 TABLESPOON ALL-PURPOSE FLOUR

½ CUP CASHEW BUTTER

¼ CUP CHOPPED TOASTED CASHEWS, PLUS MORE FOR GARNISH

3 CUPS CHICKEN STOCK (SEE PAGE 440)

1 CUP HEAVY CREAM

SALT AND PEPPER, TO TASTE

CRUSTY BREAD, FOR SERVING

1. Place the butter in a large pot and melt it over medium heat. Add the celery, leek, and shallot and cook, stirring occasionally, until they have softened, about 5 minutes. Add the flour and cook, stirring frequently, for 5 minutes.
2. Add the cashew butter, cashews, and stock and bring the soup to a boil.
3. Reduce the heat so that the soup simmers and cook for 15 minutes.
4. Add the cream, season with salt and pepper, and stir to combine.
5. Ladle the soup into warmed bowls, garnish with celery leaves and additional toasted cashews, and serve with crusty bread.

Oaxacan Black Bean Soup

YIELD: 4 TO 6 SERVINGS / **ACTIVE TIME:** 30 MINUTES / **TOTAL TIME:** 1 HOUR AND 30 MINUTES

10 CUPS WATER, PLUS MORE AS NEEDED

1½ CUPS DRIED BLACK BEANS

½ CUP FINELY DICED FENNEL

½ CUP FINELY DICED ANDOUILLE SAUSAGE

1 ONION, FINELY DICED

2 CUPS EXTRA-VIRGIN OLIVE OIL

6 CORN TORTILLAS, SLICED INTO ⅛-INCH STRIPS

24 SHRIMP, SHELLED, DEVEINED, AND FINELY DICED

½ LB. COOKED CRABMEAT

FRESH CILANTRO, CHOPPED, FOR GARNISH

QUESO FRESCO OR FETA CHEESE, CRUMBLED, FOR GARNISH

1. Place the water and beans in a large pot and bring the mixture to a simmer. Add the fennel, sausage, and onion and cook until the beans are tender, about 1 hour.
2. Place the olive oil in a small skillet and warm it over medium-high heat. Add the tortillas and cook, turning them frequently, until they are crispy, about 5 minutes. Remove the crispy tortillas from the skillet and transfer them to a paper towel–lined plate to drain and cool.
3. Transfer the soup to a food processor and pulse until smooth, adding more water if necessary. Place the soup in a clean pan and bring it to a simmer. Add the shrimp and crab and cook until the shrimp are tender, about 4 minutes.
4. Ladle the soup into warmed bowls, garnish with the tortilla crisps, cilantro, and queso fresco or feta cheese, and serve.

Lentil Stew

YIELD: 6 SERVINGS / **ACTIVE TIME:** 10 MINUTES / **TOTAL TIME:** 8 HOURS

1 CUP BROWN LENTILS

½ CUP GREEN LENTILS

4 CUPS VEGETABLE STOCK (SEE PAGE 441)

3 CARROTS, PEELED AND CHOPPED

1 LARGE YELLOW ONION, CHOPPED

3 GARLIC CLOVES, MINCED

3-INCH PIECE OF FRESH GINGER, PEELED AND GRATED

ZEST AND JUICE OF 1 LEMON

3 TABLESPOONS SMOKED PAPRIKA

2 TABLESPOONS CINNAMON

1 TABLESPOON CORIANDER

1 TABLESPOON TURMERIC

1 TABLESPOON CUMIN

1½ TEASPOONS ALLSPICE

2 BAY LEAVES

SALT AND PEPPER, TO TASTE

1 (14 OZ.) CAN OF CANNELLINI BEANS, DRAINED AND RINSED

FRESH MINT, CHOPPED, FOR GARNISH

GOAT CHEESE, CRUMBLED, FOR GARNISH

1. Place the lentils in a fine-mesh sieve, rinse them well, and pick them over to remove any debris or shriveled lentils.
2. Place all of the ingredients, except for the cannellini beans and the garnishes, in a slow cooker. Cover and cook on low for 7½ hours.
3. After 7½ hours, stir in the cannellini beans. Cover and cook on low for 30 another minutes.
4. Ladle the stew into warmed bowls and garnish with fresh mint and goat cheese.

Potage of Lentils with Confit Lemon Rinds

YIELD: 4 TO 6 SERVINGS / **ACTIVE TIME:** 30 MINUTES / **TOTAL TIME:** 1 HOUR

¼ CUP LEMON-INFUSED OLIVE OIL FROM CONFIT LEMON RINDS

1 ONION, FINELY DICED

2 CELERY STALKS, FINELY DICED

2 CARROTS, PEELED AND DICED

4 GARLIC CLOVES, MINCED

1 POTATO, PEELED AND FINELY DICED

1 CUP RED LENTILS

1 BAY LEAF

2 TABLESPOONS FRESH LEMON JUICE

½ TEASPOON CUMIN

½ TEASPOON TABASCO

6 CUPS VEGETABLE STOCK (SEE PAGE 441)

SALT AND PEPPER, TO TASTE

FRESH PARSLEY, CHOPPED, FOR GARNISH

CONFIT LEMON RINDS (SEE PAGE 468), FOR SERVING

1. Place the olive oil in a medium pot and warm it over medium heat. Add the onion and cook, stirring occasionally, until it has softened, about 5 minutes. Add the celery, carrots, garlic, and potato and cook, stirring occasionally, until they have softened, about 5 minutes. Add the lentils, bay leaf, lemon juice, cumin, and Tabasco and 4 cups of the stock and bring the soup to a boil.
2. Reduce the heat so that the soup simmers and cook until the potato and lentils are tender, about 15 to 20 minutes. Remove the bay leaf and ½ cup of the solids from the pot. Discard the bay leaf and set the solids aside.
3. Transfer the soup to a food processor, pulse until smooth, and strain it back into the pot through a fine-mesh sieve. Bring the soup to a simmer, add the remaining stock, and season with salt and pepper.
4. Add the reserved solids to the soup and ladle it into warmed bowls. Garnish with parsley and serve with Confit Lemon Rinds.

Chickpea & Leftover Turkey Chili

YIELD: 6 SERVINGS / **ACTIVE TIME:** 35 MINUTES / **TOTAL TIME:** 2 HOURS AND 35 MINUTES

1 TABLESPOON EXTRA-VIRGIN OLIVE OIL

1 YELLOW ONION, DICED

5 GARLIC CLOVES, MINCED

1 TABLESPOON CHOPPED FRESH OREGANO

BLACK PEPPER, TO TASTE

1 TABLESPOON CUMIN

2 TEASPOONS CHILI POWDER

2 CUPS CHICKEN STOCK OR TURKEY STOCK (SEE PAGE 440 OR 446)

½ LB. TOMATOES

3 DRIED NEW MEXICO CHILE PEPPERS, STEMMED, SEEDED, AND TORN

1 RED BELL PEPPER, STEMMED, SEEDED, AND DICED

PINCH OF KOSHER SALT

1 (14 OZ.) CAN OF CHICKPEAS, DRAINED AND RINSED

1 LB. LEFTOVER TURKEY

2 CUPS SHREDDED CHEDDAR CHEESE, TO TOP

1 CUP SOUR CREAM, TO TOP

CORNBREAD (SEE PAGE 469), FOR SERVING

1. Place the olive oil in a Dutch oven and warm it over medium-high heat. Add the onion, garlic, oregano, pepper, cumin, and chili powder and cook, stirring frequently, until the onion has softened, about 5 minutes.
2. Add the stock, tomatoes, chiles, bell pepper, salt, chickpeas, and turkey. Stir the chili, cover the Dutch oven, and reduce the heat to low. Cook until the chili has thickened and the flavor has developed to your liking, about 2 hours, stirring occasionally.
3. Ladle the chili into warmed bowls, top each portion with some of the cheese and sour cream, and serve with the Cornbread.

Moroccan Legume Soup

YIELD: 4 SERVINGS / **ACTIVE TIME:** 45 MINUTES / **TOTAL TIME:** 24 HOURS

1½ TABLESPOONS EXTRA-VIRGIN OLIVE OIL

1 ONION, FINELY DICED

¼ TEASPOON PEELED AND MINCED FRESH GINGER

¼ TEASPOON TURMERIC

½ TEASPOON CINNAMON

⅛ TEASPOON SAFFRON THREADS

1 (14 OZ.) CAN OF DICED TOMATOES

1 TEASPOON SUGAR

½ CUP DRIED CHICKPEAS, SOAKED OVERNIGHT

½ CUP DRIED FAVA BEANS, SOAKED OVERNIGHT

4 CUPS BEEF STOCK (SEE PAGE 442)

⅓ CUP BROWN LENTILS

1 TABLESPOON FINELY CHOPPED FRESH CILANTRO

1 TABLESPOON FINELY CHOPPED FRESH PARSLEY

SALT AND PEPPER, TO TASTE

1. Place the olive oil in a medium pot and warm it over medium heat. Add the onion and cook, stirring occasionally, until it has softened, about 5 minutes. Add the ginger, turmeric, cinnamon, saffron, tomatoes, sugar, chickpeas, fava beans, and stock and bring the soup to a boil.
2. Reduce the heat so that the soup simmers, cover it, and cook until the chickpeas and fava beans are tender, 45 minutes to 1 hour.
3. Add the lentils and cook until they are tender, 15 to 20 minutes. Add the cilantro and parsley and season with salt and pepper.
4. Ladle the soup into warmed bowls and serve.

Ribollita

YIELD: 6 SERVINGS / **ACTIVE TIME:** 30 MINUTES / **TOTAL TIME:** 24 HOURS

2 LBS. DRIED CANNELLINI BEANS, SOAKED OVERNIGHT AND DRAINED

SALT AND PEPPER, TO TASTE

¼ CUP EXTRA-VIRGIN OLIVE OIL, PLUS MORE FOR GARNISH

2 SMALL WHITE ONIONS, SLICED

3 CARROTS, PEELED AND SLICED

2 CELERY STALKS, SLICED

2 SPRIGS OF FRESH ROSEMARY

2 LBS. MIXED LEAFY GREEN VEGETABLES, STEMLESS AND CHOPPED

4 MEDIUM POTATOES, PEELED AND DICED

6 CUPS VEGETABLE STOCK (SEE PAGE 441)

1 CUP WHOLE PEELED TOMATOES, CRUSHED BY HAND

8 THICK SLICES OF STALE BREAD

1. Place the beans in a large pot, cover them with cold water, and bring to a boil. Reduce the heat and simmer the beans until they are tender, 45 minutes to 1 hour, seasoning them with salt halfway through. Drain the beans and set them aside.
2. Place the olive oil in a medium saucepan and warm it over medium heat. Add the onions, carrots, celery, and rosemary and cook, stirring occasionally, until they have softened, about 6 minutes.
3. Add the leafy greens and potatoes, and then add the stock and tomatoes. Season the soup with salt and pepper, cover the pan, and cook until the potatoes and carrots are tender, 15 to 20 minutes.
4. Place half of the beans in a bowl and mash them.
5. Remove the rosemary and discard it. Add the beans, season the soup with salt and pepper, and cook for 10 minutes.
6. Arrange half of the bread in a Dutch oven and cover it with half of the soup.
7. Top with the remaining bread and ladle the remaining soup over it.
8. Cover the pot and let the ribollita rest at room temperature for 1 hour.
9. Place the pot on the stove and cook the ribollita over medium heat until it is hot, about 10 minutes. Ladle the ribollita into warmed bowls, drizzle additional olive oil over each portion, and serve.

Cabbage & Cannellini Bean Soup

YIELD: 4 TO 6 SERVINGS / **ACTIVE TIME:** 30 MINUTES / **TOTAL TIME:** 1 HOUR

1 TABLESPOON DRIED ROSEMARY

2 TEASPOONS CUMIN

2 TEASPOONS DRIED CORIANDER

1 TEASPOON DRIED OREGANO

⅛ TEASPOON KOSHER SALT, PLUS MORE TO TASTE

1 TABLESPOON EXTRA-VIRGIN OLIVE OIL

2 ITALIAN SAUSAGES

1 ONION, FINELY DICED

¼ CUP FINELY DICED LEEKS, TRIMMED AND RINSED WELL BEFORE CUTTING

1 CARROT, PEELED AND DICED

1 CELERY STALK, FINELY DICED

1 GARLIC CLOVE, MINCED

1 (14 OZ.) CAN OF DICED TOMATOES

4 CUPS CHICKEN STOCK (SEE PAGE 440)

2 CUPS CHOPPED SAVOY CABBAGE

1 (14 OZ.) CAN OF CANNELLINI BEANS, DRAINED AND RINSED

BLACK PEPPER, TO TASTE

1. Place the rosemary, cumin, coriander, oregano, and salt in a small mixing bowl and stir to combine. Set the mixture aside.
2. Place the olive oil in a medium pot and warm it over medium heat. Add the sausages and cook, stirring frequently, until they have browned, about 5 minutes. Remove the sausages from the pot, let them cool slightly, and then slice them. Set the sausages aside.
3. Add the onion, leeks, carrot, celery, and garlic to the pot and cook, stirring occasionally, until the vegetables have softened, about 5 minutes. Add the herb mixture, tomatoes, and stock and bring the soup to a boil.
4. Reduce the heat so that the soup simmers, add the cabbage, and cook until it is tender, about 15 minutes. Add the sausages and beans, season with salt and pepper, and cook until the sausages are cooked through, 5 to 10 minutes.
5. Ladle the soup into warmed bowls and serve.

Spicy Baby Spinach & Rice Soup

YIELD: 4 SERVINGS / **ACTIVE TIME:** 15 MINUTES / **TOTAL TIME:** 45 MINUTES

2 TABLESPOONS WATER

12 CUPS BABY SPINACH

3 TABLESPOONS EXTRA-VIRGIN OLIVE OIL

1 ONION, FINELY DICED

2 GARLIC CLOVES, MINCED

1 RED CHILE PEPPER, STEMMED, SEEDED, AND SLICED THIN

4 CUPS VEGETABLE STOCK (SEE PAGE 441)

⅓ CUP ARBORIO RICE

SALT AND PEPPER, TO TASTE

ROMANO CHEESE, GRATED, FOR GARNISH

1. Place the water and spinach in a large skillet and cook over medium-high heat, stirring occasionally, until the spinach has wilted, about 5 minutes. Remove the spinach from the skillet, let it cool, and then finely chop it.
2. Place the olive oil in a large pot and warm it over medium heat. Add the onion, garlic, and chile and cook, stirring frequently, until the onion has softened, about 5 minutes.
3. Add the stock and rice and bring the soup to a boil, stirring frequently.
4. Reduce the heat so that the soup simmers and cook for 15 minutes. Add the spinach and cook until the rice is tender, about 5 minutes.
5. Ladle the soup into warmed bowls, add salt and pepper to taste, garnish with Romano, and serve.

Split Pea Soup with Smoked Ham

YIELD: 4 SERVINGS / **ACTIVE TIME:** 30 MINUTES / **TOTAL TIME:** 1 HOUR AND 30 MINUTES

2 TABLESPOONS UNSALTED BUTTER

1 ONION, FINELY DICED

1 CARROT, PEELED AND DICED

1 CELERY STALK, FINELY DICED

5 CUPS CHICKEN STOCK (SEE PAGE 440), PLUS MORE AS NEEDED

1 CUP DRIED SPLIT PEAS

6 OZ. SMOKED HAM, FINELY DICED

2 TABLESPOONS FINELY CHOPPED FRESH PARSLEY, PLUS MORE FOR GARNISH

1 BAY LEAF

1 TEASPOON FRESH THYME

SALT AND PEPPER, TO TASTE

LEMON WEDGES, FOR SERVING

1. Place the butter in a medium pot and melt it over medium heat. Add the onion, carrot, and celery and cook, stirring occasionally, until the onion has softened, about 5 minutes.
2. Add the stock, split peas, ham, parsley, bay leaf, and thyme and bring the soup to a boil.
3. Reduce the heat so that the soup simmers and cook, stirring occasionally, until the peas are tender, adding more stock as necessary, about 45 minutes.
4. Remove the bay leaf from the pot, discard it, and season with salt and pepper.
5. Ladle the soup into warmed bowls, garnish with additional parsley, and serve with lemon wedges.

White Bean Soup

YIELD: 4 SERVINGS / **ACTIVE TIME:** 30 MINUTES / **TOTAL TIME:** 24 HOURS

2 TABLESPOONS UNSALTED BUTTER

1 ONION, FINELY DICED

1 GARLIC CLOVE, MINCED

1 CARROT, PEELED AND FINELY DICED

1 CELERY STALK, FINELY DICED

½ CUP DRIED WHITE BEANS, SOAKED OVERNIGHT

2½ CUPS VEGETABLE STOCK (SEE PAGE 441)

2 (14 OZ.) CANS OF TOMATOES, FINELY DICED AND JUICE RESERVED

½ TEASPOON FINELY CHOPPED FRESH ROSEMARY

½ TEASPOON FRESH THYME

1 BAY LEAF

SALT AND PEPPER, TO TASTE

FRESH OREGANO, CHOPPED, FOR GARNISH

1. Place the butter in a medium pot and melt it over medium heat. Add the onion, garlic, carrot, and celery and cook, stirring occasionally, until they have softened, about 5 minutes. Add the beans, stock, tomatoes, rosemary, thyme, and bay leaf and bring the soup to a boil.
2. Reduce the heat so that the soup simmers and cook until the beans are tender, about 1 hour.
3. Season the soup with salt and pepper and ladle it into warmed bowls. Garnish with oregano and serve.

Split Pea & Barley Soup

YIELD: 4 SERVINGS / **ACTIVE TIME:** 45 MINUTES / **TOTAL TIME:** 24 HOURS

½ CUP YELLOW SPLIT PEAS, SOAKED OVERNIGHT

¼ CUP PEARL BARLEY

6 CUPS HAM STOCK (SEE PAGE 447)

¼ LB. THICK-CUT BACON, FINELY DICED

2 TABLESPOONS UNSALTED BUTTER

1 ONION, FINELY DICED

1 GARLIC CLOVE, MINCED

1½ CUPS PEELED AND FINELY DICED PARSNIPS

1 TABLESPOON FINELY CHOPPED FRESH OREGANO

SALT AND PEPPER, TO TASTE

CRUSTY BREAD, FOR SERVING

1. Bring the split peas, barley, and stock to a boil in a large pot. Reduce the heat so that the soup simmers.
2. Place the bacon in a large skillet and cook it over medium heat, stirring occasionally, until it is crispy, about 5 minutes. Remove the bacon from the skillet and transfer it to a paper towel–lined plate to drain.

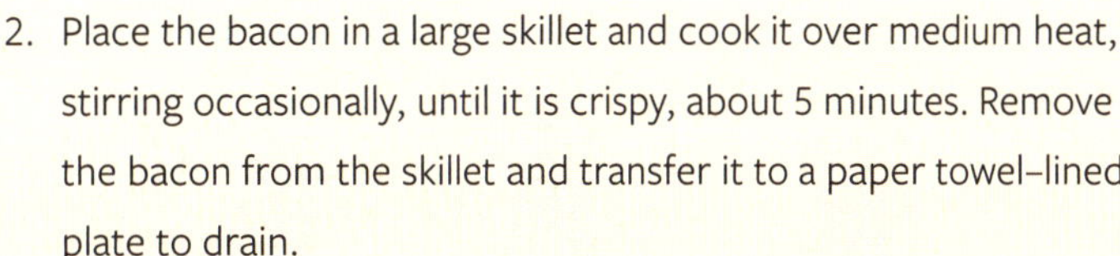

3. Add the butter to the pan and let it melt. Add the onion and garlic and cook, stirring occasionally, until the onion has softened, about 5 minutes. Add the parsnips and cook, stirring occasionally, until the onion is lightly browned, about 8 minutes.
4. Place the bacon and parsnip mixture in the pot and cook until the split peas and barley are tender, 20 to 30 minutes.
5. Add the oregano and season with salt and pepper. Ladle the soup into warmed bowls and serve with crusty bread.

Barley, Dill & Pork Soup

YIELD: 4 TO 6 SERVINGS / **ACTIVE TIME:** 20 MINUTES / **TOTAL TIME:** 2 HOURS

1 TABLESPOON EXTRA-VIRGIN OLIVE OIL

1¾ LBS. BONELESS PORK SHOULDER, CUBED

1 ONION, FINELY DICED

2 CELERY STALKS, FINELY DICED

2 CARROTS, PEELED AND DICED

¼ CUP PERNOD

1 GARLIC CLOVE, MINCED

2 TEASPOONS FRESH THYME

8 CUPS BEEF STOCK (SEE PAGE 442)

½ LB. PEARL BARLEY

½ CUP FINELY CHOPPED FRESH DILL

SALT AND PEPPER, TO TASTE

1. Place the olive oil in a large pot and warm it over medium-high heat. Add the pork and cook, stirring occasionally, until it is browned all over, about 5 minutes. Remove the pork from the pot and set it aside.
2. Add the onion, celery, and carrots to the pot and cook, stirring occasionally, until the onion has softened, about 5 minutes. Add the Pernod, garlic, and thyme and cook, stirring occasionally, until the Pernod has reduced by half. Add the pork, stock, and barley to the pot and bring the soup to a boil.
3. Reduce the heat so that the soup simmers, cover the pot, and cook until the pork is very tender, about 1 hour and 30 minutes.
4. Add the dill and season with salt and pepper. Ladle the soup into warmed bowls and serve.

Cauliflower & Quinoa Soup

YIELD: 4 SERVINGS / **ACTIVE TIME:** 30 MINUTES / **TOTAL TIME:** 1 HOUR

2 TABLESPOONS EXTRA-VIRGIN OLIVE OIL

1 ONION, FINELY DICED

2 GARLIC CLOVES, MINCED

1 HEAD OF CAULIFLOWER, CUT INTO FLORETS AND CHOPPED

4 CUPS CHICKEN STOCK (SEE PAGE 440)

¾ CUP QUINOA

2 TEASPOONS FRESH THYME

½ CUP HEAVY CREAM

SALT AND PEPPER, TO TASTE

FRESH CHIVES, CHOPPED, FOR GARNISH

1. Place the olive oil in a medium pot and warm it over medium heat. Add the onion and cook, stirring occasionally, until it has softened, about 5 minutes. Add the garlic and cook, stirring frequently, for 2 minutes. Add the cauliflower, stock, quinoa, and thyme and bring the soup to a boil.
2. Reduce the heat so that the soup simmers, cover the pot, and cook until the cauliflower and quinoa are tender, about 15 minutes.
3. Add the heavy cream, stir to combine, and season with salt and pepper.
4. Ladle the soup into warmed bowls, garnish with chives, and serve.

Peanut & Quinoa Soup

YIELD: 4 SERVINGS / **ACTIVE TIME:** 20 MINUTES / **TOTAL TIME:** 45 MINUTES

1 TABLESPOON EXTRA-VIRGIN OLIVE OIL

1 TABLESPOON UNSALTED BUTTER

1 RED ONION, FINELY DICED

1 CUP FINELY DICED SWEET POTATO

1 GREEN BELL PEPPER, STEMMED, SEEDED, AND FINELY DICED

1 JALAPEÑO PEPPER, STEMMED, SEEDED, AND SLICED THIN

2 CELERY STALKS, FINELY DICED

1 ZUCCHINI, PEELED AND FINELY DICED

1 GARLIC CLOVE, MINCED

6 CUPS CHICKEN STOCK (SEE PAGE 440)

¾ CUP QUINOA

1 TEASPOON CUMIN

½ CUP PEANUT BUTTER

SALT AND PEPPER, TO TASTE

FRESH OREGANO, CHOPPED, FOR GARNISH

ROASTED PEANUTS, CHOPPED, FOR GARNISH

1. Place the olive oil and butter in a medium pot and warm the mixture over medium heat. Add the onion, potato, peppers, celery, zucchini, and garlic and cook, stirring occasionally, until the vegetables have softened, about 10 minutes.
2. Add the stock and bring the soup to a boil. Reduce the heat so that the soup simmers and add the quinoa and cumin. Cover the pot and cook until the quinoa is tender, about 15 minutes.
3. Add the peanut butter, season with salt and pepper, and stir until fully combined.
4. Ladle the soup into warmed bowls, garnish with oregano and roasted peanuts, and serve.

African Peanut Soup

YIELD: 4 SERVINGS / **ACTIVE TIME:** 20 MINUTES / **TOTAL TIME:** 1 HOUR

½ CUP PEANUT BUTTER

2 TABLESPOONS TOMATO PASTE

6 CUPS CHICKEN STOCK (SEE PAGE 440)

1 ONION, FINELY DICED

2 TEASPOONS FRESH THYME

1 BAY LEAF

⅛ TEASPOON CAYENNE PEPPER

1 SWEET POTATO, PEELED AND FINELY DICED

6 FRESH OKRA PODS, TRIMMED AND FINELY DICED

SALT AND PEPPER, TO TASTE

EDIBLE FLOWERS, FOR GARNISH

1. Place the peanut butter, tomato paste, and stock in a medium pot and stir until fully combined.
2. Bring the soup to a simmer, add the onion, thyme, bay leaf, and cayenne, and cook, stirring occasionally, for 30 minutes.
3. Add the sweet potato and cook for 10 minutes. Add the okra and cook until the sweet potato and okra are tender, 5 to 10 minutes.
4. Season the soup with salt and pepper and ladle it into warmed bowls. Garnish with edible flowers and serve.

Persian Barley Soup

YIELD: 4 SERVINGS / **ACTIVE TIME:** 20 MINUTES / **TOTAL TIME:** 1 HOUR AND 30 MINUTES

2 TABLESPOONS EXTRA-VIRGIN OLIVE OIL

2 ONIONS, FINELY DICED

2 CARROTS, PEELED AND DICED

1 CUP PEARL BARLEY

3 TABLESPOONS TOMATO PASTE

1 TEASPOON TURMERIC

8 CUPS CHICKEN STOCK (SEE PAGE 440)

½ CUP SOUR CREAM

⅓ CUP FINELY CHOPPED FRESH PARSLEY

SALT AND PEPPER, TO TASTE

LIME WEDGES, FOR SERVING

1. Place the olive oil in a large pot and warm it over medium heat. Add the onions and cook, stirring occasionally, until they have softened, about 5 minutes. Add the carrots, barley, tomato paste, and turmeric and cook, stirring occasionally, for 2 minutes. Add the stock and bring the soup to a boil.
2. Reduce the heat so that the soup simmers and cook until the barley is tender, about 1 hour.
3. Remove the pot from heat, stir in the sour cream and parsley, and season with salt and pepper.
4. Ladle the soup into warmed bowls and serve with lime wedges.

Rocky Mountain Chili

YIELD: 4 TO 6 SERVINGS / **ACTIVE TIME:** 30 MINUTES / **TOTAL TIME:** 1 HOUR AND 30 MINUTES

- 1 TABLESPOON EXTRA-VIRGIN OLIVE OIL
- 1 ONION, FINELY DICED
- 1 LB. GROUND TURKEY
- 2 GARLIC CLOVES, MINCED
- 1 TABLESPOON CHILI POWDER
- BOUQUET GARNI (SEE PAGE 469)
- 4 TOMATOES, FINELY DICED
- 2 CUPS TOMATO SAUCE (SEE PAGE 458)
- ½ CUP TOMATO PASTE
- 1 (14 OZ.) CAN OF KIDNEY BEANS
- 1 (14 OZ.) CAN OF WHITE BEANS
- 1 (14 OZ.) CAN OF BLACK BEANS
- SALT AND PEPPER, TO TASTE
- CHEDDAR CHEESE, GRATED, FOR GARNISH
- SOUR CREAM, FOR GARNISH
- FRESH CHIVES, CHOPPED, FOR GARNISH
- CORNBREAD (SEE PAGE 469), FOR SERVING

1. Place the olive oil in a large pot and warm it over medium-high heat. Add the onion and turkey and cook, breaking up the turkey with a wooden spoon, until the meat has browned, about 5 minutes. Add the garlic and cook, stirring occasionally, for 2 minutes. Add the chili powder, Bouquet Garni, tomatoes, tomato sauce, tomato paste, and beans and bring the chili to a boil.
2. Reduce the heat so that the chili simmers and cook until the meat is fully cooked through and the flavor has developed to your liking, 20 to 30 minutes. Season the chili with salt and pepper.
3. Ladle the chili into warmed bowls, garnish with cheddar cheese, sour cream, and chives, and serve with the Cornbread.

Parsnip & Barley Soup

YIELD: 6 SERVINGS / **ACTIVE TIME:** 20 MINUTES / **TOTAL TIME:** 1 HOUR

¼ CUP UNSALTED BUTTER

1 SMALL ONION, FINELY DICED

½ LEEK, TRIMMED, RINSED WELL, AND FINELY DICED

6 PARSNIPS, PEELED AND FINELY DICED

1 BAY LEAF

1 POTATO, PEELED AND FINELY DICED

6 CUPS CHICKEN STOCK (SEE PAGE 440)

1 CINNAMON STICK

½ CUP BARLEY

½ CUP HEAVY CREAM

SALT AND PEPPER, TO TASTE

FRESHLY GRATED NUTMEG, FOR GARNISH

CELERY HEARTS, CHOPPED, FOR GARNISH

1. Place the butter in a medium pot and melt it over medium heat. Add the onion, leek, and parsnips and cook, stirring occasionally, until the onion has softened, about 5 minutes.
2. Add the bay leaf and potato and cook, stirring occasionally, for 5 minutes. Add the stock, cinnamon stick, and barley and bring the soup to a boil.
3. Reduce the heat so that the soup simmers and cook until the barley is tender, 20 to 30 minutes. Remove the cinnamon stick from the pot and discard it.
4. Transfer the soup to a food processor, pulse until smooth, and strain it back into the pot through a fine-mesh sieve. Bring the soup to a simmer, add the cream, and season with salt and pepper.
5. Ladle the soup into warmed bowls, garnish with nutmeg and celery hearts, and serve.

Vegan Chili

YIELD: 4 TO 6 SERVINGS / **ACTIVE TIME:** 15 MINUTES / **TOTAL TIME:** 45 MINUTES

2 TABLESPOONS EXTRA-VIRGIN OLIVE OIL

2 RED ONIONS, FINELY DICED

1 RED BELL PEPPER, STEMMED, SEEDED, AND FINELY DICED

1 YELLOW BELL PEPPER, STEMMED, SEEDED, AND FINELY DICED

2 GARLIC CLOVES, MINCED

2 HEADS OF CAULIFLOWER, CUT INTO FLORETS AND FINELY CHOPPED

4 (14 OZ.) CANS OF STEWED TOMATOES

2 CUPS VEGETABLE STOCK (SEE PAGE 441)

1 TABLESPOON CHILI POWDER

2 (14 OZ.) CANS OF BLACK BEANS, RINSED AND DRAINED

SALT AND PEPPER, TO TASTE

FRESH PARSLEY, CHOPPED, FOR GARNISH

1. Place the olive oil in a large pot and warm it over medium heat. Add the onions, bell peppers, and garlic and cook, stirring occasionally, until the onions and bell peppers have softened, 5 to 7 minutes.
2. Add the cauliflower and cook, stirring occasionally, until it is lightly browned, about 5 minutes. Add the tomatoes, stock, and chili powder and bring the chili to a boil.
3. Reduce the heat so that the chili simmers, cover the pot, and cook for 15 minutes.
4. Uncover the pot and cook until the chili begins to thicken and the cauliflower is tender, about 15 minutes.
5. Add the beans, cook for 3 minutes, and season with salt and pepper.
6. Ladle the chili into warmed bowls, garnish with parsley, and serve.

Quinoa & Black Bean Soup

YIELD: 4 SERVINGS / **ACTIVE TIME:** 20 MINUTES / **TOTAL TIME:** 1 HOUR

1 TABLESPOON EXTRA-VIRGIN OLIVE OIL

1 ONION, FINELY DICED

2 CELERY STALKS, FINELY DICED

2 CARROTS, PEELED AND DICED

2 GARLIC CLOVES, MINCED

1 TEASPOON PAPRIKA

1 TEASPOON RED PEPPER FLAKES

6 CUPS CHICKEN STOCK (SEE PAGE 440)

¾ CUP QUINOA

1 (14 OZ.) CAN OF STEWED TOMATOES, FINELY CHOPPED

1 (14 OZ.) CAN OF BLACK BEANS, RINSED AND DRAINED

1 CUP CANNED CORN

SALT AND PEPPER, TO TASTE

1. Place the olive oil in a medium pot and warm it over medium heat. Add the onion, celery, and carrots and cook, stirring occasionally, until they have softened, about 5 minutes.
2. Add the garlic, paprika, and red pepper flakes and cook, stirring occasionally, for 2 minutes. Add the stock and quinoa and bring the soup to a boil.
3. Reduce the heat so that the soup simmers and cook until the quinoa is tender, about 15 minutes.
4. Stir in the tomatoes, beans, and corn and cook for 10 minutes.
5. Season the soup with salt and pepper, ladle it into warmed bowls, and serve.

Lamb Leg & Lentil Soup

YIELD: 4 SERVINGS / **ACTIVE TIME:** 20 MINUTES / **TOTAL TIME:** 1 HOUR AND 30 MINUTES

4 CUPS VEGETABLE STOCK (SEE PAGE 441)

1 LB. BUTTERFLIED LEG OF LAMB, DICED

1 ONION, FINELY DICED

2 GARLIC CLOVES, MINCED

2 BAY LEAVES

4 WHOLE CLOVES

4 TEASPOONS FRESH THYME

1 POTATO, PEELED AND FINELY DICED

½ CUP RED LENTILS

2 TABLESPOONS FINELY CHOPPED FRESH PARSLEY

SALT AND PEPPER, TO TASTE

1. Bring the stock, lamb, onion, garlic, bay leaves, cloves, and thyme to a boil in a large pot. Reduce the heat so that the soup simmers and cook until the lamb is tender, about 45 minutes.
2. Remove the cloves from the pot and discard them. Add the potato and lentils, cover the pot, and cook until they are tender, 15 to 20 minutes.
3. Add the parsley and season with salt and pepper. Ladle the soup into warmed bowls and serve.

French Lentil Soup

YIELD: 4 TO 6 SERVINGS / **ACTIVE TIME:** 25 MINUTES / **TOTAL TIME:** 1 HOUR AND 15 MINUTES

2 TABLESPOONS EXTRA-VIRGIN OLIVE OIL

1 ONION, FINELY DICED

1 GARLIC CLOVE, MINCED

1 CARROT, PEELED AND FINELY DICED

1 LEEK, TRIMMED, RINSED WELL, AND FINELY DICED

1 CELERY STALK, FINELY DICED

1 TABLESPOON TOMATO PASTE

1½ CUPS FRENCH LENTILS

6 CUPS CHICKEN STOCK (SEE PAGE 440)

SACHET D'ÉPICES (SEE PAGE 465)

1 BAY LEAF

2 TEASPOONS FRESH THYME

¼ TEASPOON CARAWAY SEEDS

½ LEMON, SLICED THIN

½ OZ. APPLE CIDER VINEGAR

¼ CUP RIESLING

SALT AND PEPPER, TO TASTE

WATER CRACKERS, FOR SERVING

1. Place the olive oil in a medium pot and warm it over medium heat. Add the onion and garlic and cook, stirring occasionally, until the onion has softened, about 5 minutes. Add the carrot, leek, and celery and cook, stirring occasionally, until they have softened, about 5 minutes.
2. Add the tomato paste and cook, stirring occasionally, for 2 minutes. Add the lentils, stock, Sachet d'Épices, bay leaf, thyme, caraway seeds, and lemon and bring the soup to a boil.
3. Reduce the heat so that the soup simmers and cook until the lentils are tender, about 30 minutes.
4. Remove the Sachet d'Épices and lemon from the pot and discard them. Add the vinegar and Riesling and season with salt and pepper.
5. Ladle the soup into warmed bowls and serve with water crackers.

Vegetable Quinoa Soup

YIELD: 4 SERVINGS / **ACTIVE TIME:** 20 MINUTES / **TOTAL TIME:** 1 HOUR

2 TABLESPOONS EXTRA-VIRGIN OLIVE OIL

1 ONION, FINELY DICED

2 CARROTS, PEELED AND DICED

2 CELERY STALKS, FINELY DICED

½ CUP CORN KERNELS

½ CUP ZUCCHINI, FINELY DICED

½ CUP FINELY DICED RED BELL PEPPER

½ CUP FINELY DICED GREEN BELL PEPPER

4 GARLIC CLOVES, MINCED

2 TEASPOONS FRESH THYME

2 (14 OZ.) CANS OF DICED TOMATOES, DRAINED

1 CUP QUINOA

6 CUPS VEGETABLE STOCK (SEE PAGE 441)

1 BAY LEAF

PINCH OF RED PEPPER FLAKES

1 (14 OZ.) CAN OF CHICKPEAS, RINSED AND DRAINED

1½ CUPS FINELY CHOPPED KALE

JUICE OF ½ LEMON

SALT AND PEPPER, TO TASTE

PARMESAN CHEESE, GRATED, FOR GARNISH

1. Place the olive oil in a medium pot and warm it over medium heat. Add the onion, carrots, celery, corn, zucchini, and bell peppers and cook, stirring occasionally, until they have softened, about 8 minutes.
2. Add the garlic and thyme and cook, stirring occasionally, for 2 minutes. Add the tomatoes, quinoa, stock, bay leaf, and red pepper flakes and bring the soup to a boil.
3. Reduce the heat so that the soup simmers, cover the pot, and cook for 25 minutes.
4. Uncover the pot, add the chickpeas and kale, and cook for 5 minutes. Season the soup with the lemon juice and salt and pepper.
5. Ladle the soup into warmed bowls, garnish with Parmesan cheese, and serve.

Chicken & Corn Succotash Soup

YIELD: 4 SERVINGS / **ACTIVE TIME:** 20 MINUTES / **TOTAL TIME:** 1 HOUR

¼ CUP UNSALTED BUTTER

4 SLICES OF THICK-CUT BACON, FINELY DICED

2 ONIONS, FINELY DICED

2 GARLIC CLOVES, MINCED

2 BONELESS, SKINLESS CHICKEN BREASTS, DICED

¼ CUP ALL-PURPOSE FLOUR

4 CUPS CHICKEN STOCK (SEE PAGE 440)

KERNELS FROM 4 EARS OF CORN

1 (14 OZ.) CAN OF KIDNEY BEANS, RINSED AND DRAINED

1 CUP HEAVY CREAM

3 TABLESPOONS FINELY CHOPPED FRESH PARSLEY

SALT AND PEPPER, TO TASTE

1. Place the butter in a medium pot and melt it over medium heat. Add the bacon, onions, and garlic and cook, stirring occasionally, until the onions have softened, about 5 minutes. Add the chicken and cook, stirring occasionally, for 5 minutes.
2. Add the flour and cook, stirring frequently, for 5 minutes. Slowly add the stock, stirring continually, and bring the soup to a boil.
3. Reduce the heat so that the soup simmers, add the corn kernels and beans, and cook until the corn is tender, 5 to 10 minutes.
4. Add the heavy cream and parsley, season with salt and pepper, and stir until combined. Ladle the soup into warmed bowls and serve.

Chicken Chili

YIELD: 4 TO 6 SERVINGS / **ACTIVE TIME:** 15 MINUTES / **TOTAL TIME:** 45 MINUTES

3 (14 OZ.) CANS OF KIDNEY BEANS, DRAINED AND RINSED

2 TABLESPOONS EXTRA-VIRGIN OLIVE OIL

1 LB. BONELESS, SKINLESS CHICKEN BREASTS, DICED

1 ONION, FINELY DICED

2 GARLIC CLOVES, MINCED

4 CUPS CHICKEN STOCK (SEE PAGE 440)

1 (4 OZ.) CAN OF DICED GREEN CHILE PEPPERS

2 TEASPOONS CUMIN

1 TABLESPOON FINELY CHOPPED FRESH OREGANO

1 TEASPOON CAYENNE PEPPER

MONTEREY JACK CHEESE, GRATED, TO TOP

SALT AND PEPPER, TO TASTE

JALAPEÑO CHILE PEPPERS, SLICED, FOR GARNISH

1. Place 1 can of the beans in a bowl, mash them until they are thoroughly combined, and set them aside.
2. Place the olive oil in a Dutch oven and warm it over medium-high heat. Add the chicken and onion and cook, stirring occasionally, until the chicken has browned, about 5 minutes. Add the garlic and cook, stirring frequently, for 2 minutes.
3. Add the stock, peppers, cumin, oregano, and cayenne pepper and bring the chili to a boil. Reduce the heat so that the chili simmers, add the mashed beans and the remaining beans, and cook until the chicken is tender, 15 to 20 minutes.
4. Set the oven's broiler to high.
5. Sprinkle Monterey Jack over the chili, place the pot in the oven, and broil until the cheese has melted, 1 to 2 minutes. Remove the pot from the oven and ladle the chili into warmed bowls. Add salt and pepper to taste, garnish with jalapeños and serve.

Rabbit & Lentil Stew

YIELD: 4 SERVINGS / **ACTIVE TIME:** 20 MINUTES / **TOTAL TIME:** 1 HOUR

¼ CUP ALL-PURPOSE FLOUR

TENDERLOINS AND THIGHS FROM 2 RABBITS, BONES REMOVED, DICED

6 PIECES OF THICK-CUT BACON, FINELY DICED

1 ONION, FINELY DICED

1 GARLIC CLOVE, MINCED

1 CUP RED WINE

4 CUPS CHICKEN STOCK (SEE PAGE 440)

1 CUP LE PUY LENTILS

1 BAY LEAF

1 TEASPOON FINELY CHOPPED FRESH ROSEMARY

1 TABLESPOON FRESH LEMON JUICE

SALT AND PEPPER, TO TASTE

CRUSTY BREAD, FOR SERVING

1. Place the flour and rabbit in a medium mixing bowl, dredge the rabbit until it is fully coated, and set it aside.
2. Place the bacon in a medium pot and cook over medium heat, stirring occasionally, until it is crispy, about 5 minutes. Remove the bacon from the pot and set it aside. Add the rabbit and cook, turning it as necessary, until it has browned, about 5 minutes. Remove the rabbit from the pot and set it aside.
3. Place the onion and garlic in the pot and cook, stirring occasionally, until the onion has softened, about 5 minutes. Add the wine and cook, stirring occasionally, until it has reduced by half, about 5 minutes. Add the stock, lentils, bay leaf, and rosemary and bring the soup to a boil.
4. Reduce the heat so that the soup simmers, add the rabbit, bacon, and lemon juice, and cook until the lentils are tender, 25 to 30 minutes. Season the soup with salt and pepper.
5. Ladle the soup into warmed bowls and serve with crusty bread.

Butternut Squash, Quinoa & Chicken Soup

YIELD: 4 SERVINGS / **ACTIVE TIME:** 20 MINUTES / **TOTAL TIME:** 1 HOUR AND 15 MINUTES

1 BUTTERNUT SQUASH, HALVED AND SEEDED

3 TABLESPOONS EXTRA-VIRGIN OLIVE OIL

2 BONELESS, SKINLESS CHICKEN BREASTS, DICED

1 ONION, FINELY DICED

2 GARLIC CLOVES, MINCED

1 (14 OZ.) CAN OF DICED TOMATOES, DRAINED

1 TEASPOON FINELY CHOPPED FRESH OREGANO

4 CUPS CHICKEN STOCK (SEE PAGE 440)

⅔ CUP QUINOA

SALT AND PEPPER, TO TASTE

1. Preheat the oven to 375°F. Place the squash in a baking dish, flesh side down, drizzle 1 tablespoon of the olive oil over it, and cover the dish with aluminum foil. Place the squash in the oven and roast until a knife inserted into it can pass easily to its center, about 35 to 40 minutes.
2. Place the remaining olive oil in a medium pot and warm it over medium heat. Add the chicken and cook, stirring occasionally, until it has browned evenly, about 5 minutes. Remove the chicken from the pot and set it aside.
3. Place the onion in the pot and cook, stirring occasionally, until it has softened, about 5 minutes. Add the garlic and cook, stirring frequently, for 2 minutes. Add the tomatoes, the oregano, and 3 cups of the stock and bring the soup to a boil. Reduce the heat so that the soup simmers.
4. Remove the squash from the oven and let it cool. Once the squash is cool enough to handle, scrape the cooked flesh out of the squash.
5. Place the squash and remaining stock in a food processor, pulse until smooth, and strain the mixture into the pot through a fine-mesh sieve. Add the chicken and quinoa and cook until the quinoa is tender, about 15 minutes.
6. Season the soup with salt and pepper, ladle it into warmed bowls, and serve.

Fava Bean Soup with Grilled Halloumi Cheese

YIELD: 4 SERVINGS / **ACTIVE TIME:** 30 MINUTES / **TOTAL TIME:** 24 HOURS

1½ CUPS DRIED FAVA BEANS, SOAKED OVERNIGHT

6 CUPS VEGETABLE STOCK (SEE PAGE 441)

4 GARLIC CLOVES, MINCED

5 TABLESPOONS EXTRA-VIRGIN OLIVE OIL

1 SHALLOT, MINCED

ZEST AND JUICE OF 1 LEMON

SALT AND PEPPER, TO TASTE

2 TABLESPOONS FINELY CHOPPED FRESH PARSLEY

½ LB. HALLOUMI CHEESE, CUT INTO 4 PIECES

LEMON WEDGES, FOR SERVING

1. Drain the fava beans and place them in a large saucepan with the stock and garlic. Bring to a boil, reduce the heat so that the soup simmers, cover, and cook until the beans are so tender that they are starting to fall apart, about 1 hour.
2. While the soup is simmering, place ¼ cup of the olive oil in a skillet and warm over medium heat. When the oil starts to shimmer, add the shallot and sauté until it starts to soften, about 5 minutes. Remove the pan from heat, stir in the lemon zest, and let the mixture sit for 1 hour.
3. Transfer the soup to a food processor and blitz until smooth. Return the soup to a clean saucepan, season with salt and pepper, and bring it to a gentle simmer. Stir in the shallot mixture, lemon juice, and parsley, cook until heated through, and remove the soup from heat.
4. Warm a skillet over medium heat. Place the remaining olive oil in a small bowl, add the cheese, and toss to coat. Place the cheese in the pan and cook until browned on both sides, about 2 minutes per side. Serve alongside the soup, along with lemon wedges.

Walnut Soup with Chive & Shallot Oil

YIELD: 4 SERVINGS / **ACTIVE TIME:** 20 MINUTES / **TOTAL TIME:** 1 HOUR AND 15 MINUTES

3 TABLESPOONS UNSALTED BUTTER

1 TABLESPOON FINELY CHOPPED SHALLOT

1 CELERY STALK, FINELY DICED

3 TABLESPOONS ALL-PURPOSE FLOUR

6 CUPS CHICKEN STOCK (SEE PAGE 440)

1 BAY LEAF

1 CUP CHOPPED TOASTED WALNUTS, PLUS MORE FOR GARNISH

2 CUPS HEAVY CREAM

SALT AND PEPPER, TO TASTE

CHIVE & SHALLOT OIL (SEE PAGE 470), FOR GARNISH

1. Place the butter in a large pot and melt it over medium heat. Add the shallot and celery and cook, stirring occasionally, until they have softened, about 3 minutes. Add the flour and cook, stirring occasionally, for 3 minutes. Add the stock, bay leaf, and walnuts and bring the soup to a boil.
2. Reduce the heat so that the soup simmers, add the cream, and cook for 30 minutes. Remove the bay leaf from the pot and discard it.
3. Transfer the soup to a food processor, pulse until smooth, and strain it back into the pot through a fine-mesh sieve. Bring the soup to a simmer and season it with salt and pepper.
4. Ladle the soup into warmed bowls, garnish with additional walnuts and the Chive & Shallot Oil, and serve.

BEEF, LAMB & MUTTON

Chili con Carne

YIELD: 4 TO 6 SERVINGS / **ACTIVE TIME:** 20 MINUTES / **TOTAL TIME:** 2 HOURS

¼ CUP EXTRA-VIRGIN OLIVE OIL

1 GREEN BELL PEPPER, STEMMED, SEEDED, AND FINELY DICED

1 ONION, FINELY DICED

2 LBS. GROUND BEEF

2 BEEF BOUILLON CUBES, CRUSHED

1 CUP RED WINE

2 (14 OZ.) CANS OF DICED TOMATOES, DRAINED

2 GARLIC CLOVES, MINCED

6 TABLESPOONS TOMATO PASTE

1 TEASPOON PAPRIKA

2 TEASPOONS CHILI POWDER

1 TEASPOON CAYENNE PEPPER

2 TEASPOONS FINELY CHOPPED FRESH BASIL

1 TEASPOON FINELY CHOPPED FRESH OREGANO

2 TABLESPOONS FINELY CHOPPED FRESH PARSLEY

½ TEASPOON TABASCO

1 (14 OZ.) CAN OF KIDNEY BEANS, DRAINED AND RINSED

3 TABLESPOONS ALL-PURPOSE FLOUR

2 TABLESPOONS CORNMEAL

½ CUP WATER

SALT AND PEPPER, TO TASTE

MOZZARELLA CHEESE, SHREDDED, TO TOP

TORTILLA CHIPS, FOR SERVING

1. Place the olive oil in a large pot and warm it over medium heat. Add the bell pepper and onion and cook, stirring occasionally, until the onion has softened, about 5 minutes.

2. Add the beef and cook, stirring occasionally, until it is cooked through, about 10 minutes. Add the bouillon cubes and red wine and cook, stirring frequently, for 2 minutes. Add the tomatoes, garlic, tomato paste, paprika, chili powder, cayenne pepper, basil, oregano, parsley, and Tabasco and bring the chili to a boil. Reduce the heat to its lowest setting, cover the pot, and cook for 1 hour.

3. Add the kidney beans and cook for 15 minutes. Place the flour, cornmeal, and water in a mixing bowl and stir until fully combined. Add the cornmeal mixture to the pot, stir to combine, and cook until the chili has thickened, about 10 minutes. Season the chili with salt and pepper.

4. Set the oven's broiler to high. Top the chili with mozzarella, place the pot in the oven, and cook until the cheese has melted, 1 to 2 minutes.

5. Ladle the chili into warmed bowls and serve with tortilla chips.

Honey, Huckleberry & Veal Soup

YIELD: 4 SERVINGS / **ACTIVE TIME:** 20 MINUTES / **TOTAL TIME:** 45 MINUTES

2 TABLESPOONS EXTRA-VIRGIN OLIVE OIL

1 LB. VEAL BUTT TENDERS, DICED

1 LARGE ONION, FINELY DICED

1 TABLESPOON UNSALTED BUTTER

4 CUPS BEEF STOCK (SEE PAGE 442)

1 CUP FRESH HUCKLEBERRIES

4 TEASPOONS HONEY

SALT AND PEPPER, TO TASTE

1. Place the olive oil in a medium pot and warm it over medium heat. Add the veal and cook, turning it as necessary, until it has browned, about 5 minutes. Remove the veal from the pot and set it aside.
2. Reduce the heat to low, add the onion and butter, and cook, stirring occasionally, until the onion has softened, about 5 minutes. Add the stock and huckleberries and bring the soup to a boil.
3. Reduce the heat so that the soup simmers and cook for 20 minutes.
4. Stir in the veal and honey and cook until the veal is warmed through, about 3 minutes. Season the soup with salt and pepper, ladle it into warmed bowls, and serve.

Santa Fe Chili

YIELD: 4 SERVINGS / **ACTIVE TIME:** 45 MINUTES / **TOTAL TIME:** 2 HOURS AND 30 MINUTES

1 TABLESPOON EXTRA-VIRGIN OLIVE OIL

1 LB. BONE-IN BEEF SHANKS

1 ONION, FINELY DICED

1 CUP CORN KERNELS

½ CUP FINELY DICED GREEN BELL PEPPER

½ TEASPOON CUMIN

2 GARLIC CLOVES, MINCED

1 TABLESPOON TOMATO PASTE

6 CUPS BEEF STOCK (SEE PAGE 442)

1 TOMATO, DICED

⅛ TEASPOON RED PEPPER FLAKES

⅛ TEASPOON TABASCO

SALT AND PEPPER, TO TASTE

CORNBREAD (SEE PAGE 469), FOR SERVING

1. Place the olive oil in a large pot and warm it over medium heat. Add the beef and cook, turning it as necessary, until it has browned, about 5 minutes. Remove the beef from the pot and set it aside.
2. Add the onion to the pot and cook, stirring occasionally, until it is translucent, about 3 minutes. Add the corn, bell pepper, cumin, and garlic and cook, stirring occasionally, until the vegetables have softened, about 3 minutes.
3. Add the beef, tomato paste, and stock, reduce the heat so that the soup simmers, and cook until the beef is very tender, about 2 hours.
4. Remove the beef shanks from the pot, remove the meat from the bones, and finely dice it. Add the diced beef and tomato to the pot and cook for 10 minutes.
5. Skim all the fat off of the soup, stir in the red pepper flakes and Tabasco, and season with salt and pepper.
6. Ladle the soup into warmed bowls and serve with the Cornbread.

Venison & Barley Soup

YIELD: 4 TO 6 SERVINGS / **ACTIVE TIME:** 20 MINUTES / **TOTAL TIME:** 2 HOURS

1 TABLESPOON EXTRA-VIRGIN OLIVE OIL

1¾ LBS. VENISON SHOULDER, DICED

1 ONION, FINELY DICED

2 CELERY STALKS, FINELY DICED

2 CARROTS, PEELED AND DICED

½ CUP RED WINE

1 GARLIC CLOVE, MINCED

1 TEASPOON CHILI POWDER

1 TEASPOON CUMIN

2 TEASPOONS FRESH THYME

½ LB. PEARL BARLEY

8 CUPS BEEF STOCK (SEE PAGE 442)

SALT AND PEPPER, TO TASTE

1. Place the olive oil in a large pot and warm it over medium-high heat. Add the venison and cook, stirring occasionally, until it has browned, about 5 minutes. Remove the venison from the pot and set it aside.
2. Add the onion, celery, and carrots to the pot and cook, stirring occasionally, until the onion has softened, about 5 minutes. Add the wine, garlic, chili powder, and cumin and cook, stirring occasionally, until the wine has reduced by half.
3. Add the venison, thyme, barley, and stock and bring the soup to a boil. Reduce the heat so that the soup simmers, cover the pot, and cook until the venison is very tender, about 1 hour and 30 minutes.
4. Season the soup with salt and pepper, ladle it into warmed bowls, and serve.

Cincinnati Chili

YIELD: 4 TO 6 SERVINGS / **ACTIVE TIME:** 15 MINUTES / **TOTAL TIME:** 1 HOUR AND 30 MINUTES

2 TABLESPOONS EXTRA-VIRGIN OLIVE OIL

1 ONION, FINELY DICED

1½ LBS. GROUND BEEF

2 TABLESPOONS CHILI POWDER

1 TEASPOON CINNAMON

1 TEASPOON CUMIN

¼ TEASPOON ALLSPICE

¼ TEASPOON GROUND CLOVES

2 BAY LEAVES

2 CUPS BEEF STOCK (SEE PAGE 442)

1 CUP TOMATO SAUCE (SEE PAGE 458)

2 TABLESPOONS APPLE CIDER VINEGAR

¼ TEASPOON CAYENNE PEPPER

1 OZ. BAKER'S CHOCOLATE

SALT AND PEPPER, TO TASTE

CHEDDAR CHEESE, GRATED, FOR GARNISH

FRESH PARSLEY, CHOPPED, FOR GARNISH

SPAGHETTI, COOKED, FOR SERVING

1. Place the olive oil in a medium pot and warm it over medium heat. Add the onion and cook, stirring occasionally, until it has softened, about 5 minutes. Add the beef and cook, stirring frequently, until it has browned, about 5 minutes.
2. Add the chili powder, cinnamon, cumin, allspice, cloves, bay leaves, stock, tomato sauce, vinegar, and cayenne pepper and bring the chili to a boil. Reduce the heat so that the chili simmers, cover the pot, and cook for 1 hour.
3. Remove the chili from heat, stir in the chocolate, and season with salt and pepper.
4. Ladle the chili into warmed bowls, garnish with cheddar cheese and parsley, and serve with spaghetti.

Cincinnati Chili

SEE PAGE 209

Mexican Beef Chili with Nachos

YIELD: 4 SERVINGS / **ACTIVE TIME:** 20 MINUTES / **TOTAL TIME:** 1 HOUR AND 15 MINUTES

3 TABLESPOONS EXTRA-VIRGIN OLIVE OIL

1 LB. BEEF ROUND, DICED

3 ONIONS, FINELY DICED

3 GARLIC CLOVES, MINCED

2 RED CHILE PEPPERS, STEMMED, SEEDED, AND SLICED THIN

1 TEASPOON CAYENNE PEPPER

1 TEASPOON CUMIN

6 CUPS BEEF STOCK (SEE PAGE 442)

2 BAY LEAVES

3 TABLESPOONS TOMATO PASTE

1 (14 OZ.) CAN OF CANNELLINI BEANS, RINSED AND DRAINED

1 (14 OZ.) CAN OF BLACK BEANS, RINSED AND DRAINED

SALT AND PEPPER, TO TASTE

TORTILLA CHIPS, FOR GARNISH

MONTEREY JACK CHEESE, GRATED, FOR GARNISH

JALAPEÑO CHILE PEPPERS, SLICED THIN, FOR GARNISH

FRESH CILANTRO, CHOPPED, FOR GARNISH

SOUR CREAM, FOR GARNISH

1. Place the olive oil in a large pot and warm it over medium-high heat. Add the beef and cook, turning it as necessary, until it has browned, about 5 minutes. Reduce the heat to medium, add the onions, garlic, and peppers, and cook, stirring occasionally, until the onions have softened, about 5 minutes.
2. Add the cayenne and cumin and cook, stirring occasionally, for 2 minutes. Add the stock, bay leaves, and tomato paste and bring the soup to a boil. Reduce the heat so that the soup simmers and cook until the beef is tender, 30 to 40 minutes.
3. Preheat the oven to 350°F. Place one-third of the cannellini beans and one-third of the black beans in a small mixing bowl and mash until fully combined. Add the mashed beans and the remaining beans to the pot, season with salt and pepper, and stir to combine.
4. Ladle the soup into warmed bowls and garnish with tortilla chips, Monterey Jack, jalapeños, cilantro, and sour cream.

Moroccan Beef & Bean Stew

YIELD: 4 SERVINGS / **ACTIVE TIME:** 45 MINUTES / **TOTAL TIME:** 24 HOURS

1 MARROW BONE

¾ LB. BEEF SIRLOIN, DICED

1 ONION, FINELY CHOPPED

¼ CUP DRIED KIDNEY BEANS, SOAKED OVERNIGHT AND DRAINED

¼ CUP BROWN LENTILS, RINSED WELL

2 TOMATOES, FINELY DICED

1 CELERY STALK, FINELY DICED

2 TEASPOONS TOMATO PASTE

⅛ TEASPOON GROUND GINGER

⅛ TEASPOON SAFFRON THREADS

3 TABLESPOONS ALL-PURPOSE FLOUR

¼ CUP LONG-GRAIN RICE

¼ CUP FINELY CHOPPED FRESH CILANTRO

2 TABLESPOONS FINELY CHOPPED FRESH PARSLEY

SALT AND PEPPER, TO TASTE

LEMON WEDGES, FOR SERVING

1. Bring 6 cups of water to a boil in a large pot. Add the marrow bone to the boiling water and cook for 5 minutes. Remove the marrow bone from the pot, let it cool, and discard the water.
2. Add the marrow bone, sirloin, onion, kidney beans, and 6 cups of water to the pot and bring to a boil. Reduce the heat so that the broth simmers and cook for 1 hour.
3. Add the lentils, tomatoes, celery, tomato paste, ginger, and saffron to the pot and cook, adding water as necessary, until the lentils have softened, about 15 minutes.
4. Place the flour and ½ cup of the simmering broth in a small mixing bowl and stir until smooth. Add another ½ cup of the simmering broth, stir to combine, and set the mixture aside.
5. Add the rice to the pot and cook until it is tender, about 20 minutes.
6. Add the flour mixture, cilantro, and parsley and stir until fully combined. Remove the marrow bone from the pot and discard it.
7. Add salt and pepper to taste, ladle the soup into warmed bowls, and serve with lemon wedges.

Avikas

YIELD: 6 SERVINGS / **ACTIVE TIME:** 1 HOUR / **TOTAL TIME:** 24 HOURS

1 TABLESPOON EXTRA-VIRGIN OLIVE OIL

1 LB. BEEF CHUCK, CUBED

1 TABLESPOON KOSHER SALT

1 YELLOW ONION, CHOPPED

1 TABLESPOON TOMATO PASTE

½ CUP DRIED CANNELLINI BEANS, SOAKED OVERNIGHT AND DRAINED

¼ TEASPOON BLACK PEPPER

LONG-GRAIN RICE, COOKED, FOR SERVING

1. Place the olive oil in a large saucepan and warm it over medium-high heat.
2. Season the meat with 1 teaspoon of the salt, place it in the pan, and cook until well browned all over, turning it as needed. Transfer the meat to a plate and set it aside.
3. Add the onion to the pan and cook, stirring occasionally, until golden brown, about 10 minutes. Add the tomato paste and cook until it has caramelized, about 2 minutes.
4. Return the meat to the pot and stir in the beans, pepper, and remaining salt. Cover with water, bring the soup to a boil, and then reduce the heat. Cover the pan and gently simmer until the soup has thickened and the beans and meat are tender, about 30 minutes.
5. Ladle the soup into bowls and serve with rice.

Mansaf

YIELD: 4 SERVINGS / **ACTIVE TIME:** 30 MINUTES / **TOTAL TIME:** 1 HOUR AND 30 MINUTES

2 TABLESPOONS EXTRA-VIRGIN OLIVE OIL

1 ONION, CHOPPED

2 LBS. LAMB SHOULDER, CUBED

6 CUPS BEEF STOCK (SEE PAGE 442)

SEEDS FROM 2 CARDAMOM PODS

1 CUP FULL-FAT GREEK YOGURT

SALT AND PEPPER, TO TASTE

2 CUPS COOKED LONG-GRAIN RICE

¼ CUP PINE NUTS, TOASTED, FOR GARNISH

FRESH PARSLEY, FINELY CHOPPED, FOR GARNISH

1. Place the olive oil in a saucepan and warm over medium-high heat. Add the onion and cook, stirring frequently, until it starts to soften, about 5 minutes. Add the lamb and cook until it is browned all over, about 8 minutes.
2. Add the stock and cardamom and bring the soup to a boil. Reduce the heat to medium-low, cover the pan, and simmer until the lamb is very tender, about 1 hour.
3. Stir in the yogurt, season with salt and pepper, and remove the soup from heat. Divide the rice among the serving bowls, ladle the soup over the rice, and garnish with the pine nuts and parsley.

Tomato & Beef Soup

YIELD: 4 SERVINGS / **ACTIVE TIME:** 20 MINUTES / **TOTAL TIME:** 45 MINUTES

2 TABLESPOONS EXTRA-VIRGIN OLIVE OIL

1 LB. SIRLOIN STEAK, SLICED

4 CUPS BEEF STOCK (SEE PAGE 442)

2 TABLESPOONS TOMATO PASTE

6 TOMATOES, DICED

2 TEASPOONS SUGAR

1 TABLESPOON CORNSTARCH

1 TABLESPOON COLD WATER

1 TABLESPOON WORCESTERSHIRE SAUCE

1 TABLESPOON DIJON MUSTARD

CAYENNE PEPPER, TO TASTE

SALT AND PEPPER, TO TASTE

SESAME OIL, FOR GARNISH

FRESH SCALLIONS, TRIMMED AND SLICED, FOR GARNISH

SESAME SEEDS, TOASTED, FOR GARNISH

1. Preheat the oven to 350°F. Place the olive oil in a cast-iron skillet and warm it over medium heat. Add the steak and cook, turning it as needed, until it is browned, about 8 minutes. Place the pan in the oven and cook until the steak is cooked to your liking. Remove the steak from the oven and set it aside.
2. Place the stock, tomato paste, tomatoes, and sugar in a medium pot and bring the soup to a boil, stirring occasionally.
3. Place the cornstarch and water in a small mixing bowl and stir until the mixture is smooth.
4. Reduce the heat so that the soup simmers and cook for 2 minutes. Add the slurry and stir until the soup thickens.
5. Transfer the soup to a food processor, add the Worcestershire sauce and mustard, and pulse until smooth. Strain the soup back into the pot through a fine-mesh sieve, bring it to a simmer, and season with cayenne, salt, and pepper.
6. Ladle the soup into warmed bowls, garnish with sesame oil, scallions, and toasted sesame seeds, and top each portion with some of the steak.

Spicy Eggplant & Beef Soup

YIELD: 4 SERVINGS / **ACTIVE TIME:** 45 MINUTES / **TOTAL TIME:** 3 HOURS

- 8 CUPS BEEF STOCK (SEE PAGE 442)
- 3-INCH PIECE OF FRESH GINGER, PEELED AND MINCED
- 1 CINNAMON STICK
- 2 STAR ANISE PODS
- ½ TEASPOON BLACK PEPPERCORNS
- SEEDS OF 4 CARDAMOM PODS, CRUSHED
- 1 MAKRUT LIME LEAF
- 1 LEMONGRASS STALK, CRUSHED
- 1-INCH PIECE OF FRESH GALANGAL, PEELED AND MINCED
- 1 LB. BRISKET
- 1 TABLESPOON SOY SAUCE
- 3 TABLESPOONS TUK TREY (SEE PAGE 471)
- 1 TABLESPOON EXTRA-VIRGIN OLIVE OIL
- 2 DRIED NEW MEXICO CHILE PEPPERS, SOAKED FOR 30 MINUTES, DRAINED, STEMMED, SEEDED, AND SLICED THIN
- 1 SHALLOT, FINELY DICED
- 2 TABLESPOONS TAMARIND CONCENTRATE
- 1 TABLESPOON JAGGERY
- 8 THAI EGGPLANTS, STEMMED AND FINELY DICED
- 1 TEASPOON FINELY CHOPPED FRESH CURRY LEAVES, PLUS MORE FOR GARNISH
- ½ BUNCH OF WATERCRESS
- SALT AND PEPPER, TO TASTE
- RED CHILE PEPPERS, STEMMED, SEEDED, AND SLICED THIN, FOR GARNISH
- TOASTED PEANUTS, CHOPPED, FOR GARNISH

1. Place the stock, ginger, cinnamon, star anise, peppercorns, cardamom, lime leaf, lemongrass, and galangal root in a large pot and bring to a boil. Reduce the heat so that the broth simmers. Add the brisket, cover the pot, and cook for 1 hour.
2. Uncover the pot, add the soy sauce and Tuk Trey, and cook until the stock has reduced by half, about 45 minutes.
3. Remove the brisket from the pot, slice it thin, and set it aside. Skim the excess fat from the broth, strain the broth through a fine-mesh sieve, and set it aside.
4. Place the olive oil in a medium pot and warm it over medium heat. Add the New Mexico chiles and shallot and cook, stirring occasionally, until they have softened, about 5 minutes. Add the broth and bring the soup to a simmer.
5. Add the tamarind concentrate, jaggery, brisket, and eggplants and cook until the eggplants are tender, about 20 minutes.
6. Add the curry leaves and watercress, season with salt and pepper, and cook for 2 minutes.
7. Ladle the soup into warmed bowls, garnish with additional curry leaves, red chiles, and toasted peanuts, and serve.

Hungarian Goulash

YIELD: 4 SERVINGS / **ACTIVE TIME:** 30 MINUTES / **TOTAL TIME:** 2 HOURS

1 LB. BEEF CHUCK, DICED

¼ CUP ALL-PURPOSE FLOUR

2 TABLESPOONS EXTRA-VIRGIN OLIVE OIL

1 ONION, FINELY DICED

1 GREEN BELL PEPPER, STEMMED, SEEDED, AND FINELY DICED

2 CARROTS, PEELED AND DICED

1 CELERY STALK, FINELY DICED

1 CUP RED WINE

2 TEASPOONS PAPRIKA

3 TABLESPOONS TOMATO PASTE

1 TEASPOON FRESH THYME

1 TEASPOON FINELY CHOPPED FRESH PARSLEY

4 CUPS BEEF STOCK (SEE PAGE 442)

1 (14 OZ.) CAN OF DICED TOMATOES, DRAINED

1 TABLESPOON WORCESTERSHIRE SAUCE

CAYENNE PEPPER, TO TASTE

SALT AND PEPPER, TO TASTE

SOUR CREAM, FOR SERVING

CRUSTY BREAD, FOR SERVING

1. Preheat the oven to 350°F. Place the beef and flour in a medium mixing bowl and toss until the beef is coated.
2. Place the olive oil in a large pot and warm it over medium heat. Add the onion, bell pepper, carrots, and celery and cook, stirring occasionally, until the onion has softened, about 5 minutes. Add the beef and cook, stirring occasionally, until it has browned, about 8 minutes.
3. Add the wine and cook, stirring occasionally, for 5 minutes. Add the paprika, tomato paste, thyme, and parsley and cook, stirring occasionally, for 2 minutes. Add the stock, tomatoes, and Worcestershire sauce, bring the soup to a simmer, and cover the pot. Cook for 45 minutes.
4. Uncover the pot, stir the soup, and then cook until the beef is very tender, about 45 minutes.
5. Season with cayenne, salt, and pepper, ladle the soup into warmed bowls, and serve with sour cream and crusty bread.

Cholent

YIELD: 4 SERVINGS / **ACTIVE TIME:** 15 MINUTES / **TOTAL TIME:** 2 DAYS

1½ LBS. FATTY BEEF CHUCK, CUBED

4 MARROW BONES

2 LARGE YUKON GOLD OR RUSSET POTATOES, PEELED AND CUT INTO CHUNKS

1 ONION, PEELED

4 GARLIC CLOVES, PEELED

2 CUPS PEARL BARLEY

1 CUP DRIED KIDNEY BEANS, SOAKED OVERNIGHT AND DRAINED; SOAKING WATER RESERVED

⅓ CUP KETCHUP

1 TABLESPOON PAPRIKA

3 CUPS WATER

2 TEASPOONS KOSHER SALT

1 TEASPOON BLACK PEPPER

1 TEASPOON GARLIC POWDER

1 LB. PACKAGED KISHKE

1. Coat the inside of a slow cooker with nonstick cooking spray. Add the beef, marrow bones, and potatoes to the slow cooker, followed by the onion, garlic, barley, kidney beans, and water the beans soaked in.
2. In a bowl, combine the ketchup, the paprika, and 2½ cups of the water and add to the slow cooker. Stir in the salt, pepper, and garlic powder and arrange the kishke on top.
3. Set the slow cooker to low and cook overnight, for 8 to 10 hours. Check it in the morning and add the remaining water if the stew seems too dry.
4. Ladle the stew into warmed bowls and enjoy.

Clear Oxtail Soup

YIELD: 4 SERVINGS / **ACTIVE TIME:** 25 MINUTES / **TOTAL TIME:** 3 HOURS AND 45 MINUTES

- 2 TABLESPOONS EXTRA-VIRGIN OLIVE OIL
- 2½ LBS. OXTAIL
- 3 CARROTS, PEELED AND DICED
- 1 ONION, FINELY DICED
- 3 CELERY STALKS, FINELY DICED
- 6 CUPS BEEF STOCK (SEE PAGE 442)
- 1 TOMATO, FINELY DICED
- SACHET D'ÉPICES (SEE PAGE 465)
- 1 CUP FINELY DICED CELERY ROOT
- 1 CUP FINELY DICED PARSNIPS
- 3 EGG WHITES
- ⅛ CUP WHITE WINE VINEGAR
- ¼ LB. GROUND BEEF
- SALT AND PEPPER, TO TASTE
- 2 TABLESPOONS SHERRY
- FRESH CHIVES, CHOPPED, FOR GARNISH
- HORSERADISH OIL (SEE PAGE 472), FOR GARNISH

1. Place the olive oil in a large pot and warm it over medium heat. Add the oxtail and cook, turning it as necessary, until it has browned, about 5 minutes.
2. Add 2 of the carrots, the onion, and 2 of the celery stalks and cook, stirring occasionally, until the onion has softened, about 5 minutes. Add the stock, tomato, and Sachet d'Épices and bring the broth to a boil.
3. Reduce the heat so that the soup simmers and cook until the oxtail is tender, about 2 hours. Strain the soup through a fine-mesh sieve, set the solids aside, and chill the broth in the refrigerator, skimming the fat off the top as it rises to the surface. Remove the meat from the oxtail and finely dice it.
4. Bring 8 cups of water to a boil in a large pot. Add the remaining celery stalks, the remaining carrot, the celery root, and the parsnips and cook until they are tender, about 5 minutes. Remove the solids from the pot, let them cool, and set them aside.
5. Place the egg whites, vinegar, and beef and 2 cups of water in a medium mixing bowl, season with salt, and stir until fully combined.
6. Place the broth and egg white mixture in a medium pot and stir to combine. Bring the soup to a low simmer and cook for 45 minutes.
7. Strain the soup into a clean pot through a fine-mesh sieve. Add the oxtail meat, reserved vegetables, and sherry, season with salt and pepper, and bring the soup to a boil.
8. Ladle the soup into warmed bowls, garnish with chives and the Horseradish Oil, and serve.

Bone Marrow & Matzo Ball Soup

YIELD: 8 SERVINGS / **ACTIVE TIME:** 35 MINUTES / **TOTAL TIME:** 24 HOURS

4 LBS. MARROW BONES

2 TEASPOONS KOSHER SALT, PLUS MORE TO TASTE

2 EGGS, SEPARATED

2 TABLESPOONS CHOPPED FRESH PARSLEY

1 TEASPOON BLACK PEPPER

DASH OF FRESHLY GRATED NUTMEG

1 CUP MATZO MEAL

8 CUPS CHICKEN STOCK (SEE PAGE 440)

1 GARLIC CLOVE

1. Place the marrow bones in a saucepan, add a few pinches of salt, and cover the bones with cold water. Let the bones soak overnight.
2. Preheat the oven to 400°F. Pat the bones dry, arrange them on a baking sheet, and place them in the oven. Roast for 30 minutes, remove from the oven, and let the marrow bones cool slightly.
3. Using a spoon or a table knife, remove the roasted marrow from the bones and place it in a small bowl. Continue until you have about ½ cup of marrow.
4. Place half of the marrow in a mixing bowl and mash it with a fork until it is smooth. Add the egg yolks, parsley, salt, pepper, and nutmeg and stir until combined. Add the matzo and work the mixture until it comes together as a soft dough.
5. Cover the bowl with plastic wrap and chill it in the refrigerator for 2 hours.
6. Place the egg whites in a mixing bowl and whip them until they hold soft peaks. Add them to the matzo dough and gently fold to incorporate them.
7. Place the stock in a large saucepan and stir in the garlic and the remaining marrow. Bring the stock to a simmer.
8. Form the dough into small balls and drop them into the simmering stock in batches of five. Cook each batch in the simmering stock until cooked through and tender, 10 to 15 minutes. Transfer the cooked matzo balls to a serving bowl.
9. When all of the matzo balls have been cooked, divide them among the serving bowls. Ladle the stock over each portion and enjoy.

Msoki de Pesaj

YIELD: 6 SERVINGS / **ACTIVE TIME:** 45 MINUTES / **TOTAL TIME:** 3 HOURS

2½ LBS. BONELESS LAMB SHOULDER, CUT INTO 3-INCH CUBES

1 TABLESPOON KOSHER SALT, PLUS MORE TO TASTE

½ TEASPOON BLACK PEPPER, PLUS MORE TO TASTE

2 TABLESPOONS AVOCADO OIL

2 LARGE YELLOW ONIONS, CHOPPED

2 CARROTS, PEELED AND CHOPPED

1 TURNIP, PEELED AND CHOPPED

1 GARLIC CLOVE, MINCED

1 CINNAMON STICK

2 TEASPOONS HARISSA SAUCE (SEE PAGE 461)

2 LBS. SPINACH LEAVES, FINELY CHOPPED

2 LEEKS, TRIMMED, RINSED WELL, AND MINCED

1 ZUCCHINI, CHOPPED

1 FENNEL BULB, TRIMMED AND CHOPPED

3 CELERY STALKS, CHOPPED

1½ CUPS FAVA BEANS

1 CUP GREEN PEAS

4 ARTICHOKE HEARTS, CUT INTO WEDGES

¼ BUNCH OF FRESH PARSLEY, CHOPPED

¼ BUNCH OF FRESH CILANTRO, CHOPPED

¼ BUNCH OF FRESH MINT LEAVES, FINELY CHOPPED

2 TEASPOONS ORANGE BLOSSOM WATER

1. Season the lamb with the salt and pepper. Place the avocado oil in a large Dutch oven and warm it over medium-high heat. Working in batches to avoid crowding the pot, add the lamb and cook until browned all over, about 8 minutes for each batch, turning it as necessary. Using a slotted spoon, transfer the browned lamb to a bowl.
2. Add the onions, carrots, turnip, and garlic and cook, stirring frequently, until the vegetables are tender, 15 to 20 minutes.
3. Add the cinnamon stick and harissa and cook, stirring frequently, for 5 minutes.
4. Add the spinach, leeks, zucchini, fennel, and celery and cook until the fennel is tender, about 15 minutes.
5. Stir in the fava beans, peas, artichoke hearts, parsley, cilantro, mint, and orange blossom water. Add water until the liquid reaches three-quarters of the way up the mixture. Bring the stew to a simmer and let it cook, stirring occasionally, until the liquid has reduced to one-quarter of the original amount.
6. Season the stew with salt and pepper, ladle it into warmed bowls, and enjoy.

Beef & Braised Cabbage Soup

YIELD: 6 SERVINGS / **ACTIVE TIME:** 30 MINUTES / **TOTAL TIME:** 2 HOURS AND 20 MINUTES

2 LBS. RED CABBAGE, CORED AND FINELY DICED

2 ONIONS, FINELY DICED

1 LARGE APPLE, PEELED, CORED, AND FINELY DICED

3 TABLESPOONS BROWN SUGAR

2 GARLIC CLOVES, MINCED

¼ TEASPOON FRESHLY GRATED NUTMEG

½ TEASPOON CARAWAY SEEDS

3 TABLESPOONS APPLE CIDER VINEGAR

4 CUPS BEEF STOCK (SEE PAGE 442)

SALT AND PEPPER, TO TASTE

2 TABLESPOONS EXTRA-VIRGIN OLIVE OIL

1½ LBS. SIRLOIN STEAK

FRESH WATERCRESS, FOR GARNISH

HORSERADISH CREAM (SEE PAGE 471), FOR SERVING

1. Preheat the oven to 300°F. Place the cabbage, onions, apple, brown sugar, garlic, nutmeg, caraway seeds, and vinegar and ½ cup of the stock in a large mixing bowl and toss to combine. Season with salt and pepper, place the cabbage mixture in a large baking dish, and cover the dish. Place the dish in the oven and cook for 1 hour and 30 minutes.
2. Remove the cabbage mixture from the oven, let it cool, and set it aside.
3. Preheat the oven to 450°F. Place the olive oil in a medium skillet and warm it over medium heat. Season the steak with salt and pepper, add it to the skillet, and cook, turning occasionally, until it is browned on both sides, about 4 minutes. Remove the steak from the skillet and set it aside.
4. Place the cabbage mixture and the remaining stock in a large pot and bring the soup to a boil. Reduce the heat so that the soup simmers.
5. Place the steak in a baking dish, place the dish in the oven, and cook until it is to your liking. Remove the steak from the oven and let it cool. Once the steak has cooled, slice it thin and set it aside.
6. Ladle the soup into warmed bowls and top each bowl with sliced steak. Garnish with watercress and serve with the Horseradish Cream.

Lamb Stew

YIELD: 10 SERVINGS / **ACTIVE TIME:** 30 MINUTES / **TOTAL TIME:** 1 HOUR

2 TABLESPOONS RED WINE

1 TABLESPOON FRESH LEMON JUICE

½ TEASPOON LEMON ZEST

1 TABLESPOON BERBERE SEASONING

1 TEASPOON SMOKED PAPRIKA

1 TEASPOON DIJON MUSTARD

3½ LBS. BONELESS LEG OF LAMB, CUBED

1 TEASPOON KOSHER SALT, PLUS MORE TO TASTE

½ TEASPOON BLACK PEPPER, PLUS MORE TO TASTE

¼ CUP EXTRA-VIRGIN OLIVE OIL

2 ONIONS, SLICED THIN

6 GARLIC CLOVES, MINCED

2 TEASPOONS CHOPPED FRESH ROSEMARY

2 TEASPOONS FRESH THYME

2 PLUM TOMATOES, DICED

1 ORANGE BELL PEPPER, STEM AND SEEDS REMOVED, DICED

1 LARGE SHALLOT, SLICED THIN

1. Place the wine, lemon juice, lemon zest, berbere, paprika, and mustard in a small bowl and stir until well combined.
2. Season the lamb with the salt and pepper. Place the olive oil in a large Dutch oven and warm it over medium-high heat. Working in two batches, add the lamb and cook until browned all over, about 8 minutes for each batch, turning it as necessary. Using a slotted spoon, transfer the browned lamb to a bowl.
3. Add the onions, garlic, rosemary, and thyme and a generous pinch of salt and pepper to the pot, reduce the heat to medium, and cook, stirring occasionally, until the onions have softened and are starting to brown, about 8 minutes.
4. Return the lamb and any juices that have accumulated to the pot, along with the wine mixture, tomatoes, bell pepper, and shallot. Cook, stirring, until the bell pepper has softened and the lamb is just cooked through, about 10 minutes.
5. Taste, adjust the seasoning as necessary, and enjoy.

Dafina

YIELD: 4 SERVINGS / **ACTIVE TIME:** 20 MINUTES / **TOTAL TIME:** 24 HOURS

2 (14 OZ.) CANS OF CHICKPEAS, DRAINED AND RINSED

12 LARGE RED POTATOES, PEELED

2 LBS. BONE-IN FLANKEN SHORT RIBS

4 CHICKEN DRUMSTICKS

4 EGGS, LEFT WHOLE

4 PITTED DATES

1 TABLESPOON KOSHER SALT

1 TEASPOON BLACK PEPPER

1 TEASPOON PAPRIKA

1 TEASPOON CUMIN

1 TEASPOON TURMERIC

1 TEASPOON HONEY

1 TEASPOON CINNAMON

3 GARLIC CLOVES

2 TABLESPOONS AVOCADO OIL

1. Place the chickpeas on the bottom of a slow cooker. Place the potatoes against the wall of the slow cooker and then place the short ribs meat, chicken, eggs, and dates in the center.
2. Place the remaining ingredients in a mixing bowl, stir to combine, and add the mixture to the slow cooker, making sure to keep all of the ingredients in their particular place. Add water until the mixture is covered by ¼ inch.
3. Set the slow cooker to low and cook for 24 hours.
4. Ladle the stew into warmed bowls and enjoy.

Korean Beef & Rice Soup

YIELD: 4 SERVINGS / **ACTIVE TIME:** 15 MINUTES / **TOTAL TIME:** 30 MINUTES

2 TABLESPOONS SESAME SEEDS

1 TEASPOON RED PEPPER FLAKES

1 STAR ANISE POD

1 CINNAMON STICK

2 TABLESPOONS SESAME OIL

2 TABLESPOONS FISH SAUCE

2 TABLESPOONS SOY SAUCE

1 TABLESPOON RICE VINEGAR

2 TABLESPOONS EXTRA-VIRGIN OLIVE OIL

1 LB. BONELESS BEEF CHUCK, CUBED

2 GARLIC CLOVES, MINCED

8 CUPS BEEF STOCK (SEE PAGE 442)

1 CUP LONG-GRAIN RICE

4 SCALLIONS, TRIMMED AND SLICED THIN, WHITES AND GREENS SEPARATED

4 CELERY STALKS, FINELY DICED

SALT AND PEPPER, TO TASTE

1. Place the sesame seeds, red pepper flakes, star anise, and cinnamon stick in a small skillet and cook over medium heat, stirring continually, until the mixture is fragrant, about 3 minutes. Remove the pan from heat, add the sesame oil, fish sauce, soy sauce, and vinegar and half of the olive oil, and stir to combine. Set the infused oil aside.
2. Place the remaining olive oil in a medium pot and warm it over medium-high heat. Add the beef and cook, stirring occasionally, until it has browned, 3 to 5 minutes. Add the garlic, stock, and rice and bring the soup to a boil.
3. Reduce the heat so that the soup simmers and cook until the rice is tender, about 15 minutes. Add the scallion whites and celery and cook until the celery is tender, about 5 minutes.
4. Season the soup with salt and pepper and ladle it into warmed bowls. Garnish with the infused oil and scallion greens and serve.

Short Rib & Okra Stew

YIELD: 6 SERVINGS / **ACTIVE TIME:** 30 MINUTES / **TOTAL TIME:** 3 HOURS

2¼ LBS. BONELESS SHORT RIBS

1 TEASPOON KOSHER SALT, PLUS MORE TO TASTE

½ TEASPOON BLACK PEPPER, PLUS MORE TO TASTE

¼ CUP PLUS 5 TABLESPOONS AVOCADO OIL

3 GARLIC CLOVES, SMASHED

¼ CUP TOMATO PASTE

¾ LB. TOMATOES, QUARTERED

1½ CUPS WATER

JUICE OF 1 LEMON, PLUS MORE TO TASTE

1 TEASPOON SWEET PAPRIKA

3 BAY LEAVES

1 SMALL JALAPEÑO CHILE PEPPER, STEM AND SEEDS REMOVED, SLICED THIN

1 TEASPOON SUGAR

1 LB. OKRA, TRIMMED

1 BUNCH OF FRESH MINT

1 CUP BASMATI RICE

1 TEASPOON CORIANDER SEEDS

1½ CUPS BOILING WATER

1. Preheat the oven to 350°F. Slice the short ribs into 2-inch cubes and season with the salt and pepper.
2. Place ¼ cup of the avocado oil in a Dutch oven and warm it over medium-high heat. Working in batches to avoid crowding the pot, add the short ribs and cook until browned all over, about 5 minutes, turning the meat as necessary. Transfer the browned short ribs to a plate.
3. Add the garlic to the pot and cook until it is fragrant, about 1 minute. Add the tomato paste and cook for 30 seconds, stirring constantly. Add the tomatoes a little bit at a time, crushing them in your hands before adding them to the pot.
4. Add the water, the lemon juice, the paprika, 1 of the bay leaves, and 3 to 5 slices of the jalapeño. Return the short ribs to the pot and sprinkle the sugar over them. Reduce the heat to low and let the stew simmer while preparing the okra.
5. Add 3 tablespoons of the avocado oil to a large skillet and warm it over high heat. Add the okra and cook, tossing it frequently, until it is bright green and lightly blistered, 1 to 2 minutes. Remove the pan from heat, season it with salt and lemon juice, and toss to coat.
6. Add the okra to the stew, making sure it is evenly distributed. Add 6 to 10 mint leaves, cover the pot, and place it in the oven. Braise for 2 hours, checking the stew every 30 minutes and adding water as necessary if the liquid has reduced too much.
7. After 2 hours, the meat should be fork-tender. Turn on the broiler and broil the stew until it is dark and caramelized, about 10 minutes.
8. While the stew is in the oven, place the remaining avocado oil in a small saucepan and warm it over high heat. Add the rice and toast it, stirring continuously, until the grains are too hot to touch, about 2 minutes. Add the remaining bay leaves, the

coriander seeds, and the boiling water, bring the rice to a boil, and cover the pan. Reduce the heat and simmer the rice until it is tender, about 20 minutes.

9. Remove the rice from heat and let it stand, covered, for 10 minutes. Gently fluff the rice with a fork and cover until ready to serve.

10. Remove the stew from the oven. Season with salt and pepper and sprinkle the remaining mint over it. Serve with the rice and enjoy.

Chamin

YIELD: 4 SERVINGS / **ACTIVE TIME:** 30 MINUTES / **TOTAL TIME:** 24 HOURS

1½ TABLESPOONS EXTRA-VIRGIN OLIVE OIL

1 ONION, FINELY DICED

5 GARLIC CLOVES, MINCED

¾ CUP FINELY DICED PARSNIPS

¾ CUP PEELED AND DICED CARROTS

1 TEASPOON CUMIN

¼ TEASPOON TURMERIC

1½ TABLESPOONS PEELED AND MINCED FRESH GINGER

5 OZ. BRISKET, DICED

5 OZ. LAMB SHOULDER, DICED

4 CUPS BEEF STOCK (SEE PAGE 442)

½ CUP DRIED CHICKPEAS, SOAKED OVERNIGHT AND DRAINED

1 POTATO, PEELED AND FINELY DICED

1 ZUCCHINI, PEELED AND FINELY DICED

½ LB. TOMATOES, FINELY DICED

2 TABLESPOONS BROWN LENTILS

1 BAY LEAF

½ BUNCH OF FRESH CILANTRO, FINELY CHOPPED

SALT AND PEPPER, TO TASTE

FRESH CHILE PEPPERS, SLICED THIN, FOR GARNISH

RICE, COOKED, FOR SERVING

FRESH LEMON WEDGES, FOR SERVING

1. Preheat the oven to 250°F. Place the olive oil in a Dutch oven and warm it over medium heat. Add the onion, garlic, parsnips, carrots, cumin, turmeric, and ginger and cook, stirring frequently, for 2 minutes. Add the brisket and lamb and cook, stirring occasionally, until they have browned, about 5 minutes.
2. Add the stock and bring the soup to a simmer. Add the chickpeas, potato, zucchini, tomatoes, lentils, bay leaf, and cilantro, cover the Dutch oven, and place it in the oven. Cook until the meat is tender, about 1 hour and 15 minutes.
3. Remove the soup from the oven, uncover the Dutch oven, and skim off any excess fat. Season the soup with salt and pepper.
4. Ladle the soup into warmed bowls, garnish with chiles, and serve with rice and lemon wedges.

Beef, Barley & Portobello Mushroom Soup

YIELD: 4 TO 6 SERVINGS / **ACTIVE TIME:** 20 MINUTES / **TOTAL TIME:** 2 HOURS

1 TABLESPOON EXTRA-VIRGIN OLIVE OIL

1¾ LBS. BEEF STEW MEAT, DICED

1 ONION, FINELY DICED

2 CELERY STALKS, FINELY DICED

2 CARROTS, PEELED AND DICED

½ CUP RED WINE

1 GARLIC CLOVE, MINCED

2 TEASPOONS FRESH THYME

8 CUPS BEEF STOCK (SEE PAGE 442)

¾ CUP PEARL BARLEY

1 LB. PORTOBELLO MUSHROOMS, FINELY DICED

SALT AND PEPPER, TO TASTE

1. Place the olive oil in a large pot and warm it over medium-high heat. Add the beef and cook, stirring occasionally, until it has browned, about 5 minutes. Remove the beef from the pot and set it aside.
2. Add the onion, celery, and carrots and cook, stirring occasionally, until the onion has softened, about 5 minutes. Add the red wine, garlic, and thyme and cook, stirring occasionally, until the wine has reduced by half.
3. Add the beef, stock, and barley and bring the soup to a boil. Reduce the heat so that the soup simmers, cover the pot, and cook until the beef is very tender, about 1 hour and 30 minutes.
4. Add the mushrooms and cook for 10 minutes. Season the soup with salt and pepper, ladle it into warmed bowls, and serve.

Corned Beef & Barley Soup

YIELD: 4 SERVINGS / **ACTIVE TIME:** 20 MINUTES / **TOTAL TIME:** 2 HOURS AND 15 MINUTES

3 TABLESPOONS EXTRA-VIRGIN OLIVE OIL

1 LB. CORNED BEEF

4 CUPS BEEF STOCK (SEE PAGE 442)

SACHET D'ÉPICES (SEE PAGE 465)

SALT AND PEPPER, TO TASTE

1 ONION, FINELY DICED

1 CELERY STALK, FINELY DICED

½ CUP BARLEY

1 TOMATO, DICED

2 TABLESPOONS FINELY CHOPPED FRESH PARSLEY

CRÈME FRAÎCHE, FOR GARNISH

1. Place 2 tablespoons of the olive oil in a medium pot and warm it over medium heat. Add the beef and cook, turning it as necessary, until it has browned, about 8 minutes.
2. Add the stock and Sachet d'Épices, season with salt and pepper, and bring the broth to a simmer. Cook the broth for 1 hour, skimming off any excess fat as it accumulates.
3. Remove the beef from the pot, finely dice it, and set it aside. Strain the broth through a fine-mesh sieve and set it aside.
4. Place the remaining olive oil in a medium pot and warm it over medium heat. Add the onion and celery and cook, stirring occasionally, until they have softened, about 5 minutes. Add the broth, beef, and barley and bring the soup to a boil.
5. Reduce the heat so that the soup simmers and cook until the barley is tender, about 15 minutes. Add the tomato and cook for 10 minutes.
6. Stir in the parsley and season with salt and pepper. Ladle the soup into warmed bowls and serve with crème fraîche.

Lamb Sharba

YIELD: 6 SERVINGS / **ACTIVE TIME:** 30 MINUTES / **TOTAL TIME:** 2 HOURS

2 TABLESPOONS EXTRA-VIRGIN OLIVE OIL

¾ LB. BONELESS LEG OF LAMB, CUT INTO 1-INCH CUBES

1 ONION, CHOPPED

1 TOMATO, QUARTERED, SEEDED, AND SLICED THIN

1 GARLIC CLOVE, MINCED

1 TABLESPOON TOMATO PASTE

1 BUNCH OF FRESH MINT, TIED WITH TWINE, PLUS MORE FOR GARNISH

2 CINNAMON STICKS

1¼ TEASPOONS TURMERIC

1¼ TEASPOONS PAPRIKA

½ TEASPOON CUMIN

8 CUPS CHICKEN STOCK (SEE PAGE 440)

1 (14 OZ.) CAN OF CHICKPEAS, DRAINED AND RINSED

¾ CUP ORZO

SALT AND PEPPER, TO TASTE

1. Place the olive oil in a Dutch oven and warm it over medium-high heat. Add the lamb and cook, turning it as necessary, until it is browned all over, about 5 minutes. Remove the lamb with a slotted spoon and place it on a paper towel–lined plate.
2. Add the onion to the pot and cook, stirring occasionally, until it starts to soften, about 5 minutes. Add the tomato, garlic, tomato paste, mint, cinnamon sticks, turmeric, paprika, and cumin and cook, stirring continually, for 1 minute.
3. Add the stock and bring the mixture to a boil. Return the seared lamb to the pot, reduce the heat, and simmer until the lamb is tender, about 30 minutes.
4. Add the chickpeas and orzo and cook until the orzo is tender, about 10 minutes.
5. Remove the mint and discard it. Season the soup with salt and pepper and ladle it into warmed bowls. Garnish with additional mint and enjoy.

Quick Lamb Stew

YIELD: 4 SERVINGS / **ACTIVE TIME:** 15 MINUTES / **TOTAL TIME:** 30 MINUTES

2 TABLESPOONS EXTRA-VIRGIN OLIVE OIL

1 ONION, FINELY DICED

1 LB. LAMB LOIN, TRIMMED AND DICED

2 GARLIC CLOVES, MINCED

1 TABLESPOON CUMIN

1 TABLESPOON FINELY CHOPPED FRESH ROSEMARY, PLUS MORE FOR GARNISH

2 (14 OZ.) CANS OF DICED TOMATOES, WITH THEIR LIQUID

4 CUPS BEEF STOCK (SEE PAGE 442)

2 POTATOES, PEELED AND FINELY DICED

2 CUPS CHOPPED GREEN BEANS

JUICE OF 1 LEMON

SALT AND PEPPER, TO TASTE

1. Place the olive oil in a medium pot and warm it over medium heat. Add the onion and lamb and cook, stirring occasionally, until the lamb has browned, about 5 minutes. Add the garlic, cumin, rosemary, and tomatoes and cook, stirring frequently, for 5 minutes.
2. Add the stock and potatoes and bring to a boil. Reduce the heat so that the soup simmers and cook until the potatoes are tender, 10 to 15 minutes.
3. Add the green beans and cook for 5 minutes. Add the lemon juice, season with salt and pepper, and stir to combine.
4. Ladle the soup into warmed bowls, garnish with additional rosemary, and serve.

Mulligatawny with Lamb

YIELD: 4 SERVINGS / **ACTIVE TIME:** 20 MINUTES / **TOTAL TIME:** 1 HOUR

4 TEASPOONS POPPY SEEDS

½ TEASPOON CUMIN SEEDS

1 TEASPOON CORIANDER SEEDS

¼ TEASPOON TURMERIC

1 ONION, FINELY DICED

4 GARLIC CLOVES, MINCED

1-INCH PIECE OF FRESH GINGER, PEELED AND MINCED

¼ CUP EXTRA-VIRGIN OLIVE OIL

¾ LB. LAMB LOIN, DICED

⅛ TEASPOON CAYENNE PEPPER

2 CUPS LAMB STOCK (SEE PAGE 450)

2 CUPS BEEF STOCK (SEE PAGE 442)

¼ CUP LONG-GRAIN RICE

4 TEASPOONS FRESH LEMON JUICE

¼ CUP COCONUT MILK

SALT AND PEPPER, TO TASTE

SHREDDED COCONUT, FOR GARNISH

FRESH CILANTRO, CHOPPED, FOR GARNISH

1. Place the poppy seeds, cumin seeds, and coriander seeds in a small skillet and toast over medium heat until they are fragrant, 30 seconds to 1 minute, shaking the pan frequently.
2. Place the toasted seeds, turmeric, onion, garlic, and ginger and half of the olive oil in a food processor, pulse until the mixture is a smooth paste, and set it aside.
3. Place the remaining olive oil in a medium pot and warm it over medium-high heat. Add the lamb and cook, stirring frequently, until it has browned, about 5 minutes.
4. Add the paste and cook, stirring continually, for 2 minutes. Add the cayenne pepper and stocks and bring the soup to a boil. Reduce the heat so that the soup simmers, add the rice, and cook until it is tender, about 20 minutes.
5. Stir in the lemon juice and coconut milk and season the soup with salt and pepper.
6. Ladle the soup into warmed bowls, garnish with coconut and cilantro, and serve.

Lamb & Barley Soup

YIELD: 4 TO 6 SERVINGS / **ACTIVE TIME:** 20 MINUTES / **TOTAL TIME:** 1 HOUR AND 15 MINUTES

2 TABLESPOONS EXTRA-VIRGIN OLIVE OIL

1 ONION, FINELY DICED

2 CARROTS, PEELED AND DICED

2 CELERY STALKS, FINELY DICED

1½ LBS. GROUND LAMB

2 TEASPOONS FRESH THYME

2 (14 OZ.) CANS OF DICED TOMATOES, DRAINED

3 CUPS LAMB STOCK (SEE PAGE 450)

3 CUPS BEEF STOCK (SEE PAGE 442)

½ CUP PEARL BARLEY

½ TEASPOON CUMIN

½ TEASPOON CHILI POWDER

¼ CUP FINELY CHOPPED FRESH PARSLEY

SALT AND PEPPER, TO TASTE

1. Place the olive oil in a medium pot and warm it over medium heat. Add the onion, carrots, and celery and cook, stirring occasionally, until they have softened, about 5 minutes. Add the lamb and cook, breaking it up with a wooden spoon, until it has browned, about 5 minutes.
2. Add the thyme, tomatoes, stocks, barley, cumin, and chili powder and bring the soup to a boil. Reduce the heat so that soup simmers and cook until the barley is tender, about 30 minutes.
3. Add the parsley and stir to combine. Season the soup with salt and pepper, ladle it into warmed bowls, and serve.

Lamb & Okra Stew

YIELD: 4 SERVINGS / **ACTIVE TIME:** 15 MINUTES / **TOTAL TIME:** 55 MINUTES

2 TABLESPOONS EXTRA-VIRGIN OLIVE OIL

2 ONIONS, FINELY DICED

1½ LBS. BONELESS LAMB SHOULDER, DICED

2 TABLESPOONS TURMERIC

½ CUP TOMATO PASTE

4 CUPS LAMB STOCK (SEE PAGE 450)

2 GARLIC CLOVES, MINCED

20 OKRA PODS, TRIMMED AND SLICED THIN

SALT AND PEPPER, TO TASTE

1. Place the olive oil in a medium pot and warm it over medium heat. Add the onions and cook, stirring occasionally, until they have softened, about 5 minutes. Add the lamb and turmeric and cook, stirring frequently, until the lamb has browned, about 5 minutes.
2. Add the tomato paste, stock, and garlic and bring the soup to a boil. Reduce the heat so that the soup simmers and cook until the lamb is tender, about 30 minutes.
3. Add the okra and cook until it is tender, about 5 minutes.
4. Season the soup with salt and pepper, ladle it into warmed bowls, and serve.

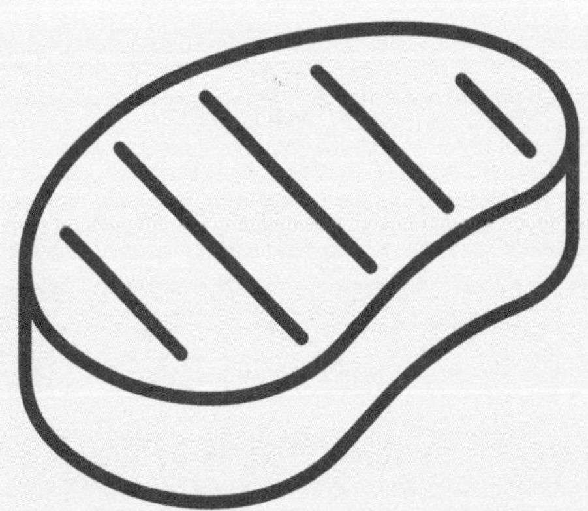

Lamb & Cannellini Soup

YIELD: 4 SERVINGS / **ACTIVE TIME:** 20 MINUTES / **TOTAL TIME:** 24 HOURS

2 TABLESPOONS EXTRA-VIRGIN OLIVE OIL

1 ONION, CHOPPED

2 GARLIC CLOVES, MINCED

1½ LBS. GROUND LAMB

3 CARROTS, PEELED AND CHOPPED

3 CELERY STALKS, CHOPPED

1 (14 OZ.) CAN OF STEWED TOMATOES, DRAINED

¼ CUP FINELY CHOPPED FRESH PARSLEY

2 TABLESPOONS FINELY CHOPPED FRESH THYME

½ LB. DRIED CANNELLINI BEANS, SOAKED OVERNIGHT AND DRAINED

6 CUPS CHICKEN STOCK (SEE PAGE 440)

½ LB. BABY SPINACH

¼ CUP SLICED KALAMATA OLIVES

SALT AND PEPPER, TO TASTE

FETA CHEESE, CRUMBLED, FOR GARNISH

1. Place the olive oil in a large saucepan and warm over medium heat. Add the onion and cook, stirring frequently, until it starts to soften, about 5 minutes. Stir in the garlic, cook for 2 minutes, and then add the lamb. Cook until it starts to brown, about 5 minutes, and add the carrots and celery.
2. Cook for 5 minutes, stir in the tomatoes, herbs, cannellini beans, and stock, and bring the soup to a boil. Reduce the heat to medium-low, cover the pan, and simmer until the beans are tender, about 1 hour.
3. Add the spinach and olives and cook until the spinach wilts, about 2 minutes. Season the soup with salt and pepper, ladle it into warmed bowls, and garnish each portion with feta cheese.

Lamb & Cannellini Soup

SEE PAGE 245

Fresh Cucumber & Lamb Soup

YIELD: 4 SERVINGS / **ACTIVE TIME:** 20 MINUTES / **TOTAL TIME:** 45 MINUTES

1 LB. LAMB LOIN, DICED

2 TABLESPOONS SOY SAUCE

2 TABLESPOONS MIRIN

1 TEASPOON SESAME OIL

4 CUPS CHICKEN STOCK (SEE PAGE 440)

1 LEMONGRASS STALK, CRUSHED

½ CUCUMBER, SLICED THIN

4 SCALLIONS, TRIMMED AND SLICED, WHITES AND GREENS SEPARATED

4 TEASPOONS RICE VINEGAR

SALT AND PEPPER, TO TASTE

FRESH CILANTRO, CHOPPED, FOR GARNISH

LIME WEDGES, FOR SERVING

1. Place the lamb, soy sauce, mirin, and sesame oil in a mixing bowl, stir to combine, and let the lamb marinate for 20 minutes.
2. Bring the stock and lemongrass to a boil in a medium pot. Reduce the heat so that the broth simmers, add the marinated lamb, and cook for 3 minutes.
3. Add the cucumber and scallion whites and cook until the lamb is medium-rare, 2 to 3 minutes. Stir in the vinegar and season with salt and pepper.
4. Ladle the soup into warmed bowls, garnish with the scallion greens and cilantro, and serve with lime wedges.

Italian Lamb Stew

YIELD: 4 TO 6 SERVINGS / **ACTIVE TIME:** 30 MINUTES / **TOTAL TIME:** 1 HOUR AND 30 MINUTES

2 TABLESPOONS EXTRA-VIRGIN OLIVE OIL

2 LBS. BONELESS LEG OF LAMB, DICED

4 GARLIC CLOVES, MINCED

¾ CUP RED WINE

2 CUPS CHICKEN STOCK (SEE PAGE 440)

3 (14 OZ.) CANS OF DICED TOMATOES, WITH THEIR LIQUID

2 TEASPOONS DRIED OREGANO

2 BAY LEAVES

6 POTATOES, PEELED AND FINELY DICED

2 CUPS CHOPPED GREEN BEANS

2 RED BELL PEPPERS, STEMMED, SEEDED, AND DICED

2 ZUCCHINI, SLICED THIN

¼ CUP FINELY CHOPPED FRESH PARSLEY

SALT AND PEPPER, TO TASTE

CRUSTY BREAD, FOR SERVING

1. Place the olive oil in a large pot and warm it over medium-high heat. Add the lamb and cook, stirring frequently, until it has browned, about 5 minutes. Add the garlic and cook, stirring frequently, for 2 minutes. Add the wine and cook, stirring occasionally, until it has reduced by half.
2. Add the stock, tomatoes, oregano, and bay leaves, reduce the heat so that the soup simmers, and cook until the lamb is tender, about 45 minutes.
3. Raise the heat to medium-high, add the potatoes, beans, bell peppers, and zucchini, and cook until the potatoes are tender, about 15 minutes. Remove the bay leaves from the soup, discard them, and stir in the parsley.
4. Season the soup with salt and pepper, ladle it into warmed bowls, and serve with crusty bread.

Lamb, Spinach & Lentil Stew

YIELD: 4 TO 6 SERVINGS / **ACTIVE TIME:** 20 MINUTES / **TOTAL TIME:** 45 MINUTES

2 TABLESPOONS EXTRA-VIRGIN OLIVE OIL

2 LBS. BONELESS LAMB SHOULDER, DICED

2 ONIONS, FINELY DICED

4 CARROTS, PEELED AND DICED

4 GARLIC CLOVES, MINCED

1½ CUPS RED LENTILS

6 CUPS CHICKEN STOCK (SEE PAGE 440)

2 (14 OZ.) CANS OF DICED TOMATOES, DRAINED

2 TEASPOONS FRESH THYME

1 TEASPOON FINELY CHOPPED FRESH SAGE

4 CUPS BABY SPINACH, CHOPPED

ZEST AND JUICE OF 2 LEMONS

SALT AND PEPPER, TO TASTE

RICOTTA CHEESE, FOR GARNISH

1. Place the olive oil in a medium pot and warm it over medium heat. Add the lamb and cook, stirring frequently, until it has browned, about 5 minutes.
2. Add the onions, carrots, and garlic and cook, stirring frequently, until the onion has softened, about 5 minutes. Add the lentils, stock, tomatoes, thyme, and sage and bring the soup to a boil.
3. Reduce the heat so that the soup simmers and cook until the lentils are tender, about 20 minutes.
4. Stir in the spinach, lemon zest, and lemon juice and season with salt and pepper. Cook until the spinach has wilted, about 2 minutes.
5. Ladle the soup into warmed bowls, garnish with ricotta cheese, and serve.

Mutton Soup

YIELD: 6 SERVINGS / **ACTIVE TIME:** 20 MINUTES / **TOTAL TIME:** 2 HOURS AND 15 MINUTES

2 LBS. BONELESS LEG OF MUTTON, DICED

2 CARROTS, PEELED AND DICED

1 ONION, FINELY DICED

2 LEEKS, TRIMMED, RINSED WELL, AND FINELY DICED

1 TABLESPOON PEARL BARLEY

8 CUPS WATER

SALT AND PEPPER, TO TASTE

FRESH PARSLEY, CHOPPED, FOR GARNISH

1. Bring all of the ingredients, except for the parsley, to a boil in a large pot. Reduce the heat so that the soup simmers, cover the pot, and cook until the mutton is tender, 1 to 2 hours.
2. Season the soup with salt and pepper and ladle it into warmed bowls. Garnish with parsley and serve.

South Indian Mutton Soup

YIELD: 4 TO 6 SERVINGS / **ACTIVE TIME:** 30 MINUTES / **TOTAL TIME:** 1 HOUR AND 15 MINUTES

¼ CUP EXTRA-VIRGIN OLIVE OIL

1½ LBS. BONELESS MUTTON SHOULDER, DICED

2 FRESH CURRY LEAVES

2 TEASPOONS BLACK PEPPERCORNS

2 TEASPOONS CUMIN SEEDS

2 TABLESPOONS FENNEL SEEDS

SEEDS OF 4 CARDAMOM PODS, CRUSHED

2 CINNAMON STICKS

4 WHOLE CLOVES

2 BAY LEAVES

8 CUPS LAMB STOCK (SEE PAGE 450)

4 SHALLOTS, FINELY DICED

4 GARLIC CLOVES, MINCED

1-INCH PIECE OF FRESH GINGER, PEELED AND MINCED

2 TOMATOES, FINELY DICED

½ TEASPOON TURMERIC

2 TEASPOONS GROUND CUMIN

2 TEASPOONS PAPRIKA

2 CUPS PEELED AND FINELY DICED POTATOES

SALT AND PEPPER, TO TASTE

FRESH CILANTRO, CHOPPED, FOR GARNISH

1. Place half of the olive oil in a large pot and warm it over medium heat. Add the mutton and cook, stirring frequently, until it has browned, about 5 minutes. Add the curry leaves, peppercorns, cumin seeds, fennel seeds, cardamom, cinnamon sticks, cloves, and bay leaves and cook, stirring continually, until the mixture is fragrant, about 3 minutes.
2. Add the stock and bring the soup to a boil. Reduce the heat so that the soup simmers and cook for 10 minutes.
3. Place the remaining olive oil in a medium skillet and warm it over medium heat. Add the shallots, garlic, and ginger and cook, stirring frequently, until the mixture is fragrant, about 3 minutes. Reduce the heat to low, add the tomatoes, turmeric, ground cumin, and paprika, and cook until the tomatoes have collapsed, about 10 minutes.
4. Add the contents of the skillet to the pot and bring the soup to a boil. Reduce the heat so that the soup simmers and cook for 15 minutes. Add the potatoes and cook until the mutton and potatoes are tender, about 20 minutes.
5. Season the soup with salt and pepper and ladle it into warmed bowls. Garnish with cilantro and serve.

Bulgarian Sour Lamb Soup

YIELD: 4 SERVINGS / **ACTIVE TIME:** 25 MINUTES / **TOTAL TIME:** 1 HOUR AND 35 MINUTES

- 2 TABLESPOONS EXTRA-VIRGIN OLIVE OIL
- 1 LB. BONELESS LAMB SHOULDER, DICED
- 1 ONION, FINELY DICED
- 2 TABLESPOONS ALL-PURPOSE FLOUR
- 1 TABLESPOON PAPRIKA
- 4 CUPS LAMB STOCK (SEE PAGE 450)
- 3 TABLESPOONS FINELY CHOPPED FRESH PARSLEY
- 4 SCALLIONS, TRIMMED AND SLICED THIN
- ¼ CUP FINELY CHOPPED FRESH DILL, PLUS MORE FOR GARNISH
- ¼ CUP LONG-GRAIN RICE
- 2 EGGS, BEATEN
- 2 TO 3 TABLESPOONS WHITE VINEGAR
- SALT AND PEPPER, TO TASTE

1. Place the olive oil in a medium pot and warm it over medium heat. Add the lamb and cook, stirring frequently, until it has browned, about 5 minutes. Add the onion and cook, stirring occasionally, until it has softened, about 5 minutes.
2. Add the flour and paprika and cook, stirring continually, for 2 minutes. Add the stock and stir until fully combined. Bring the soup to a simmer and cook for 10 minutes.
3. Tie the parsley, scallions, and dill together with kitchen twine. Add the bunch of herbs and rice to the pot and bring the soup to a boil.
4. Reduce the heat so that the soup simmers and cook until the lamb is tender, 30 to 40 minutes.
5. Remove the pot from heat, add the eggs and vinegar, and stir to combine. Remove the tied herbs from the pot, discard them, and season the soup with salt and pepper.
6. Ladle the soup into warmed bowls, garnish with additional dill, and serve.

Lamb Shank & Barley Soup

YIELD: 4 TO 6 SERVINGS / **ACTIVE TIME:** 30 MINUTES / **TOTAL TIME:** 2 HOURS

2 TABLESPOONS EXTRA-VIRGIN OLIVE OIL

2 LAMB SHANKS, TRIMMED

1 ONION, FINELY DICED

2 GARLIC CLOVES, MINCED

2 CARROTS, PEELED AND DICED

2 CELERY STALKS, FINELY DICED

1 LEEK, TRIMMED, RINSED WELL, AND FINELY DICED

½ CUP RED WINE

8 CUPS LAMB STOCK (SEE PAGE 450)

½ CUP PEARL BARLEY

1½ TABLESPOONS FINELY CHOPPED FRESH ROSEMARY

SALT AND PEPPER, TO TASTE

1. Place the olive oil in a large pot and warm it over medium heat. Add the lamb and cook, turning it as necessary, until it is browned all over, about 5 minutes. Remove the lamb from the pot and set it aside.
2. Add the onion, garlic, carrots, celery, and leek to the pot and cook, stirring occasionally, until the onion has softened, about 5 minutes. Add the wine and cook, stirring occasionally, for 5 minutes. Add the lamb, stock, barley, and rosemary and bring the soup to a boil.
3. Reduce the heat so that the soup simmers, cover the pot, and cook until the lamb is very tender, about 1 hour and 30 minutes.
4. Remove the lamb from the pot, remove the meat from the shanks, and add the lamb meat to the pot.
5. Season the soup with salt and pepper, ladle it into warmed bowls, and serve.

Lamb & Potato Stew

YIELD: 4 TO 6 SERVINGS / **ACTIVE TIME:** 30 MINUTES / **TOTAL TIME:** 2 HOURS

⅓ CUP ALL-PURPOSE FLOUR

2 LBS. BONELESS LEG OF LAMB, DICED

¼ CUP UNSALTED BUTTER

1 ONION, FINELY DICED

1 CARROT, PEELED AND DICED

½ LEEK, TRIMMED, RINSED WELL, AND FINELY DICED

½ LB. CREAMER POTATOES, HALVED

5 GARLIC CLOVES, MINCED

1 CUP RED WINE

2 CUPS LAMB STOCK (SEE PAGE 450)

2 BAY LEAVES

2 TABLESPOONS FRESH THYME

1 TABLESPOON EXTRA-VIRGIN OLIVE OIL

½ LB. LAMB OR PORK SAUSAGE, SLICED

½ CUP PITTED AND CHOPPED KALAMATA OLIVES

1 TABLESPOON SHERRY VINEGAR

SALT AND PEPPER, TO TASTE

1. Preheat the oven to 250°F. Place the flour and lamb in a mixing bowl and toss until the lamb is evenly coated. Place the butter in a Dutch oven and melt it over medium heat. Add the lamb and cook, stirring frequently, until it has browned, about 5 minutes.
2. Add the onion, carrot, leek, potatoes, and garlic and cook, stirring occasionally, until the onion has softened, about 5 minutes. Add the wine and cook, stirring occasionally, for 5 minutes. Add the stock, bay leaves, and thyme and bring the soup to a boil.
3. Cover the Dutch oven, place it in the oven, and cook, stirring every 15 minutes, for 1 hour.
4. Place the olive oil in a small skillet and warm it over medium-high heat. Add the sausage and cook, stirring frequently, until it has browned, about 5 minutes.
5. Remove the Dutch oven from the oven, uncover it, and increase the oven's temperature to 325°F. Add the sausage, olives, and vinegar to the Dutch oven, place it in the oven, and cook until the lamb is tender, about 20 minutes.
6. Remove the Dutch oven from the oven and skim off any excess fat. Remove the thyme and bay leaves from the Dutch oven, discard them, and season with salt and pepper.
7. Ladle the stew into warmed bowls and serve.

Doenjang Jjigae

YIELD: 6 SERVINGS / **ACTIVE TIME:** 15 MINUTES / **TOTAL TIME:** 30 MINUTES

1 TABLESPOON CANOLA OIL, PLUS MORE AS NEEDED

6 OZ. BEEF BRISKET, TRIMMED AND SLICED THIN

3 GARLIC CLOVES, MINCED

⅔ CUP PEELED AND DICED POTATO

1 CUP DICED ONION

⅓ CUP DOENJANG

1 TEASPOON GOCHUJANG (OPTIONAL)

½ CUP SLICED BUTTON MUSHROOMS

1 CUP DICED ZUCCHINI

1 CUP CUBED MEDIUM-FIRM TOFU

1 GREEN CHILE PEPPER, STEMMED AND SEEDED, SLICED

1 SCALLION, TRIMMED AND CHOPPED

SALT, TO TASTE

RICE, COOKED, FOR SERVING

1. Place the canola oil in a Dutch oven and warm it over medium-high heat. Add the beef and garlic and stir-fry until the beef is no longer pink, about 2 minutes.
2. Add 2 cups of water, cover the pot, and reduce the heat to medium-low. Cook for 10 to 12 minutes, making sure not to let it come to a boil.
3. Add the potato, onion, doenjang, and gochujang (if desired), cover the pot, and simmer for 5 minutes.
4. Add the mushrooms and zucchini, cover the pot, and simmer for 5 to 6 minutes.
5. Add the tofu, chile, and scallion and simmer, uncovered, until the stew starts to bubble, the tofu has softened, and the potato is tender.
6. Taste and adjust the seasoning as necessary. Ladle the stew over rice and serve.

Lamb & Rice Soup

YIELD: 6 SERVINGS / **ACTIVE TIME:** 30 MINUTES / **TOTAL TIME:** 2 HOURS AND 30 MINUTES

2 MARROW BONES

4 CUPS WATER, PLUS MORE AS NEEDED

1 LB. BONELESS LAMB SHOULDER, TRIMMED AND DICED

SALT AND PEPPER, TO TASTE

⅓ CUP LONG-GRAIN RICE, RINSED

3 TABLESPOONS UNSALTED BUTTER

3 GARLIC CLOVES, MINCED

3 TABLESPOONS WHITE WINE VINEGAR

3 TABLESPOONS FINELY CHOPPED FRESH PARSLEY

PITA BREAD (SEE PAGE 460), TOASTED, FOR SERVING

1. Bring 4 cups of water to a boil in a large pot. Add the marrow bones, let the water return to a boil, and cook for 5 minutes. Remove the bones from the pot, let them cool, and discard the water in the pot.
2. Place the water in the pot, bring to a boil, and add the blanched marrow bones to the pot.
3. Reduce the heat so that the water simmers, add the lamb, and cook, adding water as necessary to ensure that the bones are submerged, until the lamb is tender, about 2 hours. Season the soup with salt and pepper.
4. Remove the marrow bones from the pot and discard them. Add the rice and cook until it is tender, 10 to 15 minutes.
5. Place the butter in a small skillet and melt it over low heat. Add the garlic and cook, stirring continually, until it is fragrant, about 3 minutes. Add the vinegar and bring the mixture to a boil.
6. Divide the garlic mixture among warmed bowls and ladle the soup over the top. Garnish with parsley and serve with the Pita Bread.

Mutton & Barley Stew

YIELD: 4 SERVINGS / **ACTIVE TIME:** 20 MINUTES / **TOTAL TIME:** 1 HOUR AND 30 MINUTES

4 CUPS LAMB STOCK (SEE PAGE 450)

1 LB. BONELESS LEG OF MUTTON, DICED

1 ONION, FINELY DICED

2 GARLIC CLOVES, MINCED

2 BAY LEAVES

4 WHOLE CLOVES

4 SPRIGS OF FRESH THYME

1 POTATO, PEELED AND FINELY DICED

½ CUP BARLEY

2 TABLESPOONS FINELY CHOPPED FRESH PARSLEY

SALT AND PEPPER, TO TASTE

1. Place the stock, mutton, onion, garlic, bay leaves, cloves, and thyme in a large pot and bring to a boil. Reduce the heat so that the soup simmers and cook until the mutton is tender, about 45 minutes.
2. Remove the bay leaves, thyme, and cloves from the pot and discard them. Add the potato and barley, cover the pot, and cook until the barley and potatoes are tender, about 15 minutes.
3. Stir in the parsley and season with salt and pepper. Ladle the soup into warmed bowls and serve.

Irish Country Soup

YIELD: 4 SERVINGS / **ACTIVE TIME:** 30 MINUTES / **TOTAL TIME:** 1 HOUR AND 15 MINUTES

1 TABLESPOON EXTRA-VIRGIN OLIVE OIL

1 LB. LAMB LOIN, DICED

1 ONION, FINELY DICED

2 LEEKS, TRIMMED, RINSED WELL, AND FINELY DICED

2 CARROTS, PEELED AND DICED

4 CUPS BEEF STOCK (SEE PAGE 442)

2 POTATOES, PEELED AND DICED

4 TEASPOONS FRESH THYME

1 TABLESPOON UNSALTED BUTTER

SALT AND PEPPER, TO TASTE

FRESH PARSLEY, CHOPPED, FOR GARNISH

1. Place the olive oil in a medium pot and warm it over medium-high heat. Add the lamb and cook, stirring frequently, until it has browned, about 5 minutes. Add the onion, leeks, and carrots and cook, stirring occasionally, until they have softened, about 5 minutes.
2. Add the stock and bring the soup to a boil. Reduce the heat so that the soup simmers and cook until the lamb is tender, about 45 minutes.
3. Add the potatoes and thyme and cook until the potatoes are tender, about 15 minutes. Remove the pot from heat and let the soup stand for 5 minutes.
4. Skim off the excess fat, strain the soup into a clean pot through a fine-mesh sieve, and reserve the meat and vegetables.
5. Add the butter, meat, and vegetables to the pot, stir to combine, and season with salt and pepper.
6. Ladle the soup into warmed bowls, garnish with parsley, and serve.

POULTRY

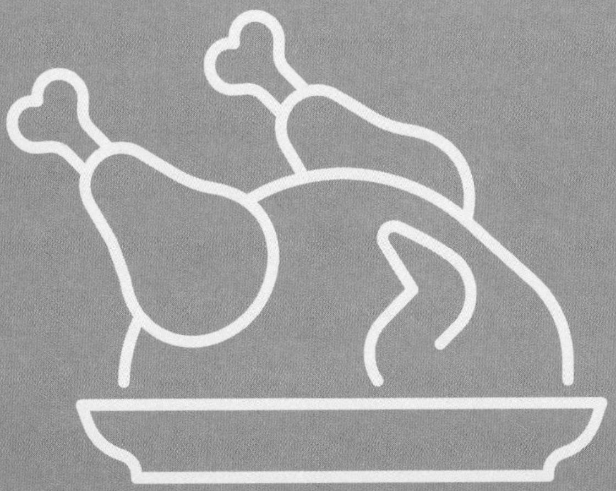

Chicken Consommé

YIELD: 4 SERVINGS / **ACTIVE TIME:** 30 MINUTES / **TOTAL TIME:** 1 HOUR AND 30 MINUTES

2 CELERY STALKS, FINELY DICED

1 CUP FINELY DICED PARSNIPS

3 CARROTS, PEELED AND DICED

1 ONION, FINELY DICED

½ LB. LEAN GROUND CHICKEN

1 TOMATO, FINELY DICED

6 CUPS CHICKEN STOCK (SEE PAGE 440)

SACHET D'ÉPICES (SEE PAGE 465), 1 WHOLE CLOVE AND 1 ALLSPICE BERRY ADDED

5 EGG WHITES, BEATEN

SALT AND PEPPER, TO TASTE

FRESH CHIVES, CHOPPED, FOR GARNISH

1. Bring water to a boil in a medium pot. Add the celery, parsnips, carrots, and onion and cook until they have softened, about 5 minutes. Remove the vegetables from the pot, transfer them to a colander, and let them cool and dry.
2. Place the chicken, tomato, stock, Sachet d'Épices, and egg whites in a large pot and stir to combine. Bring to a simmer and cook for 45 minutes.
3. Strain the broth into a clean pot through a fine-mesh sieve, add the cooked vegetables, and bring the soup to a boil. Remove the pot from heat and season with salt and pepper.
4. Ladle the soup into warmed bowls, garnish with chives, and serve.

Thai Chicken & Coconut Soup

YIELD: 4 SERVINGS / **ACTIVE TIME:** 15 MINUTES / **TOTAL TIME:** 30 MINUTES

2 TABLESPOONS EXTRA-VIRGIN OLIVE OIL

2 BONELESS, SKINLESS CHICKEN BREASTS, DICED

1 ONION, FINELY DICED

4 CUPS CHICKEN STOCK (SEE PAGE 440)

2-INCH PIECE OF FRESH GINGER, PEELED AND MINCED

2 THAI CHILE PEPPERS, STEMMED, SEEDED, AND FINELY DICED

2 LEMONGRASS STALKS, HALVED AND CRUSHED

4 CARROTS, PEELED AND FINELY DICED

2 (14 OZ.) CANS OF COCONUT MILK

3 TABLESPOONS FISH SAUCE

JUICE OF 1 LIME

SALT AND PEPPER, TO TASTE

FRESH THAI BASIL, FINELY CHOPPED, FOR GARNISH

1. Place the olive oil in a medium pot and warm it over medium heat. Add the chicken and onion and cook, stirring occasionally, until the chicken has browned, about 5 minutes. Add the stock, ginger, chiles, lemongrass, and carrots and bring to a boil.
2. Reduce the heat so that the soup simmers and cook for 5 minutes. Add the coconut milk and cook until the carrots are tender, about 5 minutes.
3. Remove the lemongrass from the pot and discard it. Stir in the fish sauce and lime juice and season with salt and pepper.
4. Ladle the soup into warmed bowls, garnish with Thai basil, and serve.

Tuscan Chicken & White Bean Stew

YIELD: 6 SERVINGS / **ACTIVE TIME:** 45 MINUTES / **TOTAL TIME:** 24 HOURS

1 LB. DRIED CANNELLINI BEANS, SOAKED OVERNIGHT

2 LBS. CHICKEN THIGHS, BONES AND SKIN REMOVED, BONES RESERVED

2 BAY LEAVES

1 TABLESPOON KOSHER SALT, PLUS MORE TO TASTE

2 SPRIGS OF FRESH ROSEMARY

BLACK PEPPER, TO TASTE

2 TABLESPOONS EXTRA-VIRGIN OLIVE OIL, PLUS MORE TO TASTE

1 YELLOW ONION, DICED

3 CARROTS, PEELED AND DICED

2 CELERY STALKS, DICED

1 YELLOW BELL PEPPER, STEMMED, SEEDED, AND DICED

1 ORANGE BELL PEPPER, STEMMED, SEEDED, AND DICED

3 GARLIC CLOVES, MINCED

1 TEASPOON RED PEPPER FLAKES

4 SMALL ROMA TOMATOES, DICED

2 TABLESPOONS FINELY CHOPPED FRESH SAGE

1½ OZ. ASIAGO CHEESE, GRATED

¼ CUP FRESH BASIL LEAVES, CHOPPED

1. Drain the cannellini beans and rinse them. Place them in a Dutch oven, cover with water, and cook over medium heat. Add the chicken bones, bay leaves, salt, and rosemary. Cover and cook, stirring occasionally, until the beans are tender and starting to fall apart, about 1 hour.
2. While the beans are cooking, season the chicken with salt and pepper and let it rest at room temperature for about 20 minutes.
3. When the beans are done, drain them, reserve the cooking liquid, and transfer the beans to a bowl. Remove the chicken bones, rosemary sprigs, and bay leaves and discard them.
4. Place the Dutch oven back on the stove and add the olive oil. Warm it over medium heat and then add the chicken. Cook until the chicken is browned all over and cooked through, 10 to 12 minutes, turning it over once. Remove the chicken from the pot and let it cool. When the chicken is cool enough to handle, dice the chicken.
5. Place the onion, carrots, celery, bell peppers, garlic, red pepper flakes, tomatoes, and sage in the pot and cook until the vegetables are tender and have released their juices, about 20 minutes.
6. While the vegetables are cooking, transfer the beans to a blender and puree until smooth, adding the reserved cooking liquid as needed to get the desired consistency. Place the puree in the pot and then stir in the Asiago and basil. Season the stew with salt and pepper and cook until the cheese has melted, 7 to 10 minutes.
7. Return the chicken to the pot and cook until it is warmed through. Drizzle olive oil over the stew, ladle it into warmed bowls, and serve.

Chicken Stew with Potatoes & Radishes

YIELD: 4 SERVINGS / **ACTIVE TIME:** 30 MINUTES / **TOTAL TIME:** 2 HOURS AND 30 MINUTES

4 CHICKEN LEGS

SALT AND PEPPER, TO TASTE

2 TABLESPOONS EXTRA-VIRGIN OLIVE OIL, PLUS MORE TO TASTE

1 LARGE ONION, CHOPPED

5 GARLIC CLOVES, SLICED THIN

2 TABLESPOONS HUNGARIAN PAPRIKA (HOT OR SWEET), PLUS MORE TO TASTE

1 (28 OZ.) CAN OF WHOLE PEELED TOMATOES, WITH THEIR LIQUID

3 CUPS CHICKEN STOCK (SEE PAGE 440), PLUS MORE AS NEEDED

1½ LBS. NEW POTATOES

½ LEMON

¾ CUP SOUR CREAM, FOR SERVING

6 RADISHES, SLICED THIN, FOR SERVING

1. Season the chicken legs generously with salt. Place the olive oil in a large Dutch oven and warm it over medium-high heat. Working in two batches, add the chicken and cook until the skin is golden brown, 8 to 10 minutes. Transfer the chicken to a plate and set it aside.
2. Add the onion and cook, stirring occasionally, until it is browned, 8 to 10 minutes. Add the garlic and cook, stirring frequently, until softened, about 1 minute. Add the paprika and cook, stirring continually, until fragrant, about 30 seconds.
3. Add the tomatoes and cook, breaking them up with a wooden spoon until no pieces are bigger than ½ inch. Bring the mixture to a simmer and cook until the liquid in the pan has thickened slightly, 6 to 8 minutes.
4. Add the stock, potatoes, and chicken and return to a simmer. Cook, stirring occasionally, until the chicken is very tender and the potatoes are creamy, about 1½ hours. Add more stock to the pot as necessary to keep the potatoes submerged. Remove the pot from heat and season the stew with salt and paprika.
5. Squeeze the lemon into a small bowl and stir in the sour cream. Season the mixture with salt. In another small bowl, combine the radishes with a pinch of salt and toss to coat.
6. To serve, ladle the stew into warmed bowls, season each portion generously with pepper, and drizzle some olive oil over the top. Serve with the sour cream and radishes.

Chicken Tortilla Soup

YIELD: 6 SERVINGS / **ACTIVE TIME:** 30 MINUTES / **TOTAL TIME:** 1 HOUR AND 45 MINUTES

8 CORN TORTILLAS

3 TABLESPOONS EXTRA-VIRGIN OLIVE OIL

2 TABLESPOONS KOSHER SALT, PLUS MORE TO TASTE

3 GARLIC CLOVES, MINCED

6 BONELESS, SKINLESS CHICKEN THIGHS

½ LARGE YELLOW ONION, DICED

1 POBLANO CHILE PEPPER, STEMMED, SEEDED, AND DICED

1 ANAHEIM CHILE PEPPER, STEMMED, SEEDED, AND DICED

4 PLUM TOMATOES, DICED

2 TABLESPOONS ADOBO SAUCE

1 TABLESPOON CUMIN

2 DRIED CHILES DE ÁRBOL, STEMMED, SEEDED, AND MINCED

4 CUPS CHICKEN STOCK (SEE PAGE 440)

1 CUP WATER

COTIJA CHEESE, FOR GARNISH

FRESH CILANTRO, CHOPPED, FOR GARNISH

1. Preheat the oven to 375°F. Cut six of the tortillas in half and cut each half into small strips. Line a baking sheet with parchment paper and place the tortilla strips on the pan. Brush the strips with 1 tablespoon of the olive oil and then season with salt. Place the pan in the oven and bake until the tortilla strips are crispy, 15 to 20 minutes. Remove the crispy tortilla strips from the oven and set them aside.
2. Place the remaining olive oil in a medium saucepan and warm it over medium-high heat. Add the garlic and cook, stirring frequently, for 2 minutes.
3. Add the chicken to the pan and sear until it is browned on both sides, about 8 minutes, turning it over once. Remove the chicken from the pan and set it aside. The chicken will cook further in the soup, so don't worry if it's not cooked through.
4. Add the onion, fresh chiles, tomatoes, adobo sauce, cumin, and dried chiles to the pan and cook, stirring occasionally, until the tomatoes start to collapse, 10 to 15 minutes.
5. Return the chicken to the pan. Add the salt, stock, and water and simmer the soup until the chicken comes apart when pressed against the side of the pan with a wooden spoon, about 1 hour.
6. Add the remaining tortillas and cook, stirring occasionally, until they dissolve, about 10 minutes.
7. Ladle the soup into warmed bowls, garnish with the cotija cheese, cilantro, and crispy tortilla strips, and serve.

Harira

YIELD: 6 SERVINGS / **ACTIVE TIME:** 30 MINUTES / **TOTAL TIME:** 1 HOUR

3 TABLESPOONS UNSALTED BUTTER

1½ LBS. BONELESS, SKINLESS CHICKEN THIGHS

SALT AND PEPPER, TO TASTE

1 LARGE ONION, FINELY DICED

5 GARLIC CLOVES, MINCED

1-INCH PIECE OF FRESH GINGER, PEELED AND GRATED

2 TEASPOONS TURMERIC

1 TEASPOON CUMIN

½ TEASPOON CINNAMON

⅛ TEASPOON CAYENNE PEPPER

¾ CUP FINELY CHOPPED FRESH CILANTRO

½ CUP FINELY CHOPPED FRESH PARSLEY

4 CUPS CHICKEN STOCK (SEE PAGE 440)

4 CUPS WATER

1 (14 OZ.) CAN OF CHICKPEAS, DRAINED AND RINSED

1 CUP BROWN LENTILS, PICKED OVER AND RINSED

1 (28 OZ.) CAN OF CRUSHED TOMATOES

½ CUP VERMICELLI, BROKEN INTO 2-INCH PIECES

2 TABLESPOONS FRESH LEMON JUICE, PLUS MORE TO TASTE

1. Place the butter in a Dutch oven and melt it over medium-high heat. Season the chicken thighs with salt and pepper, place them in the pot, and cook until browned on both sides, about 8 minutes. Remove the chicken from the pot and set it on a plate.
2. Add the onion and cook, stirring occasionally, until it starts to brown, about 8 minutes. Add the garlic and ginger and cook until fragrant, about 1 minute. Stir in the turmeric, cumin, cinnamon, and cayenne pepper and cook for 1 minute. Add ½ cup of the cilantro and ¼ cup of the parsley and cook for 1 minute.
3. Stir in the stock, water, chickpeas, and lentils and bring the soup to a simmer. Return the chicken to the pot, reduce the heat to medium-low, partially cover the Dutch oven, and gently simmer, stirring occasionally, until the lentils are just tender, about 20 minutes.
4. Add the tomatoes and vermicelli and simmer, stirring occasionally, until the pasta is tender, about 10 minutes.
5. Stir in the lemon juice and the remaining cilantro and parsley. Taste, adjust the seasoning as necessary, and enjoy.

Chicken & Tomato Stew

YIELD: 4 SERVINGS / **ACTIVE TIME:** 45 MINUTES / **TOTAL TIME:** 3 HOURS TO 24 HOURS

4 BONE-IN, SKIN-ON CHICKEN LEGS

SALT, TO TASTE

¼ CUP EXTRA-VIRGIN OLIVE OIL

1 LARGE ONION, SLICED THIN

6 GARLIC CLOVES, HALVED

2 TABLESPOONS HONEY

1 TABLESPOON TOMATO PASTE

¾ TEASPOON TURMERIC

½ TEASPOON CINNAMON

1 (14 OZ.) CAN OF WHOLE PEELED TOMATOES, WITH THEIR JUICES

3 CUPS CHICKEN STOCK (SEE PAGE 440)

1 LEMON

1½ TEASPOONS SUGAR

1 TABLESPOON TOASTED SESAME SEEDS, TO TOP

½ CUP TORN FRESH MINT LEAVES, TO TOP

PITA BREAD (SEE PAGE 460), FOR SERVING

1. Pat the chicken dry and season it with salt. Let the chicken sit at room temperature for at least 15 minutes and up to 1 hour, or cover and refrigerate for up to 24 hours.
2. Place 2 tablespoons of the olive oil in a large Dutch oven and warm it over medium-high heat. Add the chicken and cook until it is a deep golden brown on both sides, about 12 minutes, adjusting the heat as necessary to avoid burning.
3. Transfer the chicken to a plate, leaving the drippings in the pan.
4. Place the onion in the pot and cook, stirring frequently, until it has softened, 6 to 8 minutes. Add the garlic and cook, stirring frequently, until the onion begins to brown around the edges, about 3 minutes. Stir in the honey, tomato paste, turmeric, and cinnamon and cook until fragrant, about 2 minutes. Add the tomatoes and their juices and smash the tomatoes with a wooden spoon until they break down into pieces no larger than 1 inch.
5. Return the chicken to the pot, add the stock (it should barely cover the chicken), and bring to a simmer. Reduce the heat to low, partially cover the pot, and simmer until the chicken is tender and the sauce has thickened, about 1 hour.
6. While the chicken is simmering, trim the top and bottom from the lemon and cut it into quarters. Remove the seeds and the white pith in the center. Slice the quarters crosswise into quarter moons.
7. Place the lemon pieces in a medium skillet, cover them with water, and bring to a boil. Cook for 3 minutes, drain, and pat dry with paper towels. Transfer the lemon pieces to a small bowl, sprinkle the sugar over them, and toss to coat.
8. Wipe out the skillet and warm the remaining olive oil over medium-high heat. Arrange the lemon pieces in a single layer in the skillet. Cook, turning halfway through, until they are deeply browned all over, about 3 minutes. Return the lemon to the bowl and season with salt. Ladle the stew into bowls, top with the caramelized lemon, sesame seeds, and mint, and serve with the Pita Bread.

Chicken & Shrimp Gumbo

YIELD: 4 SERVINGS / **ACTIVE TIME:** 30 MINUTES / **TOTAL TIME:** 1 HOUR

⅓ CUP ALL-PURPOSE FLOUR

1 TABLESPOON EXTRA-VIRGIN OLIVE OIL

6 OZ. ANDOUILLE SAUSAGE, CHOPPED

½ LB. BONELESS, SKINLESS CHICKEN BREASTS, DICED

1 ONION, FINELY DICED

¾ CUP FINELY DICED GREEN BELL PEPPER

¾ CUP FINELY DICED CELERY

2 SCALLIONS, TRIMMED AND SLICED

2 GARLIC CLOVES, MINCED

½ CUP THINLY SLICED OKRA

1 TOMATO, FINELY DICED

6 CUPS CHICKEN STOCK (SEE PAGE 440)

½ CUP LONG-GRAIN RICE

1 BAY LEAF

¼ TEASPOON DRIED OREGANO

¼ TEASPOON ONION POWDER

⅛ TEASPOON DRIED THYME

⅛ TEASPOON DRIED BASIL

¾ LB. SHRIMP, SHELLED, DEVEINED, AND FINELY DICED

SALT AND PEPPER, TO TASTE

1. Preheat the oven to 375°F. Place the flour on a baking sheet, place the pan in the oven, and toast until the flour is dark brown, 5 to 8 minutes. Remove the pan from the oven and let the flour cool.
2. Place the olive oil in a medium pot and warm it over medium heat. Add the sausage and chicken and cook, stirring frequently, until they have browned, about 5 minutes. Add the onion, bell pepper, celery, scallions, garlic, okra, and tomato and cook, stirring occasionally, until the vegetables have softened, about 8 minutes.
3. Add the toasted flour and cook, stirring continually, for 4 minutes. Add the stock, stir until well combined, and bring the soup to a boil.
4. Reduce the heat so that the soup simmers, add the rice, bay leaf, oregano, onion powder, thyme, and basil, and cook until the rice is tender, 15 to 20 minutes.
5. Add the shrimp and cook until they are cooked through, about 3 minutes.
6. Season the soup with salt and pepper, ladle it into warmed bowls, and serve.

Chicken Curry Soup

YIELD: 4 SERVINGS / **ACTIVE TIME:** 20 MINUTES / **TOTAL TIME:** 45 MINUTES

¼ CUP UNSALTED BUTTER

1 ONION, FINELY DICED

2 CARROTS, PEELED AND DICED

2 CELERY STALKS, FINELY DICED

2 TABLESPOONS ALL-PURPOSE FLOUR

1 TABLESPOON CURRY POWDER

1 TABLESPOON POPPY SEEDS

1 TEASPOON CUMIN

4 CUPS CHICKEN STOCK (SEE PAGE 440)

⅓ CUP LONG-GRAIN RICE

1 APPLE, PEELED, CORED, AND FINELY DICED

1 CUP CHOPPED COOKED CHICKEN

¼ TEASPOON DRIED THYME

½ CUP HEAVY CREAM

SALT AND PEPPER, TO TASTE

FRESH CILANTRO, FOR GARNISH

CASHEWS, FOR GARNISH

1. Place the butter in a large pot and melt it over medium heat. Add the onion, carrots, and celery and cook, stirring occasionally, until they have softened, about 5 minutes. Add the flour, curry, poppy seeds, and cumin and cook, stirring continually, for 2 minutes.
2. Add the stock and bring the soup to a boil. Reduce the heat so that the soup simmers, add the rice, and cook until it is tender, about 15 minutes.
3. Add the apple, chicken, and thyme and cook for 10 minutes. Stir in the cream and season with salt and pepper.
4. Ladle the soup into warmed bowls, garnish with cilantro and cashews, and serve.

Turkey & Couscous Soup

YIELD: 4 SERVINGS / **ACTIVE TIME:** 20 MINUTES / **TOTAL TIME:** 1 HOUR

2 TABLESPOONS EXTRA-VIRGIN OLIVE OIL

1 ONION, FINELY DICED

2 GARLIC CLOVES, MINCED

2 CARROTS, PEELED AND DICED

2 CELERY STALKS, FINELY DICED

⅓ CUP FINELY DICED RED BELL PEPPER

⅓ CUP FINELY DICED GREEN BELL PEPPER

6 CUPS TURKEY STOCK (SEE PAGE 446)

ZEST AND JUICE OF 1 LEMON

½ CUP ISRAELI COUSCOUS

2 CUPS CHOPPED COOKED TURKEY

4 CUPS SPINACH

SALT AND PEPPER, TO TASTE

1. Place the olive oil in a medium pot and warm it over medium heat. Add the onion and cook, stirring occasionally, until it has softened, about 5 minutes. Add the garlic and cook, stirring frequently, for 2 minutes. Add the carrots, celery, and bell peppers and cook, stirring occasionally, until they are tender, about 5 minutes.
2. Add the stock, lemon zest, and couscous and bring the soup to a boil. Reduce the heat so that the soup simmers and cook for 15 minutes.
3. Stir in the turkey and lemon juice and cook for 5 minutes. Add the spinach and cook until it has wilted, about 2 minutes.
4. Season the soup with salt and pepper, ladle it into warmed bowls, and serve.

Turkey & Couscous Soup

SEE PAGE 277

Aromatic Duck Broth with Egg Noodles

YIELD: 4 SERVINGS / **ACTIVE TIME:** 45 MINUTES / **TOTAL TIME:** 1 HOUR AND 30 MINUTES

2 DUCK BREASTS

2-INCH PIECE OF FRESH GINGER, PEELED AND MINCED

2 GARLIC CLOVES, MINCED

2 LEMONGRASS STALKS, CRUSHED

8 CUPS DUCK STOCK (SEE PAGE 451)

2 TABLESPOONS FISH SAUCE

1 TABLESPOON SOY SAUCE

1 TEASPOON FIVE-SPICE POWDER

2 TEASPOONS SUGAR

4 SCALLIONS, TRIMMED AND SLICED, WHITES AND GREENS SEPARATED

SALT AND PEPPER, TO TASTE

2 BOK CHOY, TRIMMED AND HALVED

½ LB. THIN EGG NOODLES

RED CHILE PEPPERS, SLICED THIN, FOR GARNISH

1. Place the duck breasts in a large pot, skin side down, and cook over low heat until the skin is crispy, about 10 minutes. Flip the breasts over and cook for 5 minutes. Remove the breasts from the pot, thinly slice the meat, and set it aside.
2. Add the ginger and garlic to the pot and cook, stirring continually, for 1 minute. Add the lemongrass and stock and bring the soup to a boil. Reduce the heat so that the soup simmers, add the fish sauce, soy sauce, five-spice powder, sugar, and scallion whites, and cook for 30 minutes, skimming off any fat that rises to the surface.
3. Strain the broth into a clean pot through a fine-mesh sieve and bring it to a boil. Reduce the heat so that the broth simmers and season it with salt and pepper.
4. Bring water to a boil in a medium pot. Add the bok choy and cook for 3 minutes. Remove the bok choy from the pot with a strainer, transfer it to a colander, and let it drain.
5. Add the noodles to the boiling water and cook until they are al dente, 6 to 8 minutes. Drain the noodles and divide them among warmed bowls. Top with the bok choy and sliced duck and ladle the broth over the top. Garnish with the scallion greens and chiles and serve.

Chicken Noodle Soup

YIELD: 4 SERVINGS / **ACTIVE TIME:** 20 MINUTES / **TOTAL TIME:** 1 HOUR

1 TABLESPOON EXTRA-VIRGIN OLIVE OIL

½ ONION, FINELY DICED

1 CARROT, PEELED AND DICED

1 CELERY STALK, FINELY DICED

1 TEASPOON FRESH THYME

4 CUPS CHICKEN STOCK (SEE PAGE 440)

1½ CUPS WIDE EGG NOODLES

1 COOKED CHICKEN BREAST, DICED

SALT AND PEPPER, TO TASTE

1. Place the olive oil in a medium pot and warm it over medium heat. Add the onion and cook, stirring occasionally, until it has softened, about 5 minutes. Add the carrot and celery and cook, stirring occasionally, until they are tender, 5 to 10 minutes.
2. Add the thyme and stock and bring the soup to a boil. Reduce the heat so that the soup simmers and cook for 20 minutes.
3. Bring the soup back to a boil, add the noodles, and cook until the noodles are al dente, 8 to 10 minutes. Add the chicken to the soup, season with salt and pepper, and cook until it is warmed through.
4. Ladle the soup into warmed bowls and serve.

Chicken Noodle Soup

SEE PAGE 281

Cream of Pheasant & Mushroom Soup

YIELD: 4 SERVINGS / **ACTIVE TIME:** 30 MINUTES / **TOTAL TIME:** 3 HOURS AND 15 MINUTES

2½-LB. PHEASANT, LEGS SEPARATED

2 TABLESPOONS UNSALTED BUTTER

1 CARROT, PEELED AND DICED

1 ONION, FINELY DICED

2 CELERY STALKS, FINELY DICED

1 TABLESPOON FINELY CHOPPED FRESH ROSEMARY

1 TABLESPOON FRESH THYME

2 GARLIC CLOVES, MINCED

1 CUP WHITE PORT

1 LB. PORTOBELLO MUSHROOMS, FINELY DICED

1 CUP HEAVY CREAM

SALT AND PEPPER, TO TASTE

FRESH CHIVES, CHOPPED, FOR GARNISH

1. Preheat the oven to 400°F. Place the pheasant in a baking dish, place the dish in the oven, and cook until it is golden brown and cooked through (the interior is 165°F), about 45 minutes. Remove the dish from the oven, let the pheasant cool, and set it aside.
2. Place the butter in a large pot and melt it over medium heat. Add the carrot, onion, celery, rosemary, thyme, and garlic and cook, stirring occasionally, until the vegetables have softened, about 5 minutes. Add the port and cook, stirring occasionally, for 5 minutes.
3. Add the pheasant and enough water to cover it, bring the broth to a simmer, and cook for 2 hours. Strain the broth through a fine-mesh sieve and set it aside.
4. Place 6 cups of the pheasant broth and the mushrooms in a food processor and pulse until smooth, adding more broth as necessary. Place the mixture in a clean pot and bring it to a boil.
5. Reduce the heat so that the soup simmers and cook for 10 minutes. Stir in the cream, return the soup to a simmer, and season the soup with salt and pepper.
6. Cut up the pheasant breasts and stir them into the soup. Cook until they are warmed through, about 5 minutes.
7. Ladle the soup into warmed bowls, garnish with chives, and serve.

Duck a l'Orange Soup

YIELD: 4 SERVINGS / **ACTIVE TIME:** 45 MINUTES / **TOTAL TIME:** 1 HOUR AND 45 MINUTES

4-LB. DUCK, BROKEN DOWN INTO BREASTS AND LEGS

1 ONION, FINELY DICED

2 CARROTS, PEELED AND DICED

2 CELERY STALKS, FINELY DICED

1 GARLIC CLOVE, MINCED

1 CUP WHITE WINE

6 CUPS DUCK STOCK (SEE PAGE 451)

ZEST AND JUICE OF 2 ORANGES

1 TABLESPOON HONEY

2 TEASPOONS FRESH THYME

2 TEASPOONS FINELY CHOPPED FRESH MARJORAM

½ TEASPOON GROUND CORIANDER

½ TEASPOON CUMIN

SALT AND PEPPER, TO TASTE

FRESH CHIVES, CHOPPED, FOR GARNISH

1. Place the duck breasts in a large pot, skin side down, and cook over low heat until the skin is crispy, about 10 minutes. Flip the breasts over and cook for 5 minutes. Remove the breasts from the pot and set them aside.
2. Raise the heat to medium, add the onion, carrots, celery, and garlic to the pot, and cook, stirring occasionally, until they have softened, about 5 minutes. Add the wine and cook, stirring occasionally, until it has reduced by half. Add the stock, orange zest, orange juice, honey, thyme, marjoram, coriander, and cumin and bring the soup to a boil.
3. Reduce the heat so that the soup simmers, add the duck legs, and cook until they are very tender, about 45 minutes.
4. Remove the duck legs from the pot and let them cool. Once they are cool enough to handle, remove the meat from the duck legs, finely dice it, and add it and the duck breasts to the pot. Cook for 5 minutes.
5. Season the soup with salt and pepper and ladle it into warmed bowls. Garnish with chives and serve.

Tom Kha Kai

YIELD: 4 TO 6 SERVINGS / **ACTIVE TIME:** 20 MINUTES / **TOTAL TIME:** 45 MINUTES

2 (14 OZ.) CANS OF COCONUT MILK

2 CUPS FINELY DICED SHIITAKE MUSHROOMS

4 SCALLIONS, TRIMMED AND SLICED THIN

1 LEMONGRASS STALK, CRUSHED

1-INCH PIECE OF FRESH GALANGAL, PEELED

1 RED CHILE PEPPER, STEMMED, SEEDED, AND SLICED THIN

1 MAKRUT LIME LEAF

2 TEASPOONS MINCED FRESH GINGER

½ CUP FISH SAUCE, OR TO TASTE

JUICE OF 2 LIMES

1 LB. BONELESS, SKINLESS CHICKEN BREASTS, DICED

1 TEASPOON SUGAR

HANDFUL OF BEAN SPROUTS

1. Bring the coconut milk to a simmer in a medium pot. Add the mushrooms, scallions, lemongrass, galangal, pepper, lime leaf, and ginger and cook, stirring occasionally, until the mixture is fragrant, about 5 minutes.
2. Raise the heat to medium-high, add the fish sauce, lime juice, chicken, and sugar, and cook until the chicken is cooked through, about 10 minutes.
3. Remove the lemongrass and galangal from the pot and discard them. Add the bean sprouts and cook for 2 minutes.
4. Ladle the soup into warmed bowls and serve.

Goose, Dates & Nut Soup

YIELD: 4 SERVINGS / **ACTIVE TIME:** 20 MINUTES / **TOTAL TIME:** 3 HOURS

2 TABLESPOONS EXTRA-VIRGIN OLIVE OIL

THIGHS AND WINGS FROM 2 GEESE

7 CUPS CHICKEN STOCK (SEE PAGE 440)

1 (14 OZ.) CAN OF COCONUT MILK

6 TABLESPOONS FISH SAUCE

2 LEMONGRASS STALKS, CRUSHED

16 CHESTNUTS, HULLED

¼ CUP ROASTED CASHEWS

¼ CUP ROASTED ALMONDS

¼ CUP ROASTED PEANUTS

16 DATES, PITTED

SALT AND PEPPER, TO TASTE

FRESH THAI BASIL, FOR GARNISH

1. Place the olive oil in a large pot and warm it over medium-high heat. Add the geese and cook, turning occasionally, until they are golden brown, about 10 minutes.
2. Add the stock, coconut milk, fish sauce, and lemongrass and bring the soup to a simmer. Cover the pot and cook until the geese are very tender, about 2 hours.
3. Remove the lemongrass from the pot and discard it. Remove the geese from the pot, remove the meat from the bones, and add the goose meat to the pot. Add the nuts and dates and cook until the chestnuts are tender, about 30 minutes.
4. Season the soup with salt and pepper and ladle it into warmed bowls. Garnish with Thai basil and serve.

Cream of Duck Soup

YIELD: 4 SERVINGS / **ACTIVE TIME:** 30 MINUTES / **TOTAL TIME:** 1 HOUR AND 15 MINUTES

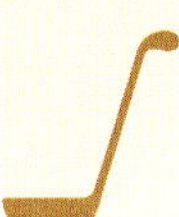

4-LB. DUCK, BROKEN DOWN INTO BREASTS AND LEGS

4 STRIPS OF THICK-CUT BACON, CHOPPED

1 ONION, FINELY DICED

2 GARLIC CLOVES, MINCED

2 CARROTS, PEELED AND DICED

2 CELERY STALKS, FINELY DICED

1 TABLESPOON TOMATO PASTE

1 TABLESPOON ALL-PURPOSE FLOUR

3 TABLESPOONS CRÈME DE CASSIS

1 CUP RED WINE

½ CUP PORT

4 CUPS DUCK STOCK (SEE PAGE 451)

1 BAY LEAF

2 TEASPOONS FRESH THYME

⅔ CUP HEAVY CREAM

SALT AND PEPPER, TO TASTE

FRESH PARSLEY, CHOPPED, FOR GARNISH

BLACK CURRANT PRESERVES, FOR GARNISH

1. Place the duck breasts in a large pot, skin side down, and cook over low heat until the skin is crispy, about 10 minutes. Flip the breasts over and cook for 5 minutes. Remove the breasts from the pot and let them cool slightly. When the breasts are cool enough to handle, slice the meat from them and set it aside.
2. Add the bacon, onion, garlic, carrots, and celery to the pot and cook, stirring occasionally, until the vegetables have softened, about 5 minutes. Add the tomato paste and duck legs and cook, stirring frequently, for 5 minutes.
3. Add the flour and cook, stirring continually, for 2 minutes. Add the crème de cassis, red wine, and port and cook, stirring occasionally, until half of the liquid has evaporated, about 5 minutes. Add the stock, bay leaf, and thyme and bring the soup to a boil.
4. Reduce the heat so that the soup simmers and cook until the duck legs are cooked through, about 30 minutes. Remove the bay leaf and discard it. Remove the duck legs and set them aside.
5. Transfer the soup to a food processor, pulse until smooth, and strain it into a clean pot through a fine-mesh sieve. Add the cream and bring the soup to a simmer.
6. Remove the meat from the duck legs and chop it. Season the soup with salt and pepper, add the duck meat, and cook for 2 minutes.
7. Ladle the soup into warmed bowls, garnish with parsley and black currant preserves, and serve.

Cream of Duck Soup

SEE PAGE 289

Squab & Root Vegetable Soup

YIELD: 4 SERVINGS / **ACTIVE TIME:** 30 MINUTES / **TOTAL TIME:** 2 HOURS

2 TABLESPOONS EXTRA-VIRGIN OLIVE OIL

2 (1 LB.) SQUABS

2 TABLESPOONS UNSALTED BUTTER

1 ONION, FINELY DICED

4 CARROTS, PEELED AND DICED

1 TURNIP, PEELED AND FINELY DICED

2 PARSNIPS, FINELY DICED

4 CELERY STALKS, FINELY DICED

2 TABLESPOONS ALL-PURPOSE FLOUR

2 TABLESPOONS TOMATO PASTE

6 CUPS CHICKEN STOCK (SEE PAGE 440)

1 CUP APPLE CIDER

2 TABLESPOONS CALVADOS

1 TABLESPOON FRESH THYME

1 TABLESPOON FINELY CHOPPED FRESH SAGE

1 TABLESPOON FINELY CHOPPED FRESH CHIVES

2 TABLESPOONS FINELY CHOPPED FRESH PARSLEY

SALT AND PEPPER, TO TASTE

1. Place the olive oil in a large pot and warm it over medium-high heat. Add the squabs and cook, turning occasionally, until they are browned on both sides, about 5 minutes. Remove the squabs from the pot, let them cool, and set them aside.

2. Add the butter to the pot and melt it over medium heat. Add the onion, carrots, turnip, parsnips, and celery and cook, stirring occasionally, until they have softened, about 10 minutes. Add the flour and cook, stirring continually, for 2 minutes. Add the tomato paste, stock, cider, Calvados, thyme, and sage and bring the soup to a boil. Reduce the heat so that the soup simmers and add the squabs to the pot. Cover the pot and cook for 1 hour and 30 minutes.

3. Remove the squabs from the pot and let them cool. Once they are cool enough to handle, remove the meat from the squabs, finely chop it, and add the squab meat to the pot. Stir in the chives and parsley.

4. Season the soup with salt and pepper, ladle it into warmed bowls, and serve.

Quail & Ginseng Root Soup

YIELD: 4 SERVINGS / **ACTIVE TIME:** 10 MINUTES / **TOTAL TIME:** 1 HOUR

6 CUPS CHICKEN STOCK (SEE PAGE 440)

½ CUP SHERRY

4 WHOLE QUAIL, DISJOINTED

1-INCH PIECE OF FRESH GINGER, PEELED AND MINCED

⅓ CUP PEELED AND MINCED GINSENG ROOT

1 TABLESPOON SOY SAUCE

SALT AND PEPPER, TO TASTE

FRESH CHIVES, CHOPPED, FOR GARNISH

1. Bring the stock and sherry to a boil in a medium pot. Reduce the heat so that the broth simmers and add the quail. Cover the pot and cook for 15 minutes.
2. Add the ginger, ginseng root, and soy sauce and cook for 30 minutes.
3. Remove the quail from the pot and divide them among warmed bowls. Ladle the soup into the bowls, add salt and pepper to taste, garnish with chives, and serve.

Guinea Hen & Wild Rice Soup

YIELD: 4 SERVINGS / **ACTIVE TIME:** 20 MINUTES / **TOTAL TIME:** 1 HOUR

2 TABLESPOONS EXTRA-VIRGIN OLIVE OIL

2 GUINEA HEN BREASTS, HALVED

SALT AND PEPPER, TO TASTE

¼ CUP UNSALTED BUTTER

2 CUPS FINELY DICED LEEKS, TRIMMED AND RINSED WELL BEFORE DICING

1 CUP DICED CARROTS

1 CUP FINELY DICED CELERY

2 TABLESPOONS ALL-PURPOSE FLOUR

8 CUPS CHICKEN STOCK (SEE PAGE 440)

1 CUP WILD RICE

1 CUP HEAVY CREAM

2 TABLESPOONS SHERRY

FRESH CHIVES, CHOPPED, FOR GARNISH

1. Place the olive oil in a small skillet and warm it over medium heat. Add the guinea hen breasts, season with salt and pepper, and cook, turning occasionally, until they are fully cooked through, about 10 minutes. Remove the breasts from the skillet and set them aside.
2. Place the butter in a large pot and melt it over medium heat. Add the leeks, carrots, and celery and cook, stirring occasionally, until they have softened, about 5 minutes. Add the flour and cook, stirring continually, for 3 minutes. Add the stock, stir until fully combined, and bring the soup to a boil.
3. Reduce the heat so that the soup simmers, add the rice, and cook until the rice is tender, about 20 minutes.
4. Stir in the cream and sherry and season the soup with salt and pepper.
5. Ladle the soup into warmed bowls, garnish with chives, and top each portion with one of the guinea hen breasts.

Guinea Hen & Roasted Grape Stew

YIELD: 4 SERVINGS / **ACTIVE TIME:** 20 MINUTES / **TOTAL TIME:** 1 HOUR AND 15 MINUTES

⅓ CUP ALL-PURPOSE FLOUR

2 GUINEA HENS, BROKEN DOWN INTO BREASTS AND LEGS

6 SLICES OF THICK-CUT BACON, FINELY DICED

2 CUPS RED GRAPES

2 CUPS WHITE WINE

1 CUP FINELY DICED WILD MUSHROOMS

1 FINELY DICED ONION

2 CARROTS, PEELED AND DICED

1 CUP ORANGE JUICE

2 CUPS CHICKEN STOCK (SEE PAGE 440)

SALT AND PEPPER, TO TASTE

RICE, COOKED, FOR SERVING

1. Preheat the oven to 350°F. Place the flour and guinea hens in a mixing bowl and toss until the guinea hens are fully coated. Set them aside.
2. Place the bacon in a Dutch oven and cook over medium heat, stirring occasionally, until it is crispy, about 8 minutes. Remove the bacon from the pot and set it aside.
3. Add the guinea hens to the pot and cook, turning as necessary, until they are browned all over, about 5 minutes. Remove the guinea hens from the pot and set them aside.
4. Add the grapes and wine to the pot and cook, stirring occasionally, until the liquid has reduced by half, about 5 minutes. Remove the grapes from the pot and set them aside. Add the mushrooms, onion, carrots, orange juice, and stock and bring the soup to a simmer. Place the Dutch oven in the oven and braise for 20 minutes.
5. Add the bacon, guinea hens, and grapes to the pot, stir to combine, and braise until the guinea hens are cooked through and the vegetables are tender, about 30 minutes.
6. Remove the pot from the oven and season the soup with salt and pepper. Ladle it into warmed bowls and serve with rice.

Pheasant, Morel & Olive Broth

YIELD: 4 SERVINGS / **ACTIVE TIME:** 20 MINUTES / **TOTAL TIME:** 45 MINUTES

½ CUP ALL-PURPOSE FLOUR

4 PHEASANT BREASTS

2 TABLESPOONS EXTRA-VIRGIN OLIVE OIL

1 ONION, FINELY DICED

1½ CUPS FINELY DICED MOREL MUSHROOMS

3 GARLIC CLOVES, MINCED

1 CUP WHITE WINE

4 CUPS CHICKEN STOCK (SEE PAGE 440)

½ CUP CHOPPED BLACK OLIVES

SALT AND PEPPER, TO TASTE

1. Place the flour and pheasants in a mixing bowl and toss until the pheasants are fully coated.
2. Place the olive oil in a large pot and warm it over medium-high heat. Add the pheasants and cook, turning as necessary, until they have browned all over, about 5 minutes. Add the onion, mushrooms, and garlic and cook, stirring occasionally, until the onion has softened, about 5 minutes.
3. Add the wine and cook, stirring occasionally, until it has reduced by half. Add the stock and bring the soup to a boil. Reduce the heat so that the soup simmers and cook until the pheasant is fully cooked through, about 20 minutes.
4. Stir in the olives, season with salt and pepper, and cook for 3 minutes.
5. Ladle the soup into warmed bowls and serve.

Preserved Lime & Duck Leg Soup

YIELD: 4 SERVINGS / **ACTIVE TIME:** 20 MINUTES / **TOTAL TIME:** 1 HOUR AND 15 MINUTES

1 TABLESPOON EXTRA-VIRGIN OLIVE OIL

4 DUCK LEGS

2-INCH PIECE OF FRESH GINGER, PEELED AND MINCED

2 GARLIC CLOVES, MINCED

8 CUPS DUCK STOCK (SEE PAGE 451)

8 PRESERVED LIMES (SEE PAGE 473), QUARTERED

4 SCALLIONS, TRIMMED AND SLICED THIN, WHITES AND GREENS RESERVED

SALT AND PEPPER, TO TASTE

1. Place the olive oil in a large pot and warm it over medium-high heat. Add the duck and cook, turning as necessary, until it has browned all over, about 10 minutes. Remove the duck from the pot and set it aside.
2. Add the ginger and garlic to the pot and cook, stirring continually, for 2 minutes. Add the stock and bring the soup to a boil.
3. Reduce the heat so that the soup simmers, add the duck and Preserved Limes, and cook until the duck is very tender, about 45 minutes.
4. Add the scallion whites, season with salt and pepper, and cook for 5 minutes.
5. Divide the duck legs among warmed bowls and ladle the soup over the top. Garnish with the scallions greens and serve.

Southwestern Chicken Soup

YIELD: 4 SERVINGS / **ACTIVE TIME:** 15 MINUTES / **TOTAL TIME:** 45 MINUTES

2 CUPS CHOPPED COOKED CHICKEN

4 CUPS CHICKEN STOCK (SEE PAGE 440)

2 (14 OZ.) CANS OF DICED TOMATOES, DRAINED

2 PLUM TOMATOES, FINELY DICED

½ JALAPEÑO CHILE PEPPER, STEMMED, SEEDED, AND FINELY DICED

1 ONION, FINELY DICED

2 GARLIC CLOVES, MINCED

JUICE OF 1 LIME

½ TEASPOON CAYENNE PEPPER

½ TEASPOON CUMIN

FLESH OF 2 AVOCADOS, DICED

SALT AND PEPPER, TO TASTE

SOUR CREAM, FOR GARNISH

FRESH CILANTRO, CHOPPED, FOR GARNISH

MONTEREY JACK CHEESE, SHREDDED, FOR GARNISH

CORNBREAD (SEE PAGE 469), FOR SERVING

1. Place the chicken, stock, tomatoes, chile, onion, garlic, lime juice, cayenne pepper, and cumin in a large pot and bring the soup to a boil. Reduce the heat so that the soup simmers and cook for 25 minutes.
2. Stir in the avocados and cook until the soup thickens slightly, about 10 minutes.
3. Season the soup with salt and pepper and ladle it into warmed bowls. Garnish with sour cream, cilantro, and Monterey Jack and serve with the Cornbread.

Turkey & Wild Rice Soup

YIELD: 4 SERVINGS / **ACTIVE TIME:** 20 MINUTES / **TOTAL TIME:** 1 HOUR

6 CUPS TURKEY STOCK (SEE PAGE 446)

8 SCALLIONS, TRIMMED AND SLICED

½ CUP WILD RICE

4 TEASPOONS FRESH THYME

8 SLICES OF THICK-CUT BACON, FINELY DICED

¼ CUP UNSALTED BUTTER

½ CUP ALL-PURPOSE FLOUR

1 CUP WHOLE MILK

1 CUP HEAVY CREAM

2 CUPS CHOPPED COOKED TURKEY

2 TABLESPOONS SHERRY

SALT AND PEPPER, TO TASTE

EDIBLE FLOWERS, FOR GARNISH

1. Place the stock, scallions, rice, and thyme in a large pot and bring to a boil. Reduce the heat so that the soup simmers and cook until the rice is tender, about 30 minutes.
2. Place the bacon in a medium skillet and cook over medium heat, stirring occasionally, until it is crispy, about 8 minutes. Remove the bacon from the skillet and set it aside. Add the butter to the skillet and melt it. Add the flour and cook, stirring continually, for 2 minutes.
3. Add the milk and cream and cook, stirring continually, for 2 minutes. Add the cream mixture to the soup and bring to a boil. Reduce the heat so that the soup simmers and cook until it has thickened slightly, about 5 minutes.
4. Stir in the turkey and sherry and season with salt and pepper. Cook until the turkey is warmed through, 3 to 5 minutes.
5. Ladle the soup into warmed bowls, garnish with the bacon and edible flowers, and serve.

Velvety Chicken & Chestnut Soup

YIELD: 4 SERVINGS / **ACTIVE TIME:** 45 MINUTES / **TOTAL TIME:** 3 HOURS AND 15 MINUTES

3½-LB. CHICKEN, BROKEN DOWN

2 TABLESPOONS UNSALTED BUTTER

1 CARROT, PEELED AND DICED

1 ONION, FINELY DICED

2 CELERY STALKS, FINELY DICED

3 TABLESPOONS FINELY DICED FRESH ROSEMARY

1 TABLESPOON FRESH THYME

2 GARLIC CLOVES, MINCED

1 CUP RIESLING

1 LB. ROASTED CHESTNUTS, ¼ LB. CHOPPED AND RESERVED FOR GARNISH

1 CUP HEAVY CREAM

SALT AND PEPPER, TO TASTE

1. Preheat the oven to 400°F. Place the chicken in a baking dish, place it in the oven, and bake until the chicken is golden brown and cooked through (the interior is 165°F), about 45 minutes. Remove the chicken from the oven and set it aside.
2. Place the butter in a large pot and melt it over medium heat. Add the carrot, onion, celery, rosemary, thyme, and garlic and cook, stirring frequently, until the vegetables have softened, about 5 minutes. Add the Riesling and cook, stirring occasionally, for 5 minutes.
3. Add the chicken, cover the solids with water, and bring the soup to a simmer. Cook until the soup is very flavorful, about 2 hours.
4. Strain the soup through a fine-mesh sieve and set the chicken aside. Place 4 cups of the soup and the whole chestnuts in a food processor. Pulse until the mixture is smooth.
5. Transfer the soup to a clean pot and bring to a boil. Stir in the cream and chicken and season with salt and pepper.
6. Ladle the soup into warmed bowls, garnish with the chopped chestnuts, and serve.

Coconut & Chicken Curry Soup

YIELD: 4 SERVINGS / **ACTIVE TIME:** 45 MINUTES / **TOTAL TIME:** 1 HOUR AND 30 MINUTES

2 TABLESPOONS EXTRA-VIRGIN OLIVE OIL

2 BONELESS, SKINLESS CHICKEN BREASTS

1 ONION, FINELY DICED

1 CARROT, PEELED AND DICED

1 GARLIC CLOVE, MINCED

2 CUPS CHICKEN STOCK (SEE PAGE 440)

1 (14 OZ.) CAN OF COCONUT MILK

½ CUP FINELY CHOPPED FRESH CILANTRO, PLUS MORE FOR GARNISH

2 FRESH LIME LEAVES

1 TABLESPOON CURRY POWDER

½ JALAPEÑO CHILE PEPPER, STEMMED, SEEDED, AND FINELY DICED

JUICE OF ½ LIME

SALT AND PEPPER, TO TASTE

SCALLION GREENS, SLICED, FOR GARNISH

BAMBOO SHOOTS, CHOPPED, FOR GARNISH

RICE, COOKED, FOR SERVING

NAAN (SEE PAGE 474), FOR SERVING

1. Place the olive oil in a medium pot and warm it over medium heat. Add the chicken and cook, turning as necessary, until it has browned, about 10 minutes. Remove the chicken from the pot, chop it, and set it aside.
2. Add the onion, carrot, and garlic to the pot and cook, stirring occasionally, until they have softened, about 5 minutes. Add the stock and coconut milk and bring the soup to a boil. Reduce the heat so that the soup simmers, add the cilantro, lime leaves, curry powder, and jalapeño, and cook for 15 minutes.
3. Remove the lime leaves from the pot and discard them. Transfer the soup to a food processor, pulse until smooth, and strain it back into the pot through a fine-mesh sieve. Bring the soup to a simmer, stir in the chicken and lime juice, and cook until the chicken is completely cooked through, about 10 minutes.
4. Season the soup with salt and pepper and ladle it into warmed bowls. Garnish with scallion greens, bamboo shoots, and additional cilantro and serve with rice and the Naan.

Mulligatawny with Squab

YIELD: 4 SERVINGS / **ACTIVE TIME:** 30 MINUTES / **TOTAL TIME:** 1 HOUR AND 30 MINUTES

2 (1 LB.) SQUABS

2 TABLESPOONS EXTRA-VIRGIN OLIVE OIL

GARAM MASALA, TO TASTE

¼ LB. BASMATI RICE

1 TEASPOON CORIANDER SEEDS

1 TEASPOON CUMIN SEEDS

1 ONION, FINELY DICED

2 GARLIC CLOVES, MINCED

1 THAI CHILE PEPPER, STEMMED, SEEDED, AND FINELY SLICED

1 TEASPOON TURMERIC

1 BAY LEAF

4 OZ. RED LENTILS

4 CUPS CHICKEN STOCK (SEE PAGE 440)

1 (14 OZ.) CAN OF COCONUT MILK

JUICE OF 1 LEMON

SALT AND PEPPER, TO TASTE

YOGURT, FOR GARNISH

FRESH CILANTRO, CHOPPED, FOR GARNISH

1. Preheat the oven to 375°F. Place the squabs in a baking dish, drizzle half of the olive oil over them, and season with garam masala. Place the dish in the oven and bake for 20 minutes.
2. Remove the squabs from the oven and let them cool. When they are cool enough to handle, remove the meat from the squabs, chop it, and set it aside.
3. Cook the rice according to the instructions on the package.
4. Place the coriander seeds and cumin seeds in a small, dry skillet and cook over low heat, stirring continually, until they are fragrant, 2 to 4 minutes. Remove the toasted seeds from the pan and grind them into a fine powder, using a mortar and pestle or spice grinder.
5. Place the remaining olive oil in a medium pot and warm it over medium heat. Add the onion and garlic and cook, stirring occasionally, until they have softened, about 5 minutes. Add the toasted seed powder, chile, turmeric, bay leaf, lentils, and stock and bring the soup to a boil.
6. Reduce the heat so that the soup simmers and cook until the lentils are tender, about 20 minutes.
7. Stir in the coconut milk and cook for 5 minutes. Add the chopped squabs and lemon juice, season with salt and pepper, and cook until the squabs are warmed through.
8. Divide the rice among warmed bowls and ladle the soup over the top. Garnish with yogurt and cilantro and serve.

Truffled White Bean & Chicken Soup

YIELD: 4 TO 6 SERVINGS / **ACTIVE TIME:** 20 MINUTES / **TOTAL TIME:** 24 HOURS

¼ CUP EXTRA-VIRGIN OLIVE OIL

2 BONELESS, SKINLESS CHICKEN THIGHS

8 CUPS CHICKEN STOCK (SEE PAGE 440)

¾ CUP DRIED WHITE BEANS, SOAKED OVERNIGHT AND DRAINED

2 ONIONS, FINELY DICED

4 CELERY STALKS, FINELY DICED

2 PARSNIPS, PEELED AND FINELY DICED

2 TABLESPOONS TRUFFLE PASTE

2 TABLESPOONS TRUFFLE OIL, PLUS MORE FOR GARNISH

SALT AND PEPPER, TO TASTE

ALFALFA SPROUTS, FOR GARNISH

PAPRIKA, FOR GARNISH

1. Place the olive oil in a medium pot and warm it over medium heat. Add the chicken and cook, turning as necessary, until it has browned all over, about 6 minutes. Add the stock and bring to a boil.
2. Reduce the heat so that the soup simmers, add the beans, and cook for 15 minutes.
3. Add the onions, celery, and parsnips and cook until the beans and vegetables are tender, 15 to 25 minutes. Remove the chicken from the pot and let it cool. When it is cool enough to handle, chop the chicken and set it aside.
4. Transfer the soup to a food processor, pulse until it is smooth, and strain it back into the pot through a fine-mesh sieve. Bring the soup to a simmer, stir in the truffle paste and truffle oil, and season it with salt and pepper.
5. Ladle the soup into warmed bowls and top each portion with some chicken. Garnish with alfalfa sprouts, paprika, and additional truffle oil and serve.

Aromatic Chicken Stew

YIELD: 4 SERVINGS / **ACTIVE TIME:** 30 MINUTES / **TOTAL TIME:** 1 HOUR AND 15 MINUTES

3 TABLESPOONS UNSALTED BUTTER

1 BONELESS, SKINLESS CHICKEN BREAST, DICED

1 ONION, FINELY DICED

1 GARLIC CLOVE, MINCED

2 GREEN BELL PEPPERS, STEMMED, SEEDED, AND FINELY DICED

¼ TEASPOON ALLSPICE

½ TEASPOON GROUND CLOVES

½ TEASPOON CINNAMON

¼ TEASPOON FRESH THYME, PLUS MORE FOR GARNISH

½ THAI CHILE PEPPER, STEMMED, SEEDED, AND FINELY DICED

¼ CUP CHOPPED KALAMATA OLIVES

4 CUPS CHICKEN STOCK (SEE PAGE 440)

1½ CUPS DICED TOMATOES

SALT AND PEPPER, TO TASTE

FETA CHEESE, CRUMBLED, FOR GARNISH

KATSAMAKI (SEE PAGE 473), FOR SERVING

1. Place one-third of the butter in a large pot and melt it over medium heat. Add the chicken and cook, stirring occasionally, until it has browned, about 8 minutes. Remove the chicken from the pot and set it aside.
2. Add another one-third of the butter to the pot and let it melt. Add the onion, garlic, and bell peppers and cook, stirring occasionally, until they have softened, about 8 minutes. Add the chicken, allspice, cloves, cinnamon, thyme, and chile and cook, stirring continually, for 2 minutes.
3. Add the olives and stock, bring the soup to a simmer, and cook until the chicken is tender, about 40 minutes.
4. Stir in the remaining butter and tomatoes and season with salt and pepper.
5. Ladle the soup into warmed bowls, garnish with feta and additional thyme, and serve with Katsamaki.

Lemongrass Chicken & Rice Soup

YIELD: 4 SERVINGS / **ACTIVE TIME:** 30 MINUTES / **TOTAL TIME:** 2 HOURS AND 30 MINUTES

2 BONE-IN CHICKEN THIGHS, SKIN REMOVED

8 CUPS CHICKEN STOCK (SEE PAGE 440)

1-INCH PIECE OF FRESH GINGER, PEELED AND MINCED

3 LEMONGRASS STALKS, CRUSHED

1 THAI CHILE PEPPER, PIERCED, PLUS MORE, CHOPPED, FOR GARNISH

3 TABLESPOONS FISH SAUCE

½ CUP LONG-GRAIN RICE

FRESH CILANTRO, CHOPPED, FOR GARNISH

LIME WEDGES, FOR SERVING

NAAN (SEE PAGE 474), FOR SERVING

1. Place the chicken, stock, ginger, lemongrass, chile, and fish sauce in a large pot and bring to a boil. Reduce the heat so that the soup simmers and cook, skimming away the fat as it rises to the surface, until the chicken is tender, about 2 hours.
2. Remove the chicken from the pot and let it cool. When it is cool enough to handle, chop the chicken and set it aside.
3. Strain the soup into a clean pot through a fine-mesh sieve and bring it to a boil. Reduce the heat so that the soup simmers, add the rice, and cook until the rice is tender, about 30 minutes.
4. Stir in the chicken and cook until it is warmed through, 2 to 3 minutes.
5. Ladle the soup into warmed bowls, garnish with cilantro and additional chiles, and serve with lime wedges and the Naan.

PORK

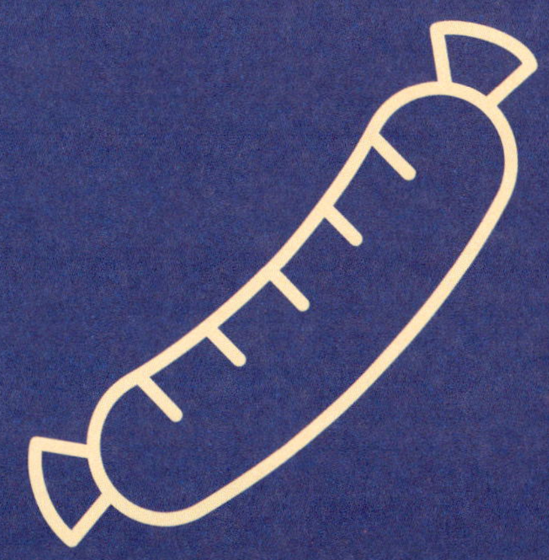

Pork Sinigang

YIELD: 4 SERVINGS / **ACTIVE TIME:** 15 MINUTES / **TOTAL TIME:** 1 HOUR

1 TABLESPOON EXTRA-VIRGIN OLIVE OIL

1½ LBS. BONELESS PORK CHOPS, DICED

1 ONION, FINELY DICED

1-INCH PIECE OF FRESH GINGER, PEELED AND MINCED

2 PLUM TOMATOES, FINELY DICED

6 CUPS HAM STOCK (SEE PAGE 447)

1 TABLESPOON TAMARIND CONCENTRATE

1 TABLESPOON SOY SAUCE

2 TABLESPOONS FISH SAUCE

2 CUPS TRIMMED AND CHOPPED GREEN BEANS

SALT AND PEPPER, TO TASTE

1. Place the olive oil in a medium pot and warm it over medium-high heat. Add the pork and cook, stirring occasionally, until it has browned, about 5 minutes. Add the onion and cook, stirring occasionally, until it has softened, about 5 minutes.
2. Add the ginger, tomatoes, stock, and tamarind concentrate and bring the soup to a boil.
3. Reduce the heat so that the soup simmers and cook until the pork is tender, about 30 minutes.
4. Stir in the soy sauce, fish sauce, and green beans and cook until the green beans are just tender, about 5 minutes.
5. Season the soup with salt and pepper, ladle it into warmed bowls, and serve.

Spicy Sausage Stew with Summer Vegetables

YIELD: 6 SERVINGS / **ACTIVE TIME:** 35 MINUTES / **TOTAL TIME:** 1 HOUR

2 TABLESPOONS UNSALTED BUTTER

1 ONION, DICED

2 GARLIC CLOVES, MINCED

1 LB. HOT ITALIAN SAUSAGE, SLICED

2 TEASPOONS CHILI POWDER

½ TEASPOON CAYENNE PEPPER

2 RED BELL PEPPERS, STEMMED, SEEDED, AND DICED

KERNELS FROM 3 EARS OF CORN

1 SMALL ZUCCHINI, CUT INTO THIN HALF-MOONS

4 TOMATOES, SEEDED AND CHOPPED

SALT AND PEPPER, TO TASTE

FRESH PARSLEY, CHOPPED, FOR GARNISH

1. Place the butter in a large, deep skillet and melt it over medium-high heat. Add the onion and garlic and cook, stirring frequently, until they have softened, about 5 minutes.
2. Add the sausage and cook until it is browned all over, about 5 minutes, turning it as necessary.
3. Stir in the chili powder and cayenne and cook for 1 minute. Add the bell peppers, corn, zucchini, and tomatoes, stir to combine, and season with salt and pepper.
4. Cover the skillet, reduce the heat to medium, and cook until the sausage is cooked through and the vegetables are tender, about 20 minutes.
5. Garnish with parsley and serve.

Chorizo & Cabbage Soup

YIELD: 4 SERVINGS / **ACTIVE TIME:** 15 MINUTES / **TOTAL TIME:** 30 MINUTES

2 TABLESPOONS EXTRA-VIRGIN OLIVE OIL

1 ONION, FINELY DICED

4 TEASPOONS FRESH THYME

1 LB. SMOKED CHORIZO, SLICED THIN

1 GREEN CABBAGE, SLICED THIN

1 TABLESPOON CUMIN SEEDS

1 CINNAMON STICK

6 CUPS CHICKEN STOCK (SEE PAGE 440)

SALT AND PEPPER, TO TASTE

1. Place the olive oil in a medium pot and warm it over medium heat. Add the onion and cook, stirring occasionally, until it has softened, about 5 minutes. Add the thyme, chorizo, cabbage, cumin seeds, and cinnamon stick, cover the pot, and cook, stirring occasionally, for 5 minutes.
2. Add the stock and bring to a boil. Reduce the heat so that the soup simmers and cook for 10 minutes.
3. Season the soup with salt and pepper, ladle it into warmed bowls, and serve.

Albondigas Soup

YIELD: 4 SERVINGS / **ACTIVE TIME:** 45 MINUTES / **TOTAL TIME:** 2 HOURS

FOR THE MEATBALLS

2 CUPS DAY-OLD BREAD PIECES, CRUST REMOVED

½ CUP MILK

1 LB. GROUND PORK

½ CUP GRATED ZAMORANO CHEESE

¼ CUP CHOPPED FRESH PARSLEY

2 TABLESPOONS MINCED SHALLOTS

2 TABLESPOONS EXTRA-VIRGIN OLIVE OIL

1 TEASPOON KOSHER SALT

½ TEASPOON BLACK PEPPER

1 EGG

FOR THE SOUP

1 TABLESPOON EXTRA-VIRGIN OLIVE OIL

1 ONION, CHOPPED

2 CELERY STALKS, CHOPPED

2 RED BELL PEPPERS, STEMS AND SEEDS REMOVED, CUT INTO ¼-INCH-WIDE STRIPS

2 GARLIC CLOVES, MINCED

1½ TEASPOONS PAPRIKA

¼ TEASPOON SAFFRON

2 PINCHES OF RED PEPPER FLAKES

½ CUP WHITE WINE

6 CUPS CHICKEN STOCK (SEE PAGE 440)

¼ CUP CHOPPED FRESH PARSLEY

SALT AND PEPPER, TO TASTE

1. To begin preparations for the meatballs, place the bread and milk in a mixing bowl. Let the bread soak for 10 minutes.
2. Use a fork to mash the bread until it is very soft and broken down. Add the remaining ingredients and work the mixture with your hands until thoroughly combined. Cover the bowl with plastic wrap and chill it in the refrigerator for 30 minutes.
3. Line a baking sheet with parchment paper. Remove the mixture from the refrigerator and form tablespoons of it into balls. Place the meatballs on the baking sheet, cover them with plastic wrap, and refrigerate for 30 minutes.
4. To begin preparations for the soup, place the olive oil in a large saucepan and warm it over medium-high heat. Add the onion and cook, stirring frequently, for 2 minutes. Add the celery and bell peppers and cook, stirring occasionally, until the vegetables are soft, about 8 minutes.
5. Add the garlic, paprika, saffron, and red pepper flakes and cook, stirring continually, for 45 seconds. Add the wine and cook until the alcohol has been cooked off, 1 to 2 minutes. Add the stock and bring the soup to a boil.
6. Reduce the heat, add the meatballs, and simmer until they are cooked through, 15 to 20 minutes.
7. Stir in the parsley, season the soup with salt and pepper, and ladle it into warmed bowls.

Ham & Vegetable Soup

YIELD: 4 SERVINGS / **ACTIVE TIME:** 35 MINUTES / **TOTAL TIME:** 1 HOUR AND 5 MINUTES

1 TABLESPOON EXTRA-VIRGIN OLIVE OIL

1 ONION, FINELY DICED

½ CUP FINELY DICED GREEN BELL PEPPER

½ CUP FINELY DICED ZUCCHINI

½ CUP PEELED AND DICED CARROT

½ CUP FINELY DICED LEEKS, TRIMMED AND RINSED WELL BEFORE CUTTING

½ CUP FINELY DICED CELERY

½ CUP PEELED AND FINELY DICED POTATO

1 GARLIC CLOVE, MINCED

1 TEASPOON FRESH THYME

1 CUP V8

4 CUPS HAM STOCK (SEE PAGE 447)

SALT AND PEPPER, TO TASTE

LEEK OIL (SEE PAGE 475), FOR GARNISH

1. Place the olive oil in a medium pot and warm it over medium heat. Add the onion, bell pepper, zucchini, carrot, leeks, celery, potato, garlic, and thyme and cook, stirring occasionally, until the vegetables have softened, about 10 minutes.
2. Add the V8 and cook, stirring occasionally, for 5 minutes. Add the stock, bring the soup to a simmer, and cook for 15 minutes.
3. Season the soup with salt and pepper and ladle it into warmed bowls. Garnish with the Leek Oil and serve.

Tanuki Jiru

YIELD: 4 SERVINGS / **ACTIVE TIME:** 20 MINUTES / **TOTAL TIME:** 40 MINUTES

2 TABLESPOONS SESAME OIL

½ LB. BONELESS PORK LOIN, DICED

6-INCH PIECE OF FRESH BURDOCK ROOT, PEELED AND MINCED

½ CUP FINELY DICED DAIKON RADISH, PLUS MORE FOR GARNISH

4 SHIITAKE MUSHROOMS, FINELY DICED

2½ CUPS FISH STOCK (SEE PAGE 454)

¾ CUP TOFU, FINELY DICED

¼ CUP WHITE MISO

SALT AND PEPPER, TO TASTE

FRESH SCALLIONS, TRIMMED AND SLICED, FOR GARNISH

1. Place the sesame oil in a medium pot and warm it over medium heat. Add the pork, burdock root, daikon, and mushrooms and cook, stirring occasionally, until the pork is browned, about 5 minutes.
2. Add the stock and tofu and bring the soup to a boil. Reduce the heat so that the soup simmers and cook until the pork is cooked through, about 10 minutes.
3. Place the miso and ¼ cup of the broth in a small mixing bowl and stir until the mixture is smooth. Stir the mixture into the soup.
4. Ladle the soup into warmed bowls, add salt and pepper to taste, garnish with scallions and additional daikon, and serve.

Carne Adovada

YIELD: 4 TO 6 SERVINGS / **ACTIVE TIME:** 30 MINUTES / **TOTAL TIME:** 24 HOURS

2 TABLESPOONS EXTRA-VIRGIN OLIVE OIL

3 TABLESPOONS ALL-PURPOSE FLOUR

¼ CUP NEW MEXICO CHILE POWDER

6 CUPS HAM STOCK (SEE PAGE 447)

4 GARLIC CLOVES, MINCED

1 TABLESPOON FINELY CHOPPED FRESH OREGANO

½ TEASPOON CUMIN

SALT AND PEPPER, TO TASTE

2½ LBS. BONELESS PORK SHOULDER, DICED

1. Place the olive oil in a medium pot and warm it over medium heat. Add the flour and cook, stirring continually, until it is golden brown, about 5 minutes.
2. Add the chile powder, stock, garlic, oregano, and cumin, season with salt and pepper, and bring the soup to a boil.
3. Reduce the heat so that the soup simmers and cook for 2 minutes. Remove the pot from heat and let the soup cool. Place the pork in a baking dish, pour the soup into the dish, and cover it with aluminum foil. Let the pork marinate in the refrigerator overnight.
4. Preheat the oven to 300°F. Place the baking dish in the oven and cook, stirring occasionally, until the pork is very tender, at least 4 hours.
5. Ladle the soup into warmed bowls and serve.

Pozole

YIELD: 8 SERVINGS / **ACTIVE TIME:** 30 MINUTES / **TOTAL TIME:** 24 HOURS

2 TABLESPOONS EXTRA-VIRGIN OLIVE OIL

2 LBS. BONELESS PORK SHOULDER, CUBED

1 ONION, FINELY DICED

SALT AND PEPPER, TO TASTE

4 DRIED CHIPOTLE CHILE PEPPERS, STEMMED, SEEDED, AND SLICED THIN

2 CUPS DRIED HOMINY, SOAKED OVERNIGHT AND DRAINED

2 TABLESPOONS FRESH THYME

2 TABLESPOONS CUMIN

4 GARLIC CLOVES, MINCED

FRESH CILANTRO, CHOPPED, FOR GARNISH

LIME WEDGES, FOR GARNISH

1. Place the olive oil in a large pot and warm it over medium-high heat. Add the pork and onion, season with salt and pepper, and cook, stirring frequently, until they have browned, about 15 minutes.
2. Add the chiles, hominy, thyme, and cumin and enough water to cover the solids by an inch and bring the soup to a boil.
3. Reduce the heat so that the soup simmers and cook, stirring occasionally and adding water as necessary, until the pork and hominy are tender, at least 1 hour and 30 minutes.
4. Add the garlic, season with salt and pepper, and cook for 3 minutes.
5. Ladle the soup into warmed bowls, garnish with cilantro and lime wedges, and serve.

Ham Hock & Collard Green Soup

YIELD: 4 SERVINGS / **ACTIVE TIME:** 30 MINUTES / **TOTAL TIME:** 1 HOUR AND 35 MINUTES

1 LB. COLLARD GREENS OR KALE, FINELY CHOPPED

SALT AND PEPPER, TO TASTE

1 TABLESPOON EXTRA-VIRGIN OLIVE OIL

2 OZ. SALT PORK

½ CUP FINELY DICED ONION

¼ CUP FINELY DICED CELERY

½ CUP ALL-PURPOSE FLOUR

8 CUPS CHICKEN STOCK (SEE PAGE 440)

2 SMOKED HAM HOCKS

SACHET D'ÉPICES (SEE PAGE 465)

½ CUP HEAVY CREAM

1. Bring water to a boil in a medium pot. Add the collard greens or kale, season with salt, and cook until the greens have softened, about 4 minutes. Drain the greens and set them aside.
2. Place the olive oil and salt pork in a large pot and warm the mixture over medium heat until the salt pork has melted. Add the onion and celery and cook, stirring occasionally, until they have softened, about 5 minutes.
3. Add the flour and cook, stirring frequently, for 4 minutes. Add the stock, stir to fully combine, and bring the soup to a boil.
4. Reduce the heat so that the soup simmers, add the ham hocks and Sachet d'Épices, and cook for 1 hour.
5. Remove the ham hocks from the pot, remove the meat from the ham hocks, and finely dice it. Remove the Sachet d'Épices from the pot and discard it.
6. Add the collard greens or kale, ham meat, and heavy cream to the pot and season the soup with salt and pepper. Cook until the soup is warmed through.
7. Ladle the soup into warmed bowls and serve.

Sweet & Sour Pork Soup

YIELD: 4 SERVINGS / **ACTIVE TIME:** 30 MINUTES / **TOTAL TIME:** 50 MINUTES

2 SHALLOTS, FINELY DICED

2 GARLIC CLOVES, MINCED

½ TEASPOON BLACK PEPPERCORNS

2 TEASPOONS SHRIMP PASTE

1-INCH PIECE OF FRESH GINGER, PEELED AND MINCED

½ CUP WATER

1 TEASPOON SUGAR

1 TEASPOON TAMARIND CONCENTRATE

1 TABLESPOON EXTRA-VIRGIN OLIVE OIL

4 CUPS CHICKEN STOCK (SEE PAGE 440)

1 LB. PORK TENDERLOIN, SLICED THIN

3 CUPS FINELY DICED RIPE PAPAYA

1 TEASPOON HONEY

JUICE OF 1 LIME

1 SMALL THAI CHILE PEPPER, STEMMED, SEEDED, AND SLICED THIN, PLUS MORE FOR GARNISH

2 SCALLIONS, TRIMMED AND SLICED THIN, PLUS MORE FOR GARNISH

SALT AND PEPPER, TO TASTE

1. Place the shallots, garlic, peppercorns, shrimp paste, ginger, water, sugar, and tamarind concentrate in a food processor, pulse until smooth, and strain it through a fine-mesh sieve. Set the mixture aside.
2. Place the olive oil in a medium pot and warm it over medium heat. Add the shallot mixture and cook, stirring frequently, for 2 minutes. Add the stock and bring the soup to a boil.
3. Reduce the heat so that the soup simmers, add the pork and papaya, and cook until the pork is cooked through, 10 to 15 minutes.
4. Add the honey, lime juice, chile, and scallions and season with salt and pepper.
5. Ladle the soup into warmed bowls, garnish with additional chiles and scallions, and serve.

Apple & Pork Stew

YIELD: 4 TO 6 SERVINGS / **ACTIVE TIME:** 20 MINUTES / **TOTAL TIME:** 1 HOUR AND 15 MINUTES

1½ LBS. BONELESS PORK SHOULDER, DICED

⅓ CUP ALL-PURPOSE FLOUR

2 TABLESPOONS EXTRA-VIRGIN OLIVE OIL

2 TABLESPOONS UNSALTED BUTTER

2 ONIONS, FINELY DICED

4 GARLIC CLOVES, MINCED

1 TABLESPOON FRESH THYME

1 TABLESPOON FINELY CHOPPED FRESH ROSEMARY

2 POTATOES, PEELED AND FINELY DICED

1 CUP RED WINE

6 CUPS BEEF STOCK (SEE PAGE 442)

2 APPLES, PEELED, CORED, AND FINELY DICED

SALT AND PEPPER, TO TASTE

1. Place the pork and flour in a medium mixing bowl and toss until the pork is fully coated. Place the olive oil in a large pot and warm it over medium-high heat. Add the pork and cook, stirring occasionally, until it has browned, about 5 minutes. Remove the pork from the pot and set it aside.
2. Reduce the heat to medium, add the butter, onions, and garlic to the pot, and cook, stirring frequently, until the onions have softened, about 5 minutes. Add the thyme, rosemary, and potatoes and cook, stirring occasionally, for 5 minutes.
3. Add the wine and cook, stirring occasionally, until it has reduced by half, about 5 minutes. Add the stock and bring the soup to a boil. Reduce the heat so that the soup simmers. Add the pork, cover the pot, and cook until it is cooked through, about 20 minutes.
4. Add the apples and cook until they are soft, about 15 minutes.
5. Season the soup with salt and pepper, ladle it into warmed bowls, and serve.

Lotus Root & Pork Rib Broth

YIELD: 4 SERVINGS / **ACTIVE TIME:** 20 MINUTES / **TOTAL TIME:** 3 HOURS

12 CUPS HAM STOCK (SEE PAGE 447)

1½ LBS. PORK RIBS

1 OZ. DRIED SQUID, SOAKED FOR 30 MINUTES AND DRAINED

¼ CUP FISH SAUCE

1 TABLESPOON SOY SAUCE

¾ LB. FRESH LOTUS ROOT, PEELED AND SLICED THIN

SALT AND PEPPER, TO TASTE

THAI CHILE PEPPERS, STEMMED, SEEDED, AND SLICED THIN, FOR GARNISH

FRESH THAI BASIL, CHOPPED, FOR GARNISH

1. Place the stock, pork ribs, squid, fish sauce, and soy sauce in a large pot and bring to a boil. Reduce the heat so that the broth simmers, cover the pot, and cook for 1 hour and 30 minutes.
2. Remove the pork ribs from the pot, remove the meat from the pork ribs, and finely dice it. Skim any excess fat off of the broth and then strain the broth into a clean pot through a fine-mesh sieve.
3. Bring the broth to a simmer, add the lotus root, and cook until it is tender, about 30 minutes. Add the meat from the pork ribs and season with salt and pepper.
4. Ladle the soup into warmed bowls, garnish with chiles and Thai basil, and serve.

Chili Verde

YIELD: 4 SERVINGS / **ACTIVE TIME:** 20 MINUTES / **TOTAL TIME:** 1 HOUR AND 15 MINUTES

1 JALAPEÑO CHILE PEPPER, FOR GARNISH

1 TABLESPOON EXTRA-VIRGIN OLIVE OIL

1 LB. BONELESS PORK SHOULDER, DICED

1 ONION, FINELY DICED

2 GARLIC CLOVES, MINCED

1 (14 OZ.) CAN OF STEWED TOMATOES, DICED

2 TOMATILLOS, HUSKED AND CHOPPED

4 CUPS CHICKEN STOCK (SEE PAGE 440)

1 TEASPOON FINELY CHOPPED FRESH OREGANO

PINCH OF GROUND CLOVES

SALT AND PEPPER, TO TASTE

RICE, COOKED, FOR SERVING

1. Roast the jalapeño over an open flame or in the oven until it is charred all over. Let it cool slightly. When it is cool enough to handle, remove the stem and seeds and slice the jalapeño into thin strips. Set it aside.
2. Place the olive oil in a medium pot and warm it over medium-high heat. Add the pork and cook, turning it as necessary, until it is browned all over, about 5 minutes. Add the onion and garlic and cook, stirring occasionally, until the onion has softened, about 5 minutes. Add the tomatoes, tomatillos, stock, oregano, and cloves and bring the chili to a boil.
3. Reduce the heat so that the chili simmers, cover the pot, and cook, stirring occasionally, for 20 minutes.
4. Transfer 2 cups of the chili, without any pork in it, to a food processor and pulse until smooth. Stir the puree back into the pot and cook, stirring occasionally, until the pork is tender, about 25 minutes.
5. Ladle the chili into warmed bowls, add salt and pepper to taste, garnish with the charred jalapeño, and serve with rice.

Chili Verde

SEE PAGE 325

Ham Hock Soup

YIELD: 4 TO 6 SERVINGS / **ACTIVE TIME:** 30 MINUTES / **TOTAL TIME:** 2 HOURS AND 45 MINUTES

2 TABLESPOONS EXTRA-VIRGIN OLIVE OIL

4 HAM HOCKS

1 ONION, FINELY DICED

2 CARROTS, PEELED AND DICED

2 CELERY STALKS, FINELY DICED

1 GREEN BELL PEPPER, STEMMED, SEEDED, AND FINELY DICED

4 TEASPOONS FRESH THYME

8 CUPS HAM STOCK (SEE PAGE 447)

2 POTATOES, PEELED AND FINELY DICED

1 (14 OZ.) CAN OF DICED TOMATOES, DRAINED

1 (14 OZ.) CAN OF KIDNEY BEANS, RINSED AND DRAINED

SALT AND PEPPER, TO TASTE

CRUSTY BREAD, FOR SERVING

1. Place the olive oil in a large pot and warm it over medium-high heat. Add the ham hocks and cook, turning them as necessary, until they have browned, about 5 minutes. Remove the ham hocks from the pot and set them aside.
2. Add the onion, carrots, celery, bell pepper, and thyme and cook, stirring occasionally, until the onion has softened, about 5 minutes. Add the ham hocks and stock and bring the soup to a boil.
3. Reduce the heat so that the soup simmers, cover the pot, and cook, adding water as necessary to cover the ham hocks, until the ham meat is very tender, about 2 hours.
4. Remove the ham hocks from the pot and let them cool. Once they are cool enough to handle, remove the meat from the ham hocks, finely dice it, and set it aside.
5. Add the potatoes to the pot and cook until they are tender, about 15 minutes. Add the ham hock meat, tomatoes, and beans and cook until everything is warmed through, about 5 minutes.
6. Season the soup with salt and pepper, ladle it into warmed bowls, and serve with crusty bread.

Pigs' Trotter Stew

YIELD: 4 SERVINGS / **ACTIVE TIME:** 20 MINUTES / **TOTAL TIME:** 1 HOUR AND 20 MINUTES

2 TABLESPOONS EXTRA-VIRGIN OLIVE OIL

1 ONION, FINELY DICED

2 CARROTS, PEELED AND DICED

2 CELERY STALKS, FINELY DICED

1-INCH PIECE OF FRESH GINGER, PEELED AND MINCED

2 GARLIC CLOVES, MINCED

3 LBS. PIG TROTTERS, RINSED WELL

4 CUPS HAM STOCK (SEE PAGE 447)

1 CUP WHITE WINE VINEGAR

⅓ CUP SOY SAUCE

SACHET D'ÉPICES (SEE PAGE 465)

SALT AND PEPPER, TO TASTE

FRESH CHIVES, CHOPPED, FOR GARNISH

RICE, COOKED, FOR SERVING

1. Place the olive oil in a large pot and warm it over medium heat. Add the onion, carrots, and celery and cook, stirring occasionally, until the onion has softened, about 5 minutes. Add the ginger and garlic and cook, stirring occasionally, for 2 minutes. Add the pig trotters, stock, vinegar, soy sauce, and Sachet d'Épices and bring the soup to a boil.
2. Reduce the heat so that the soup simmers and cook until the broth has thickened and the meat is very tender, about 1 hour.
3. Remove the pig trotters from the pot and let them cool. When they are cool enough to handle, remove the meat from the pig trotters, finely dice it, and add the meat to the pot. Remove the Sachet d'Épices, discard it, and season with salt and pepper.
4. Ladle the soup into warmed bowls, garnish with chives, and serve with rice.

Italian Sausage Soup

YIELD: 4 SERVINGS / **ACTIVE TIME:** 20 MINUTES / **TOTAL TIME:** 1 HOUR

2 TABLESPOONS EXTRA-VIRGIN OLIVE OIL

1 LB. HOT ITALIAN SAUSAGE

1 ONION, FINELY DICED

2 CARROTS, PEELED AND DICED

1 CELERY STALK, FINELY DICED

2 GARLIC CLOVES, MINCED

6 CUPS BEEF STOCK (SEE PAGE 442)

1 ZUCCHINI, FINELY DICED

1 (14 OZ.) CAN OF DICED TOMATOES, DRAINED

1 (14 OZ.) CAN OF CANNELLINI BEANS, RINSED AND DRAINED

2 CUPS SPINACH

SALT AND PEPPER, TO TASTE

1. Place the olive oil in a medium pot and warm it over medium heat. Add the sausage and cook, turning it as necessary, until it has browned, about 5 minutes. Remove the sausage from the pot, slice it thin, and set it aside.
2. Add the onion, carrots, celery, and garlic and cook, stirring occasionally, until the onion has softened, about 5 minutes. Add the stock and bring the soup to a boil.
3. Reduce the heat so that the soup simmers and cook for 10 minutes. Add the zucchini, tomatoes, and beans and cook for 15 minutes.
4. Add the sausage and spinach and cook until the sausage is cooked through, 5 to 10 minutes.
5. Season the soup with salt and pepper, ladle it into warmed bowls, and serve.

Swedish Meatball Soup

YIELD: 4 TO 6 SERVINGS / **ACTIVE TIME:** 30 MINUTES / **TOTAL TIME:** 1 HOUR AND 15 MINUTES

FOR THE MEATBALLS

1 CUP PANKO

½ CUP HEAVY CREAM

2 TABLESPOONS EXTRA-VIRGIN OLIVE OIL

1 ONION, FINELY DICED

½ LB. GROUND BEEF

½ LB. GROUND PORK

1 EGG

⅛ TEASPOON ALLSPICE

SALT AND PEPPER, TO TASTE

FOR THE SOUP

¼ CUP UNSALTED BUTTER

2 CARROTS, PEELED AND DICED

2 CELERY STALKS, FINELY DICED

2 CUPS FINELY DICED BUTTON MUSHROOMS

2 GARLIC CLOVES, MINCED

⅓ CUP ALL-PURPOSE FLOUR

6 CUPS BEEF STOCK (SEE PAGE 442)

¾ CUP HEAVY CREAM

1 TEASPOON WORCESTERSHIRE SAUCE

½ TEASPOON PAPRIKA

½ TEASPOON RED PEPPER FLAKES

SALT AND PEPPER, TO TASTE

FRESH PARSLEY, CHOPPED, FOR GARNISH

1. To begin preparations for the meatballs, place the panko and cream in a large mixing bowl and stir to combine. Let the panko soak for 10 minutes.
2. Place half of the olive oil in a small skillet and warm it over medium heat. Add the onion and cook, stirring occasionally, until it has softened, about 5 minutes. Remove the onion from the skillet and let it cool. Once it has cooled, add the onion, beef, pork, egg, and allspice to the mixing bowl, season with salt and pepper, and stir until fully combined. Form the mixture into 24 balls.
3. Place the remaining olive oil in a large skillet and warm it over medium-high heat. Add the meatballs and cook, turning them as necessary, until they have browned, about 5 minutes. Remove the meatballs from the skillet and set them aside.
4. To begin preparations for the soup, place the butter in a large pot and melt it over medium heat. Add the carrots and celery and cook, stirring occasionally, for 3 minutes. Add the mushrooms and garlic and cook, stirring occasionally, until the celery and carrots have softened, about 3 minutes. Add the flour and cook, stirring frequently, for 3 minutes. Stir in the stock and bring the soup to a boil.
5. Reduce the heat so that the soup simmers, add the meatballs, and cook until they are cooked through, about 15 minutes.
6. Add the cream, Worcestershire sauce, paprika, and red pepper flakes, season with salt and pepper, and cook for 5 minutes.
7. Ladle the soup into warmed bowls, garnish with parsley, and serve.

Spicy Hot & Sour Soup

YIELD: 4 SERVINGS / **ACTIVE TIME:** 20 MINUTES / **TOTAL TIME:** 45 MINUTES

6 DRIED WOOD EAR MUSHROOMS, SOAKED IN WARM WATER, DRAINED, AND FINELY DICED

6 DRIED SHIITAKE MUSHROOMS, SOAKED IN WARM WATER, DRAINED, AND FINELY DICED

6 DRIED TIGER LILY BUDS, SOAKED IN WARM WATER, DRAINED, AND TORN

4 CUPS CHICKEN STOCK (SEE PAGE 440)

¼ CUP FINELY DICED BAMBOO SHOOTS

½ CUP GROUND PORK

1 TEASPOON SOY SAUCE

½ TEASPOON SUGAR

2 TABLESPOONS RED WINE VINEGAR

2 TABLESPOONS CORNSTARCH

¼ CUP WATER

½ LB. TOFU, DICED

1 EGG, BEATEN

SALT AND PEPPER, TO TASTE

SCALLIONS, TRIMMED AND SLICED THIN, FOR GARNISH

SESAME OIL, FOR GARNISH

1. Place the mushrooms, tiger lily buds, stock, bamboo shoots, and pork in a medium pot and bring to a boil. Reduce the heat so that the soup simmers and cook for 10 minutes.
2. Place the soy sauce, sugar, vinegar, cornstarch, and water and ¼ cup of the broth in a small mixing bowl and stir until fully combined. Stir the slurry and tofu into the pot and cook for 2 minutes.
3. Remove the pot from heat, add the egg, and stir until fully combined.
4. Ladle the soup into warmed bowls, add salt and pepper to taste, garnish with scallions and sesame oil, and serve.

Pork & Zucchini Soup

YIELD: 4 SERVINGS / **ACTIVE TIME:** 20 MINUTES / **TOTAL TIME:** 45 MINUTES

1½ LBS. PORK TENDERLOIN, DICED

⅓ CUP ALL-PURPOSE FLOUR

2 TABLESPOONS EXTRA-VIRGIN OLIVE OIL

1 ONION, FINELY DICED

2 GARLIC CLOVES, MINCED

½ CUP STEMMED, SEEDED, AND FINELY DICED RED BELL PEPPER

½ CUP STEMMED, SEEDED, AND FINELY DICED GREEN BELL PEPPER

2 ZUCCHINI, FINELY DICED

1 (14 OZ.) CAN OF DICED TOMATOES, DRAINED

2 TABLESPOONS FINELY DICED SUN-DRIED TOMATOES IN OLIVE OIL

2 CUPS FINELY DICED BUTTON MUSHROOMS

4 CUPS CHICKEN STOCK (SEE PAGE 440)

2 TABLESPOONS OYSTER SAUCE

1 TABLESPOON FINELY CHOPPED FRESH BASIL

1 TEASPOON FINELY CHOPPED FRESH OREGANO

SALT AND PEPPER, TO TASTE

PARMESAN CHEESE, GRATED, FOR GARNISH

1. Place the pork and flour in a mixing bowl and toss until the pork is completely coated.
2. Place the olive oil in a medium pot and warm it over medium-high heat. Add the onion, garlic, and pork and cook, stirring frequently, until the pork has browned, about 5 minutes.
3. Add the bell peppers, zucchini, tomatoes, and mushrooms and cook, stirring occasionally, for 5 minutes. Add the stock, stir until fully combined, and bring the soup to a boil.
4. Reduce the heat so that the soup simmers, add the oyster sauce, and cook for 15 minutes.
5. Stir in the basil and oregano and season the soup with salt and pepper.
6. Ladle the soup into warmed bowls, garnish with Parmesan, and serve.

Prosciutto & Onion Soup

YIELD: 4 SERVINGS / **ACTIVE TIME:** 20 MINUTES / **TOTAL TIME:** 1 HOUR

6 OZ. PROSCIUTTO, CHOPPED

1 TABLESPOON EXTRA-VIRGIN OLIVE OIL

2 TABLESPOONS UNSALTED BUTTER

2 ONIONS, FINELY DICED

1 TABLESPOON MAPLE SYRUP

6 CUPS HAM STOCK (SEE PAGE 447)

1 (14 OZ.) CAN OF DICED TOMATOES, DRAINED

SALT AND PEPPER, TO TASTE

PECORINO CHEESE, GRATED, FOR GARNISH

FRESH BASIL, FINELY CHOPPED, FOR GARNISH

1. Place the prosciutto in a medium pot and cook, stirring occasionally, over low heat for 5 minutes.
2. Add the olive oil, butter, and onions, cover the pot, and cook, stirring occasionally, for 20 minutes.
3. Add the syrup, stock, and tomatoes and cook for 15 minutes.
4. Season the soup with salt and pepper and ladle it into warmed bowls. Garnish with pecorino and basil and serve.

Prosciutto & Onion Soup

SEE PAGE 335

Liver & Bacon Soup

YIELD: 4 SERVINGS / **ACTIVE TIME:** 30 MINUTES / **TOTAL TIME:** 1 HOUR

2 TABLESPOONS EXTRA-VIRGIN OLIVE OIL

4 SLICES OF THICK-CUT BACON, FINELY DICED

1 ONION, FINELY DICED

2 GARLIC CLOVES, MINCED

2 TABLESPOONS ALL-PURPOSE FLOUR

6 CUPS WATER

2 TABLESPOONS WORCESTERSHIRE SAUCE

2 TABLESPOONS SOY SAUCE

1 TABLESPOON FRESH THYME

½ LB. CHICKEN OR DUCK LIVERS, FINELY DICED

SALT AND PEPPER, TO TASTE

4 SLICES OF BAGUETTE

1 CUP GRATED GRUYÈRE CHEESE

1. Place half of the olive oil and the bacon in a large pot and cook over medium heat for 3 minutes. Add the onion and garlic and cook, stirring frequently, until the onion has softened, about 5 minutes. Add half of the flour and cook, stirring continually, for 2 minutes.

2. Add the water, Worcestershire sauce, soy sauce, and thyme, stir to combine, and bring the soup to a boil. Set the oven's broiler to high. Reduce the heat so that the soup simmers and cook for 30 minutes.

3. Place the livers and remaining flour in a mixing bowl and toss until the livers are completely coated.

4. Place the remaining olive oil in a small skillet and warm it over medium-high heat. Add the livers and cook, stirring frequently, until they are golden brown, about 5 minutes. Remove the livers from the skillet, add them to the soup, and season with salt and pepper.

5. Place the baguette slices on a baking sheet and top them with the Gruyère. Place the pan in the oven and broil until the cheese has melted, 1 to 2 minutes. Remove the pan from the oven and let the baguette slices cool.

6. Ladle the soup into warmed bowls and serve with the baguette slices.

Sauerkraut & Chorizo Soup

YIELD: 4 SERVINGS / **ACTIVE TIME:** 25 MINUTES / **TOTAL TIME:** 1 HOUR AND 10 MINUTES

1 TABLESPOON EXTRA-VIRGIN OLIVE OIL

1 POTATO, PEELED AND FINELY DICED

1 ONION, FINELY DICED

½ LB. DRIED CHORIZO SAUSAGES, DICED

3 GARLIC CLOVES, MINCED

1 BAY LEAF

1 TEASPOON CARAWAY SEEDS

2 TABLESPOONS SWEET PAPRIKA

LARGE PINCH OF CAYENNE PEPPER

4 CUPS WATER

1 LB. SAUERKRAUT

SALT AND PEPPER, TO TASTE

SOUR CREAM, FOR GARNISH

1. Place the olive oil in a large pot and warm it over medium heat. Add the potato and onion and cook, stirring occasionally, until the onion has softened, about 5 minutes.
2. Add the chorizo and garlic and cook, stirring frequently, for 3 minutes. Add the bay leaf and caraway seeds and cook, stirring occasionally, for 2 minutes.
3. Add the paprika, cayenne pepper, water, and sauerkraut and bring the soup to a simmer. Cover the pot and cook for 45 minutes.
4. Season the soup with salt and pepper and ladle it into warmed bowls. Garnish with sour cream and serve.

SEAFOOD

Mussel Cappuccino

YIELD: 4 SERVINGS / **ACTIVE TIME:** 30 MINUTES / **TOTAL TIME:** 40 MINUTES

2 TABLESPOONS UNSALTED BUTTER

2 SHALLOTS, FINELY CHOPPED

1 GARLIC CLOVE, MINCED

½ CUP WHITE WINE

2 TABLESPOONS FINELY CHOPPED FRESH CILANTRO

2 LBS. MUSSELS

½ CUP HEAVY CREAM

1½ CUPS WHOLE MILK

SALT AND PEPPER, TO TASTE

FIVE SPICE POWDER, FOR GARNISH

CRACKERS, FOR SERVING

1. Place the butter in a medium pot and melt it over medium heat. Add the shallots and garlic and cook, stirring frequently, until the shallots are translucent, about 3 minutes.
2. Add the wine and cilantro and bring the soup to a simmer. Add the mussels, cover the pot, and cook until the majority of the mussels have opened, about 5 minutes. Remove the mussels from the pot and let them cool. Discard any mussels that did not open.
3. When the mussels are cool enough to handle, remove the meat from them, chop it, and set it aside.
4. Place the soup, mussels, and cream and half of the milk in a food processor, pulse until smooth, and strain it into a clean pot through a fine-mesh sieve.
5. Bring the soup to a simmer and season with salt and pepper. Stir in the remaining milk and use an immersion blender to froth the soup.
6. Ladle the soup into warmed cups. Garnish with five-spice powder and serve with crackers.

Creamy Haddock Chowder

YIELD: 4 SERVINGS / **ACTIVE TIME:** 30 MINUTES / **TOTAL TIME:** 1 HOUR

4 SLICES OF THICK-CUT BACON, FINELY DICED

1 ONION, FINELY DICED

4 CUPS PEELED AND FINELY DICED POTATOES

4 CUPS FISH STOCK (SEE PAGE 454)

1½ LBS. HADDOCK FILLETS, SKIN REMOVED, DICED

2 TABLESPOONS FINELY CHOPPED FRESH PARSLEY

1 TABLESPOON FINELY CHOPPED FRESH CHIVES, PLUS MORE FOR GARNISH

1 TABLESPOON FINELY CHOPPED FRESH TARRAGON

2 CUPS HEAVY CREAM

SALT AND PEPPER, TO TASTE

CRACKERS, FOR SERVING

1. Place the bacon in a medium pot and cook over low heat, stirring occasionally, until it is crispy, 10 to 12 minutes. Add the onion and potatoes and cook, stirring occasionally, until the onion has softened, about 8 minutes.
2. Add the stock and bring the soup to a boil. Reduce the heat so that the soup simmers and cook until the potatoes have softened, about 10 minutes. Add the haddock, parsley, chives, and tarragon and cook until the haddock is cooked through, about 10 minutes.
3. Stir in the cream, season with salt and pepper, and bring the soup to a gentle simmer.
4. Ladle the soup into warmed bowls, garnish with additional chives, and serve with crackers.

Chilled Niçoise Soup

YIELD: 4 SERVINGS / **ACTIVE TIME:** 25 MINUTES / **TOTAL TIME:** 1 HOUR

SALT AND PEPPER, TO TASTE

16 GREEN BEANS

8 CREAMER OR FINGERLING POTATOES, QUARTERED

4 CUPS VEGETABLE STOCK (SEE PAGE 441)

3 GARLIC CLOVES, MINCED

2 TEASPOONS RED WINE VINEGAR

2 TEASPOONS DIJON MUSTARD

2 TABLESPOONS KALAMATA OLIVE BRINE

2 TEASPOONS FRESH LEMON JUICE

DASH OF WORCESTERSHIRE SAUCE

2 TABLESPOONS EXTRA-VIRGIN OLIVE OIL

½ LB. YELLOWFIN TUNA FILLETS, CUT INTO 4 PIECES

1 PLUM TOMATO, FINELY DICED

8 ANCHOVIES IN OLIVE OIL, DRAINED

8 BLACK OLIVES, PITTED AND CHOPPED

MICROGREENS, FOR GARNISH

POACHED EGGS, FOR SERVING

CRUSTY BREAD, FOR SERVING

1. Bring water to a boil in a small pot. Add salt and let the water return to a boil. Add the green beans and cook until they are just tender, 2 to 3 minutes. Remove the green beans with a strainer, rinse them under cold water, and cut them in half. Set the green beans aside.
2. Add the potatoes to the boiling water and cook until they are tender, about 10 minutes. Drain the potatoes and set them aside.
3. Place the stock, garlic, vinegar, mustard, brine, lemon juice, and Worcestershire sauce in a medium pot, bring to a simmer, and cook for 10 minutes.
4. Strain the soup into a bowl through a fine-mesh sieve, season with salt and pepper, and set it aside.
5. Place half of the olive oil in a small skillet and warm it over medium-high heat. Add the tuna, season it with salt and pepper, and sear it on both sides, turning it over just once. Remove the tuna from the skillet and set it aside.
6. Place the green beans, potatoes, tomato, anchovies, olives, and remaining olive oil in a mixing bowl, season with salt and pepper, and toss to combine.
7. Divide the tossed ingredients and tuna among chilled bowls, ladle the soup over the top, garnish with microgreens, and serve with poached eggs and crusty bread.

Sweet Corn Chowder with Scallops

YIELD: 6 SERVINGS / **ACTIVE TIME:** 30 MINUTES / **TOTAL TIME:** 45 MINUTES

6 TABLESPOONS UNSALTED BUTTER

1 LARGE ONION, DICED

6 SLICES OF BACON, COOKED AND DICED

2 CELERY STALKS, CHOPPED

2 GARLIC CLOVES, MINCED

¼ CUP ALL-PURPOSE FLOUR

3 CUPS FRESH CORN KERNELS

3 SPRIGS OF FRESH THYME

2 LARGE POTATOES, PEELED AND DICED

½ CUP HEAVY CREAM

½ CUP MILK

SALT AND PEPPER, TO TASTE

1 TABLESPOON EXTRA-VIRGIN OLIVE OIL

6 SCALLOPS

1. Place the butter in a large cast-iron skillet and melt it over medium heat. Add the onion and cook, stirring occasionally, until it gives off a nutty aroma and starts to brown, about 8 minutes.
2. Add the bacon, celery, and garlic and cook, stirring frequently, until the bacon starts to brown, about 5 minutes.
3. Stir in the flour and then add the corn, thyme, potatoes, cream, and milk. Bring the chowder to a simmer, season it with salt and pepper, and cook, stirring occasionally, until the potatoes are fork-tender, about 15 minutes.
4. Place the olive oil in a medium cast-iron skillet and warm it over medium-high heat.
5. Pat the scallops dry and season them with salt. Place the scallops in the cast-iron pan and cook until golden brown on both sides, about 2 minutes per side.
6. Remove the sprigs of thyme from the chowder and discard them. Ladle the chowder into warmed bowls and top each portion with a scallop.

Canh Chua Cá

YIELD: 4 SERVINGS / **ACTIVE TIME:** 30 MINUTES / **TOTAL TIME:** 45 MINUTES

1 LB. CATFISH FILLETS, SKIN REMOVED, DICED

SALT AND PEPPER, TO TASTE

CHILI POWDER, TO TASTE

2 TABLESPOONS EXTRA-VIRGIN OLIVE OIL

4 GARLIC CLOVES, MINCED

1 THAI CHILE PEPPER, STEMMED, SEEDED, AND SLICED THIN

3 TOMATOES, 1 DICED, 2 QUARTERED

6 CUPS VEGETABLE STOCK (SEE PAGE 441)

1 TABLESPOON TAMARIND PASTE

¼ CUP SUGAR

¼ CUP FISH SAUCE, PLUS MORE TO TASTE

1 CUP CHOPPED PINEAPPLE

6 OKRA, TRIMMED AND SLICED THIN

2 OZ. BEAN SPROUTS

1 BUNCH OF FRESH THAI BASIL, FINELY CHOPPED

2 SPRING ONIONS, TRIMMED AND FINELY DICED

1. Season the catfish with salt, pepper, and chili powder and set it aside.
2. Place the olive oil in a medium pot and warm it over medium heat. Add the garlic and cook, stirring frequently, for 2 minutes. Transfer the garlic and olive oil to a small mixing bowl, add the chile, and set the mixture aside.
3. Add the diced tomato to the pot and cook, stirring occasionally, for 3 minutes. Add the stock and bring to a boil.
4. Reduce the heat so that the soup simmers, add the tamarind paste, sugar, fish sauce, pineapple, and okra, and cook for 2 minutes. Add the catfish and cook until it is cooked through, 3 to 5 minutes.
5. Add the bean sprouts and cook for 2 minutes. Stir in the basil and onions and season with salt, pepper, and fish sauce.
6. Ladle the soup into warmed bowls, garnish with the garlic-and-chile oil and quartered tomatoes, and serve.

Spicy Clam Soup

YIELD: 6 SERVINGS / **ACTIVE TIME:** 30 MINUTES / **TOTAL TIME:** 1 HOUR

2 TABLESPOONS EXTRA-VIRGIN OLIVE OIL

1 ONION, FINELY DICED

2 GARLIC CLOVES, MINCED

2 THAI CHILE PEPPERS, STEMMED, SEEDED, AND SLICED THIN

⅔ CUP THINLY SLICED DRIED CHORIZO

1 CUP WHITE WINE

1 (14 OZ.) CAN OF DICED TOMATOES, WITH THEIR LIQUID

1½ CUPS PEELED AND FINELY DICED POTATOES

2 CUPS CRAB STOCK (SEE PAGE 452)

4 LBS. LITTLENECK CLAMS, SCRUBBED AND RINSED WELL

1 TABLESPOON FINELY CHOPPED FRESH CILANTRO

1 TABLESPOON FINELY CHOPPED FRESH PARSLEY, PLUS MORE FOR GARNISH

SALT AND PEPPER, TO TASTE

LEMON WEDGES, FOR SERVING

CRUSTY BREAD, FOR SERVING

1. Place the olive oil in a medium pot and warm it over medium heat. Add the onion and cook, stirring occasionally, until it has softened, about 5 minutes. Add the garlic, chiles, and chorizo and cook, stirring frequently, for 2 minutes. Add the wine and bring to a boil. Reduce the heat so that the liquid simmers and cook, stirring occasionally, for 2 minutes.
2. Add the tomatoes, potatoes, and stock and bring the soup to a boil. Reduce the heat so that the soup simmers, cover the pot, and cook until the soup has thickened and the potatoes are very tender, about 45 minutes.
3. Add the clams and cook until the majority of them have opened, about 5 minutes. Discard any clams that did not open.
4. Stir in the cilantro and parsley and season with salt and pepper.
5. Ladle the soup into warmed bowls, garnish with additional parsley, and serve with lemon wedges and crusty bread.

Spicy Clam Soup

SEE PAGE 349

Seafarers' Stew

YIELD: 4 SERVINGS / **ACTIVE TIME:** 30 MINUTES / **TOTAL TIME:** 45 MINUTES

½ LB. SMOKED MACKEREL, SKIN REMOVED, DICED

½ LB. SWORDFISH FILLETS, SKIN REMOVED, DICED

¼ LB. SMALL SHRIMP, SHELLED AND DEVEINED

3 CUPS LOBSTER STOCK (SEE PAGE 443)

3 CUPS FISH STOCK (SEE PAGE 454)

8 CLAMS, RINSED WELL AND SCRUBBED

8 MUSSELS, RINSED WELL AND SCRUBBED

1 TABLESPOON EXTRA-VIRGIN OLIVE OIL

2 SHALLOTS, FINELY CHOPPED

4 SLICES OF THICK-CUT BACON, FINELY DICED

3 CUPS PEELED AND GRATED CARROTS

¾ CUP HEAVY CREAM

SALT AND PEPPER, TO TASTE

FRESH PARSLEY, CHOPPED, FOR GARNISH

1. Place the mackerel, swordfish, shrimp, and stocks in a large pot, bring to a simmer, and cook for 5 minutes. Add the clams, cover the pot, and cook for 3 minutes. Add the mussels, cover the pot, and cook until the majority of the clams and mussels have opened, 3 to 5 minutes. Discard any clams and/or mussels that did not open. Strain the broth into a bowl through a fine-mesh sieve and set it and the solids aside.
2. Place the olive oil in a clean large pot and warm it over medium-high heat. Add the shallots and bacon and cook, stirring occasionally, until the bacon is crispy, 6 to 8 minutes.
3. Add the broth and bring the soup to a boil. Reduce the heat so that the soup simmers, add the carrots, and cook for 5 minutes. Add the reserved solids and the cream and stir to combine.
4. Ladle the soup into warmed bowls, add salt and pepper to taste, garnish with parsley, and serve.

Sole & Pasta Soup

YIELD: 4 SERVINGS / **ACTIVE TIME:** 30 MINUTES / **TOTAL TIME:** 1 HOUR AND 30 MINUTES

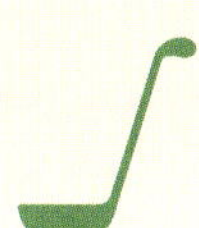

1 RED BELL PEPPER

2 TABLESPOONS EXTRA-VIRGIN OLIVE OIL

1 ONION, FINELY DICED

1 GARLIC CLOVE, MINCED

½ LEEK, TRIMMED, RINSED WELL, AND FINELY DICED

4 CUPS VEGETABLE STOCK (SEE PAGE 441)

1 (14 OZ.) CAN OF DICED TOMATOES, WITH THEIR LIQUID

1 TEASPOON HERBES DE PROVENCE

⅛ TEASPOON SAFFRON THREADS

2 CUPS FARFALLE

1½ LBS. SOLE FILLETS, SKIN REMOVED, HALVED LENGTHWISE

16 MUSSELS, RINSED WELL AND SCRUBBED

SALT AND PEPPER, TO TASTE

CRUSTY BREAD, FOR SERVING

1. Prepare a gas or charcoal grill for medium-high heat (about 450°F). Place the bell pepper on the grill and cook, turning occasionally, until it is lightly charred, about 10 minutes. Remove the bell pepper from the grill and let it cool slightly. When it is cool enough to handle, remove the stem, seeds, and skin and dice the remaining flesh. Set the bell pepper aside.
2. Place the olive oil in a large pot and warm it over medium heat. Add the onion, garlic, and leek and cook, stirring occasionally, until they have softened, about 5 minutes. Add the stock, tomatoes, herbes de Provence, and saffron and bring the soup to a boil. Add the pasta and cook for 8 minutes.
3. Reduce the heat so that the soup simmers, add the roasted pepper, sole, and mussels, and cook until the fish is cooked through and the majority of the mussels have opened, 5 to 10 minutes. Discard any mussels that did not open.
4. Season the soup with salt and pepper, ladle it into warmed bowls, and serve with crusty bread.

Smoked Mackerel & Tomato Soup

YIELD: 4 SERVINGS / **ACTIVE TIME:** 25 MINUTES / **TOTAL TIME:** 30 MINUTES

6 CUPS VEGETABLE STOCK (SEE PAGE 441)

1 LEMONGRASS STALK, CRUSHED

2-INCH PIECE OF FRESH GALANGAL, PEELED AND MINCED

4 SHALLOTS, FINELY CHOPPED

2 GARLIC CLOVES, MINCED

¾ LB. SMOKED MACKEREL, SKIN REMOVED, DICED

4 TOMATOES, FINELY DICED

½ TEASPOON RED PEPPER FLAKES

2 TABLESPOONS FISH SAUCE

2 TEASPOONS BROWN SUGAR

2 TABLESPOONS TAMARIND PASTE

8 SCALLIONS, TRIMMED

SALT AND PEPPER, TO TASTE

1. Place the stock, lemongrass, galangal root, shallots, and garlic in a medium pot and bring to a boil. Reduce the heat so that the soup simmers and cook for 10 minutes.
2. Add the mackerel, tomatoes, red pepper flakes, fish sauce, brown sugar, and tamarind paste and cook for 5 minutes. Add the scallions and cook for 2 minutes.
3. Remove the scallions, galangal root, and lemongrass from the pot and discard them.
4. Season the soup with salt and pepper, ladle it into warmed bowls, and serve.

Smoked Trout & Mushroom Soup

YIELD: 6 SERVINGS / **ACTIVE TIME:** 30 MINUTES / **TOTAL TIME:** 1 HOUR

2 TABLESPOONS UNSALTED BUTTER

1 ONION, FINELY DICED

1 GARLIC CLOVE, MINCED

½ CUP FINELY DICED RED BELL PEPPER

½ CUP FINELY DICED GREEN BELL PEPPER

½ TEASPOON TABASCO

¼ CUP ALL-PURPOSE FLOUR

3 CUPS FISH STOCK (SEE PAGE 454)

1 (14 OZ.) CAN OF DICED TOMATOES, WITH THEIR LIQUID

¾ CUP FINELY DICED BEECH MUSHROOMS

¾ CUP FINELY DICED BABY BROWN PEARL MUSHROOMS

1 CUP WHOLE MILK

¾ LB. HADDOCK FILLETS, SKIN REMOVED, DICED

¼ LB. SMOKED TROUT, DICED

12 MUSSELS, RINSED WELL AND SCRUBBED

SALT AND PEPPER, TO TASTE

FRESH PARSLEY, CHOPPED, FOR GARNISH

GRUYÈRE CHEESE, GRATED, FOR GARNISH

CRUSTY BREAD, FOR SERVING

1. Place the butter in a medium pot and melt it over medium heat. Add the onion and garlic and cook, stirring frequently, until they have softened, about 5 minutes.
2. Add the bell peppers and Tabasco and cook, stirring frequently, for 2 minutes. Add the flour and cook, stirring continually, for 3 minutes. Add the stock, tomatoes, mushrooms, and milk and bring the soup to a boil.
3. Reduce the heat so that the soup simmers and cook until the vegetables have softened, about 5 minutes.
4. Add the haddock and trout and cook for 2 to 3 minutes. Add the mussels and cook until the majority of the mussels have opened, about 5 minutes. Discard any mussels that did not open.
5. Season the soup with salt and pepper and ladle it into warmed bowls. Garnish with parsley and Gruyère and serve with crusty bread.

Bouillabaisse

YIELD: 6 SERVINGS / **ACTIVE TIME:** 25 MINUTES / **TOTAL TIME:** 1 HOUR AND 30 MINUTES

6 TABLESPOONS EXTRA-VIRGIN OLIVE OIL

1 ONION, CHOPPED

1 CUP CHOPPED LEEKS

½ CUP SLICED CELERY

1 CUP CHOPPED FENNEL

2 GARLIC CLOVES, MINCED

BOUQUET GARNI (SEE PAGE 469)

ZEST OF 1 ORANGE

1 TOMATO, PEELED, SEEDED, AND CHOPPED

PINCH OF SAFFRON

3 CUPS FISH STOCK (SEE PAGE 454)

3 CUPS LOBSTER STOCK (SEE PAGE 443)

2 TEASPOONS PERNOD

1 TABLESPOON TOMATO PASTE

1 LB. MONKFISH, CUT INTO 1-INCH CUBES

12 SMALL SHRIMP, SHELLS REMOVED, DEVEINED

12 STEAMER CLAMS

24 MUSSELS

SALT AND PEPPER, TO TASTE

FRESH PARSLEY, CHOPPED, FOR GARNISH

CRUSTY BREAD, TOASTED, FOR SERVING

1. Place ¼ cup of the olive oil in a large saucepan and warm it over medium heat. Add the onion, leeks, celery, and fennel and cook, stirring occasionally, until the vegetables have softened, about 10 minutes.
2. Add the garlic, Bouquet Garni, orange zest, and tomato and cook, stirring continually, for 1 minute. Stir in the saffron, stocks, Pernod, and tomato paste and bring the soup to a boil. Reduce the heat and simmer the soup for 20 minutes.
3. While the soup is simmering, place the remaining olive oil in a skillet and warm it over medium heat. Add the monkfish and shrimp and cook for 2 minutes on each side. Remove the shrimp and monkfish from the pan and set them aside.
4. Add the clams to the soup and cook for 3 minutes. Add the mussels and cook until the majority of the clams and mussels have opened, 3 to 4 minutes. Discard any clams and mussels that did not open.
5. Add the monkfish and shrimp to the soup and cook until warmed through.
6. Season the soup with salt and pepper and ladle it into warmed bowls. Garnish each portion with parsley and serve with toasted crusty bread.

Lobster Cioppino

YIELD: 6 SERVINGS / **ACTIVE TIME:** 30 MINUTES / **TOTAL TIME:** 1 HOUR AND 30 MINUTES

1¼-LB. FRESH LOBSTER

2 CUPS WATER

1 LB. PEI MUSSELS, RINSED WELL AND DEBEARDED

12 LITTLENECK CLAMS, RINSED WELL AND SCRUBBED

2 TABLESPOONS EXTRA-VIRGIN OLIVE OIL

½ LARGE BULB OF FENNEL, TRIMMED AND SLICED THIN

2 SHALLOTS, MINCED

3 GARLIC CLOVES, MINCED

1 (6 OZ.) CAN OF TOMATO PASTE

1 CUP RED WINE

1 (28 OZ.) CAN OF WHOLE SAN MARZANO TOMATOES, WITH THEIR LIQUID, LIGHTLY CRUSHED BY HAND

1 CUP WHITE WINE

2 CUPS FISH STOCK (SEE PAGE 454)

2 BAY LEAVES

1 TEASPOON RED PEPPER FLAKES

SALT AND PEPPER, TO TASTE

1 LB. HALIBUT FILLETS, CHOPPED

CRUSTY BREAD, FOR SERVING

1. Place 3 inches of water in a cast-iron Dutch oven and bring to a boil. Place the lobster, headfirst, in the pot, cover the pot, and cook the lobster until the shell is bright red, about 6 minutes. Remove the lobster from the pot and set aside. Discard the cooking liquid and return the Dutch oven to the stove.
2. Add the water to the pot and bring it to a boil. Add the mussels and clams, cover the pot, and cook until the majority of the mussels and clams have opened, about 5 minutes. Drain the mussels and clams, reserve the liquid, and set aside the mussels and clams. Discard any mussels and clams that did not open.
3. Place the Dutch oven over medium-high heat and add the olive oil. When the oil is warm, add the fennel and cook, stirring occasionally, until the fennel has softened, about 5 minutes.
4. Add the shallots and cook, stirring occasionally, until they have softened, about 5 minutes.
5. Add the garlic and tomato paste and cook, stirring continually, for 1 minute. Deglaze the pot with the red wine, scraping up any browned bits from the bottom of the pot. Cook until the wine has almost evaporated, about 5 minutes.
6. Add the tomatoes, white wine, stock, bay leaves, and red pepper flakes and a pinch of salt and pepper. Reduce the heat to medium-low, cover the pot, and cook for 30 minutes.
7. While the stew is cooking, remove the meat from the tail and claws of the lobster. Set it aside.
8. Remove the legs from the lobster and add the remaining carcass to the pot. Uncover the pot and cook the stew for 20 minutes.
9. Add the halibut to the pot and cook until it is cooked through, about 5 minutes. Add the lobster meat, clams, mussels, and reserved cooking liquid and cook for 2 minutes. Ladle the stew into warmed bowls and serve with crusty bread.

Caribbean Rice Stew with Salt Cod

YIELD: 4 SERVINGS / **ACTIVE TIME:** 45 MINUTES / **TOTAL TIME:** 1 HOUR

1½ TABLESPOONS ALL-PURPOSE FLOUR

½ LB. SALT COD, DICED

2 TEASPOONS EXTRA-VIRGIN OLIVE OIL

¼ CUP UNSALTED BUTTER

3 OZ. THICK-CUT BACON, CHOPPED

1 ONION, FINELY DICED

1 GARLIC CLOVE, MINCED

1 RED CHILE PEPPER, STEMMED, SEEDED, AND SLICED THIN

¾ CUP LONG-GRAIN RICE

2 TEASPOONS FRESH THYME

1 CINNAMON STICK

1 (14 OZ.) CAN OF BLACK-EYED PEAS, DRAINED AND RINSED

4 CUPS WATER

1 CUP COCONUT MILK

4 CUPS BABY SPINACH

SALT AND PEPPER, TO TASTE

1. Place the flour and cod in a small mixing bowl and toss until the cod is fully coated.
2. Place the olive oil and butter in a medium pot and warm the mixture over medium heat. Add the bacon and cook, stirring occasionally, until it is crispy, about 8 minutes. Add the onion, garlic, and chile and cook, stirring occasionally, for 3 to 4 minutes.
3. Stir in the rice and cook for 2 minutes. Add the thyme, cinnamon stick, and peas and cook for 2 minutes. Add the water and bring the soup to a boil.
4. Reduce the heat to low and cook until the rice is tender, about 20 minutes.
5. Bring the soup to a simmer, add the coconut milk and cod, and cook for 5 minutes.
6. Remove the cinnamon stick from the pot and discard it. Stir in the spinach, season with salt and pepper, and cook for 3 minutes.
7. Ladle the soup into warmed bowls and serve.

Thai Seafood Soup

YIELD: 4 SERVINGS / **ACTIVE TIME:** 20 MINUTES / **TOTAL TIME:** 45 MINUTES

4 CUPS FISH STOCK (SEE PAGE 454)

2 LEMONGRASS STALKS, CRUSHED

ZEST AND JUICE OF 2 LIMES

1-INCH PIECE OF FRESH GALANGAL, PEELED AND MINCED

6 TABLESPOONS FINELY CHOPPED FRESH CILANTRO

1 FRESH MAKRUT LIME LEAF

2 MONKFISH FILLETS, SKIN REMOVED, DICED

12 SMALL SHRIMP, SHELLED AND DEVEINED

2 THAI CHILE PEPPERS, STEMMED, SEEDED, AND SLICED THIN

1 TABLESPOON RICE VINEGAR

¼ CUP FISH SAUCE

HANDFUL OF BEAN SPROUTS

FRESH CILANTRO, CHOPPED, FOR GARNISH

TOASTED SESAME SEEDS, FOR GARNISH

SESAME OIL, FOR GARNISH

1. Place the stock, lemongrass, lime zest, galangal root, cilantro, and lime leaf in a medium pot and bring to a boil. Reduce the heat so that the soup simmers and cook for 5 minutes. Remove the pot from heat and let the soup rest for 15 minutes.

2. Strain the soup into a clean pot through a fine-mesh sieve and bring it to a boil. Reduce the heat so that the soup simmers, add the lime juice, fish, shrimp, peppers, vinegar, fish sauce, and bean sprouts, and cook until the fish is cooked through, 3 to 4 minutes.

3. Ladle the soup into warmed bowls, garnish with cilantro, toasted sesame seeds, and sesame oil, and serve.

Thai Seafood Soup

SEE PAGE 361

New England Clam Chowder

YIELD: 4 TO 6 SERVINGS / **ACTIVE TIME:** 45 MINUTES / **TOTAL TIME:** 1 HOUR AND 30 MINUTES

4 LBS. STEAMER CLAMS, RINSED WELL AND SCRUBBED

2 CUPS WHITE WINE

2 CUPS FINELY DICED ONIONS

¼ CUP UNSALTED BUTTER

1 TEASPOON FRESH THYME

2 CUPS PEELED AND FINELY DICED YUKON GOLD POTATOES

4 CUPS HEAVY CREAM

SALT AND PEPPER, TO TASTE

FRESH PARSLEY, CHOPPED, FOR GARNISH

OYSTER CRACKERS, FOR SERVING

1. Place the clams, the wine, and half of the onions in a medium pot, cover the pot, and cook over medium-high heat until the majority of the clams have opened, about 5 minutes. Discard any clams that did not open.
2. Strain the mixture through a fine-mesh sieve and set the cooking liquid aside. Remove the meat and bellies from the clams, chop them, and set them aside.
3. Place the butter in a clean medium pot and melt it over medium heat. Add the remaining onions and cook, stirring occasionally, until they have softened, about 5 minutes. Add the reserved cooking liquid and thyme, bring to a simmer, and cook until the liquid has been reduced by half, about 5 minutes.
4. Add the potatoes and cook until they are tender, about 15 minutes.
5. Add the cream and clam meat and bellies and season the soup with salt and pepper. Cook until the soup is warmed through.
6. Ladle the soup into warmed bowls, garnish with parsley, and serve with oyster crackers.

Manhattan Clam Chowder

YIELD: 4 SERVINGS / **ACTIVE TIME:** 45 MINUTES / **TOTAL TIME:** 1 HOUR AND 30 MINUTES

15 STEAMER CLAMS, RINSED WELL AND SCRUBBED

2 CUPS WATER

⅓ CUP CHOPPED SALT PORK

¾ CUP FINELY DICED ONION

⅓ CUP PEELED AND DICED CARROTS

1 CUP FINELY DICED LEEKS, TRIMMED AND RINSED WELL BEFORE CUTTING

⅓ CUP FINELY DICED GREEN BELL PEPPER

1 GARLIC CLOVE, MINCED

1 CUP TOMATO JUICE

½ CUP FINELY DICED TOMATO

1 BAY LEAF

1 TEASPOON FRESH THYME

1 TEASPOON OREGANO

1 CUP PEELED AND FINELY DICED POTATOES

⅛ TEASPOON TABASCO

⅛ TEASPOON WORCESTERSHIRE SAUCE

⅛ TEASPOON OLD BAY SEASONING

SALTINES, FOR SERVING

1. Place the clams and water in a medium pot, cover the pot, and cook over medium-high heat until the majority of the clams have opened, about 5 minutes. Discard any clams that did not open. Strain the mixture through a fine-mesh sieve and set the cooking liquid aside. Remove the meat and bellies from the clams, chop the meat, and set the meat and bellies aside.
2. Place the salt pork in a clean medium pot and melt it over medium heat. Add the onion, carrots, leeks, bell pepper, and garlic and cook, stirring occasionally, until they have softened, about 5 minutes.
3. Add the cooking liquid, tomato juice, tomato, bay leaf, thyme, and oregano, bring the soup to a simmer, and cook for 10 minutes. Add the potatoes and cook until it is tender, about 15 minutes.
4. Remove the bay leaf, thyme, and oregano and discard them. Stir in the clam meat and bellies, Tabasco, Worcestershire sauce, and Old Bay Seasoning and cook until the soup is warmed through.
5. Ladle the soup into warmed bowls and serve with saltines.

Crab Bisque with Caviar & Crème Fraîche

YIELD: 4 SERVINGS / **ACTIVE TIME:** 20 MINUTES / **TOTAL TIME:** 1 HOUR

¼ CUP UNSALTED BUTTER

1 CUP FINELY DICED LEEKS, TRIMMED AND RINSED WELL BEFORE CUTTING

1 CUP PEELED AND DICED CARROTS

¾ CUP CHOPPED FENNEL

2 TABLESPOONS RIESLING

1 CUP FINELY DICED TOMATOES

1 TABLESPOON TOMATO PASTE

½ CUP WHITE WINE

6 CUPS CRAB STOCK (SEE PAGE 452)

1 TEASPOON FINELY CHOPPED FRESH TARRAGON

½ CUP HEAVY CREAM

1½ CUPS CANNED CRABMEAT, PICKED OVER

SALT AND PEPPER, TO TASTE

CRÈME FRAÎCHE, FOR GARNISH

CAVIAR, FOR GARNISH

1. Place the butter in a medium pot and melt it over medium heat. Add the leeks, carrots, and fennel and cook, stirring occasionally, until they have softened, about 5 minutes. Add the Riesling, tomatoes, tomato paste, wine, stock, and tarragon and bring to a boil.
2. Reduce the heat so that the soup simmers and cook for 30 minutes.
3. Transfer the soup to a food processor, pulse until smooth, and strain it into a clean pot through a fine-mesh sieve.
4. Stir in the cream and crabmeat, season with salt and pepper, and stir to combine.
5. Ladle the soup into warmed bowls, garnish with crème fraîche and caviar, and serve.

Finnish Salmon Soup

YIELD: 4 SERVINGS / **ACTIVE TIME:** 20 MINUTES / **TOTAL TIME:** 50 MINUTES

2 TABLESPOONS UNSALTED BUTTER

1 ONION, FINELY DICED

4 CUPS FISH STOCK (SEE PAGE 454)

1 POTATO, PEELED AND FINELY DICED

¾-LB. SALMON FILLET, SKIN REMOVED, DICED

1 CUP HEAVY CREAM

SALT AND PEPPER, TO TASTE

FENNEL FRONDS, FOR GARNISH

FENNEL POLLEN, FOR GARNISH

SALMON ROE, FOR GARNISH

CRÈME FRAÎCHE, FOR GARNISH

CRUSTY BREAD, TOASTED, FOR SERVING

1. Place the butter in a large pot and melt it over medium heat. Add the onion and cook, stirring occasionally, until it has softened, about 5 minutes. Add the stock and bring to a boil.
2. Reduce the heat so that the soup simmers, add the potato, and cook until it is tender, 10 to 15 minutes.
3. Add the salmon and cook until it is cooked through, 4 to 5 minutes. Stir in the cream, season with salt and pepper, and stir to combine.
4. Ladle the soup into warmed bowls, garnish with fennel fronds, fennel pollen, salmon roe, and crème fraîche, and serve with toasted bread.

Lobster Bisque

YIELD: 4 TO 6 SERVINGS / **ACTIVE TIME:** 25 MINUTES / **TOTAL TIME:** 1 HOUR AND 15 MINUTES

6 LOBSTER CARCASSES

¼ CUP UNSALTED BUTTER

1 ONION, DICED

1 GARLIC CLOVE, MINCED

4 CUPS CHOPPED TOMATOES

½ CUP CHOPPED FENNEL

½ TEASPOON FRESH THYME

2 TEASPOONS CHOPPED FRESH PARSLEY

2 TEASPOONS CHOPPED FRESH TARRAGON

½ CUP RIESLING

1 CUP BRANDY

4 CUPS LOBSTER STOCK (SEE PAGE 443)

4 CUPS HEAVY CREAM

¼ TEASPOON CAYENNE PEPPER

1 TABLESPOON FRESH LEMON JUICE

SALT AND PEPPER, TO TASTE

1 CUP COOKED LOBSTER MEAT

FENNEL FRONDS, FOR GARNISH

CRÈME FRAÎCHE, FOR GARNISH

1. Preheat the oven to 400°F. Place the lobsters on a baking sheet, place the pan in the oven, and roast the lobsters for 15 minutes. Remove them from the oven and set them aside.
2. Place the butter in a large stockpot and melt it over medium heat. Add the onion, garlic, tomatoes, fennel, and fresh herbs and cook, stirring frequently, until the onion starts to brown, about 10 minutes.
3. Add the Riesling and brandy and cook until the liquid has reduced by half.
4. Add the roasted lobsters, stock, and heavy cream and bring to a boil. Reduce the heat so that the soup simmers and cook for 45 minutes.
5. Using tongs, remove the lobsters from the soup. Squeeze as much liquid as possible from them into the soup, and then discard the lobsters.
6. Transfer the soup to a food processor, blitz until smooth and creamy, and strain into a clean pot through a fine-mesh sieve.
7. Bring the soup to a simmer, stir in the cayenne pepper and lemon juice, season with salt and pepper, and then stir in the lobster meat.
8. Cook until it is warmed through, about 2 minutes, ladle the soup into warmed bowls, and garnish each portion with fennel fronds and crème fraîche.

Cod Chowder

YIELD: 6 TO 8 SERVINGS / **ACTIVE TIME:** 20 MINUTES / **TOTAL TIME:** 1 HOUR

SALT AND WHITE PEPPER, TO TASTE

1 POTATO, PEELED AND CHOPPED

½ LB. BACON, CHOPPED

½ CUP UNSALTED BUTTER

1 LARGE ONION, DICED

1 CUP DICED CELERY

2 CARROTS, PEELED AND DICED

¾ CUP ALL-PURPOSE FLOUR

2 CUPS FISH STOCK OR VEGETABLE STOCK (SEE PAGE 454 OR 441)

1 CUP HEAVY CREAM

2 CUPS WHOLE MILK

1 LB. COD, CHOPPED

1 TEASPOON PAPRIKA

½ TEASPOON CAYENNE PEPPER

1 TABLESPOON FRESH LEMON JUICE

1. Bring water to a boil in a large saucepan. Add salt and the potato and parboil until the potato is almost tender, about 10 minutes. Drain the potato and set it aside.
2. Place the bacon in a Dutch oven and cook over medium heat until the fat has rendered and it is crispy, about 8 minutes, stirring as necessary.
3. Add the butter, onion, celery, and carrots, season with salt and white pepper, and cook, stirring occasionally, until the onion is translucent, about 3 minutes.
4. Add the flour and stir continually until the flour begins to brown and gives off a nutty aroma.
5. Add the stock, cream, and milk and bring to a gentle simmer. Cook until the flour develops to your liking and the broth thickens, 15 to 20 minutes.
6. Add the cod, reduce the heat to low, and simmer until it is cooked through, 8 to 10 minutes.
7. Stir in the potato, paprika, cayenne, and lemon juice and cook until the potato is tender, about 5 minutes.
8. Taste, adjust the seasoning as necessary, and serve.

Seafood Minestrone with Basil Pesto

YIELD: 4 TO 6 SERVINGS / **ACTIVE TIME:** 45 MINUTES / **TOTAL TIME:** 1 HOUR AND 30 MINUTES

½ CUP WHITE WINE

30 MUSSELS, RINSED WELL AND SCRUBBED

1 TABLESPOON EXTRA-VIRGIN OLIVE OIL

4 SLICES OF THICK-CUT BACON, FINELY CHOPPED

1 GARLIC CLOVE, MINCED

1 ONION, FINELY DICED

2 CELERY STALKS, FINELY DICED

1 TABLESPOON TOMATO PASTE

1 TEASPOON FINELY DICED FRESH ROSEMARY

1 TEASPOON FRESH THYME

1 BAY LEAF

1 TEASPOON FRESH LEMON JUICE

½ CUP CANNED KIDNEY BEANS, RINSED AND DRAINED

6 TABLESPOONS ARBORIO RICE

⅔ CUP FINELY DICED TOMATOES

6 CUPS FISH STOCK (SEE PAGE 454)

6 OZ. SHRIMP, SHELLED AND DEVEINED

12 OYSTERS, RINSED WELL AND SCRUBBED

SALT AND PEPPER, TO TASTE

FRESH BASIL, FOR GARNISH

PARMESAN CHEESE, GRATED, FOR GARNISH

PESTO (SEE PAGE 462), FOR SERVING

1. Place the wine and mussels in a large skillet, cover the skillet, and cook over medium heat until the majority of the mussels have opened. Remove the mussels from the skillet, remove the meat, and set it aside. Reserve the cooking liquid. Discard any mussels that did not open.
2. Place the olive oil in a medium pot and warm it over medium heat. Add the bacon and cook, stirring occasionally, for 4 minutes. Add the garlic, onion, and celery and cook until they are tender, about 5 minutes.
3. Add the tomato paste, rosemary, thyme, bay leaf, lemon juice, beans, rice, and tomatoes and cook, stirring frequently, for 2 minutes. Add the stock and bring to a boil.
4. Reduce the heat so that the soup simmers and cook until the rice is tender, about 12 minutes.
5. Add the mussel meat, shrimp, and oysters, season the soup with salt and pepper, and cook until the shrimp and oysters are cooked through, about 4 minutes. Discard any oysters that did not open.
6. Ladle the soup into warmed bowls, garnish with basil and Parmesan, and serve with Pesto.

Oyster Stew with Herb Butter

YIELD: 4 TO 6 SERVINGS / **ACTIVE TIME:** 45 MINUTES / **TOTAL TIME:** 1 HOUR AND 30 MINUTES

1½ CUPS QUARTERED CREAMER OR FINGERLING POTATOES

2 CUPS WHOLE MILK

2 CUPS HEAVY CREAM

1 CUP FINELY DICED GREEN BELL PEPPER

1 CUP ONION, FINELY DICED

1 GARLIC CLOVE, MINCED

25 OYSTERS, SHUCKED, LIQUOR RESERVED

1 TEASPOON PAPRIKA, PLUS MORE FOR GARNISH

2 TOMATOES, FINELY DICED

1 TEASPOON FRESH LEMON JUICE

1 TABLESPOON CHOPPED CAPERS

SALT AND PEPPER, TO TASTE

FRESH PARSLEY, CHOPPED, FOR GARNISH

1. Bring water to a boil in a medium pot. Add the potatoes and cook until they have softened slightly, 5 to 10 minutes. Drain the potatoes and set them aside.
2. Place the milk, cream, bell pepper, onion, garlic, and oyster liquor in a medium pot and cook over low heat, stirring occasionally, until the bell pepper is tender, about 10 minutes.
3. Add the potatoes and oysters and cook, stirring occasionally, until the oysters are plump, 3 to 4 minutes. Stir in the paprika, tomatoes, lemon juice, and capers and season with salt and pepper. Cook until the soup is warmed through.
4. Ladle the soup into warmed bowls, garnish with parsley and additional paprika, and serve.

Broccoli & Anchovy Soup

YIELD: 4 SERVINGS / **ACTIVE TIME:** 20 MINUTES / **TOTAL TIME:** 45 MINUTES

1 TABLESPOON EXTRA-VIRGIN OLIVE OIL

1 TABLESPOON UNSALTED BUTTER

1 ONION, CHOPPED

1 GARLIC CLOVE, MINCED

1½ CUPS CHOPPED PORTOBELLO MUSHROOMS

1 BIRD'S EYE CHILE PEPPER, STEMS AND SEEDS REMOVED, CHOPPED

2 ANCHOVIES IN OLIVE OIL, DRAINED AND MINCED

1 CUP CHOPPED TOMATO

¼ CUP WHITE WINE

4 CUPS CHICKEN STOCK OR VEGETABLE STOCK (SEE PAGE 440 OR 441)

2 CUPS BROCCOLI FLORETS

SALT AND PEPPER, TO TASTE

PARMESAN CHEESE, GRATED, FOR GARNISH

1. Place the olive oil and butter in a saucepan and warm over low heat. When the butter has melted, add the onion, garlic, mushrooms, chile, and anchovies and cook, stirring frequently, until the onion starts to soften, about 5 minutes.
2. Stir in the tomato and white wine and simmer, stirring occasionally, for 10 minutes.
3. Add the stock, raise the heat to medium-high, and bring the soup to a boil. Reduce the heat so that the soup simmers. Add the broccoli florets and cook for 10 minutes.
4. Season with salt and pepper, ladle into warmed bowls, and garnish with Parmesan cheese.

Sunchoke & Scallop Soup

YIELD: 4 SERVINGS / **ACTIVE TIME:** 30 MINUTES / **TOTAL TIME:** 1 HOUR

½ CUP UNSALTED BUTTER

2 ONIONS, FINELY DICED

2 LBS. SUNCHOKES, PEELED AND CHOPPED

2 CUPS FISH STOCK (SEE PAGE 454)

2 CUPS WHOLE MILK

¼ TEASPOON SAFFRON THREADS

1½ TABLESPOONS EXTRA-VIRGIN OLIVE OIL

12 SCALLOPS

1 CUP HEAVY CREAM

SALT AND PEPPER, TO TASTE

FRESH TARRAGON, CHOPPED, FOR GARNISH

CAVIAR, FOR GARNISH

1. Place the butter in a medium saucepan and melt it over medium heat. Add the onions and cook, stirring occasionally, until they start to soften, about 5 minutes.
2. Drain the sunchokes and add them to the pan. Cook, stirring occasionally, for 5 minutes. Add the stock, milk, and saffron and bring to a boil. Reduce the heat so that the soup simmers and cook until the sunchokes are tender, about 10 minutes.
3. Place the olive oil in a large skillet and warm it over medium-high heat. Add the scallops and sear on each side for 1½ minutes. Remove the scallops from the pan and set them aside.
4. Transfer the soup to a food processor, add half of the scallops, and blitz until smooth. Strain into a clean saucepan through a fine-mesh sieve and bring to a simmer.
5. Stir in the cream and remaining scallops, season the soup with salt and pepper, and ladle it into warmed bowls. Garnish with tarragon and caviar and serve.

Cream of Langoustine Soup

YIELD: 4 SERVINGS / **ACTIVE TIME:** 25 MINUTES / **TOTAL TIME:** 50 MINUTES

1 TABLESPOON EXTRA-VIRGIN OLIVE OIL

1½ LBS. LANGOUSTINES, SHELLED

1 ONION, FINELY DICED

1 CARROT, PEELED AND DICED

1 CELERY STALK, FINELY DICED

2 TABLESPOONS BRANDY

2 TABLESPOONS RIESLING

5 CUPS LOBSTER STOCK (SEE PAGE 443)

⅛ TEASPOON FRESH LEMON JUICE

1 TABLESPOON TOMATO PASTE

BOUQUET GARNI (SEE PAGE 469)

½ CUP HEAVY CREAM

SALT AND PEPPER, TO TASTE

FRESH CHIVES, CHOPPED, FOR GARNISH

CRUSTY BREAD, GRILLED OR TOASTED, FOR SERVING

1. Place the olive oil in a medium pot and warm it over medium-high heat. Add the langoustines and cook, turning occasionally, until they are cooked through, about 2 minutes.
2. Remove the langoustines from the pot, let them cool, and set them aside. Reduce the heat to medium, add the onion, carrot, and celery, and cook, stirring occasionally, until the vegetables have softened, about 5 minutes.
3. Add the brandy and Riesling and cook, stirring occasionally, for 2 minutes. Add the stock, lemon juice, tomato paste, and Bouquet Garni and bring to a boil. Reduce the heat so that the soup simmers and cook for 10 minutes.
4. Transfer the soup to a food processor, add half of the langoustines, and pulse until smooth. Strain the soup into a clean pot through a fine-mesh sieve and bring it to a simmer. Stir in the cream and cook for 3 minutes.
5. Add the remaining langoustines, season with salt and pepper, and stir to combine.
6. Ladle the soup into warmed bowls, garnish with chives, and serve with grilled bread.

Seafood & Sausage Gumbo

YIELD: 4 TO 6 SERVINGS / **ACTIVE TIME:** 30 MINUTES / **TOTAL TIME:** 1 HOUR

½ CUP EXTRA-VIRGIN OLIVE OIL

½ CUP ALL-PURPOSE FLOUR

¼ CUP UNSALTED BUTTER

1 ONION, FINELY DICED

1 CUP FINELY DICED GREEN BELL PEPPER

1 CUP FINELY DICED RED BELL PEPPER

2 CELERY STALKS, FINELY DICED

1 LB. ANDOUILLE SAUSAGE, SLICED THIN

2 GARLIC CLOVES, MINCED

1 BAY LEAF

¼ TEASPOON FRESH THYME

½ TEASPOON CAYENNE PEPPER

3 CUPS LOBSTER STOCK (SEE PAGE 443)

1 CUP FINELY DICED TOMATOES

1 CUP CHOPPED OKRA

1½ CUPS LONG-GRAIN RICE

1½ LBS. SHRIMP, SHELLED AND DEVEINED

½ LB. CANNED CRABMEAT, PICKED OVER

½ LB. SMALL SQUID, HALVED

SALT AND PEPPER, TO TASTE

TABASCO, TO TASTE

1. Place the olive oil in a medium skillet and warm it over medium heat. Add the flour and cook, stirring continually, until the roux is golden brown, 5 to 10 minutes. Remove the skillet from heat and set the roux aside.
2. Place the butter in a medium pot and melt it over medium heat. Add the onion, bell peppers, and celery and cook, stirring occasionally, until they have softened, about 5 minutes. Add the sausage and garlic and cook, stirring occasionally, for 5 minutes.
3. Add the bay leaf, thyme, cayenne, stock, tomatoes, and okra and bring the soup to a boil. Reduce the heat so that the soup simmers and cook for 10 minutes.
4. Cook the rice according to the instructions on the package.
5. Stir the roux into the soup and bring to a boil, stirring continually. Reduce the heat so that the soup simmers and cook for 5 minutes.
6. Add the shrimp, crab, and squid and cook until the shrimp turn pink and the squid begins to curl, 3 to 4 minutes. Season the soup with salt, pepper, and Tabasco.
7. Divide the rice among warmed bowls, ladle the soup over the top, and serve.

Oyster Bisque

YIELD: 4 TO 6 SERVINGS / **ACTIVE TIME:** 45 MINUTES / **TOTAL TIME:** 1 HOUR AND 30 MINUTES

1½ CUPS WATER

24 OYSTERS, RINSED WELL AND SCRUBBED

6 TABLESPOONS UNSALTED BUTTER

1 ONION, CHOPPED

6 CUPS CRAB STOCK (SEE PAGE 452)

¾ CUP LONG-GRAIN RICE

3 CUPS HEAVY CREAM

¼ TEASPOON TABASCO

¼ TEASPOON WORCESTERSHIRE SAUCE

SALT AND PEPPER, TO TASTE

FRESH PARSLEY, CHOPPED, FOR GARNISH

1. Place the water and oysters in a large pot, cover it, and cook over medium heat until the majority of the oysters have opened, 6 to 8 minutes.
2. Strain the oysters through a fine-mesh sieve, making sure to reserve the cooking liquid. When the oysters are cool enough to handle, remove the meat from the shells. Discard any oysters that did not open.
3. Place the butter in a medium saucepan and melt it over medium heat. Add the onion and cook, stirring occasionally, until it has softened, about 5 minutes.
4. Add the stock, reserved cooking liquid, and rice and bring to a boil. Reduce the heat so that the soup simmers and cook until the rice is tender, about 20 minutes.
5. Transfer the soup to a food processor and blitz until smooth. Strain the soup back into the pan and bring it to a simmer. Stir in the cream, Tabasco, and Worcestershire sauce and season with salt and pepper.
6. Ladle the soup into warmed bowls, garnish with parsley, and serve.

Pumpkin Soup with Scallops

YIELD: 4 SERVINGS / **ACTIVE TIME:** 25 MINUTES / **TOTAL TIME:** 1 HOUR AND 15 MINUTES

2 TABLESPOONS UNSALTED BUTTER

3 CUPS PEELED AND DICED PUMPKIN

1 ONION, DICED

1 CARROT, PEELED AND DICED

1 SMALL APPLE, PEELED AND DICED

½ GARLIC CLOVE, MINCED

1 TEASPOON FRESH THYME

¼ CUP WHITE WINE

2 CUPS CHICKEN STOCK (SEE PAGE 440)

1 TABLESPOON EXTRA-VIRGIN OLIVE OIL

8 SCALLOPS

SALT AND PEPPER, TO TASTE

1 CUP HEAVY CREAM

⅛ TEASPOON FRESHLY GRATED NUTMEG

PINCH OF CINNAMON

CRÈME FRAÎCHE, FOR GARNISH

FRESH ROSEMARY, CHOPPED, FOR GARNISH

1. Place the butter in a medium pot and melt it over low heat. Add the pumpkin, onion, carrot, apple, garlic, and thyme and cook, stirring frequently, for 10 minutes.
2. Raise the heat to medium and add the white wine. Cook, scraping up any browned bits from the bottom of the pan, until the wine has nearly evaporated. Add the stock and reduce the heat so that the soup gently simmers. Cook until all of the vegetables are tender, about 30 minutes.
3. While the soup is simmering, place the olive oil in a medium skillet and warm it over high heat.
4. Season the scallops with salt and pepper and place them in the pan. Sear on each side until they are golden brown and just cooked through, 3 to 4 minutes. Transfer the scallops to a paper towel–lined plate to drain.
5. Transfer the soup to a food processor, blitz until smooth, and strain it back into the pot. Stir in the cream, nutmeg, and cinnamon and season with salt and pepper.
6. Place two scallops in the center of each warmed bowl and ladle the soup over the top. Garnish with crème fraîche and rosemary and serve.

Hatteras Clam Chowder

YIELD: 4 TO 6 SERVINGS / **ACTIVE TIME:** 20 MINUTES / **TOTAL TIME:** 45 MINUTES

8 SLICES OF THICK-CUT BACON, FINELY CHOPPED

2 ONIONS, FINELY DICED

2 CELERY STALKS, FINELY DICED

2 CARROTS, PEELED AND FINELY DICED

8 CUPS CLAM JUICE

2 LBS. LITTLENECK CLAMS, RINSED WELL AND SCRUBBED

2 CUPS PEELED AND FINELY DICED POTATOES

4 TEASPOONS FRESH THYME

SALT AND PEPPER, TO TASTE

FRESH PARSLEY, CHOPPED, FOR GARNISH

1. Place the bacon in a large pot and cook, stirring occasionally, over medium heat for 5 minutes. Add the onions, celery, and carrots and cook, stirring occasionally, until they have softened, about 5 minutes.
2. Raise the heat to medium-high, add half of the clam juice, and bring to a boil.
3. Reduce the heat so that chowder simmers, add the clams, and cover the pot. Cook until the majority of the clams have opened, about 5 minutes. Remove the clams from the pot, shuck them, and set the meat aside. Discard any clams that did not open.
4. Add the potatoes, thyme, and the remaining clam juice and cook until the potatoes are tender, 10 to 15 minutes.
5. Stir in the clam meat, season with salt and pepper, and cook for 2 minutes.
6. Ladle the chowder into warmed bowls, garnish with parsley, and serve.

Romesco de Peix

YIELD: 6 SERVINGS / **ACTIVE TIME:** 25 MINUTES / **TOTAL TIME:** 40 MINUTES

½ CUP SLIVERED ALMONDS

½ TEASPOON SAFFRON

¼ CUP BOILING WATER

½ CUP EXTRA-VIRGIN OLIVE OIL

1 LARGE YELLOW ONION, CHOPPED

2 LARGE RED BELL PEPPERS, STEMS AND SEEDS REMOVED, CHOPPED

2½ TEASPOONS SWEET PAPRIKA

1 TABLESPOON SMOKED PAPRIKA

1 BAY LEAF

2 TABLESPOONS TOMATO PASTE

½ CUP SHERRY

2 CUPS FISH STOCK (SEE PAGE 454)

1 (28 OZ.) CAN OF CHOPPED TOMATOES, WITH THEIR LIQUID

SALT AND PEPPER, TO TASTE

1½ LBS. MONKFISH FILLETS, CHOPPED INTO LARGE PIECES

1 LB. MUSSELS, RINSED WELL AND DEBEARDED

FRESH CILANTRO, FINELY CHOPPED, FOR GARNISH

1. Place the almonds in a large cast-iron skillet and toast them over medium heat until they are just browned. Transfer them to a food processor and pulse until they are finely ground.
2. Place the saffron and boiling water in a bowl and let the mixture steep.
3. Place the olive oil in a Dutch oven and warm over medium heat. Add the onion and bell peppers and cook, stirring occasionally, until the peppers are tender, about 15 minutes.
4. Add the sweet paprika, smoked paprika, bay leaf, and tomato paste and cook, stirring constantly, for 1 minute. Add the sherry and bring the mixture to a boil. Boil for 5 minutes and then stir in the stock, tomatoes, saffron, and soaking liquid. Stir to combine, season with salt and pepper, and reduce the heat so that the soup simmers.
5. Stir in the ground almonds and cook until the mixture thickens slightly, about 8 minutes. Add the fish and mussels, stir gently to incorporate, and simmer until the fish is cooked through and a majority of the mussels have opened, about 5 minutes. Discard any mussels that did not open.
6. Ladle the mixture into warmed bowls, garnish with cilantro, and enjoy.

Saffron & Mussel Soup

YIELD: 4 SERVINGS / **ACTIVE TIME:** 20 MINUTES / **TOTAL TIME:** 45 MINUTES

3 LBS. MUSSELS, RINSED WELL AND DEBEARDED

3 CUPS WHITE WINE

4 TABLESPOONS UNSALTED BUTTER

2 LEEKS, TRIMMED, RINSED WELL, AND CHOPPED

2 CELERY STALKS, CHOPPED

¾ CUP CHOPPED FENNEL

1 CARROT, PEELED AND MINCED

2 GARLIC CLOVES, MINCED

⅛ TEASPOON SAFFRON

2 CUPS HEAVY CREAM

SALT AND PEPPER, TO TASTE

3 TOMATOES, CHOPPED

FRESH PARSLEY, FINELY CHOPPED, FOR GARNISH

MICROGREENS, FOR GARNISH

RADISH, FOR GARNISH

LEMON WEDGES, FOR SERVING

1. Place the mussels and wine in a large saucepan, cover, and cook over medium heat, shaking the pan occasionally, for 4 to 5 minutes, until the majority of the mussels have opened.
2. Discard any unopened mussels. Drain, reserve the cooking liquid, and remove the meat from all but 18 of the mussels. Reserve the 18 mussels in their shells for garnish.
3. Add the butter to the saucepan and melt it over medium heat. Add the leeks, celery, fennel, carrot, and garlic and cook, stirring frequently, until the vegetables start to soften, about 5 minutes.
4. Strain the reserved liquid through a fine-mesh sieve and add it to the saucepan. Cook for 10 minutes, until the liquid has reduced by one-quarter.
5. Add the saffron and cream and bring the soup to a boil. Reduce the heat to low, season with salt and pepper, add the mussels and tomatoes, and cook gently until heated through.
6. Ladle the soup into warmed bowls, garnish with parsley, microgreens, radish, and the reserved mussels, and serve with lemon wedges.

Seafood & Leek Soup

YIELD: 4 TO 6 SERVINGS / **ACTIVE TIME:** 30 MINUTES / **TOTAL TIME:** 1 HOUR AND 30 MINUTES

2 TABLESPOONS EXTRA-VIRGIN OLIVE OIL

½ LB. MEDIUM SHRIMP, SHELLS REMOVED AND RESERVED, DEVEINED

¾ CUP WHITE WINE

2 CUPS CLAM JUICE

3 CUPS WATER

1 LEEK, TRIMMED, HALVED, RINSED WELL, AND SLICED THIN

6 OZ. PANCETTA, CHOPPED

2 TABLESPOONS TOMATO PASTE

1 TEASPOON GRATED FRESH GINGER

1 TEASPOON CORIANDER

1 TEASPOON PAPRIKA

½ TEASPOON TURMERIC

2 PINCHES OF RED PEPPER FLAKES

½ LB. COD, SKIN REMOVED, CUT INTO ½-INCH CUBES

10 OZ. SQUID, HALVED IF LARGE

1 TEASPOON FRESH LEMON JUICE

SALT AND PEPPER, TO TASTE

CRUSTY BREAD, FOR SERVING

1. Place half of the olive oil in a medium saucepan and warm over medium heat. Add the shrimp shells and cook, stirring frequently, until the bottom of the pan starts to brown, about 4 minutes. Remove the shells from the pan and discard them.
2. Add the white wine and cook until it has evaporated, scraping any browned bits up from the bottom of the pan.
3. Add the clam juice and water and bring the broth to a boil. Reduce the heat and simmer.
4. Place the remaining olive oil in a separate pan and warm it over medium-high heat. Add the leek and pancetta and cook, stirring frequently, until the leek has softened and the pancetta is lightly browned, 6 to 8 minutes.
5. Stir in the tomato paste, ginger, coriander, paprika, turmeric, and red pepper flakes and cook, stirring continually, for 1 minute. Add the mixture to the broth and simmer for 20 minutes.
6. Add the cod and cook for 2 minutes. Add the shrimp and cook for another 2 minutes.
7. Remove the pan from heat, add the squid, and cover the pan. Let the soup sit until the squid is cooked through, 4 to 6 minutes.
8. Stir in the lemon juice, season the soup with salt and pepper, and ladle it into warmed bowls. Serve with crusty bread and enjoy.

Shrimp Bisque

YIELD: 4 SERVINGS / **ACTIVE TIME:** 30 MINUTES / **TOTAL TIME:** 1 HOUR

- 1 TABLESPOON EXTRA-VIRGIN OLIVE OIL
- 1½ LBS. SHRIMP, SHELLED AND DEVEINED
- 1 ONION, FINELY DICED
- 1 CARROT, PEELED AND FINELY DICED
- 1 CELERY STALK, FINELY DICED
- 2 TABLESPOONS BRANDY
- 2 TABLESPOONS RIESLING
- 2 CUPS CRAB STOCK (SEE PAGE 452)
- 3 CUPS LOBSTER STOCK (SEE PAGE 443)
- ⅛ TEASPOON FRESH LEMON JUICE
- 1 TABLESPOON TOMATO PASTE
- BOUQUET GARNI (SEE PAGE 469)
- ½ CUP HEAVY CREAM
- SALT AND PEPPER, TO TASTE
- CRÈME FRAÎCHE, FOR SERVING

1. Place the olive oil in a medium pot and warm it over medium-high heat. Add the shrimp and cook, turning occasionally, until it is cooked through, 3 to 4 minutes. Remove the shrimp from the pot and set it aside.
2. Reduce the heat to medium, add the onion, carrot, and celery, and cook, stirring occasionally, until they have softened, about 5 minutes. Add the brandy and Riesling and cook, stirring occasionally, for 2 minutes. Add the stocks, lemon juice, tomato paste, and Bouquet Garni and bring to a boil. Reduce the heat so that the soup simmers and cook for 10 minutes.
3. Transfer the soup to a food processor, add half of the shrimp, and pulse until smooth. Strain the soup into a clean pot through a fine-mesh sieve and bring it to a simmer. Stir in the cream and cook for 3 minutes. Add the remaining shrimp, season with salt and pepper, and stir to combine.
4. Ladle the soup into warmed bowls and serve with crème fraîche.

Seafood Wonton Soup

YIELD: 4 SERVINGS / **ACTIVE TIME:** 40 MINUTES / **TOTAL TIME:** 1 HOUR

FOR THE WONTONS

¼ LB. SHRIMP, PEELED, DEVEINED, AND FINELY CHOPPED

¼ LB. COOKED CRABMEAT, FINELY CHOPPED

1 TABLESPOON MINCED SHALLOTS

1 TABLESPOON FINELY CHOPPED CHIVES

1 TABLESPOON FISH SAUCE

2 TABLESPOONS WHITE MISO

1 TABLESPOON SHRIMP PASTE

2 TABLESPOONS FINELY DICED RADISH

1 TABLESPOON TOASTED SESAME SEEDS

1 TEASPOON SESAME OIL

1 TEASPOON SHERRY

12 WONTON WRAPPERS

FOR THE SOUP

1 TABLESPOON SESAME OIL

1 ONION, FINELY DICED

2 CARROTS, PEELED AND FINELY DICED

2 GARLIC CLOVES, MINCED

1 CUP SAKE

4 CUPS FISH STOCK (SEE PAGE 454)

1 LEMONGRASS STALK, CRUSHED

1 TABLESPOON SOY SAUCE

1 TABLESPOON FISH SAUCE

SALT AND PEPPER, TO TASTE

ROMAINE LETTUCE, SHREDDED, FOR GARNISH

TOASTED SESAME SEEDS, FOR GARNISH

FRESH CILANTRO, CHOPPED, FOR GARNISH

RADISH, SHAVED, FOR GARNISH

1. To begin preparations for the wontons, place all of the ingredients, except for the wonton wrappers, in a mixing bowl and stir until well combined. Place 2 teaspoons of the wonton mixture in the center of each wonton wrapper. Moisten a finger with cold water and rub it around the entire edge of each wrapper. Bring the corners of each wrapper together and pinch to seal the wontons. Set the wontons aside.
2. To begin preparations for the soup, place the sesame oil in a medium pot and warm it over medium heat. Add the onion and carrots and cook, stirring occasionally, until they have softened, about 5 minutes. Add the garlic and cook, stirring frequently, for 2 minutes.
3. Add the sake, stock, lemongrass, soy sauce, and fish sauce, bring to a simmer, and cook for 10 minutes.
4. Remove the lemongrass from the pot and discard it. Season the soup with salt and pepper and bring it to a boil. Reduce the heat so that the soup simmers, add the wontons, and cook until they float to the surface, about 5 minutes.
5. Divide the wontons among warmed bowls and ladle the soup over the top. Garnish with romaine lettuce, toasted sesame seeds, cilantro, and shaved radish and serve.

Minorcan Clam Chowder

YIELD: 4 SERVINGS / **ACTIVE TIME:** 20 MINUTES / **TOTAL TIME:** 45 MINUTES

½ CUP CLAM JUICE

1 LB. LITTLENECK CLAMS

1 OZ. SALT PORK

1 TABLESPOON EXTRA-VIRGIN OLIVE OIL

1 TEASPOON FRESH THYME

1 TEASPOON FINELY CHOPPED FRESH BASIL

1 TEASPOON FINELY CHOPPED FRESH OREGANO

2 GARLIC CLOVES, MINCED

1 BAY LEAF

½ HABANERO CHILE PEPPER, FINELY DICED

½ GREEN BELL PEPPER, FINELY DICED

1 ONION, FINELY DICED

2 PLUM TOMATOES, FINELY DICED

1 (14 OZ.) CAN OF DICED TOMATOES, WITH THEIR LIQUID

2 CUPS FISH STOCK (SEE PAGE 454)

1 POTATO, PEELED AND FINELY DICED

SALT AND PEPPER, TO TASTE

1. Place the clam juice in a medium skillet and warm it over medium heat. Add the clams, cover the skillet, and cook until the majority of the clams have opened, about 5 minutes. Remove the clams from the skillet, shuck them, and set the clam meat aside. Reserve the cooking liquid. Discard any clams that did not open.
2. Place the salt pork and olive oil in a medium pot and warm the mixture over medium-high heat. Add the thyme, basil, oregano, garlic, bay leaf, chile, bell pepper, and onion and cook, stirring frequently, until the vegetables have softened, about 5 minutes.
3. Add the reserved cooking liquid, tomatoes, and stock and bring to a boil. Reduce the heat so that the soup simmers, add the potato, and cook until it is tender, about 15 minutes.
4. Stir in the clam meat and season with salt and pepper.
5. Ladle the soup into warmed bowls and serve.

Haddock & Lobster Chowder

YIELD: 4 SERVINGS / **ACTIVE TIME:** 30 MINUTES / **TOTAL TIME:** 24 HOURS

9 OZ. HADDOCK FILLETS, SKIN REMOVED

1½ CUPS WATER

1 CUP KOSHER SALT

2 CUPS PEELED AND FINELY DICED SWEET POTATO

1 CUP PEELED AND FINELY DICED BUTTERNUT SQUASH

¼ CUP UNSALTED BUTTER

2 CUPS WHOLE MILK

1 ONION, FINELY DICED

¼ CUP THINLY SLICED DRIED CHORIZO

1 CUP LOBSTER STOCK (SEE PAGE 443)

1 CUP CHOPPED COOKED LOBSTER MEAT

SALT AND PEPPER, TO TASTE

FRESH BASIL, FINELY CHOPPED, FOR GARNISH

1. Place the haddock, water, and salt in a large mixing bowl, stir to combine, and let the mixture rest for 10 minutes. Remove the haddock from the bowl, rinse it under cold water, and refrigerate it overnight.
2. Bring water to a boil in a medium pot. Add the potato to the boiling water and cook until it has just softened, about 5 minutes. Remove the potato from the pot, set it aside, and return the water to a boil. Add the squash to the boiling water and cook until it is tender, 3 to 5 minutes. Remove the squash from the pot, let it cool, and set it aside.
3. Place the potato, half of the butter, and half of the milk in a food processor, pulse until smooth, and set the mixture aside.
4. Place the remaining butter in a clean medium pot and melt it over medium heat. Add the onion and chorizo and cook, stirring occasionally, until the onion has softened, about 5 minutes. Add the haddock, stock, and remaining milk and bring to a boil. Reduce the heat so that the soup simmers and cook until the haddock is flaky, about 10 minutes.
5. Remove the haddock from the pot and set it aside. Add the potato mixture to the pot, stir to combine, and bring the soup to a boil. Reduce the heat so that the soup simmers, add the butternut squash, lobster, and haddock, and cook for 2 minutes.
6. Season the soup with salt and pepper and ladle it into warmed bowls. Garnish with basil and serve.

Spicy & Sour Fish Soup

YIELD: 4 SERVINGS / **ACTIVE TIME:** 40 MINUTES / **TOTAL TIME:** 1 HOUR AND 30 MINUTES

¾ LB. SWORDFISH, DICED

½ CUP FISH SAUCE

2 GARLIC CLOVES, MINCED

SALT AND PEPPER, TO TASTE

3 OZ. RICE NOODLES

1 TABLESPOON EXTRA-VIRGIN OLIVE OIL

1 OZ. DRIED SQUID, SOAKED, DRAINED, AND RINSED

4 SCALLIONS, SLICED THIN

2 SHALLOTS, FINELY CHOPPED

2 TABLESPOONS GRATED FRESH GINGER

2 LEMONGRASS STALKS, CRUSHED

4 CUPS FISH STOCK (SEE PAGE 454)

2 TABLESPOONS TAMARIND PASTE

2 THAI CHILE PEPPERS, STEMMED, SEEDED, AND SLICED THIN

¾ LB. PINEAPPLE, FINELY DICED

4 PLUM TOMATOES, FINELY DICED

1 (3 OZ.) CAN OF SLICED BAMBOO SHOOTS, DRAINED

½ LB. FRESH SQUID, FINELY DICED

2 TABLESPOONS FINELY CHOPPED FRESH CILANTRO, PLUS MORE FOR GARNISH

FRESH BEAN SPROUTS, FOR GARNISH

FRESH ALFALFA SPROUTS, FOR GARNISH

LIME WEDGES, FOR SERVING

1. Place the swordfish, 2 tablespoons of the fish sauce, and the garlic in a mixing bowl, toss until the swordfish is coated, and set it aside.
2. Bring water to a boil in a medium pot. Add salt, let the water return to a boil, and add the noodles. Cook until the noodles are al dente, 6 to 8 minutes. Drain the noodles, rinse them under cold water, and set them aside.
3. Place the olive oil in another medium pot and warm it over medium heat. Add the dried squid, scallions, shallots, ginger, and lemongrass and cook, stirring occasionally, for 2 minutes. Add the stock and bring to a boil.
4. Reduce the heat so that the soup simmers and cook for 10 minutes.
5. Strain the soup into a clean pot through a fine-mesh sieve and bring it to a boil. Reduce the heat so that the soup simmers, add the tamarind paste, chiles, and remaining fish sauce, and cook for 3 minutes. Add the pineapple, tomatoes, bamboo shoots, and fresh squid and cook for 3 minutes. Add the swordfish and cilantro and cook until the swordfish is cooked through, about 3 minutes.
6. Season the soup with salt and pepper, divide the noodles among warmed bowls, and ladle the soup over the top. Garnish with bean sprouts, alfalfa sprouts, and additional cilantro and serve with lime wedges.

Humarsúpa

YIELD: 4 SERVINGS / **ACTIVE TIME:** 20 MINUTES / **TOTAL TIME:** 45 MINUTES

2 TABLESPOONS EXTRA-VIRGIN OLIVE OIL

1 ONION, FINELY DICED

2 GARLIC CLOVES, MINCED

2 CARROTS, PEELED AND FINELY DICED

2 CELERY STALKS, FINELY DICED

2 POTATOES, PEELED AND FINELY DICED

1 TABLESPOON PAPRIKA

1 TABLESPOON CURRY POWDER

6 CUPS CRAB STOCK (SEE PAGE 452)

1 LB. LANGOUSTINES, SHELLED

1 (14 OZ.) CAN OF COCONUT MILK

SALT AND PEPPER, TO TASTE

FRESH CHIVES, FINELY CHOPPED, FOR GARNISH

CRUSTY BREAD, FOR SERVING

1. Place the olive oil in a medium pot and warm it over medium heat. Add the onion and garlic and cook, stirring frequently, until they have softened, about 5 minutes. Add the carrots, celery, and potatoes and cook, stirring occasionally, for 5 minutes.
2. Add the paprika, curry, and stock and bring to a boil. Reduce the heat so that the soup simmers and cook until the potatoes are tender, about 10 minutes. Add the langoustines and coconut milk and cook until the langoustines are cooked through, about 5 minutes.
3. Season the soup with salt and pepper and ladle it into warmed bowls. Garnish with chives and serve with crusty bread.

Crab Velouté

YIELD: 4 SERVINGS / **ACTIVE TIME:** 30 MINUTES / **TOTAL TIME:** 1 HOUR

2 TABLESPOONS UNSALTED BUTTER

2 SHALLOTS, FINELY DICED

2 TABLESPOONS ALL-PURPOSE FLOUR

4 CUPS CRAB STOCK (SEE PAGE 452)

2 TABLESPOONS BRANDY

2 TABLESPOONS TOMATO PASTE

4 EGG YOLKS

2 CUPS HEAVY CREAM

2 CUPS COOKED AND CHOPPED CRABMEAT

1 TEASPOON FRESH LEMON JUICE

PINCH OF CAYENNE PEPPER

SALT AND PEPPER, TO TASTE

CRUSTY BREAD, FOR SERVING

1. Place the butter in a medium pot and melt it over medium heat. Add the shallots and cook, stirring occasionally, until they are translucent, about 3 minutes. Add the flour and cook, stirring continually, for 3 minutes.
2. Add the stock, brandy, and tomato paste, stir to combine, and bring to a boil. Reduce the heat so that the soup simmers and cook until it thickens, about 10 minutes.
3. Strain the soup into a clean pot through a fine-mesh sieve and bring it to a simmer. Place the egg yolks, cream, and ⅓ cup of the soup in a small mixing bowl and stir until fully combined.
4. Reduce the heat to low, add the egg mixture to the pot, and cook, stirring continually, for 3 minutes. Add the crabmeat, lemon juice, and cayenne, season with salt and pepper, and stir to combine.
5. Ladle the soup into warmed bowls and serve with crusty bread.

Spicy Mussel Soup

YIELD: 6 SERVINGS / **ACTIVE TIME:** 45 MINUTES / **TOTAL TIME:** 1 HOUR AND 30 MINUTES

1½ CUPS WHITE WINE

3 LBS. FRESH MUSSELS, RINSED AND CLEANED

2 TABLESPOONS UNSALTED BUTTER

1 ONION, FINELY DICED

2 GARLIC CLOVES, MINCED

2 CELERY STALKS, FINELY DICED, LEAVES RESERVED FOR GARNISH

6 SCALLIONS, TRIMMED AND SLICED THIN

1 CUP V8

1 CUP PEELED AND FINELY DICED POTATOES

1 TABLESPOON HARISSA SAUCE (SEE PAGE 461)

1½ CUPS FINELY DICED TOMATOES

½ CUP FINELY CHOPPED FRESH PARSLEY

SALT AND PEPPER, TO TASTE

GREEK YOGURT, FOR SERVING

1. Place the wine in a large pot and bring to a boil over medium heat. Add the mussels, cover the pot, and cook until the majority of the mussels have opened, about 5 minutes. Remove the mussels from the pot, shuck most of them, leaving a few in their shells, and set the meat aside. Reserve the cooking liquid. Discard any mussels that did not open.
2. Place the butter in a medium pot and melt it over medium heat. Add the onion, garlic, celery, and scallions and cook, stirring occasionally, until they have softened, about 5 minutes. Add the reserved cooking liquid, mussel meat, V8, potatoes, Harissa Sauce, and tomatoes and bring to a boil.
3. Reduce the heat so that the soup simmers and cook until the potatoes are tender, 10 to 15 minutes.
4. Add the parsley and shelled mussels, season with salt and pepper, and stir to combine.
5. Ladle the soup into warmed bowls, garnish with celery leaves, and serve with yogurt.

Prince Edward Island Mussel Soup

YIELD: 4 TO 6 SERVINGS / **ACTIVE TIME:** 20 MINUTES / **TOTAL TIME:** 45 MINUTES

2 TABLESPOONS EXTRA-VIRGIN OLIVE OIL

8 SLICES OF THICK-CUT BACON, FINELY CHOPPED

2 SHALLOTS, FINELY DICED

1 FENNEL BULB, TRIMMED AND FINELY DICED

2 GARLIC CLOVES, MINCED

1 CUP WHITE WINE

1 CUP PEELED, FINELY DICED, AND PARBOILED POTATOES

2 CUPS HEAVY CREAM

1 TABLESPOON FINELY CHOPPED FRESH CILANTRO

2 LBS. PEI MUSSELS, RINSED WELL AND SCRUBBED

SALT AND PEPPER, TO TASTE

CRUSTY BREAD, GRILLED OR TOASTED, FOR SERVING

1. Bring water to a boil in a large pot.
2. Place the olive oil in a medium pot and warm it over medium heat. Add the bacon and cook, stirring occasionally, until it is crispy, about 8 minutes. Add the shallots, fennel, and garlic and cook, stirring occasionally, until they have softened, about 5 minutes.
3. Add the wine and cook, stirring occasionally, until it has reduced by half, about 5 minutes. Add the potatoes, cream, and cilantro and bring to a boil.
4. Add the mussels to the boiling water, cover the pot, and cook until a majority of them have opened, about 5 minutes. Remove the mussels from the pot, shuck them, and add the meat to the soup. Discard any mussels that did not open.
5. Season the soup with salt and pepper, ladle it into warmed bowls, and serve with slices of grilled bread.

Crab & Oyster Gumbo

YIELD: 4 TO 6 SERVINGS / **ACTIVE TIME:** 30 MINUTES / **TOTAL TIME:** 1 HOUR

⅓ CUP EXTRA-VIRGIN OLIVE OIL

½ CUP ALL-PURPOSE FLOUR

½ CUP GREEN BELL PEPPER

½ CUP FINELY DICED RED BELL PEPPER

1 ONION, FINELY DICED

1 CELERY STALK, FINELY DICED

1 GARLIC CLOVE, MINCED

¼ LB. ANDOUILLE SAUSAGE, SLICED THIN

3 CUPS CRAB STOCK (SEE PAGE 452)

2 CUPS LOBSTER STOCK (SEE PAGE 443)

¾ CUP ORZO

30 OYSTERS, SHUCKED, LIQUOR RESERVED

½ LB. CANNED CRABMEAT, PICKED OVER

4 SCALLIONS, FINELY CHOPPED, WHITES AND GREENS SEPARATED

1 TEASPOON TABASCO

SALT AND PEPPER, TO TASTE

1. Place the olive oil in a medium pot and warm it over medium heat. Add the flour and cook, stirring continually, until the roux has thickened and is golden brown, about 5 minutes.
2. Add the bell peppers, onion, celery, garlic, and sausage and cook, stirring occasionally, for 4 minutes. Add the stocks, stir to combine, and bring to a boil.
3. Reduce the heat so that the soup simmers and cook for 10 minutes.
4. Add the orzo and cook until it is tender, about 10 minutes. Add the oysters, oyster liquor, crabmeat, and scallion whites and cook until the oysters are cooked through, about 3 minutes.
5. Add the Tabasco, season with salt and pepper, and stir to combine.
6. Ladle the soup into warmed bowls, garnish with the scallion greens, and serve.

Rhode Island Clam Chowder

YIELD: 4 TO 6 SERVINGS / **ACTIVE TIME:** 20 MINUTES / **TOTAL TIME:** 45 MINUTES

⅓ CUP UNSALTED BUTTER

2 ONIONS, FINELY DICED

2 CELERY STALKS, FINELY DICED

4 CUPS CLAM JUICE

4 CUPS CHICKEN STOCK (SEE PAGE 440)

2 LBS. QUAHOGS

1 LB. FINGERLING POTATOES, QUARTERED

3 TABLESPOONS FINELY CHOPPED FRESH DILL

PINCH OF CAYENNE PEPPER

TABASCO, TO TASTE

SALT AND PEPPER, TO TASTE

FRESH PARSLEY, FINELY CHOPPED, FOR GARNISH

1. Place the butter in a large pot and melt it over medium heat. Add the onions and celery and cook, stirring occasionally, until they have softened, about 5 minutes. Add the clam juice and stock and bring to a boil.
2. Reduce the heat so that the soup simmers and add the quahogs and potatoes. Cover the pot and cook until the majority of the quahogs have opened, about 5 minutes. Remove the quahogs from the pot, shuck them, and set the meat aside. Discard any quahogs that did not open.
3. Cook the soup until the potatoes are tender, about 10 minutes. Add the quahog meat and cook for 2 minutes. Stir in the dill, cayenne pepper, and Tabasco and season with salt and pepper.
4. Ladle the soup into warmed bowls, garnish with parsley, and serve.

Wild Rice Soup with Crab

YIELD: 4 SERVINGS / **ACTIVE TIME:** 30 MINUTES / **TOTAL TIME:** 1 HOUR

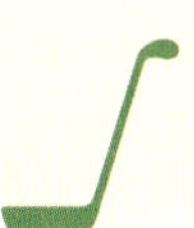

¼ CUP CLARIFIED BUTTER (SEE PAGE 475)

2 CUPS FINELY DICED LEEKS, TRIMMED AND RINSED WELL BEFORE CUTTING

1 CUP PEELED AND FINELY DICED CARROTS

1 CUP FINELY DICED CELERY

2 TABLESPOONS ALL-PURPOSE FLOUR

8 CUPS CRAB STOCK (SEE PAGE 452)

1 CUP WILD RICE

1 CUP HEAVY CREAM

2 TABLESPOONS SHERRY

½ LB. CANNED CRABMEAT, PICKED OVER

SALT AND PEPPER, TO TASTE

FRESH CHIVES, FINELY CHOPPED, FOR GARNISH

1. Place the Clarified Butter in a medium pot and melt it over medium heat. Add the leeks, carrots, and celery and cook, stirring occasionally, until they have softened, about 5 minutes.
2. Add the flour and cook, stirring continually, for 2 minutes. Add the stock, stir to combine, and bring to a boil.
3. Reduce the heat so that the soup simmers, add the rice, and cook until it is tender, about 20 minutes.
4. Stir in the cream, sherry, and crabmeat and season with salt and pepper.
5. Ladle the soup into warmed bowls, garnish with chives, and serve.

CHILLED & DESSERT SOUPS

Saffron & Almond Soup

YIELD: 4 SERVINGS / **ACTIVE TIME:** 30 MINUTES / **TOTAL TIME:** 3 HOURS

2 TABLESPOONS EXTRA-VIRGIN OLIVE OIL

2 ONIONS, FINELY DICED

1 GARLIC CLOVE, MINCED

¼ TEASPOON SAFFRON THREADS

¼ CUP FINELY CHOPPED ALMONDS

¼ CUP DRY VERMOUTH

4 CUPS VEGETABLE STOCK (SEE PAGE 441)

SALT AND PEPPER, TO TASTE

TOASTED ALMONDS, SLICED THIN, FOR GARNISH

FRESH PARSLEY, FINELY CHOPPED, FOR GARNISH

1. Place the olive oil in a medium pot and warm it over low heat. Add the onions and garlic and cook, stirring frequently, until they have softened, about 5 minutes.
2. Add the saffron and almonds and cook, stirring frequently, for 5 minutes. Add the vermouth and cook, stirring occasionally, until it has reduced by half, about 5 minutes. Add the stock and bring to a boil.
3. Reduce the heat so that the soup simmers and cook for 10 minutes. Transfer the soup to a food processor, pulse until smooth, and strain it back into the pot through a fine-mesh sieve.
4. Season the soup with salt and pepper and stir to combine. Place the soup in the refrigerator and let it chill for at least 2 hours.
5. Ladle the soup into chilled bowls, garnish with toasted almonds and parsley, and serve.

Honeydew Melon Soup

YIELD: 4 SERVINGS / **ACTIVE TIME:** 15 MINUTES / **TOTAL TIME:** 30 MINUTES

1 HONEYDEW MELON, PEELED, SEEDED, AND HALVED

1 TABLESPOON FRESH LEMON JUICE

2 CUPS CHILLED WHITE WINE

2 TABLESPOONS CASTER (SUPERFINE) SUGAR

GRAPES, FOR GARNISH

LEMON ZEST, FOR GARNISH

1. Place the melon and lemon juice in a food processor, pulse until smooth, and strain it into a mixing bowl through a fine-mesh sieve. Chill it in the refrigerator for 20 minutes.
2. Add the wine and sugar to the soup and stir to combine. Ladle the soup into chilled bowls, garnish with grapes and lemon zest, and serve.

Blueberry & Yogurt Soup

YIELD: 4 SERVINGS / **ACTIVE TIME:** 5 MINUTES / **TOTAL TIME:** 30 MINUTES

2 CUPS FRESH BLUEBERRIES, PLUS MORE FOR GARNISH

4 CUPS GREEK YOGURT

1 CUP ORANGE JUICE

1 CUP CHAMPAGNE

SEEDS OF 1 VANILLA BEAN

½ TEASPOON CINNAMON

½ TEASPOON CASTER (SUPERFINE) SUGAR

1. Place all of the ingredients in a food processor, pulse until smooth, and chill the soup in the refrigerator for 15 minutes.
2. Ladle the soup into chilled bowls, garnish with additional blueberries, and serve.

Mango Soup

YIELD: 4 SERVINGS / **ACTIVE TIME:** 5 MINUTES / **TOTAL TIME:** 25 MINUTES

FLESH OF 2 RIPE MANGOES, FINELY DICED

2 CUPS ORANGE JUICE

2 TEASPOONS AGAVE NECTAR, OR TO TASTE

1 CUP YOGURT

FRESH MINT LEAVES, FOR GARNISH

BLOOD ORANGE SEGMENTS, FOR GARNISH

KIWI, SLICED, FOR GARNISH

1. Place the mangoes, orange juice, agave nectar, and yogurt in a food processor, pulse until smooth, and chill the soup in the refrigerator for 20 minutes.
2. Ladle the soup into chilled bowls, garnish with mint, blood orange, and kiwi, and serve.

Avocado Soup with Crab & Mango Salad

YIELD: 6 SERVINGS / **ACTIVE TIME:** 25 MINUTES / **TOTAL TIME:** 1 HOUR AND 25 MINUTES

FLESH OF 3 RIPE AVOCADOS, FINELY DICED

5 CUPS VEGETABLE STOCK (SEE PAGE 441)

JUICE OF 2 LIMES

1 TEASPOON CUMIN

2 TEASPOONS KOSHER SALT

¼ TEASPOON CAYENNE PEPPER

FRESH CHIVES, FINELY CHOPPED, FOR GARNISH

CRÈME FRAÎCHE, FOR GARNISH

CRAB & MANGO SALAD (SEE PAGE 476), FOR SERVING

1. Place the avocados, stock, lime juice, cumin, salt, and cayenne pepper in a food processor, pulse until smooth, and strain into a mixing bowl through a fine-mesh sieve. Place the soup in the refrigerator and let it chill for at least 1 hour.
2. Pour the soup into chilled bowls, garnish with chives and crème fraîche, and serve with the Crab & Mango Salad.

White Chocolate Soup

YIELD: 4 SERVINGS / **ACTIVE TIME:** 10 MINUTES / **TOTAL TIME:** 25 MINUTES

3 CUPS WHOLE MILK

1 CUP HEAVY CREAM

SEEDS OF 1 VANILLA BEAN, POD RESERVED

1 LB. WHITE CHOCOLATE, CHOPPED

FRESH MINT, FOR GARNISH

1. Bring the milk, cream, and vanilla seeds and pod to a simmer in a medium pot. Remove the pot from heat and let the soup rest for 10 minutes.
2. Remove the vanilla pod from the pot, discard it, and bring the soup back to a simmer. Remove the pot from heat, add the chocolate, and stir until the soup is smooth.
3. Strain the soup into a mixing bowl through a fine-mesh sieve. Ladle the soup into warmed mugs or bowls, garnish with mint, and serve.

Cantaloupe & Ginger Soup

YIELD: 4 SERVINGS / **ACTIVE TIME:** 25 MINUTES / **TOTAL TIME:** 2 HOURS AND 25 MINUTES

2 CANTALOUPES, HALVED AND FINELY DICED, RINDS RESERVED

2 TEASPOONS GRATED FRESH GINGER

2 TABLESPOONS FRESH LEMON JUICE

4 CUPS CHILLED CHAMPAGNE

¼ CUP CASTER (SUPERFINE) SUGAR, OR TO TASTE

FRESH MINT, CHOPPED, FOR GARNISH

1. Place the cantaloupes, ginger, and lemon juice in a food processor, pulse until smooth, and strain into a mixing bowl through a fine-mesh sieve. Place the bowl in the refrigerator and let the soup chill for at least 2 hours.
2. Just before serving, remove the bowl from the refrigerator, add the champagne, and stir to combine. Add the sugar and stir until it has dissolved.
3. Ladle the soup into chilled bowls, garnish with fresh mint, and serve.

Mango, Coconut, & Curry Soup

YIELD: 4 TO 6 SERVINGS / **ACTIVE TIME:** 15 MINUTES / **TOTAL TIME:** 15 MINUTES

FOR THE COCONUT FROTH

½ CUP COCONUT MILK

½ CUP WHOLE MILK

1 TABLESPOON HEAVY CREAM

1 TABLESPOON CASTER (SUPERFINE) SUGAR

FOR THE SOUP

3 CUPS FINELY DICED RIPE MANGOES

3 (14 OZ.) CANS OF COCONUT MILK

4 TEASPOONS CURRY POWDER

1. To begin preparations for the coconut froth, place all of the ingredients in a mixing bowl and froth with an immersion blender. Set the froth aside.
2. To begin preparations for the soup, place the mangoes, coconut milk, and curry powder in a food processor, pulse until smooth, and strain into a mixing bowl through a fine-mesh sieve.
3. Ladle the soup into chilled bowls or glasses, top with the coconut froth, and serve.

Corn Soup with Garlic Custard

YIELD: 4 SERVINGS / **ACTIVE TIME:** 30 MINUTES / **TOTAL TIME:** 2 HOURS AND 15 MINUTES

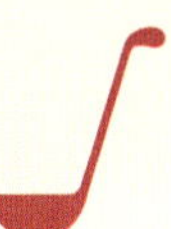

KERNELS FROM 8 EARS OF SWEET CORN, COBS RESERVED, 2 TABLESPOONS OF KERNELS RESERVED FOR GARNISH

10 CUPS WATER

1 BAY LEAF

12 SPRIGS OF FRESH THYME

6 WHOLE PEPPERCORNS

2 ONIONS, FINELY DICED

2 TABLESPOONS UNSALTED BUTTER

4 GARLIC CLOVES, MINCED

2 TABLESPOONS FRESH LEMON JUICE

SALT AND PEPPER, TO TASTE

FRESH CILANTRO, CHOPPED, FOR GARNISH

1. Place the corn cobs, water, bay leaf, thyme, and peppercorns and one of the onions in a large pot, bring to a simmer, and cook until the flavor has developed to your liking, about 1 hour. Strain the broth through a fine-mesh sieve and set it aside.
2. Place the butter in a medium pot and melt it over medium heat. Add the remaining onion and the garlic and cook, stirring frequently, until they have softened, about 5 minutes. Reduce the heat to low, add the corn kernels, and cook, stirring occasionally, for 5 minutes.
3. Transfer the mixture to a food processor, add the lemon juice and at least 4 cups of the broth, and pulse until smooth. Season with salt and pepper and chill the soup in the refrigerator for at least 1 hour.
4. Ladle the soup into chilled bowls, garnish with cilantro and the reserved corn kernels, and serve.

Curried Yogurt Soup

YIELD: 4 SERVINGS / **ACTIVE TIME:** 25 MINUTES / **TOTAL TIME:** 1 HOUR AND 45 MINUTES

- 4 CUPS GREEK YOGURT, PLUS MORE FOR SERVING
- ½ CUP CHICKPEA FLOUR
- 1 TEASPOON CHILI POWDER
- 1 TEASPOON TURMERIC
- ½ TEASPOON MINCED JALAPEÑO CHILE PEPPER
- 1 CUP VEGETABLE STOCK (SEE PAGE 441)
- ½ CUP EXTRA-VIRGIN OLIVE OIL
- 1 DRIED RED CHILE PEPPER
- 1 TEASPOON CUMIN
- 2 TEASPOONS FINELY CHOPPED DRIED CURRY LEAVES
- 6 GARLIC CLOVES, MINCED
- 2-INCH PIECE OF FRESH GINGER, PEELED AND MINCED
- ¼ CUP FINELY CHOPPED FRESH CILANTRO, PLUS MORE FOR GARNISH
- 1 TEASPOON CASTER (SUPERFINE) SUGAR
- SALT AND PEPPER, TO TASTE

1. Place the yogurt, flour, chili powder, and turmeric in a mixing bowl and stir to combine. Place the yogurt mixture, jalapeño, and stock in a medium pot, bring to a simmer, and cook, stirring occasionally, for 10 minutes.
2. Place the olive oil in a small skillet and warm it over low heat. Add the dried chile, cumin, curry leaves, garlic, and ginger and cook, stirring continually, until the curry leaves are black, about 2 minutes.
3. Stir the mixture into the pot. Add the cilantro and sugar, cover the pot, and cook for 10 minutes.
4. Strain the soup into a bowl through a fine-mesh sieve and season with salt and pepper. Chill the soup in the refrigerator for at least 1 hour.
5. Ladle the soup into chilled bowls, garnish with additional cilantro, and serve with additional yogurt.

Gazpacho with Parsley Oil

YIELD: 4 TO 6 SERVINGS / **ACTIVE TIME:** 1 HOUR / **TOTAL TIME:** 24 HOURS

4 TOMATOES, FINELY DICED

½ RED ONION, FINELY DICED

½ CUCUMBER, PEELED AND FINELY DICED

1 RED BELL PEPPER, STEMMED, SEEDED, AND FINELY DICED

1 CELERY STALK, FINELY DICED

1 CUP DICED CRUSTY BREAD

2 TABLESPOONS FINELY CHOPPED FRESH PARSLEY

2 TABLESPOONS FINELY CHOPPED FRESH CHIVES

1 GARLIC CLOVE, MINCED

¼ CUP RED WINE VINEGAR

2 TABLESPOONS EXTRA-VIRGIN OLIVE OIL

1 TEASPOON FRESH LEMON JUICE

2 CUPS TOMATO JUICE

1 TEASPOON SUGAR

2 TEASPOONS TABASCO

1 TEASPOON WORCESTERSHIRE SAUCE

SALT AND PEPPER, TO TASTE

PARSLEY OIL (SEE PAGE 476), FOR SERVING

1. Place the tomatoes, onion, cucumber, bell pepper, celery, bread, parsley, chives, garlic, vinegar, olive oil, juices, sugar, Tabasco, and Worcestershire sauce in a large mixing bowl and stir until well combined. Season with salt and pepper, cover the bowl, and chill it in the refrigerator overnight.
2. Transfer the soup to a food processor, pulse until smooth, and chill it in the refrigerator for at least 1 hour.
3. Ladle the soup into chilled bowls and serve with the Parsley Oil.

Garlic & Pine Nut Soup

YIELD: 4 SERVINGS / **ACTIVE TIME:** 35 MINUTES / **TOTAL TIME:** 1 HOUR AND 45 MINUTES

7 OZ. DAY-OLD BREAD, CRUSTS REMOVED, CHOPPED

¾ CUP PINE NUTS

6 GARLIC CLOVES, MINCED

½ CUP BLANCHED ALMONDS

½ CUP EXTRA-VIRGIN OLIVE OIL

1 TABLESPOON WHITE WINE VINEGAR

2 TABLESPOONS SHERRY

SALT AND PEPPER, TO TASTE

1. Preheat the oven to 375°F. Place the bread and 2 cups of water in a mixing bowl and let the bread soak for 8 to 10 minutes. Remove the bread from the water, squeeze it dry, and set it aside. Reserve the soaking liquid.
2. Place the pine nuts in a baking dish, place them in the oven, and toast until they have browned slightly, about 8 minutes, stirring halfway through. Remove the pine nuts from the oven and let them cool. When they are cool enough to handle, use a mortar and pestle to grind the nuts into a fine powder. Set it aside.
3. Bring water to a boil in a small pot. Add the garlic and cook for 4 minutes. Remove the garlic from the pot, let it cool, and set it aside.
4. Place the bread, almonds, ground pine nuts, garlic, olive oil, vinegar, and sherry and 2 cups of water in a food processor, pulse until smooth, and season with salt and pepper. Chill the soup in the refrigerator for at least 1 hour.
5. Ladle the soup into chilled bowls and serve.

Tomato & Raspberry Gazpacho

YIELD: 4 TO 6 SERVINGS / **ACTIVE TIME:** 10 MINUTES / **TOTAL TIME:** 24 HOURS

- 2 TO 3 LARGE HEIRLOOM TOMATOES
- 1 CUP RASPBERRIES
- 2 GARLIC CLOVES
- ½ CUP PEELED AND DICED CUCUMBER
- 2 TEASPOONS FRESH LEMON JUICE
- 2 TABLESPOONS EXTRA-VIRGIN OLIVE OIL
- 1 RED BELL PEPPER, STEMMED AND SEEDED, CHOPPED
- SALT AND PEPPER, TO TASTE
- FRESH MINT, FOR GARNISH
- HEAVY CREAM, FOR GARNISH

1. Preheat the oven to 425°F. Place the tomatoes on a baking sheet, place them in the oven, and roast until they start to collapse and their skins start to blister, 10 to 15 minutes. Remove the tomatoes from the oven and let them cool slightly.
2. Place the roasted tomatoes and the remaining ingredients, except for the garnishes, in a blender. Puree until smooth, transfer the soup to a large container, and refrigerate overnight.
3. When ready to serve, ladle the soup into bowls, season with salt and pepper, and garnish each portion with mint leaves and heavy cream.

Chilled Pea Soup

YIELD: 4 TO 6 SERVINGS / **ACTIVE TIME:** 15 MINUTES / **TOTAL TIME:** 1 HOUR AND 15 MINUTES

1 TABLESPOON EXTRA-VIRGIN OLIVE OIL

½ ONION, FINELY DICED

1 TABLESPOON FINELY CHOPPED FRESH MINT

4 CUPS VEGETABLE STOCK (SEE PAGE 441)

1 LB. FROZEN PEAS

4 CUPS SPINACH

SALT AND PEPPER, TO TASTE

1. Place the olive oil in a medium pot and warm it over medium heat. Add the onion and cook, stirring occasionally, until it has softened, about 5 minutes. Add the mint and cook, stirring continually, for 1 minute.
2. Add the stock and bring to a boil. Add the peas, stir to combine, and cook until they have thawed.
3. Transfer the soup to a food processor, add the spinach, and pulse until smooth. Strain the soup into a mixing bowl through a fine-mesh sieve, season with salt and pepper, and chill it in the refrigerator for at least 1 hour.
4. Ladle the soup into chilled bowls and serve.

Strawberry & Tomato Gazpacho

YIELD: 4 TO 6 SERVINGS / **ACTIVE TIME:** 20 MINUTES / **TOTAL TIME:** 24 HOURS

4 LBS. RIPE TOMATOES, FINELY DICED

1 ONION, FINELY DICED

2 RED BELL PEPPERS, STEMMED, SEEDED, AND FINELY DICED

6 GARLIC CLOVES, MINCED

2 TABLESPOONS BALSAMIC VINEGAR

2 TABLESPOONS EXTRA-VIRGIN OLIVE OIL

½ BAGUETTE, CHOPPED

4 CUPS FINELY DICED STRAWBERRIES

ZEST AND JUICE OF 1 LEMON

⅛ TEASPOON CAYENNE PEPPER

SALT AND PEPPER, TO TASTE

FRESH MINT, CHOPPED, FOR GARNISH

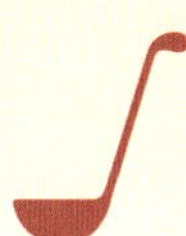

1. Place the tomatoes, onion, bell peppers, garlic, vinegar, olive oil, baguette, strawberries, lemon zest, lemon juice, and cayenne pepper in a mixing bowl and stir until well combined. Cover the bowl and chill the mixture in the refrigerator overnight.
2. Transfer the mixture to a food processor, pulse until smooth, and strain the soup into a clean mixing bowl through a fine-mesh sieve. Season with salt and pepper and chill the soup in the refrigerator for at least 1 hour.
3. Ladle the soup into chilled bowls, garnish with mint, and serve.

Cherry Soup

YIELD: 4 TO 6 SERVINGS / **ACTIVE TIME:** 30 MINUTES / **TOTAL TIME:** 1 HOUR AND 40 MINUTES

1 CUP WATER

1 CUP RIESLING

¼ CUP CASTER (SUPERFINE) SUGAR

SEEDS OF 1 VANILLA BEAN

2 CINNAMON STICKS

¼ CUP FRESH LEMON JUICE

2½ LBS. RED CHERRIES, PITTED, PLUS MORE FOR GARNISH

¼ CUP KIRSCH

2 TEASPOONS LEMON ZEST

½ CUP SOUR CREAM, PLUS MORE FOR GARNISH

FRESH MINT, FINELY CHOPPED, FOR GARNISH

1. Bring the water, Riesling, sugar, vanilla, cinnamon sticks, and lemon juice to a boil in a large pot. Reduce the heat so that the soup simmers and cook for 5 minutes.
2. Remove the pot from heat and let the soup rest for 30 minutes.
3. Strain the soup into a clean pot through a fine-mesh sieve, add the cherries, and bring the soup to a boil. Reduce the heat so that the soup simmers and cook for 5 minutes.
4. Transfer the soup to a food processor, pulse until smooth, and strain it back into the pot through a fine-mesh sieve. Stir in the kirsch and lemon zest and chill the soup in the refrigerator for at least 1 hour.
5. Add the sour cream and stir to combine. Ladle the soup into chilled bowls, garnish with mint, additional cherries, and additional sour cream, and serve.

Watermelon & Cherry Soup

YIELD: 4 SERVINGS / **ACTIVE TIME:** 20 MINUTES / **TOTAL TIME:** 1 HOUR AND 20 MINUTES

1½ CUPS FINELY DICED WATERMELON

¾ CUP PITTED CHERRIES

1 CUP RIESLING

1 CUP CHAMPAGNE

1. Place the watermelon, cherries, and Riesling in a food processor, pulse until smooth, and strain into a bowl through a fine-mesh sieve. Chill the soup in the refrigerator for at least 1 hour.
2. Stir in the champagne, ladle the soup into chilled bowls, and serve.

Vichyssoise

YIELD: 4 SERVINGS / **ACTIVE TIME:** 40 MINUTES / **TOTAL TIME:** 2 HOURS

¼ CUP UNSALTED BUTTER

6 LEEKS, TRIMMED, RINSED WELL, AND FINELY DICED

3 SHALLOTS, FINELY DICED

1 IDAHO POTATO, PEELED AND FINELY DICED

6 CUPS CHICKEN STOCK (SEE PAGE 440)

1 CUP HEAVY CREAM

PINCH OF FRESHLY GRATED NUTMEG

SALT AND PEPPER, TO TASTE

CHIVE OIL (SEE PAGE 477), FOR SERVING

CROUTONS (SEE PAGE 463), FOR SERVING

1. Place the butter in a medium pot and melt it over medium heat. Add the leeks and shallots and cook, stirring occasionally, until they have softened, about 5 minutes.
2. Add the potato and cook, stirring occasionally, for 3 minutes. Add the stock and bring to a boil.
3. Reduce the heat so that the soup simmers, cover the pot, and cook until the potato is tender, 10 to 15 minutes. Transfer the soup to a food processor, pulse until smooth, and strain it back into the pot through a fine-mesh sieve.
4. Stir in the cream and nutmeg, season with salt and pepper, and chill the soup in the refrigerator for at least 1 hour.
5. Ladle the soup into chilled bowls and serve with the Chive Oil and Croutons.

Golden Gazpacho

YIELD: 4 TO 6 SERVINGS / **ACTIVE TIME:** 30 MINUTES / **TOTAL TIME:** 2 HOURS AND 30 MINUTES

2 CUPS CANNED CORN, DRAINED

9 GOLDEN TOMATOES, FINELY DICED

2 YELLOW BELL PEPPERS, STEMMED, SEEDED, AND FINELY DICED

1 ONION, FINELY DICED

3 GARLIC CLOVES, MINCED

½ CUP EXTRA-VIRGIN OLIVE OIL

¼ CUP APPLE CIDER VINEGAR

SALT AND PEPPER, TO TASTE

FRESH PARSLEY, FINELY CHOPPED, FOR GARNISH

1. Place the corn, tomatoes, bell peppers, onion, garlic, olive oil, and vinegar in a mixing bowl, stir until well combined, and chill the mixture in the refrigerator for 1 hour.
2. Transfer the mixture to a food processor, pulse until smooth, and strain the soup into the mixing bowl through a fine-mesh sieve. Season with salt and pepper and chill the soup in the refrigerator for at least 1 hour.
3. Ladle the soup into chilled bowls, garnish with parsley, and serve.

Sour Cherry Soup

YIELD: 4 SERVINGS / **ACTIVE TIME:** 20 MINUTES / **TOTAL TIME:** 2 HOURS

¾ CUP WATER

1¼ LBS. CHERRIES, HALVED AND PITTED

¾ CUP SUGAR

1 CINNAMON STICK

2 CUPS RED WINE

¾ CUP SOUR CREAM, PLUS MORE FOR GARNISH

¼ CUP WHOLE MILK

¼ CUP HEAVY CREAM

1. Bring the water, cherries, sugar, cinnamon, and wine to a boil in a large pot. Reduce the heat so that the soup simmers and cook for 20 minutes.
2. Transfer the soup to a food processor, pulse until smooth, and strain it back into the pot through a fine-mesh sieve. Chill the soup in the refrigerator for 30 minutes.
3. Place the sour cream, milk, and heavy cream in a medium bowl and stir until well combined. Stir the cream mixture into the soup and chill the soup in the refrigerator for 1 hour.
4. Ladle the soup into chilled bowls, garnish with additional sour cream, and serve.

Golden Gazpacho

SEE PAGE 426

Almond Soup with Mixed Berry Coulis

YIELD: 4 TO 6 SERVINGS / **ACTIVE TIME:** 20 MINUTES / **TOTAL TIME:** 24 HOURS

3 CUPS ALMONDS

8 CUPS WATER

¼ CUP SUGAR

SEEDS OF 1 VANILLA BEAN

FRESH MINT, FINELY CHOPPED, FOR GARNISH

MIXED BERRY COULIS (SEE PAGE 478), FOR SERVING

1. Preheat the oven to 350°F. Place the almonds on a baking sheet, place it in the oven, and roast the almonds until they are fragrant and browned, about 15 minutes.
2. Remove the almonds from the oven and let them cool. Place the almonds, water, sugar, and vanilla in a medium bowl and let the mixture soak at room temperature overnight.
3. Place the almond mixture in a medium pot and bring to a boil. Reduce the heat so that the mixture simmers and cook for 20 minutes.
4. Transfer the mixture to a food processor, pulse until smooth, and strain it back into the pot through a fine-mesh sieve.
5. Ladle the soup into warmed bowls, garnish with mint, and serve with the Mixed Berry Coulis.

Strawberry Consommé

YIELD: 4 SERVINGS / **ACTIVE TIME:** 30 MINUTES / **TOTAL TIME:** 3 HOURS AND 30 MINUTES

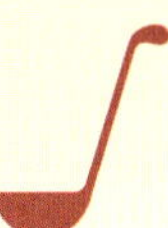

8 CUPS STRAWBERRIES, HULLED AND FINELY DICED

½ CUP CASTER (SUPERFINE) SUGAR

SEEDS OF 1 VANILLA BEAN

1 CINNAMON STICK

1 STAR ANISE POD

ZEST AND JUICE OF 2 LEMONS

1 TABLESPOON FINELY CHOPPED FRESH MINT

2 TABLESPOONS GRAND MARNIER

SHORTBREAD COOKIES, FOR SERVING

1. Bring water to a boil in a large pot.
2. Place the strawberries, sugar, vanilla, cinnamon, star anise, lemon zest, lemon juice, mint, and Grand Marnier in a large heatproof bowl and stir until fully combined. Cover the bowl with aluminum foil and place it on top of the pot, over the boiling water.
3. Reduce the heat so that the soup simmers and cook for 1 hour. Remove the bowl from heat and let the soup rest for 1 hour.
4. Strain the soup into a clean mixing bowl through a fine-mesh sieve and chill it in the refrigerator for at least 1 hour.
5. Ladle the soup into chilled bowls and serve with shortbread cookies.

Almond Soup with Mixed Berry Coulis

SEE PAGE 430

Sparkling Rhubarb Soup

YIELD: 4 SERVINGS / **ACTIVE TIME:** 45 MINUTES / **TOTAL TIME:** 2 HOURS

1 CUP WATER

4 CUPS FINELY DICED RHUBARB

1 CUP RASPBERRIES

1 CUP ORANGE JUICE

2 CUPS CHAMPAGNE

FRESH MINT, FINELY CHOPPED, FOR GARNISH

LEMON POPPY SEED MASCARPONE (SEE PAGE 477), FOR SERVING

1. Bring the water, rhubarb, raspberries, and orange juice to a boil in a medium pot. Reduce the heat so that the soup simmers and cook for 20 minutes.
2. Transfer the soup to a food processor and pulse until smooth. Strain the soup back into the pot through a fine-mesh sieve, stir in the champagne, and chill it in the refrigerator for at least 1 hour.
3. Ladle the soup into chilled bowls, garnish with fresh mint, and serve with the Lemon Poppy Seed Mascarpone.

Coconut & Tapioca Soup

YIELD: 4 TO 6 SERVINGS / **ACTIVE TIME:** 30 MINUTES / **TOTAL TIME:** 30 MINUTES

5 CUPS WHOLE MILK, PLUS MORE AS NEEDED

½ CUP SUGAR

SEEDS OF 1 VANILLA BEAN

1 CUP TAPIOCA PEARLS

1 (14 OZ.) CAN OF COCONUT MILK

FRESH MINT, FOR GARNISH

MANGO, DICED, FOR GARNISH

1. Bring the whole milk, sugar, and vanilla to a gentle boil in a large pot. Reduce the heat so that the soup simmers, add the tapioca, and cook, stirring occasionally, until it has softened, about 10 minutes.
2. Remove the pot from heat, add the coconut milk, and let the soup cool.
3. Ladle the soup into chilled bowls, garnish with mint and mango, and serve.

STOCKS

Chicken Stock

YIELD: 16 CUPS / **ACTIVE TIME:** 1 HOUR / **TOTAL TIME:** 9 HOURS

4 LBS. LEFTOVER CHICKEN BONES

32 CUPS COLD WATER

¼ CUP WHITE WINE

1 ONION, CHOPPED

1 CELERY STALK, CHOPPED

1 CARROT, CHOPPED

2 BAY LEAVES

10 SPRIGS OF FRESH PARSLEY

10 SPRIGS OF FRESH THYME

1 TEASPOON BLACK PEPPERCORNS

SALT, TO TASTE

1. Preheat the oven to 400°F. Place the chicken bones on a baking sheet, place them in the oven, and roast them until they are caramelized, about 1 hour.
2. Remove the chicken bones from the oven and place them in a stockpot. Cover them with the water and bring to a boil, skimming to remove any impurities that rise to the surface.
3. Deglaze the baking sheet with the white wine, scraping up any browned bits from the bottom. Stir the liquid into the stock, add the remaining ingredients, and reduce the heat so that the stock simmers. Simmer the stock until it has reduced by three-quarters and the flavor is to your liking, about 6 hours, skimming the surface as needed.
4. Strain the stock and either use immediately or let it cool completely and store it in the refrigerator.

Vegetable Stock

YIELD: 6 CUPS / **ACTIVE TIME:** 20 MINUTES / **TOTAL TIME:** 3 HOURS

2 TABLESPOONS EXTRA-VIRGIN OLIVE OIL

2 LARGE LEEKS, TRIMMED AND RINSED WELL

2 LARGE CARROTS, PEELED AND SLICED

2 CELERY STALKS, SLICED

2 LARGE YELLOW ONIONS, SLICED

3 GARLIC CLOVES, UNPEELED BUT SMASHED

2 SPRIGS OF FRESH PARSLEY

2 SPRIGS OF FRESH THYME

1 BAY LEAF

8 CUPS WATER

½ TEASPOON BLACK PEPPERCORNS

SALT, TO TASTE

1. Place the olive oil and vegetables in a large stockpot and cook over low heat until the liquid they release has evaporated. This will allow the flavor of the vegetables to become concentrated.
2. Add the garlic, parsley, thyme, bay leaf, water, and peppercorns and season with salt. Raise the heat to high and bring to a boil. Reduce the heat so that the stock simmers and cook for 2 hours, while skimming to remove any impurities that float to the surface.
3. Strain through a fine-mesh sieve, let the stock cool slightly, and place in the refrigerator, uncovered, to chill. Remove the fat layer and cover the stock. The stock will keep in the refrigerator for 3 to 5 days and in the freezer for up to 3 months.

Beef Stock

YIELD: 8 CUPS / **ACTIVE TIME:** 1 HOUR / **TOTAL TIME:** 10 HOURS

2 LBS. YELLOW ONIONS, CHOPPED

1 LB. CARROTS, CHOPPED

1 LB. CELERY, CHOPPED

5 LBS. BEEF BONES

2 TABLESPOONS TOMATO PASTE

16 CUPS WATER

1 CUP RED WINE

1 TABLESPOON BLACK PEPPERCORNS

2 BAY LEAVES

3 SPRIGS OF FRESH THYME

3 SPRIGS OF FRESH PARSLEY

1. Preheat the oven to 375°F. Divide the onions, carrots, and celery between two baking sheets in even layers. Place the beef bones on top, place the pans in the oven, and roast the vegetables and beef bones for 45 minutes.
2. Spread the tomato paste over the beef bones and then roast for another 5 minutes.
3. Remove the pans from the oven, transfer the vegetables and beef bones to a stockpot, and cover with the water. Bring to a boil.
4. Reduce the heat so that the stock simmers. Deglaze the pans with the red wine, scraping up any browned bits from the bottom. Stir the liquid into the stock, add the remaining ingredients, and cook, skimming any impurities that rise to the surface, until the stock has reduced by half and the flavor is to your liking, about 6 hours.
5. Strain the stock and either use immediately or let it cool completely before storing in the refrigerator.

Lobster Stock

YIELD: 8 CUPS / **ACTIVE TIME:** 30 MINUTES / **TOTAL TIME:** 4 HOURS AND 30 MINUTES

5 LBS. LOBSTER BODIES AND SHELLS

2 TABLESPOONS EXTRA-VIRGIN OLIVE OIL

½ LB. CARROTS, PEELED AND CHOPPED

½ LB. ONIONS, CHOPPED

10 TOMATOES, CHOPPED

1 CUP V8

5 SPRIGS OF FRESH THYME

5 SPRIGS OF FRESH PARSLEY

5 SPRIGS OF FRESH TARRAGON

5 SPRIGS OF FRESH DILL

1 GARLIC CLOVE

2 CUPS WHITE WINE

1. Preheat the oven to 350°F. Arrange the lobster bodies and shells on two baking sheets, place them in the oven, and roast them for 30 to 45 minutes. Remove the roasted bodies and shells from the oven and set them aside.

2. While the lobster bodies and shells are in the oven, place the olive oil in a stockpot and warm it over medium heat. Add the carrots and onions and cook, stirring occasionally, until the onions start to brown, about 10 minutes. Remove the pan from heat.

3. Add the lobster bodies and shells and the remaining ingredients to the stockpot. Add enough water to cover the mixture, raise the heat to high, and bring to a boil. Reduce the heat and simmer the stock for at least 2 hours, occasionally skimming to remove any impurities that rise to the surface.

4. When the flavor of the stock has developed to your liking, strain it through a fine-mesh sieve or a colander lined with cheesecloth. Place the stock in the refrigerator and chill until it is completely cool.

5. Remove the fat layer from the top of the cooled stock. The stock will keep in the refrigerator for 3 to 5 days and in the freezer for up to 3 months.

Lobster Stock

SEE PAGE 443

Turkey Stock

YIELD: 8 CUPS / **ACTIVE TIME:** 45 MINUTES / **TOTAL TIME:** 5 HOURS

1 LEFTOVER TURKEY CARCASS

16 CUPS WATER

2 CELERY STALKS, CHOPPED

2 CARROTS, PEELED AND CHOPPED

1 ONION, CHOPPED

2 SPRIGS OF FRESH THYME

2 BAY LEAVES

6 BLACK PEPPERCORNS

1. Place the turkey carcass in a stockpot, cover it with the water, and bring to a boil, skimming to remove any impurities that rise to the surface.
2. Add the remaining ingredients and reduce the heat so that the stock simmers. Simmer the stock until it has reduced by half and the flavor is to your liking, about 3 hours, skimming the surface as needed.
3. Strain the stock and either use immediately or let it cool completely and store it in the refrigerator.

Ham Stock

YIELD: 6 CUPS / **ACTIVE TIME:** 25 MINUTES / **TOTAL TIME:** 2 HOURS

¾ LB. HAM
8 CUPS WATER
2 GARLIC CLOVES
1 ONION, CHOPPED
1 BAY LEAF
1 SPRIG OF FRESH THYME

1. Place all of the ingredients in a stockpot and bring to a boil. Reduce the heat so that the stock simmers and cook for 1 hour, skimming any impurities that rise to the surface.
2. Strain the stock and either use immediately or let it cool completely and store it in the refrigerator.

Dashi Stock

YIELD: 6 CUPS / **ACTIVE TIME:** 10 MINUTES / **TOTAL TIME:** 40 MINUTES

8 CUPS COLD WATER
2 OZ. KOMBU
1 CUP BONITO FLAKES

1. Place the water and kombu in a medium saucepan. Soak the kombu for 20 minutes, remove it, and score it gently with a knife.
2. Return the kombu to the saucepan and bring to a boil. Remove the kombu as soon as the water boils, so that the stock doesn't become bitter.
3. Add the bonito flakes to the water and return it to a boil. Turn off the heat and let the mixture stand.
4. Strain the stock and either use immediately or let it cool completely and store it in the refrigerator.

Mushroom Stock

YIELD: 4 CUPS / **ACTIVE TIME:** 15 MINUTES / **TOTAL TIME:** 3 TO 4 HOURS

2 TABLESPOONS EXTRA-VIRGIN OLIVE OIL

3 LBS. MUSHROOMS

1 ONION, CHOPPED

1 GARLIC CLOVE, MINCED

2 BAY LEAVES

1 TABLESPOON BLACK PEPPERCORNS

2 SPRIGS OF FRESH THYME

1 CUP WHITE WINE

8 CUPS WATER

1. Place the olive oil in a large stockpot and warm it over low heat. Add the mushrooms and cook for 30 minutes, stirring occasionally.
2. Add the onion, garlic, bay leaves, peppercorns, and thyme and cook for 5 minutes, stirring occasionally. Add the white wine and cook for 5 minutes.
3. Add the water and bring to a boil. Reduce the heat so that the stock simmers and cook until it has reduced by half and the flavor is to your liking, 2 to 3 hours, skimming the surface as needed to remove any impurities.
4. Strain the stock and either use immediately or let it cool completely and store it in the refrigerator.

Lamb Stock

YIELD: 8 CUPS / **ACTIVE TIME:** 1 HOUR / **TOTAL TIME:** 7 HOURS

2 LBS. YELLOW ONIONS, CHOPPED

1 LB. CARROTS, CHOPPED

1 LB. CELERY, CHOPPED

5 LBS. LAMB BONES

2 TABLESPOONS TOMATO PASTE

16 CUPS WATER

1 CUP RED WINE

1 TABLESPOON WHOLE BLACK PEPPERCORNS

2 BAY LEAVES

3 SPRIGS OF FRESH THYME

3 SPRIGS OF FRESH PARSLEY

1. Preheat the oven to 375°F. Divide the onions, carrots, and celery between two baking sheets. Place the lamb bones on top, place the pans in the oven, and roast the vegetables and lamb bones for 45 minutes.
2. Spread the tomato paste over the lamb bones and then roast for another 5 minutes.
3. Remove the pans from the oven, transfer the vegetables and lamb bones to a stockpot, and cover with the water. Bring to a boil.
4. Reduce the heat so that the stock simmers. Deglaze the baking sheets with the red wine, scraping up any browned bits from the bottom. Stir the liquid into the stock, add the remaining ingredients, and cook, skimming any impurities that rise to the surface, until the stock has reduced by half and the flavor is to your liking, about 6 hours.
5. Strain the stock and either use immediately or let it cool completely before storing in the refrigerator.

Duck Stock

YIELD: 16 CUPS / **ACTIVE TIME:** 45 MINUTES / **TOTAL TIME:** 9 HOURS

2 YELLOW ONIONS, QUARTERED

2 CARROTS, CHOPPED

2 CELERY STALKS, CHOPPED

5 LBS. DUCK BONES

2 SPRIGS OF FRESH THYME

2 BAY LEAVES

1 TABLESPOON WHOLE BLACK PEPPERCORNS

1. Preheat the oven to 375°F. Place the onions, carrots, and celery on a baking sheet in an even layer. Place the duck bones on top, place the pan in the oven, and roast the vegetables and duck bones until they are browned, about 1 hour.
2. Remove the pan from the oven, transfer the vegetables and duck bones to a stockpot, and cover them completely with cold water. Add the remaining ingredients and bring to a boil.
3. Reduce the heat so that the stock simmers and cook, skimming to remove any impurities that rise to the surface, until the stock has reduced by half and the flavor is to your liking, about 6 hours.
4. Strain the stock and either use immediately or let it cool completely before storing in the refrigerator.

Crab Stock

YIELD: 8 CUPS / **ACTIVE TIME:** 30 MINUTES / **TOTAL TIME:** 3 TO 4 HOURS

- 2 TABLESPOONS EXTRA-VIRGIN OLIVE OIL
- 1 CARROT, PEELED AND CHOPPED
- 1 CELERY STALK, CHOPPED
- 1 ONION, CHOPPED
- SHELLS FROM 3 LBS. COOKED CRAB LEGS
- ½ CUP WHITE WINE
- ¼ CUP TOMATO PASTE
- 2 SPRIGS OF FRESH THYME
- 2 SPRIGS OF FRESH PARSLEY
- 3 SPRIGS OF FRESH TARRAGON
- 1 BAY LEAF
- ½ TEASPOON BLACK PEPPERCORNS
- 1 TEASPOON KOSHER SALT
- 8 CARDAMOM PODS

1. Place the olive oil in a large stockpot and warm it over low heat. Add the carrot and celery and cook until any moisture they release has evaporated. Add the remaining ingredients and enough water to cover the crab shells by 1 inch.
2. Raise the heat to high and bring the stock to a boil. Reduce the heat so that the stock simmers. Simmer the stock until it has reduced by half and the flavor is to your liking, 2 to 3 hours, skimming the surface as needed to remove any impurities.
3. Strain the stock and either use immediately or let it cool completely and store it in the refrigerator.

Fish Stock

YIELD: 6 CUPS / **ACTIVE TIME:** 20 MINUTES / **TOTAL TIME:** 4 HOURS

¼ CUP EXTRA-VIRGIN OLIVE OIL

1 LEEK, TRIMMED, RINSED WELL, AND CHOPPED

1 LARGE YELLOW ONION, UNPEELED, ROOT CLEANED, AND CHOPPED

2 LARGE CARROTS, PEELED AND CHOPPED

1 CELERY STALK, CHOPPED

¾ LB. WHITEFISH BODIES

4 SPRIGS OF FRESH PARSLEY

3 SPRIGS OF FRESH THYME

2 BAY LEAVES

1 TEASPOON BLACK PEPPERCORNS

1 TEASPOON KOSHER SALT

8 CUPS WATER

1. Place the olive oil in a stockpot and warm it over low heat. Add the vegetables and cook until the liquid they release has evaporated.
2. Add the whitefish bodies, aromatics, peppercorns, salt, and water to the pot, raise the heat to high, and bring to a boil. Reduce the heat so that the stock simmers and cook for 3 hours, skimming to remove any impurities that float to the surface.
3. Strain the stock through a fine-mesh sieve, let it cool slightly, and place in the refrigerator, uncovered, to chill. When the stock is completely cool, remove the fat layer from the top and cover. The stock will keep in the refrigerator for 3 to 5 days and in the freezer for up to 3 months.

APPENDIX

Sichuan Peppercorn & Chile Oil

YIELD: 1¾ CUPS / **ACTIVE TIME:** 5 MINUTES / **TOTAL TIME:** 30 MINUTES

1½ CUPS CANOLA OIL

5 STAR ANISE PODS

1 CINNAMON STICK

2 BAY LEAVES

3 TABLESPOONS SICHUAN PEPPERCORNS

⅓ CUP RED PEPPER FLAKES

1 TEASPOON KOSHER SALT

1. Place the canola oil in a saucepan and warm it over low heat for 2 minutes.
2. Add the star anise, cinnamon stick, bay leaves, and peppercorns and reduce the heat to the lowest-possible setting. Cook for 20 minutes, stirring occasionally.
3. Place the red pepper flakes in a small bowl and strain the warm oil over the flakes. Let the oil cool completely.
4. Stir in the salt and use immediately or store in an airtight container.

Tomato Sauce

YIELD: 8 CUPS / **ACTIVE TIME:** 25 MINUTES / **TOTAL TIME:** 40 MINUTES

¼ CUP EXTRA-VIRGIN OLIVE OIL

2 GARLIC CLOVES

1 (28 OZ.) CAN OF WHOLE PEELED TOMATOES, CRUSHED BY HAND

SALT, TO TASTE

RED PEPPER FLAKES, TO TASTE

HANDFUL OF FRESH BASIL, TORN

1. Place the olive oil in a medium saucepan and warm it over medium heat. Add the garlic and cook until it starts to brown.
2. Add the tomatoes, partially cover the pan, and cook the sauce for 20 minutes, stirring occasionally. Remove the garlic, season the sauce with salt and red pepper flakes, and add the basil.
3. Cook until the taste has developed to your liking and the sauce has the desired consistency, 5 to 10 minutes. During this last phase, leave the pan uncovered if the sauce is too liquid, or reduce the heat and add a splash of water if it is too thick. To serve, ladle the sauce over pasta.

Fennel Seed Yogurt

YIELD: 1 CUP / **ACTIVE TIME:** 5 MINUTES / **TOTAL TIME:** 5 MINUTES

1 CUP GREEK YOGURT

2 TABLESPOONS PERNOD

1 TEASPOON GROUND FENNEL SEEDS

1. Place all of the ingredients in a bowl and stir to combine. Use immediately or store in the refrigerator.

Parmesan Crisps

YIELD: 24 CRISPS / **ACTIVE TIME:** 10 MINUTES / **TOTAL TIME:** 25 MINUTES

2 CUPS GRATED PARMESAN CHEESE

2 TABLESPOONS ALL-PURPOSE FLOUR

1. Preheat the oven to 350°F and line a baking sheet with a silicone mat. Place the Parmesan and flour in a food processor and blitz until combined.
2. Using a 2-inch ring mold, shape the mixture into 24 rounds on the baking sheet. You want the rounds to be about ¼ inch thick.
3. Place the pan in the oven and bake until the rounds are brown and crispy, about 7 minutes. Remove from the oven and let cool before enjoying.

Tzatziki

YIELD: 2 CUPS / **ACTIVE TIME:** 5 MINUTES / **TOTAL TIME:** 1 HOUR AND 5 MINUTES

1 CUP GREEK YOGURT

¾ CUP SEEDED AND MINCED CUCUMBER

1 GARLIC CLOVE, MINCED

JUICE FROM 1 LEMON WEDGE

SALT AND WHITE PEPPER, TO TASTE

FRESH DILL, FINELY CHOPPED, TO TASTE

1. Place the yogurt, cucumber, garlic, and lemon juice in a mixing bowl and stir to combine. Taste and season with salt, white pepper, and dill.
2. Place in the refrigerator and chill for 1 hour before serving.

Pita Bread

YIELD: 8 SERVINGS / **ACTIVE TIME:** 1 HOUR / **TOTAL TIME:** 3 HOURS

1 CUP LUKEWARM WATER (90°F)

1 TABLESPOON ACTIVE DRY YEAST

1 TABLESPOON SUGAR

1¾ CUPS ALL-PURPOSE FLOUR, PLUS MORE AS NEEDED

1 CUP WHOLE WHEAT FLOUR

1 TABLESPOON KOSHER SALT

1. In a large mixing bowl, combine the water, yeast, and sugar. Let the mixture sit until it starts to foam, about 10 minutes.
2. Add the flours and salt to the mixing bowl and work the mixture until it comes together as a smooth dough. Cover the bowl with a kitchen towel and let it rise for about 15 minutes.
3. Preheat the oven to 500°F and place a baking stone on the floor of the oven.
4. Divide the dough into eight pieces and form them into balls. Place the balls on a flour-dusted work surface, press them down, and roll them until they are about ¼ inch thick.
5. Working with one pita at a time, place the pita on the baking stone and bake until it is puffy and brown, about 8 minutes.
6. Remove the pita from the oven and serve warm or at room temperature.

Minty Pickled Cucumbers

YIELD: 2 CUPS / **ACTIVE TIME:** 20 MINUTES / **TOTAL TIME:** 3 HOURS

½ CUP SUGAR

½ CUP WATER

½ CUP RICE VINEGAR

2 TABLESPOONS DRIED MINT

1 TABLESPOON CORIANDER SEEDS

1 TABLESPOON MUSTARD SEEDS

2 CUCUMBERS, SLICED

1. Place all of the ingredients, except for the cucumbers, in a small saucepan and bring to a boil, stirring to dissolve the sugar.
2. Place the cucumbers in a large mason jar. Remove the pan from heat and pour the brine over the cucumbers.
3. Let cool completely before using or storing in the refrigerator, where the pickles will keep for 1 week.

Harissa Sauce

YIELD: 1 CUP / **ACTIVE TIME:** 20 MINUTES / **TOTAL TIME:** 1 HOUR

1 HEAD OF GARLIC, HALVED AT ITS EQUATOR

2 TABLESPOONS EXTRA-VIRGIN OLIVE OIL

2 BELL PEPPERS

2 TABLESPOONS CORIANDER SEEDS

6 CHILES DE ÁRBOL

3 PASILLA CHILE PEPPERS

2 SHALLOTS, HALVED

2 TEASPOONS KOSHER SALT

1. Preheat the oven to 400ºF. Place the garlic in a piece of aluminum foil, drizzle half of the olive oil over it, and seal the foil closed.
2. Place the garlic on a baking sheet, along with the bell peppers, and place it in the oven. Roast until the garlic is very tender and the peppers are charred all over, about 30 to 40 minutes. Remove them from the oven and let them cool.
3. While the garlic and peppers are cooling, place the coriander seeds in a dry skillet and toast them over medium heat, shaking the pan frequently. Transfer the coriander seeds to a blender, along with the remaining ingredients, including the remaining olive oil.
4. Squeeze the roasted garlic cloves into the blender. Remove the skin, seeds, and stems from the roasted peppers and place the flesh in the blender.
5. Puree until the harissa paste has the desired texture and use immediately or store it in the refrigerator.

Pesto

YIELD: 1 CUP / **ACTIVE TIME:** 10 MINUTES / **TOTAL TIME:** 25 MINUTES

¼ CUP PINE NUTS

3 GARLIC CLOVES

SALT AND PEPPER, TO TASTE

2 CUPS FIRMLY PACKED FRESH BASIL LEAVES

½ CUP EXTRA-VIRGIN OLIVE OIL

¼ CUP GRATED PARMESAN CHEESE

1 TEASPOON FRESH LEMON JUICE

1. Warm a small skillet over low heat for 1 minute. Add the pine nuts and cook, shaking the pan frequently, until they begin to give off a toasty fragrance, 2 to 3 minutes. Transfer the pine nuts to a plate and let them cool completely.
2. Place the pine nuts, the garlic, salt, and pepper in a food processor or blender and pulse until the mixture is a coarse meal. Add the basil and pulse until it is finely minced. Transfer the mixture to a medium bowl and, while whisking to incorporate, add the olive oil in a thin stream.
3. Add the cheese and stir until thoroughly incorporated. Stir in the lemon juice, taste, and adjust the seasoning as necessary. To serve, toss pasta in the pesto.

Paprika Oil

YIELD: 2 CUPS / **ACTIVE TIME:** 5 MINUTES / **TOTAL TIME:** 5 MINUTES

½ CUP SWEET PAPRIKA

2 CUPS AVOCADO OIL

1. Place the paprika and avocado oil in a mason jar and shake until thoroughly combined.
2. Store the oil in a dark, dry place and always shake before using.

Croutons

YIELD: 2 CUPS / **ACTIVE TIME:** 10 MINUTES / **TOTAL TIME:** 15 MINUTES

2 CUPS CUBED DAY-OLD BREAD

EXTRA-VIRGIN OLIVE OIL, TO TASTE

SALT, TO TASTE

ITALIAN-STYLE DRIED HERBS (BASIL, PARSLEY, OREGANO) OR HERBES DE PROVENCE, TO TASTE

1. Preheat the oven to 400°F. Place the bread in a bowl, drizzle olive oil over it, and season with salt and dried herbs.
2. Place the bread on a baking sheet and place it in the oven. Bake until it is golden brown and crispy, 10 to 15 minutes, stirring occasionally.
3. Remove the croutons from the oven and use as desired.

Gremolata

YIELD: ½ CUP / **ACTIVE TIME:** 5 MINUTES / **TOTAL TIME:** 5 MINUTES

8 GARLIC CLOVES, MINCED

ZEST OF 8 LEMONS

¼ CUP CHOPPED FRESH PARSLEY

1. Place all of the ingredients in a bowl, stir to combine, and use immediately or store in the refrigerator.

Crispy Wonton Strips

YIELD: 6 SERVINGS / **ACTIVE TIME:** 10 MINUTES / **TOTAL TIME:** 25 MINUTES

CANOLA OIL, AS NEEDED

12 WONTON WRAPPERS, CUT INTO STRIPS

SALT, TO TASTE

1. Add canola oil to a Dutch oven until it is about 1 inch deep and warm it to 350°F.
2. Add the wonton wrappers and fry, turning them frequently, until they are crispy and golden brown, 3 to 5 minutes.
3. Transfer the fried wonton strips to a paper towel–lined plate, season with salt, and use as desired.

Butternut Squash Bread

YIELD: 1 LOAF / **ACTIVE TIME:** 15 MINUTES / **TOTAL TIME:** 1 HOUR AND 45 MINUTES

1½ CUPS ALL-PURPOSE FLOUR

¼ TEASPOON TABLE SALT

1 TEASPOON BAKING POWDER

¼ TEASPOON BAKING SODA

¼ TEASPOON CINNAMON

½ CUP UNSALTED BUTTER, SOFTENED

½ CUP SUGAR

½ CUP LIGHT BROWN SUGAR

2 EGGS

1 CUP MASHED BUTTERNUT SQUASH, COOLED

1. Preheat the oven to 350°F. Coat a 9 x 5–inch loaf pan with nonstick cooking spray.
2. Sift the flour, salt, baking powder, baking soda, and cinnamon into a mixing bowl. Set the mixture aside.
3. In the work bowl of a stand mixer fitted with the paddle attachment, cream the butter, sugar, and brown sugar until the mixture is light and fluffy, 2 to 3 minutes.
4. Incorporate the eggs one at a time, scraping down the work bowl as necessary. Add the squash and beat to incorporate. Add the dry mixture and beat until the resulting mixture comes together as a smooth dough.
5. Pour the dough into the loaf pan, place it in the oven, and bake until a cake tester inserted into the center of the bread comes out clean, 50 to 55 minutes.
6. Remove the bread from the oven, transfer it to a wire rack, and let it cool before slicing and serving.

Poached Pears

YIELD: 1½ CUPS / **ACTIVE TIME:** 10 MINUTES / **TOTAL TIME:** 24 HOURS

1 CUP RED WINE

¼ CUP SUGAR

1 TEASPOON FRESH LEMON JUICE

1 CINNAMON STICK

1 STAR ANISE POD

1 PEAR, PEELED AND FINELY DICED

1. Place the wine, sugar, lemon juice, cinnamon stick, and star anise in a small saucepan and bring to a boil. Remove the pan from heat and let the mixture steep for 10 minutes.
2. Add the pear and bring to a boil.
3. Remove the pan from heat and let the pear mixture cool to room temperature. Chill the mixture in the refrigerator overnight and strain before using.

Sachet d'Épices

YIELD: 1 SACHET / **ACTIVE TIME:** 5 MINUTES / **TOTAL TIME:** 5 MINUTES

3 SPRIGS OF FRESH PARSLEY

1 SPRIG OF FRESH THYME

½ BAY LEAF

¼ TEASPOON CRACKED BLACK PEPPERCORNS

½ GARLIC CLOVE

1. Place all of the ingredients on a 4-inch square of cheesecloth and fold the corners of the cloth together to make a purse.
2. Tie the sachet closed with a length of kitchen twine, tie the other end of the twine to the handle of your saucepan, and use as desired.

Herb Oil

YIELD: 1 CUP / **ACTIVE TIME:** 5 MINUTES / **TOTAL TIME:** 5 MINUTES

½ CUP FRESH BASIL

½ CUP FRESH PARSLEY

½ CUP CHOPPED FRESH CHIVES

⅓ CUP EXTRA-VIRGIN OLIVE OIL

1. Place a small metal bowl over a larger metal bowl that is filled with ice water.
2. Place all of the ingredients in a blender and puree on high until you see the olive oil start to smoke, about 1 minute.
3. Warm a small skillet over high heat. When the pan is hot, remove it from heat and carefully pour the oil into the pan. Place the pan back over high heat and cook the oil for about 20 seconds, until the bubbles in the oil start to become smaller.
4. Immediately transfer the oil to the small bowl sitting in the ice bath. Stir the oil until it is cold to the touch.
5. Strain the oil through a coffee filter or cheesecloth, letting it slowly drip through. Discard the solids and use the oil immediately.

Basil Oil

YIELD: 1 CUP / **ACTIVE TIME:** 15 MINUTES / **TOTAL TIME:** 20 MINUTES

1 CUP FRESH BASIL LEAVES

1 CUP BABY SPINACH

1 CUP EXTRA-VIRGIN OLIVE OIL

1. Bring water to a boil in a small saucepan. Prepare an ice bath.
2. Add the basil and spinach to the pan and cook for 1 minute. Drain the mixture, plunge it into the ice bath until it is cool, and let it drain again.
3. Place the mixture in a linen towel and wring the towel to remove as much water from it as possible.
4. Place the mixture in a food processor. With the food processor running on low, slowly drizzle in the olive oil and blitz until it has emulsified.
5. Strain the oil through a fine-mesh sieve and use immediately or store in an airtight container.

Poppy Seed Yogurt

YIELD: ½ CUP / **ACTIVE TIME:** 5 MINUTES / **TOTAL TIME:** 5 MINUTES

½ CUP YOGURT

1 TABLESPOON POPPY SEEDS

SALT, TO TASTE

1. Place the yogurt and poppy seeds in a bowl and stir to combine.
2. Season with salt and use immediately or store in the refrigerator.

Spicy Chickpeas

YIELD: 4 SERVINGS / **ACTIVE TIME:** 20 MINUTES / **TOTAL TIME:** 24 HOURS

1 CUP DRIED CHICKPEAS, SOAKED OVERNIGHT AND DRAINED

2 CUPS CANOLA OIL

1 TEASPOON SMOKED PAPRIKA

½ TEASPOON ONION POWDER

½ TEASPOON BROWN SUGAR

¼ TEASPOON GARLIC POWDER

¼ TEASPOON KOSHER SALT

PINCH OF CHILI POWDER

PINCH OF CAYENNE PEPPER

1. Bring 4 cups of water to a boil in a saucepan. Add the chickpeas, reduce the heat so that the water simmers, and cook until the chickpeas are tender, 45 minutes to 1 hour. Drain the chickpeas, place them on a paper towel–lined plate, and pat them dry.
2. Place the canola oil in a Dutch oven and warm it to 350°F over medium heat.
3. Place the remaining ingredients in a bowl, stir until thoroughly combined, and set the mixture aside.
4. Place the chickpeas in the hot oil and fry until golden brown, about 3 minutes. Remove and place in the bowl with the seasoning mixture. Toss to coat and serve.

Eggplant & Pine Nut Ragout

YIELD: 2 CUPS / **ACTIVE TIME:** 20 MINUTES / **TOTAL TIME:** 40 MINUTES

1 TABLESPOON EXTRA-VIRGIN OLIVE OIL

1 EGGPLANT, TRIMMED AND CHOPPED (¾-INCH CUBES)

½ TEASPOON RAS EL HANOUT

1 TABLESPOON RAISINS

2 TABLESPOONS PINE NUTS, TOASTED

1 TEASPOON LEMON ZEST

SALT AND PEPPER, TO TASTE

1. Place the olive oil in a large saucepan and warm it over medium heat. Add the eggplant, cover the pan, and cook the eggplant, stirring occasionally, for 5 minutes. Remove the cover and cook, stirring occasionally, until the eggplant is browned, about 10 minutes.
2. Stir in the remaining ingredients and cook, stirring occasionally, until the eggplant has collapsed and the flavor has developed to your liking, 10 to 15 minutes. To serve, ladle the ragù over pasta.

Confit Lemon Rinds

YIELD: 8 SERVINGS / **ACTIVE TIME:** 10 MINUTES / **TOTAL TIME:** 30 MINUTES

PEEL OF 1 LEMON, CUT INTO THIN STRIPS

½ CUP EXTRA-VIRGIN OLIVE OIL

1. Place the lemon peel and olive oil in a small saucepan, bring to a simmer, and cook for 10 minutes.
2. Remove the pan from heat and let the mixture cool. Strain before using or storing in the refrigerator.

Cornbread

YIELD: 6 TO 8 SERVINGS / **ACTIVE TIME:** 10 MINUTES / **TOTAL TIME:** 1 HOUR

½ CUP UNSALTED BUTTER

3 EGGS

2 TABLESPOONS BROWN SUGAR

1 CUP CORNMEAL

1 CUP ALL-PURPOSE FLOUR

1 TABLESPOON BAKING POWDER

1½ TEASPOONS FINE SEA SALT

½ TEASPOON MUSTARD POWDER

1 TEASPOON CHILI POWDER

½ CUP HONEY

1 CUP BUTTERMILK

2 TABLESPOONS WHOLE-MILK RICOTTA CHEESE

1. Place the butter in a large skillet and melt it over medium heat. Cook the butter until it starts to brown and give off a nutty aroma. Remove the pan from heat and let the brown butter cool completely.
2. Preheat the oven to 325°F and position a rack in the center. Coat a large cast-iron skillet with nonstick cooking spray.
3. Place the eggs and brown sugar in the work bowl of a stand mixer fitted with the whisk attachment and whisk on high until the mixture is pale and fluffy.
4. Place the cornmeal, flour, baking powder, salt, mustard powder, and chili powder in a mixing bowl, stir to combine, and set the mixture aside.
5. Add the brown butter, honey, buttermilk, and ricotta to the stand mixer's work bowl and whisk until incorporated. Add the dry mixture and whisk until the mixture comes together as a smooth batter.
6. Pour the batter into the skillet and place it in the oven. Bake until a cake tester inserted into the center of the cornbread comes out clean, about 35 minutes.
7. Remove the cornbread from the oven and invert it onto a wire rack. Let the cornbread cool slightly before slicing and serving.

Bouquet Garni

YIELD: 1 BOUQUET / **ACTIVE TIME:** 5 MINUTES / **TOTAL TIME:** 5 MINUTES

2 BAY LEAVES

3 SPRIGS OF FRESH THYME

3 SPRIGS OF FRESH PARSLEY

1. Cut a 2-inch section of kitchen twine. Tie one side of the twine around the herbs and knot it tightly.
2. To use, attach the other end of the twine to one of the pot's handles and slip the herbs into the broth. Remove before serving.

Laksa Curry Paste

YIELD: ½ CUP / **ACTIVE TIME:** 10 MINUTES / **TOTAL TIME:** 20 MINUTES

2 TEASPOONS CORIANDER SEEDS

½ TEASPOON FENNEL SEEDS

1 TEASPOON TURMERIC

1-INCH PIECE OF FRESH GINGER, PEELED AND MINCED

1 GREEN CHILE PEPPER, STEMMED, SEEDED, AND CHOPPED

½ TEASPOON CAYENNE PEPPER

1 LEMONGRASS STALK, MINCED

2 GARLIC CLOVES

2 TABLESPOONS CASHEWS, SOAKED IN WARM WATER FOR 10 MINUTES AND DRAINED

½ CUP FRESH CILANTRO

1 TEASPOON FRESH LIME JUICE

2 TABLESPOONS WATER

SALT AND PEPPER, TO TASTE

1. Place the coriander seeds and fennel seeds in a small skillet and toast until they are fragrant, about 2 minutes, shaking the pan frequently.
2. Transfer the toasted seeds to a blender, add the remaining ingredients, and puree until smooth. Use immediately or store in the refrigerator.

Chive & Shallot Oil

YIELD: ⅔ CUP / **ACTIVE TIME:** 5 MINUTES / **TOTAL TIME:** 15 MINUTES

½ CUP EXTRA-VIRGIN OLIVE OIL

1 SHALLOT, MINCED

1 TABLESPOON FINELY CHOPPED FRESH CHIVES

1. Place the olive oil in a saucepan and warm it over medium heat.
2. Add the shallot and cook, stirring occasionally, until it has softened, about 5 minutes.
3. Remove the pan from heat, stir in the chives, and use immediately or store in an airtight container.

Horseradish Cream

YIELD: 1 CUP / **ACTIVE TIME:** 5 MINUTES / **TOTAL TIME:** 5 MINUTES

2 TABLESPOONS GRATED FRESH HORSERADISH

2 TEASPOONS WHITE WINE VINEGAR

½ TEASPOON DIJON MUSTARD

1 CUP HEAVY CREAM

SALT AND PEPPER, TO TASTE

1. Combine the horseradish, vinegar, and mustard and ¼ cup of the cream in a mixing bowl.
2. In another mixing bowl, lightly whip the remaining cream and then fold this into the horseradish mixture. Season with salt and pepper and use immediately or store in the refrigerator.

Tuk Trey

YIELD: 1 CUP / **ACTIVE TIME:** 5 MINUTES / **TOTAL TIME:** 5 MINUTES

2 TEASPOONS SUGAR

3 TABLESPOONS FISH SAUCE

JUICE OF 1 LIME

¼ CUP WATER

2 GARLIC CLOVES, MINCED

½ CUP ROASTED PEANUTS, CHOPPED

1 BIRD'S EYE CHILE PEPPER, STEMMED, SEEDED, AND MINCED

1. Place all of the ingredients in a bowl, stir to combine, and use immediately or store in the refrigerator.

Horseradish Oil

YIELD: 1 CUP / **ACTIVE TIME:** 10 MINUTES / **TOTAL TIME:** 1 HOUR AND 15 MINUTES

½ CUP PEELED AND GRATED FRESH HORSERADISH

ZEST OF ½ LEMON

1 CUP EXTRA-VIRGIN OLIVE OIL

1. Place all of the ingredients in a saucepan and warm the mixture over medium heat for 5 minutes.
2. Remove the pan from heat and let the mixture steep for 1 hour.
3. Strain the oil through a fine-mesh sieve and use immediately or store in an airtight container.

Turkey Dumplings

YIELD: 4 SERVINGS / **ACTIVE TIME:** 25 MINUTES / **TOTAL TIME:** 1 HOUR AND 30 MINUTES

4 SLICES OF WHITE BREAD, CHOPPED

½ CUP FINELY CHOPPED FRESH PARSLEY

1¼ CUPS ALL-PURPOSE FLOUR

1 TEASPOON BAKING POWDER

½ CUP WHOLE MILK

1 EGG

¼ CUP UNSALTED BUTTER, MELTED

1 CUP COOKED TURKEY LEG MEAT, CHOPPED

SALT AND PEPPER, TO TASTE

4 CUPS TURKEY STOCK (SEE PAGE 446)

1. Place the bread and parsley in a food processor and pulse until combined. Add the flour and baking powder and pulse to combine.
2. Gradually add the milk, egg, and butter to the food processor and pulse to combine. Pulse until the mixture is a smooth, thick paste.
3. Add the turkey, season with salt and pepper, and fold to combine. Chill the mixture in the refrigerator for 1 hour.
4. Place the stock in a medium pot and warm it over medium heat.
5. Drop tablespoons of the turkey mixture into the stock, cover the pot, and cook until the dumplings are cooked through, about 12 minutes. Serve immediately.

Preserved Limes

YIELD: 16 SERVINGS / **ACTIVE TIME:** 15 MINUTES / **TOTAL TIME:** 2 TO 4 WEEKS

7 LIMES

1½ TEASPOONS CORIANDER SEEDS

3 TABLESPOONS KOSHER SALT

1 BAY LEAF

6 BLACK PEPPERCORNS

1. Squeeze the juice from the limes into a large bowl and save the spent halves. Add all of the remaining ingredients to the bowl and stir until the mixture is a paste.
2. Put on gloves, add the spent lime halves, and work the mixture until well combined.
3. Transfer the mixture to an airtight container and gently press down on it to make sure that the solids are completely submerged in the liquid and there are no pockets air can get into. Seal the container and store it at room temperature or chill in the refrigerator until the lime halves are tender. This will take about 2 weeks at room temperature, and a month in the refrigerator.
4. When the preserved limes are ready, mince them and use as desired.

Katsamaki

YIELD: 2 CUPS / **ACTIVE TIME:** 10 MINUTES / **TOTAL TIME:** 20 MINUTES

1¼ CUPS VEGETABLE STOCK (SEE PAGE 441)

½ CUP CORNMEAL

1 CUP GRATED KEFALOTYRI CHEESE

SALT AND PEPPER, TO TASTE

1. Place the stock in a medium pot and bring to a boil.
2. Reduce the heat to low and gradually add the cornmeal, stirring continually. Cook until the mixture has thickened and the cornmeal is tender, 5 to 7 minutes.
3. Remove the pot from heat, add the cheese, and stir until it has melted. Season with salt and pepper and serve.

Naan

YIELD: 8 SERVINGS / **ACTIVE TIME:** 45 MINUTES / **TOTAL TIME:** 2 HOURS

½ CUP WARM WATER (105°F)

¼ OZ. ACTIVE DRY YEAST

1 TEASPOON SUGAR

2¼ CUPS ALL-PURPOSE FLOUR, PLUS MORE AS NEEDED

½ CUP PLAIN YOGURT

1 TABLESPOON CANOLA OIL, PLUS MORE AS NEEDED

3 TABLESPOONS GHEE, MELTED

1. Place the warm water, yeast, and sugar in a small bowl and gently stir to combine. Let the mixture sit until it becomes frothy, about 10 minutes.
2. Place the flour on a work surface and make a well in the center. Fill the well with the yogurt, canola oil, and yeast mixture. Knead the resulting mixture until it comes together as a shiny, smooth dough, about 10 minutes.
3. Coat a bowl with canola oil and place the dough in it. Place a damp kitchen towel over the bowl and let it rest in a naturally warm spot until it has doubled in size, about 1 hour.
4. Warm a large cast-iron skillet over medium heat. Place the dough on a flour-dusted work surface and divide it into eight balls. Roll (or stretch them with your hands if you prefer a more rustic naan) each one out into a ¼-inch-thick oval.
5. Cover all but one of the naan with a kitchen towel. Lightly moisten one side of the uncovered naan with water and place it in the pan, moistened side down.
6. Cook until bubbles form on the surface, 1 to 2 minutes. Turn the naan over and cook until golden-brown spots appear, 1 to 2 minutes. If you want an authentic, slightly charred naan, grab it with a pair of tongs and hold it over an open flame for a few seconds.
7. Brush the hot naan with some of the ghee and repeat with the remaining naan. Serve immediately, once all of the naan have been cooked.

Leek Oil

YIELD: 1 CUP / **ACTIVE TIME:** 15 MINUTES / **TOTAL TIME:** 15 MINUTES

1 CUP CHOPPED LEEKS, GREEN PARTS ONLY

1 CUP SPINACH

1 CUP EXTRA-VIRGIN OLIVE OIL

1. Bring water to a boil in a small saucepan. Prepare an ice bath.
2. Add the leeks and spinach to the pan and cook for 1 minute. Drain the mixture, plunge it into the ice bath until it is cool, and then drain the mixture again.
3. Place the mixture in a food processor, add the olive oil, and blitz until smooth, about 3 minutes.
4. Strain the oil through a fine-mesh sieve and use immediately or store in an airtight container.

Clarified Butter

YIELD: ¾ CUP / **ACTIVE TIME:** 10 MINUTES / **TOTAL TIME:** 10 MINUTES

1 CUP UNSALTED BUTTER

1. Place the butter in a saucepan and melt it over medium heat.
2. Reduce the heat to the lowest-possible setting. Cook until the butter fat is very clear and the milk solids drop to the bottom of the pan.
3. Skim the foam from the surface of the butter and discard it. Transfer the butter to a container and refrigerate until ready to use.

Crab & Mango Salad

YIELD: 4 SERVINGS / **ACTIVE TIME:** 10 MINUTES / **TOTAL TIME:** 25 MINUTES

½ CUP DICED MANGO

½ RED BELL PEPPER, STEMMED, SEEDED, AND FINELY CHOPPED

3 TABLESPOONS MINCED RED ONION

1 TEASPOON MINCED FRESH CHIVES

1 TEASPOON RICE VINEGAR

2 TABLESPOONS EXTRA-VIRGIN OLIVE OIL

SALT, TO TASTE

½ LB. CANNED LUMP CRABMEAT, PICKED OVER

1. Place the mango, bell pepper, onion, chives, vinegar, and olive oil in a bowl and gently stir to combine. Season with salt and chill the salad in the refrigerator for 15 minutes.
2. Use a ring mold to make four towers out of the salad and place one on each plate. Top each tower with some of the crabmeat and serve.

Parsley Oil

YIELD: 1 CUP / **ACTIVE TIME:** 15 MINUTES / **TOTAL TIME:** 15 MINUTES

1 CUP FRESH PARSLEY, CHOPPED

1 CUP BABY SPINACH

1 CUP EXTRA-VIRGIN OLIVE OIL

1. Bring water to a boil in a small saucepan. Prepare an ice bath.
2. Add the parsley and spinach to the pan and cook for 1 minute. Drain the mixture, plunge it into the ice bath until it is cool, and then drain the mixture again.
3. Place the mixture in a food processor, add the olive oil, and blitz until smooth, about 3 minutes.
4. Strain the oil through a fine-mesh sieve and use immediately or store in an airtight container.

Chive Oil

YIELD: 1 CUP / **ACTIVE TIME:** 15 MINUTES / **TOTAL TIME:** 15 MINUTES

1 CUP CHOPPED FRESH CHIVES

1 CUP BABY SPINACH

1 CUP EXTRA-VIRGIN OLIVE OIL

1. Bring water to a boil in a small saucepan. Prepare an ice bath.
2. Add the chives and spinach to the pan and cook for 1 minute. Drain the mixture, plunge it into the ice bath until it is cool, and then drain the mixture again.
3. Place the mixture in a food processor, add the olive oil, and blitz until smooth, about 3 minutes.
4. Strain the oil through a fine-mesh sieve and use immediately or store in an airtight container.

Lemon Poppy Seed Mascarpone

YIELD: ¾ CUP / **ACTIVE TIME:** 5 MINUTES / **TOTAL TIME:** 5 MINUTES

½ CUP MASCARPONE

1 TABLESPOON FRESH LEMON JUICE

1 TABLESPOON POPPY SEEDS

1 TABLESPOON SUGAR

1. Place all of the ingredients in a bowl and whisk to combine. Use immediately or store in the refrigerator.

Mixed Berry Coulis

YIELD: 1¼ CUPS / **ACTIVE TIME:** 10 MINUTES / **TOTAL TIME:** 45 MINUTES

½ CUP STRAWBERRIES, HULLED AND CHOPPED

½ CUP BLACKBERRIES

½ CUP BLUEBERRIES

1 TABLESPOON ORANGE JUICE

½ CUP SUGAR

SEEDS OF ½ VANILLA BEAN

1 TABLESPOON FRESH LEMON JUICE

1. Place all of the ingredients in a medium pot and cook over low heat until the mixture has thickened, about 15 minutes, occasionally using a fork to mash the berries.
2. Remove the pot from heat and let the coulis cool before serving.

METRIC CONVERSION CHART

Weights

1 oz. = 28 grams

2 oz. = 57 grams

4 oz. (¼ lb.) = 113 grams

8 oz. (½ lb.) = 227 grams

16 oz. (1 lb.) = 454 grams

Volume Measures

⅛ teaspoon = 0.6 ml

¼ teaspoon = 1.23 ml

½ teaspoon = 2.5 ml

1 teaspoon = 5 ml

1 tablespoon (3 teaspoons) = ½ fluid oz. = 15 ml

2 tablespoons = 1 fluid oz. = 29.5 ml

¼ cup (4 tablespoons) = 2 fluid oz. = 59 ml

⅓ cup (5⅓ tablespoons) = 2.7 fluid oz. = 80 ml

½ cup (8 tablespoons) = 4 fluid oz. = 120 ml

⅔ cup (10⅔ tablespoons) = 5.4 fluid oz. = 160 ml

¾ cup (12 tablespoons) = 6 fluid oz. = 180 ml

1 cup (16 tablespoons) = 8 fluid oz. = 240 ml

Temperature Equivalents

°F	°C	Gas Mark
225	110	¼
250	130	½
275	140	1
300	150	2
325	170	3
350	180	4
375	190	5
400	200	6
425	220	7
450	230	8
475	240	9
500	250	10

Length Measures

¹⁄₁₆ inch = 1.6 mm

⅛ inch = 3 mm

¼ inch = 6.35 mm

½ inch = 1.25 cm

¾ inch = 2 cm

1 inch = 2.5 cm

INDEX

A

B

C

D

M

T

ABOUT CIDER MILL PRESS BOOK PUBLISHERS

Good ideas ripen with time. From seed to harvest, Cider Mill Press brings fine reading, information, and entertainment together between the covers of its creatively crafted books. Our Cider Mill bears fruit twice a year, publishing a new crop of titles each spring and fall.

"Where Good Books Are Ready for Press"

501 Nelson Place
Nashville, TN 37214

cidermillpress.com